CW00765908

Lost Fatherland

Lost Fatherland

Europeans between Empire and
Nation-States, 1867–1939

Iryna Vushko

Yale

UNIVERSITY PRESS

NEW HAVEN AND LONDON

Published with assistance from the Kingsley Trust Association Publication
Fund established by the Scroll and Key Society of Yale College and with
assistance from the foundation established in memory of Henry Weldon
Barnes of the Class of 1882, Yale College.

Copyright © 2024 by Iryna Vushko.
All rights reserved.
This book may not be reproduced, in whole or in part, including illustrations,
in any form (beyond that copying permitted by Sections 107 and 108 of the
U.S. Copyright Law and except by reviewers for the public press), without
written permission from the publishers.

Yale University Press books may be purchased in quantity for educational,
business, or promotional use. For information, please e-mail sales.press@yale
.edu (U.S. office) or sales@yaleup.co.uk (U.K. office).

Set in Fournier type by Westchester Publishing Services.
Printed in the United States of America.

Library of Congress Control Number: 2023936343
ISBN 978-0-300-26755-6 (hardcover : alk. paper)

A catalogue record for this book is available from the British Library.

This paper meets the requirements of ANSI/NISO Z39.48-1992
(Permanence of Paper).

10 9 8 7 6 5 4 3 2 1

To the memory of my mother,
Stefania Vushko (1939–2021)

Contents

A Note on Transliterations

This book addresses individuals, peoples, and places whose names, citizenships, and designations could and did change numerous times during a single lifespan. Perhaps most controversial of all are ethnic or national categorizations. I use "Ukrainian" to refer to inhabitants of Galicia who until the late nineteenth century were known, and would have referred to themselves, as Ruthenians, but who later became known as Ukrainians. When discussing the German-speaking populations of the Habsburg Empire, I have made distinctions among Germans who self-identified as German; German-speaking Austrians who defined themselves as Austrian; and Germanophone individuals who belonged to other groups—most notably, assimilated Jews from different parts of the monarchy. I have used the terms "Czechs," "Poles," "Italians," "Slovenes," "Croats," and "Serbs" for those Habsburg citizens who self-identified as belonging to these groups.

Place names are equally complicated. To take the example of the central locus and concept of this study itself: the Habsburg Empire was alternatively known as the Austrian Empire and, after 1867, as the Austro-Hungarian Empire or Austria-Hungary. I use "Habsburg Empire" consistently, except for those occasions calling for emphasis on its post-1867 federative structures. I have adopted standard English transliteration for places such as Cracow (Kraków in Polish) and have indicated the different versions of toponyms that vary from language to language: the Italian and Hungarian Fiume, German Flaum, Slovenian Reka, and Croatian Rijeka are all one place, now part of Croatia. The German Lemberg, Polish Lwów, and Ukrainian L'viv are likewise the same city, which is now part of Ukraine. Gorizia, a region in what is now Italy, is known as Gorica in Slovenian. Lundenburg (in German) and Břeclav (in Czech) are the same town, now part of the Czech Republic.

Language differences also affect the spelling of individuals' names. Joseph, Josef, Józef, and Josip, for example, are all variants of the same name, spelled and pronounced differently in different languages. As a rule, I have rendered names as spelled by the protagonists themselves whenever there is written evidence from their lifetime. The same goes for surnames of some of the figures under discussion, who may have spelled these names differently on different occasions. Redlich's first name appeared as Josef or Joseph; I have used the latter in my text. Mykola Hankevych was sometimes referred to as Hankiewicz or Hankewycz; I have used Hankevych consistently throughout the text. Mykola (Nicolaus) Wassilko appeared in different texts as Wasylko and Vasylko. I have used his official Austrian name, Wassilko, in the text.

All translations are mine unless otherwise indicated.

Cast of Characters

BATTISTI, CESARE (b. Trento, February 4, 1875; d. Trento, July 12, 1916). Italian socialist, deputy to imperial parliament. In 1915 emigrated to Italy; captured by Austrians, tried on charges of state treason, executed in July 1916; the only protagonist in this book to pass away before 1918.

BAUER, OTTO (b. Vienna, September 5, 1881; d. Paris, July 5, 1938). Austrian socialist from a family of Germanophone assimilated Jews with roots in Moravia; cofounder of Austro-Marxism; deputy to imperial parliament; Austrian Republic's first foreign minister; between 1919 and 1934, head of the Austrian Social Democratic Party.

BILIŃSKI, LEON (b. Zalishchyky, Galicia, June 15, 1846; d. Vienna, June 14, 1923). Polish conservative from a family of assimilated Jews; deputy to imperial parliament; minister of imperial railways; finance minister, head of the common Austro-Hungarian finance ministry; governor of Bosnia and Herzegovina; first finance minister of independent Poland.

CZECH, LUDWIG (b. L'viv, February 14, 1870; d. Theresienstadt concentration camp, August 20, 1942). Germanophone socialist from a family of assimilated Jews with roots in Moravia; deputy to the Moravian diet; 1919–1935, head of the German Social Democratic Party of Czechoslovakia, minister of social welfare in Czechoslovakia.

DASZYŃSKI, IGNACY (b. Zbaraż, Galicia, October 26, 1866; d. Bystre Śląskie, Poland, October 31, 1936). Polish socialist, cofounder of the Polish Social Democratic Party of Galicia and Silesia, deputy to imperial and Polish parliaments; vice speaker of parliament in Poland.

DE GASPERI, ALCIDE (b. Pieve Tesino, Trentino, April 3, 1881; d. Borgo Valsugana, Italy, August 19, 1954). Italian clerical politician, deputy to imperial and

Italian parliaments; cofounder of the People's Party of Italy after World War I; cofounder of the European Union after World War II.

DIAMAND, HERMAN (b. Lviv, March 30, 1860; d. Lviv, February 21, 1931). Polish socialist from a family of Germanophone assimilated Jews; co-founder of the Polish Social Democratic Party of Galicia and Silesia; deputy to imperial and Polish parliaments.

ELLENBOGEN, WILHELM (b. Lundenburg, Moravia, July 9, 1863; d. New York, February 25, 1951). Austrian socialist from a family of Germanophone assimilated Jews with roots in Moravia; deputy to imperial and Austrian parliaments; head of the Commission on Socialization, undersecretary for trade and commerce in Austria.

GŁĄBIŃSKI, STANISŁAW (b. Skole, Galicia, February 25, 1862; d. Kharkiv, Soviet Ukraine, August 14, 1941). Polish nationalist politician; deputy to imperial and Polish parliaments; minister of imperial railways, senator in Poland.

HANKEVYCH, MYKOLA (b. Sniatyn, Galicia, May 16, 1869; d. Shklo, Galicia, July 31, 1931). Ukrainian socialist, cofounder of the Ukrainian Social Democratic Party of Galicia, deputy to imperial parliament.

KRAMÁŘ, KAREL (b. Vysoké nad Jizerou, now Czech Republic, December 27, 1860; d. Prague, May 26, 1937). Czech nationalist politician, deputy to imperial and Czechoslovak parliaments; Czechoslovakia's first prime minister.

LAMMASCH, HEINRICH (b. Seitenstetten, Lower Austria, May 21, 1853; d. Salzburg, January 6, 1920). Austrian politician, no party affiliations; empire's last prime minister, member of the Austrian delegation at Versailles peace conference.

PITTONI, VALENTINO (b. Brazzano, Gorizia, May 23, 1872; d. Vienna, April 11, 1933). Italian socialist, leader of the Italian Socialist Democratic Party in Trieste before and immediately after World War I, deputy to imperial parliament.

REDLICH, JOSEPH (b. Göding, Moravia, June 18, 1869; d. Vienna, November 11, 1936). Austrian politician from a Germanophone family of assimilated Jews with roots in Moravia; member of different parties in different years; minister of finances in empire and Austrian republic.

REGENT, IVAN (b. Kontovel, near Trieste, January 24, 1884; d. Ljubljana, September 26, 1967). Slovene socialist turned communist; deputy to imperial and Italian parliaments.

SALATA, FRANCESCO (b. Ossero, Istria, September 17, 1876; d. Rome, March 10, 1944). Italian nationalist politician; deputy to imperial and Italian parliaments; senator in Italy; head of the Central Office for the New Provinces in Italy.

SEIPEL, IGNAZ (b. Vienna, July 19, 1876; d. Pernitz, Austria, August 2, 1932). Austrian priest and theologian. Minister of social welfare in the last imperial cabinet; head of the Austrian Christian Social Party between 1921 and 1922; twice chancellor of the Austrian Republic, 1922–1924, 1926–1929.

ŠMERAL, BOHUMÍR (b. Třebíč, Moravia, October 25, 1880; d. Moscow, May 8, 1941). Czech socialist turned communist. Deputy to imperial and Czechoslovak parliaments; founder of the Czechoslovak Communist Party.

TUMA, HENRIK (b. Ljubljana, July 9, 1858; d. Ljubljana, April 10, 1935). Slovene socialist, deputy to imperial parliament; post-1918 years in Italy and Yugoslavia.

VITYK, SEMEN (b. Verhnij Haij, Galicia, February 21, 1876; d. Verhnieural'sk, Siberia, October 10, 1937). Ukrainian socialist turned communist; cofounder of the Ukrainian Social Democratic Party, deputy to imperial parliament; in 1925 emigrated to the Soviet Union, employed in foreign ministry; tried and sentenced as a nationalist, sent to Siberia.

WASSILKO, MYKOLA (b. Lukawetz, Bukovina, March 25, 1868; d. Bad Reichenhall, Germany, August 2, 1924). Romanian turned Ukrainian, deputy to imperial parliament; after 1918, head of Ukrainian diplomatic missions to Germany, Austria, Switzerland, and Italy.

Abbreviations

GDVP	Großdeutsche Volkspartei
KSCS	Kingdom of Serbs, Croats, and Slovenes
PPI	Partito Popolare Italiano
PPS	Polska Partia Socjalistyczna
PPSD	Polska Partia Socjalno-Demokratyczna Galicji i Śląska
PSI	Partito Socialista Italiano
USDP	Ukraiins'ka social-demokratychna partiia

Lost Fatherland

Introduction

In the summer of 1928, Joseph Redlich, an Austrian lawyer and professor of law then residing in the United States, vented his frustration in a letter to a fellow Austrian, the poet and dramatist Hugo von Hofmannsthal: "We once had a Fatherland, a mission, and a history. Now . . . we have to face the remarkable decline of culture in the new Austria."[1] Born in 1869, Redlich was raised in a German-speaking family of assimilated Jews in Moravia, in the northwestern part of the Habsburg Empire. He spent most of his adult life before 1918 in Vienna, where the empire's collapse found him serving as finance minister in its final government. He and many of his contemporaries would long cherish the memory of the Habsburg Empire as a place of "perfect order and stability," and had great difficulty adjusting to the post-1918 order.[2] Yet he remained active in politics and government, doing his part to build the new Austria upon the old familiar image.

Redlich's story was typical of a large cohort of political and intellectual elites who had come of age in the Habsburg Empire, witnessed its collapse, and outlived it. Their stories are the inspiration for this study, which discusses twenty-one individuals who started in politics in the Habsburg Empire and then continued in different states across Europe. Marked by the trauma of the First World War, the vanishing of their empire, and the transition to post-1918 Europe, they produced a remarkable array of political programs, and would staff and sustain the various polities that emerged after the imperial downfall. A full generation younger, born in 1881, but of a similar background, was

Redlich's socialist peer Otto Bauer, cofounder of Austro-Marxism, and the future first foreign minister of the Republic of Austria. Also born in 1881 but of a different ethnocultural background was Alcide De Gasperi: raised in the empire's Alpine Italian-German area of Trentino, he would later cofound the European Union after the Second World War. One year their junior was Bohumír Šmeral, a Czech Social Democrat who would found the Communist Party of Czechoslovakia. Francesco Salata and Semen Vityk were born in 1876; the former, an Italian nationalist from Istria, would in the 1930s serve as Mussolini's ambassador to Vienna; the latter, a Ukrainian Social Democrat, would set out in 1925 to help build communism in Soviet Ukraine. Ivan Regent, a Slovenian socialist from Trieste, born in 1884, would turn to communism after 1918, then live in Italy, Yugoslavia, and Austria.

This book represents a portrait of a particular milieu—the intertwining political and intellectual circles from the late Habsburg Empire and interwar Europe—as a lens through which to examine broader issues of European history in the late nineteenth and first half of the twentieth centuries. It covers the Austrian part of what after 1867 became the federative Austro-Hungarian Empire, and several states of interwar Europe, including Austria, Czechoslovakia, Poland, Italy, Yugoslavia, post-1918 Ukraine, and the post-1922 Soviet Union. The focus here is the transfer of institutional models and practices across 1918, from the empire to interwar Europe and beyond. I explore how a cluster of ideas rooted in the nineteenth-century Habsburg Empire—conservatism, liberalism, nationalism, Christian socialism, Austro-Marxism, federalism, and internationalism—continued to shape European politics and society in the twentieth century.

To the usual story of Europe from the fall of its last empires to 1945 and beyond, I propose an alternate narrative, one that highlights the *connections* between the fin-de-siècle and post–Second World War eras and yields a new chronology of twentieth-century Europe. The First World War represented, of course, a landmark moment, especially in military, territorial, and human terms; but its political effects were not as radical as those of the Second World War. Even though several countries had descended into authoritarianism during the 1920s and 1930s, democracy remained alive in parts of the continent, as did the hope of restoring it across Europe. The years 1938 and 1939—the beginning of Nazi military aggression and the subsequent German-Soviet war, I argue, created a more radical break in European history than did the end of empires in 1918. The Habsburg epoch in European history, that is, may be understood to have come to an end not in 1918, but between 1938 and 1945.

This book's protagonists reflected imperial and European politics as the nineteenth century turned to the twentieth, and as the world of empires was replaced by that of nation-states. All of them belonged to a certain political and cultural milieu of elites from the empire. I draw on numerous studies that either focus on generations or are designated as collective biographies, but my book does not belong to either of these categories. Rather, it constitutes a history of overlapping circles and networks of people, many of whom shared similar values across time and space, despite generational divides.

The Habsburg Empire was a fatherland for all these figures: the space of their formative experiences, the origin point of the intellectual and political resources they all carried with them into the post-1918 period. All shared what we might call an "imperial pedigree." All were educated in the same or similar institutions; the law school of the University of Vienna, in particular, was the alma mater of many of this book's protagonists. Educational and political models in the empire, moreover, were similar from place to place: "coffeehouse politics" predominated in Vienna, Lemberg/Lwów, Prague, and Trieste, where major decisions were negotiated in crowded cafés by people who all spoke German at work and a variety of other languages at home. And although the empire's political system was imperfect and compromises often failed, violence was more or less unheard of.

These figures' formative experiences in the empire remained ingrained in them long after its collapse. They all spoke several languages, but German remained their lingua franca. Many felt "back home" in their visits to Vienna, even after settling in new states across Europe or emigrating to the United States. Divided by new borders after 1918, they continued to maintain the personal networks and political tradition they had come of age with. Electoral and parliamentary tactics; the building (or avoidance) of coalitions; constitutional and legal norms; judicial practices and party strategies; policies regarding national minorities—in the interwar period, all were reminiscent of the late empire. But above all there stood the same individuals: former Habsburg functionaries, deputies, and ministers, many of them occupying the very same positions in the post-imperial states long after 1918. The world around them was becoming progressively gloomier in the 1920s and 1930s, when many found themselves trapped between different political extremes and variants of authoritarianism: fascism and Nazism in the West and Soviet communism in the East. But it was only outright military aggression—first by the Nazis, then by the Soviets—that ultimately destroyed the hopes of restoring democracy in post-1918 Europe.

The legacy of the Austrian Empire on the continent from which it vanished in 1918 was multifaceted and contradictory, but it would be hard to overstate its influence on subsequent history. Continuities between the empire and twentieth-century Europe were numerous. Federative discussions became important especially in the late empire, and they carried on beyond 1918.[3] After 1918 Vienna became a center of the pan-European movement, which espoused a federation based on the Habsburg model.[4] Major trends in twentieth-century economics, intellectual history, and philosophy of science likewise emerged from the erstwhile Habsburg space. Neoliberalism, for instance, was a product of the late empire's economic and nationalities policies.[5] Twentieth-century European philosophy of science also built on Habsburg precedents.[6] This legacy persisted even beyond the Second World War. Some of the key European institutions from the post-1945 era, most notably the European Union, also trace their origins to the history of pre-1918 federalism and internationalism in the Habsburg Empire. Even if many imperial-era concepts went unimplemented, and others were embodied in institutions that failed, 1918 marked a point in the continuum of—and not an end to—debates from the empire.[7]

This legacy also implied a specific understanding of politics based on institutions, tolerance, and compromise. To be sure, institutions were flawed, and compromises often failed; coalitions were imperfect. The Habsburg parliament was in chaos for much of its final decades. National tensions sharpened in particular during the war; moreover, confrontations between the center right and the left escalated in the late empire. Post-Habsburg successors thus inherited not just the late empire's achievements, but also all its unresolved issues. Yet with its insistence on institutional solutions, on compromise as opposed to political violence, the Habsburg Empire stood apart from its Russian and Ottoman counterparts. Until the First World War, the problems faced by the Habsburg Empire seemed almost cosmetic in comparison with those of its neighbors.

This relative stability was a function of the fact that prior to 1914, the vast majority of Habsburg subjects were loyal to the monarchy and imperial institutions. Despite the narratives that became embedded in intellectual and

political discourse in Europe after 1918—tales of imperial oppression and nationalist dissent—irredentism was rare in the Habsburg Empire before the First
World War. Building on the rich body of recent scholarship on nationalism,
national indifference, and imperial loyalty, I show in this study that even the
Habsburgian politicians and activists who identified as nationalists remained
essentially loyal, and had more in common with their own country's conservatives and moderates than with, for example, their ostensible nationalist peers
in such neighboring states as the Russian Empire or the Kingdom of Italy.

In exploring the Austrian imperial heritage, I also draw attention to parallel developments in several countries of post-1918 Europe—polities as dispa-
rate and as geographically remote from one another as Italy and the Soviet
Union. These countries rarely appear side by side in European history narratives; their political developments and crises are not usually seen as having common roots. This book not only brings these different countries together in a
single narrative but also explains how the gradual onset of authoritarianism
in Europe and the concurrent radicalization on the left and right between Italy and the Soviet Union may be seen as stemming from the same political
developments in the pre-1918 Habsburg Empire.

The Austrian part of the post-1867 Habsburg Empire offers a unique case
to highlight the continuities across the ostensible epochal divide of 1918. No
other state save the Ottoman Empire saw its subjects and citizens dispersed
over such a diverse range of territories, and its institutions reproduced in so
many variations. Part of the lasting impact of the Habsburg Empire had to do
with its particular history and geography. In the Middle Ages, the Habsburgs
were a relatively marginal dynasty that controlled territories in what is now
Austria and Switzerland. The Austrian Empire was formed in 1526 as the result of a marital alliance between the Habsburg-ruled Duchy of Austria and
the Kingdoms of Bohemia and Moravia and of Hungary. In the centuries that
followed, the Habsburg state expanded, adding territories and various ethnic
and religious groups. It remained a continental empire, with rather limited access to maritime trade, mainly through the Adriatic port of Trieste. But by the
end of the Napoleonic period in 1815, the Habsburgs controlled much of
Europe, from the northern Adriatic coast around Trieste and Venice to the Carpathian mountains of Ukraine; their state bordered the Russian Empire in the
east, the Ottoman Empire in the south, and what would become the Kingdom
of Italy in the southwest and German Empire in the west. This polity was known
alternatively as the Habsburg monarchy, the Habsburg Empire, the Austrian

Empire, the Austro-Hungarian Empire, and Austro-Hungary (the latter names reflecting the political developments of 1867, when the unitary monarchy was reorganized as a federation of two parts, Austria and Hungary).

The regions covered in this study made up the part of the empire known after 1867 as Cisleithania, that is, the following Habsburg possessions: Lower and Upper Austria, which today constitute the Republic of Austria; Bohemia and Moravia, and the Slovak regions of the Hungarian part of Austro-Hungary, which became Czechoslovakia (after 1993, the Czech Republic and Slovakia); Trentino and South Tyrol, with a mixed German and Italian population, which were part of Italy between the wars, and are now as well; the Austrian Littoral, which became known in the Kingdom of Italy as Venezia Giulia ("the Julian March"), centering on the now Italian city of Trieste and featuring a mix of Italians, Slovenes, Croats, and Germans, and which after the Second World War was divided between Italy, Hungary, and Yugoslavia until the collapse of the latter (the former Yugoslavian littoral is now divided between Croatia and Slovenia); and Galicia, with its centers of Lemberg/Lwów/L'viv and Cracow/Kraków, which became part of Poland between the wars, and is now divided between that country and Ukraine.[8] Habsburg citizens who matured in these regions also influenced politics and society in several other neighboring states, including Germany and the Soviet Union.

This study deals with the Austrian part of what after 1867 became the federative empire of Austro-Hungary. Hungary after that point developed a substantially different political tradition; unlike its Austrian counterpart, it aspired to be a nation-state and acted as a nationalizing state. Its government promoted assimilation, curtailed administrative and cultural autonomy, and enforced centralization. Post-1918 Hungary, with its strong antiminority policies, in a way represented the logical development of the pre-1918 Hungarian part of Austro-Hungary. This was also a matter of personal succession, and a unilateral one at that: statesmen and politicians who started out in pre-1918 Hungary would remain active in post-1918 Hungary, but rarely if ever did they go on to make careers in any other states. It was rather the Austrian part of the empire that generated the political elites who would shape not just Austria, but numerous successor states across Europe.

This book takes its place among recent scholarship that explores continuities between empires and postimperial states in twentieth-century Europe, revising the continent's previous historiography, which focused on 1918 as a "point zero." The latter perception is linked to the stereotype—perpetuated by nationalists in interwar Europe and beyond—by which empires are inherently vicious, and nation-states virtuous.[9] Rejecting the imperial past legitimized the politics of the present; 1918 *had* to mark a radical break.[10] Indeed, for much of the past century, historians and intellectuals approached the Habsburg and other empires as anomalies and considered the emergence of nation-states on their ruins as a natural progression of history.[11] This paradigm, however, is the product of a radical politics that arose specifically during the First World War and the interwar era, and was hardly characteristic of the Habsburg Empire during its prewar existence. Most of this book's protagonists and the vast majority of their contemporaries operated within a different mindset. For them, the empire was the norm, and any other form of state was an anomaly—one that many would have to struggle to accept.

Just as several recent studies have demonstrated the survival of British, French, and Ottoman imperial traditions in the former possessions thereof, a cohort of scholars has explored different aspects of continuity between the Habsburg Empire and post-1918 Europe.[12] Unlike other studies, which typically focus on the succession to one particular country or another, this one brings together much of the post-Habsburg space between Italy and the Soviet Union to explore parallel developments and analogous inheritances from the Habsburg imperial legacy. In so doing, the historiographies of the Habsburg Empire and of different parts of interwar Europe—of the continent's East *and* West—can be brought into the same conversation.

This monograph is not a comprehensive history of the Habsburg Empire or its successor states. It represents rather an analysis of political durability and continuity across differing state forms. It explores certain aspects of imperial and interwar European history, but undertakes no comprehensive survey of all major events. For example, while the First World War is a crucial landmark, I address it only insofar as it relates to the continuity theme. Nor does this book provide extensive biographies of the figures under discussion: the life stories here are meant to reflect the different workings of the respective post-Habsburg states. Another topic dealt with tangentially is religion, which is addressed only to the extent that it relates to broader discussions of identity and politics between the late empire and successor states. Notably lacking in the story, moreover, are women. Part of the Habsburg political legacy and its afterlife was the exclusively male political space: parliament, government, and local assemblies, as well as the vast majority of institutions, were populated by men only. While women were active in intellectual circles and some nongovernmental institutions and initiatives, their role in official Habsburg politics was nonexistent.

Also excluded here is discussion of Zionism and Jewish identity, although persons of Jewish descent are proportionally overrepresented among this book's protagonists. (And with good reason: Jews formed an important part of the empire's political elites, both in the center and across the provinces.) Many of these leading Jewish figures vacillated between different ideologies and affiliations, and some did endorse Zionism at some point in their lives. Most, however, defined themselves as Austrians, their Jewish identity only secondary to their imperial loyalty. For this reason, the numerous Jewish figures who appear in different chapters do so first and foremost as former Austrian subjects, alongside other protagonists. This book should thus also prompt us to rethink Jewish political and intellectual involvement in Europe in the late nineteenth and first half of the twentieth centuries.

The book is organized around the empire and its afterlives. Nine chapters, divided into three parts, trace particular aspects of this theme from the 1860s to 1939. This introduction has briefly explained the protagonists and their fates, and the epilogue extends their narrative to the Second World War and beyond, ending the story in the 1950s with the founding of the European Economic Community. Each chapter features several individuals who came of age under the empire and then parted ways to different states.

Part I addresses Habsburg-era and postimperial liberalism, conservatism, internationalism, and political clericalism. Chapter 1 brings together two individuals from the empire's Austrian core: Heinrich Lammasch and Joseph Redlich. Chapter 2 then discusses two figures from the empire's Galician and Bukovina periphery: Leon Biliński and Mykola Wassilko. Chapter 3 shifts the focus to political Catholicism, discussing two clerical statesmen—the Austrian Ignaz Seipel and the Italian Alcide De Gasperi, who played particularly important roles as the "founder of the first Austrian republic" and cofounder of the European Union, respectively.

Part II shifts to nationalism and radicalism. Chapter 4 tells the story of Habsburg-era nationalists, focusing on the Pole Stanisław Głąbiński and Czech Karel Kramář. Here I explore late imperial nationalism: in particular, the compatibility in this period of national sentiment with imperial loyalty, the fact that radical opposition to Habsburg rule was a post-1918 myth, and the continuity of nationalist politics across 1918. Chapter 5 then narrows the focus to how these ideas converged in Italy. Discussing two Italian activists, each representing a particular ideology and political party, the chapter explores the role of the Habsburg legacy in post-1918 Italy, the myth of the "fascism of the frontier," and specific responses to the radicalization represented by Mussolini's fascism, particularly after 1925.

Part III examines the legacy of social democracy in six states: Austria and Czechoslovakia, Italy and Yugoslavia, and Poland and Soviet Ukraine. Chapter 6 discusses four socialists of the imperial era who parted ways after 1918: Otto Bauer, Wilhelm Ellenbogen, Bohumír Šmeral, and Ludwig Czech. Chapter 7 introduces two individuals who identified as Poles and two as Ukrainians—Ignacy Daszyński, Herman Diamand, Semen Vityk, and Mykola Hankevych. Chapter 8 returns to the Austrian-Italian borderland; its four protagonists, two Italians and two Slovenes, are Valentino Pittoni, Cesare Battisti, Henrik Tuma, and Ivan Regent. Why Austro-Marxism led to many variations and how its fate was bound up with the First World War are some of the overarching themes of this section. Austro-Marxism was of a similar importance to Habsburg-era federative internationalism in terms of its legacy in twentieth-century Europe. Debates in the 1960s and 1970s about Eurocommunism or the "third way to socialism" can be traced to the legacy of the Habsburg Empire, particularly its tradition of Austro-Marxism.[13]

Part IV, the last chapter of the book, addresses the effects of authoritarianism on post-Habsburg individuals, profiling the Habsburg political legacy as experienced in the late 1920s and 1930s. The story here is that of former imperial subjects attempting to make their way in the parlous stage of European history from the late 1920s to 1938—in fascist Italy, authoritarian Poland and Yugoslavia, an Austria wracked by civil war, and the new Soviet Ukraine. One of this book's protagonists, Cesare Battisti, died during the war. Three others, Lammasch, Biliński, and Wassilko, died in the 1920s. Seventeen others lived into the late 1920s and 1930s. This chapter discusses the latter cohort's encounter with a new type of politics, with a Europe slipping into extremes. The epilogue brings us to the Second World War and beyond.

To round out the story of these men, the epilogue introduces their children—daughters and sons whose lives were profoundly affected by their fathers' choices. Many grew up to be prominent politicians, diplomats, intellectuals, and businesspeople. Some were born out of wedlock, and some lacked paternal attention even when their fathers were technically present. Some endorsed their fathers' political choices, others went their own way. This is thus also a story of the intertwining of politics and private life, with repercussions for the rest of the century—indeed, a story of human behavior, alienation, and betrayal lasting across geographical divides and well beyond 1918.

Each of these chapters could have formed the basis for a separate book: the themes of conservativism, internationalism, nationalism, Christian socialism, and Austro-Marxism are all important in their own right. Yet the interactions between them, and specifically among this book's various protagonists, allow for a particularly nuanced analysis of the post-1918 transition, the interwar period, and the Habsburg legacy in modern Europe in general. For example, the antagonism between Christian Socials and Social Democrats that consolidated under the empire defined politics in several post-Habsburg states. Nationalism in the late empire grew out of conservatism and liberalism: understanding this succession, and the different nuances of each of these ideologies, should help us understand the radicalization and rising nationalism that evolved in several successor states. Decades after the Habsburg collapse, political alliances and coalitions would be formed with implicit reference to the defunct empire.

The twenty-one protagonists in this book were all interconnected, and each of their appearances in the narrative serves a particular historiographic purpose. Their political involvement was one major criterion of selection; interpersonal relationships was another. Most if not all were connected to one another at some point in their lives, and belonged to overlapping political circles. For example, Heinrich Lammasch and Joseph Redlich, who are discussed in the first chapter, had close personal and professional ties with Ignaz Seipel, a focus of chapter 3. Seipel also maintained an important personal and professional relationship with the leading Austrian socialist Otto Bauer, the protagonist of chapter 5. The conservative Leon Biliński (chapter 2) had close ties with Lammasch and Redlich (chapter 1) and the Polish nationalist Stanisław Głąbiński (chapter 3). The Italian Alcide De Gasperi (chapter 3) was acquainted with many representatives of the empire's inner political circles, and in post-1918 Italy he would collaborate with the Italian nationalist Francesco Salata (chapter 5). Eleven socialists that appear in three chapters of this book knew each other well, and moreover had close personal ties to many of its non-Marxist protagonists.

Other figures—who were either more prominent than those covered here, or more familiar to a general audience outside of particular national fields— have been excluded; the discursive space saved has gone to introduce new perspectives, and to consider the empire's heritage in a fresh way. For example, the socialist Karl Renner served as the first chancellor of the Republic of Austria after 1918, and in domestic politics he was more important than Otto Bauer. Yet it was Bauer who determined patterns of relationships between Austrian socialists and members of the Christian Social Party, and who greatly influenced the trajectories of socialism and communism in pre- and post-1918 Europe in general. The Slovenian Josip Vilfan appeared in an early draft of my manuscript, as he played a key role in shaping European minority politics in the interwar period. But he barely overlapped with the networks I explore in this book, and thus he does not appear in the final version.

I cannot of course claim that the selection informing my study is perfect, but the protagonists are all marshaled to pursue a particular goal: a nuanced analysis of European politics from the fin-de-siècle through the Second World War. The year 1918 created new geographical divides among many of them, but it did not destroy the networks and circles that had consolidated in the Habsburg Empire over the decades.

The monograph is based on research both in published sources and in archival collections in cities in five countries—Vienna, Rome, Prague, Warsaw, Kyiv, and L'viv—and in ten languages. Of additional use were volumes of parliamentary protocols from the empire and from Austria, Czechoslovakia, Poland, and Italy, as well as dozens of periodicals. Several of the book's protagonists, moreover, kept diaries and left memoirs; this voluminous epistolary material allows for a detailed reflection on their lives.

Joseph Redlich mourned the empire's loss for years after 1918, fearing that further decline was to come. The "lost fatherland" became a recurrent theme in post-1918 intellectual and political discourse. That theme informs the title of this study. Politically and intellectually, the Habsburg Empire, with its culture of federative internationalism, cosmopolitanism, and compromise as opposed to violence, lasted well beyond 1918. Redlich himself died before 1945, as did most of the figures discussed in this book. But the empire's legacy lived on even after the Second World War, both in Western Europe, in the lead-up to European unification; and in Europe's East, in the communist bloc, where the empire's memory and institutional traditions fueled anticommunist dissent beyond 1945.

The book moreover addresses some of the issues particularly relevant today: forced migration and resettlement; European unity (or disunity), European institutions, their successes and failures. The theme of lost fatherland has become especially resonant in recent years and months, since the beginning of Russia's war in Ukraine in 2014 and the full-scale invasion in February 2022. Affected are not only those whose homes were physically destroyed by Russian missiles or tanks, but the millions of others who were set on the move, experiencing, similar to Redlich, an overwhelming sense of loss. Just like Redlich, many anticipated the war to be short. They only slowly have come to the realization that the world that they knew—Ukraine, despite of all of its political and economic limitations, as a land of peace, relative stability, and prosperity—is no more. Redlich's and his peers' stories should give us a glimpse into what can come next. While the current war in Ukraine is situational and hopefully short-lived, its emotional, intellectual, and political repercussions will affect generations to come. This too is the legacy of an empire—not the Habsburg one but its former Russian neighbor and Soviet successor. The sense of loss is personal for me as well.

PART ONE

Liberalism, Conservatism, Internationalism, Clericalism

1. Liberalism, Conservatism, Internationalism, and the End of Empire

"We are waiting here for our friend Lammasch," wrote the Austrian writer Stefan Zweig in a letter to his French counterpart and friend, Romaine Rolland, on October 14, 1918.[1] Heinrich Lammasch was then at the center of public attention in the Habsburg Empire: an Austrian lawyer, statesman, and intellectual, he was being groomed for the position of prime minister in the Habsburg government. Born in 1853 in Lower Austria and having spent most of his life in Vienna, Lammasch had become one of the most prominent international lawyers. But he had long resisted the pull of the government. He declined two offers by Emperor Charles I, in the summer of 1917 and the summer of 1918, referring to his lack of political experience. "He has been stubborn in refusing this position until recently," commented Zweig in another letter to Rolland. "How well I understand him: he knows all too well that because of human frailty, no righteous work can be accomplished. And what he wants is justice, to build a model human society based on the Platonic ideal."[2] This model human society had long been a driving force of Lammasch's life and career—his attempt to create a war-free Europe based on international cooperation and pacifism.

It was this drive that eventually brought him to government service. In October 1918 he agreed to serve as head of what he and the emperor envisioned would be a "peace cabinet"—one that would preserve the empire's territorial integrity by leading it out of the Great War. By then the Habsburg Empire faced a multitude of challenges; it was losing the conflict abroad and facing domestic dissent at home, as its many nationalities stepped up irredentist campaigns and prepared for independence. Even so, Lammasch still believed that the empire could persevere. But as he worked out the features of the new government, it became obvious that his state would not survive the war. At this point Lammasch became head of a *liquidation* cabinet—the last premier of the Habsburg Empire.

Serving alongside him were a cohort of friends and colleagues who also had little or no government experience but decided to step in at this critical moment. Among these figures was Lammasch's friend and fellow jurist Joseph Redlich, a native of Moravia born in 1869 who, like Lammasch, had spent most of his pre-1918 life in Vienna. Lammasch and Redlich became close during the war, and in late October 1918 Redlich joined Lammasch's cabinet as finance minister. That government only survived for several days and was dismissed on October 28. But three of its members, including Lammasch and Redlich, continued in politics in the post-1918 Austria. Despite its short duration, Lammasch's cabinet would have long-term effects on post-1918 Austrian and European politics.

Focusing on these two statesmen from the empire's Austrian core, this chapter sheds light on the malleability and versatility of late imperial politics; the coexistence of nationalism and imperial loyalty, national and internationalism, autonomy and federalism; and the ways in which all these factors influenced Austrian and European politics after 1918.[3] It argues that the empire's physical collapse hardly erased imperial minds. Instead, for many, it reinforced the values of the bygone empire. Lammasch played a key role in the history of European internationalism leading up to the creation of the League of Nations in 1919.[4] Redlich served as finance minister in the empire and the Austrian republic, espousing continuities between two Austrias. Lammasch died in 1920 after participating at the Saint-Germain Conference between the Entente powers (France, Britain, and Russia) and Austria; Redlich lived through 1936. They are part of a broader political cohort discussed in this book with strong personal and professional ties to many other protagonists who appear in subsequent chapters. Their stories, set against the background of late empire and post-Habsburg Europe, illuminate the broader histories of sovereign transitions, revealing the intricate links between politics and personal lives across political and chronological divides.

Empire, Constitution, Federation

Lammasch's life and career encapsulated the empire's transition from central-ism to federalism, liberalism to nationalism, and eventual decline during the war. He was raised during the 1850s in the family of a notary, received an ed-ucation traditional for the empire's elites, and spent most of his life in Vienna. He studied law at the University of Vienna, took courses in Germany, the Neth-erlands, and England, and earned a doctorate in international law. He began his academic career in 1882 at the University of Innsbruck and until 1899 lived the life of a typical university professor. Unlike many of his peers, for whom an academic career was a springboard to politics, Lammasch for many years prioritized law and showed little interest in active politics.[5]

The constitutionalism, institutionalism, and internationalism that be-came key to Lammasch's worldview were by-products of the empire's experi-ence during and after the Revolutions of 1848. Lammasch was too young to observe the events firsthand, but what transpired in 1848 affected him and most of his contemporaries not just through the years of empire's existence but also after its collapse.

The story of 1848 is well told in the literature, but the interpretations of its long-term effects and significance have changed over time. In the early spring of 1848, demonstrators in Vienna (mostly students and intellectuals), influenced by revolutionary upheavals in France and Prussia, took to the streets to demand the end of absolutism and a transition to a constitutional monarchy. Subse-quent uprisings in Budapest, Lwów, Prague, and the Adriatic port of Trieste added a national element to the reformers' constitutional and institutional de-mands. The revolutions brought to the fore the empire's multiethnic nature and the potential hurdles inherent in its compositional heterogeneity. The em-pire had no single predominant nationality, and German speakers never formed an absolute majority. For the most part, administration and education were conducted in German, but legally the empire had no official language. German served as the lingua franca, but other languages were in use too, tolerated in the Habsburg Empire to a greater degree than were minority languages in other countries.[6] In 1848 elites in the empire's various provinces sought to under-mine Germanophone domination by securing autonomy from Vienna. These revolutions could hardly be said, however, to have somehow presaged the empire's collapse over half a century later. Most national demands, with the

Map of the Austrian Empire, 1851. Lionel Pincus and Princess Firyal Map Division, New York Public Library, "Austria," New York Public Library Digital Collections.

exception of those put forward by Hungary, were limited to autonomy and not independence.

The government in Vienna responded to the upheavals in two ways: first with repressions and then with concessions and reforms. In the years 1848–49, Vienna issued three different constitutions. None was implemented in full: in late 1849 Emperor Francis Joseph rescinded the constitution and dissolved the parliament. Ten years of neo-absolutism followed. However, absolutism proper never recovered: constitutional ideals had taken hold and were never successfully eradicated. In the early 1860s, the emperor reintroduced the regional assemblies and bicameral parliament. The October Diploma (1860) and February Patent (1862) transformed the provinces into autonomous units with varying degrees of self-administration. This political tradition based on peaceful institutional solutions and self-administration outlived the empire, affecting not just Lammasch and Redlich but all of our protagonists as well as many of their contemporaries who came of age under the Habsburgs.

The year 1848 also ushered in the empire's liberal period, when Habsburg politics was shaped by statesmen and intellectuals who believed in institutionalism, constitutionalism, and civic engagement. Now particularly valorized were the ideas of the rule of law, freedom of expression, and representation. Austrian liberalism was largely a German movement, as reforms were promoted in Vienna especially by Germanophone Austrians. But Austrian liberals also acknowledged the fact that most of those residing in this polity were not Germans.[7] The liberals led the empire's transition from absolutism to constitutionalism and from centralism to federalism.

Constitutionalism, liberalism, and federalism went hand in hand in the Habsburg Empire. The initial federalization was a by-product of Austria's military defeat by Prussia in 1866. The Habsburg dynasty, weakened by this and other military defeats, gave in to political pressure from the provinces, most notably Hungary. In 1867 the dynasty concluded a compromise with the Kingdom of Hungary, and the hitherto uniform empire became a federal state with two primary units, Austria and Hungary. The two shared the common dynasty and foreign and finance ministries, but otherwise would be governed as two separate entities. Liberals' influence in government began to decline in the wake of the 1872 economic crisis and concomitant political realignment. The collapse of liberalism in the late 1870s inaugurated the era of mass politics. However, several of the new parties that would dominate late Habsburg politics traced their roots to liberalism: German nationalism, Austrian Christian socialism, and Austrian social democracy.

The constitutional period in the empire's history that began in 1848 would last, with some interruptions, through 1918. Federative debates that started before 1867 also continued in the empire for decades, culminating during the last years of World War I.

The post-1867 Habsburg state (also known as Austro-Hungary) operated on the basis of the bicameral parliament and semiautonomous local assemblies. These institutions were hardly flawless; the imperial parliament, in particular, was wracked by chaos from the late 1890s onward, in part due to escalating national tensions that repeatedly bubbled up on the floor of that body. Emperor Francis Joseph dissolved the parliament in 1914 after the war broke out, and it would be reopened by his successor, Emperor Charles I, only in 1917. Yet despite the chaos and interruptions, parliamentary politics in the post-1867 Habsburg Empire was more functional than, for example, in the neighboring German, Russian, or Ottoman Empires. Even when the central parliament was

Austrian Imperial Parliament, 1902. Austrian National Library, Pictures (Bildarchiv Austria).

in chaos, local administrations exercised a great degree of authority in specific provinces.[8] Several successor states, but most notably republican Austria itself, built on the empire's institutional traditions, inheriting both their successes and limitations.[9]

Liberalism, Nationalism, Clericalism, Conservatism

Both Lammasch and Redlich exemplified the complex relationship between liberalism and the various movements and parties that emerged from its ruins, in particular German nationalism. Lammasch came of age under the rule of liberals, but he would only become active in politics after their downfall, in a way personifying the complicated transition in late Habsburg political history—all its constants and changes. His relationship with liberalism was correspondingly complex. On one hand, he endorsed institutionalism and constitutionalism. But he was also a devout Catholic, and the liberals' anticlericalism was alien to him. He supported the institutional church and regarded the empire as a bastion of Catholicism.

The collapse of liberalism initiated the period of Lammasch's political and ideological peregrinations. He progressed in his career in law but seemed increasingly lost in Austria's domestic politics, moving from one movement and party to another, settling for none. In the 1870s he became drawn to pan-Germanism, a radical nationalist ideology among ethnic Germans that espoused German superiority over Slavs and promoted the unification of German-speaking areas—including regions such as Bohemia, Moravia, and Trentino that were in fact quite ethnically mixed—with the German Empire (founded in 1871).[10] Many pan-Germans were former liberals who had once supported inclusiveness and tolerance but became disillusioned and shifted rightward from the 1870s on. Pan-Germanism represented one of the most radical variants of nationalism in the empire, as its adherents' endorsement of a greater German Empire to include Habsburg possessions threatened the territorial integrity and very existence of the Habsburg realm.[11]

Lammasch's choices in the postliberal period shed light on the continuity between Austrian liberalism and German nationalism. For him as for many others, nationalism replaced liberalism. Just as liberals sought unity in common values, so did those who turned to nationalism believe that it offered what Pieter Judson has described as "a compelling vision of social harmony that effectively denied class or religious differences."[12] Lammasch's own nationalism, however, went hand in hand with his loyalty to the ethnically diverse Habsburg Empire—a seeming paradox so widespread among imperial elites that it cannot really be called paradoxical. The pan-Germans' rejection of the multiethnic empire was ultimately a deal breaker for Lammasch. "History has taught us all lessons of coexistence," he wrote, "and has supplied numerous proofs that no state and no people can exist without others."[13] This understanding of coexistence as an essential feature of statehood ultimately defined his views of empire, nation, and state before and after 1918.

Parting ways with the radical nationalists, Lammasch considered becoming a member of the Christian Social Party. Also rooted in the postliberal tradition, and like pan-Germanism drawing certain of its leading personalities from among former liberals, Austrian Christian Socials were ultraloyal. With its stronghold in Vienna, the party targeted German-speaking Austrians. Especially important to Lammasch in the party program was the Christian element. He saw the monarchy as a *Civitas Christiana,* a guarantor of peace and stability, and the Catholic aspect of Christian socialism had a lasting appeal for him.[14] The Christian Socials, however, were economically conservative, while Lammasch was a fiscal liberal, and so he rejected this option as well.

Lammasch was now left with few alternatives. The Social Democrats were anticlerical, and other parties never became as influential as the postliberal trio just described.[15] Several years spent shuttling between different camps produced no lasting result. He later commented on the difficulty of taking sides: "I joined the middle party [*die Mittelpartei*] mainly because it was a party of those who belonged to no party [*parteilosen*], whose members could vote alternatively with the right- or left-wing senators."[16] And so he did, navigating between different parties and movements. In the Austrian Senate, to which he was appointed in 1899, he could be called "one of the leading members of the Conservative Party."[17]

Austrian conservatism often gets lost within most narratives of the late empire, which tend to focus on liberalism and radical nationalism and the succession between the two. But many of Lammasch's contemporaries, including former liberals, did not identify as nationalists. Lammasch's and his peers' conservatism was a response to a particular political dynamic in the late empire: its fragmentation after the collapse of liberalism. It implied the unquestionable loyalty to the empire paired with the rejection of nationalism and economic liberalism and support for institutionalism and reforms. Particular to Lammasch and unique to Austria, more broadly, was his combination of conservatism and internationalism. While many fellow conservatives across the empire shared similar values, the national element shaped the conservative vision in other provinces to a greater degree than it did in Vienna. But their impact upon the post-1918 Europe could not be overestimated.

Joseph Redlich: Between Moravia and Austria

Joseph Redlich, born in 1869, was Lammasch's junior by almost two generations. A specialist in administrative law, he too had prioritized the legal profession over politics before 1914, and distinguished himself in particular for his expertise on the British parliamentary system. Redlich and Lammasch would have known each other from the community of legal scholars in the Habsburg Empire and abroad from before 1914. Despite their differences in age and background, their ideological and political choices—or lack thereof—would turn out to be similar.

Redlich was raised in a prosperous family of assimilated Jews who owned a sugar factory in Göding, Moravia (Hodonín in Czech). The Redlichs belonged to the local Germanophone milieu and identified as Austrian. Redlich never shared his forebears' passion for industry, but a considerable allowance afforded all members of the family a financially carefree existence. Although his native town was predominantly German, early in his life Redlich become close friends with a Czech child: Tomáš Masaryk, the son of a maid, Therese Kropaczek, who worked in the Redlich household. Rumor had it, in fact, that the two were half brothers, with Masaryk allegedly born of a liaison between Therese and Redlich's father, Adolf. The Redlichs provided for Masaryk's education both in the Habsburg monarchy and Germany, facilitating his political career, which culminated in his election as Czechoslovakia's first president. He and Redlich remained in touch well beyond 1918.[18] Theirs was a friendship with political consequences.

Just like Lammasch, Redlich studied law in Vienna and Germany. In Vienna he joined the intellectual circles around the liberal *Die Neue Freie Presse.* Members of the editorial board and contributors included influential thinkers of that generation, such as writers Stefan Zweig and Karl Kraus. In the age of mass politics and nationalism, the liberals in Austria had not disappeared. Indeed, liberalism remained significant to elite intellectual and political life, particularly in Vienna. Redlich's initial cohort were liberals who were no longer dominant in government but remained prominent nevertheless.

Because of his Jewish background, the late imperial turn toward nationalism affected Redlich even more than it did Lammasch. Yet their political trajectories aligned, as Redlich for some time experimented with radical nationalism. In 1903 he converted to Catholicism, and in 1907 he became a member of the German Liberal Alliance, a nationalist organization based on the perception of Germans' civilizational superiority to Slavs.[19] When joining the nationalist camp, Redlich distanced himself from Jewish liberal circles, but continued to support the premises of liberalism such as institutional representation and admired Britain as an example of liberal democracy.[20] In retrospect, Redlich's affiliation with the German nationalists before 1914 may seem counterintuitive, given his Jewish background. Yet such paradoxes were hardly exceptional in late Habsburg politics, where loyalty to the empire was often permanent, and national identification far more transient.[21]

Redlich's view of statehood and nationalism was grounded in his trust of institutions, which he criticized only with the aim of reform and improvement.

He was elected deputy of the imperial parliament, and like many other protagonists of this book he regarded the parliament as the primary venue of democracy, however imperfect. Institutionalism and constitutionalism were as important for him as they were for Lammasch and most of this book's protagonists.

Pre-1914 Internationalism

While Redlich concerned himself with domestic politics, Lammasch's fields of expertise were international law and arbitration. Pivotal in his life and career was the year 1899, when he moved from Innsbruck to the imperial capital to assume a law professorship at the University of Vienna. He now also became a senator, and soon rumors began to circulate of his likely appointment as minister of justice.[22] But this possibility never materialized. His time spent in the senate only deepened his disappointment with Austrian politics. "The senate took little of my time, and it had even less influence," Lammasch would later comment on his service in that body.[23] He would remain something of an outsider in Austrian politics. But also in 1899, he became an Austrian delegate and legal advisor at the international conference in The Hague. The two Hague Conventions (1899 and 1907) became major events in the history of international law and interstate relations. They established regulations on warfare, including the treatment of civilians during hostilities, and became a keystone in the development of international arbitration.[24] In recognition of his efforts in the field of international law and arbitration, Lammasch was made a member of the Institute of International Law—one of the highest honors that could be bestowed on a legal scholar in the early twentieth century. He also became an Austrian delegate to the Permanent Court of Arbitration established at The Hague.[25]

At The Hague Lammasch began to actively promote the creation of an international organization to regulate relations between the "united states of the world" for the purpose of preventing war.[26] He also proposed an institution of arbitration that, while not mandatory, could serve as a venue to facilitate conflict resolution between states.[27] International arbitration became particularly relevant during the First World War and its immediate aftermath, marking an important point of continuity between the empire and post-1918 Europe.

From Pacifism to Militarism and Back

The international agreements signed at The Hague were put to the test when war broke out in August 1914. The Habsburg Empire found itself at the epicenter of what many in Europe initially believed would be a relatively short military confrontation, but which turned into a seemingly interminable conflict, prolonged by the unprecedented technical advances of modern warfare. While Germany was primarily preoccupied with the Western Front, the Habsburg war effort focused mainly on the East. The fate of post-1918 Europe, and particularly the territories east of Vienna—much of the post-Habsburg space—would be decided primarily by the war on the Eastern Front and the confrontations there between the Austrian and Russian Empires.

Lammasch and Redlich had crossed paths many times before 1914, but it was the war that truly brought them together. Before 1914 both men endorsed the monarchy but not, in general, war. For years prior to 1914, Lammasch had supported Austria's neutrality and advocated the creation of a federation of neutral states in Europe. He was by and large opposed to military solutions.[28] When war did break out, he justified Vienna's participation as an act of self-defense.[29] The Habsburgs, he claimed in an article of July 28, 1914, had to respond to the provocations of Serbia; only thus could they defend a "free and progressive Austria based on the principle of national self-governance of all peoples. We want an Austria that is truly a union of free nations. We deny any responsibility for the beginning of this war."[30]

Lammasch moved to Salzburg in 1914; his academic work became increasingly tied to politics. His writing from the early months of the war revealed his steadfast belief that the empire would survive it. In Salzburg he worked in particular on his book *National Rights after the War*.[31] From this study, it is clear that Lammasch at the time had no doubt that the international order would survive the conflict, requiring only certain legal modifications. In 1915 he published an article in the *Vienna Daily* (*Wiener Tagblatt*) that sought to look beyond the current violence and focus on what would come next: "At a time when a civil war of brother against brother has torn Europe apart, it is worthwhile to distance ourselves from the pressure and concerns of the present, and take a glimpse into the future—not the future of a single state, or even of the several states currently involved in mortal combat with one another, but the future of Europe and of humanity as a whole."[32] This theme of European unity would define Lammasch's thinking through the war and after its end until his death in 1920.

Like Lammasch, Redlich initially endorsed the war. He was part of that considerable cohort of Germanophone statesmen and intellectuals in the Habsburg and German Empires who not only justified their governments' course as necessary, but even saw the conflict as a potentially positive phenomenon. He supported the Habsburg emperor Francis Joseph as a "peaceful monarch," whose sole concern had been to preserve the integrity of his realm.[33] Early in the war, he remained a member of the (nationalist) German Liberal Alliance; he identified as German and referred to Germans as the "noblest people in the world."[34]

It took several months, but his vision of the war and Austria's role in it underwent a significant change. The first military campaigns were brutal, and the disastrous consequences of the war were soon too glaring to ignore. In the fall of 1914, Austrian and Russian forces clashed head-on in Galicia. When the fighting reached the Carpathian Mountains, the winter there would prove devastating for the Austrian side, an outcome so disastrous that it effectively destroyed the pre-1914 standing Habsburg army, and may have doomed Austria's and Germany's chances of victory in general.[35]

In the midst of it all, the Austrian government launched campaigns of persecution against its own citizens: against Ukrainians suspected of siding with Russia; Slovenes and Italians suspected of cooperating with Italy; and Czechs potentially involved in anti-Habsburg conspiracies.[36] This oppressive treatment of civilians by Austrian and German forces exceeded Redlich's worst fears. He refused to remain a bystander and pulled strings in the government to secure the release of some Czechs arrested as a result of Austrian political repressions in Bohemia.[37]

If the treatment of civilians inside the empire was harsh, Austrian policy beyond its borders was outright barbaric; an appalled Lammasch decried numerous breaches of the rules of war and military conduct established by the Hague and Geneva conventions. In its occupation of Serbia early in the war, the Austrian military disregarded the empire's civil authorities and law, openly brutalizing the civilian population.[38] The breakdown of civil administration in Austria—as described by Redlich—and the military's assertion of autonomy made for a civilian crisis at home and abroad.[39] By 1915 both Lammasch and Redlich were looking for ways to get the Habsburg state out of the war.

Lammasch and Redlich on War and Peace

Lammasch and Redlich became closer, politically and intellectually, during their stay in Salzburg where they moved after the beginning of the war. Here they became part of the "Salzburg Circle," a cohort of Austrian statesmen and intellectuals who opposed the war and advocated for Austria's exit. In 1915 Redlich became a member, and Lammasch an affiliate, of the Austrian Political Society. Founded by the Austrian coffee entrepreneur Julius Meinl, the society served as "a venue for discussion for intellectually engaged elites" who shared similar values and specifically sought ways to lead Austria out of the war.[40] In 1917 both participated in a public peace forum organized by Meinl on ending Austria's involvement in the conflict.

During these exchanges, Lammasch and Redlich developed different views of the Austrian government and its role in the war. Decrying the ruthlessness of modern warfare, in which "cruelty has become the norm" and "law has given way to repression," Lammasch nevertheless placed most of the blame for the conflict on Germany.[41] While critical of the war in general, Lammasch emphasized Vienna's domestic achievements. He asked, rhetorically, "How many Irish ministers are there in Britain? And how many Finnish ministers in Russia?" The Habsburg monarchy, he insisted, had made remarkable progress in multiethnic representation but had received no credit from international observers.

Lammasch ascribed Austria's troubles mainly to the machinations of nationalist minority upstarts, a conviction that he would maintain after the end of the empire. In 1917 he denounced "Masaryk, his consortium, and other renegades" for their alleged determination to ruin Austria's reputation abroad.[42] Lammasch tried to invoke international parallels in support of the Habsburg cause. In early 1918, during a visit by the American chargé d'affaires Charles Stetson Wilson (no relation to the president), Lammasch asked him pointedly "whether America believes all Irish claims regarding their national oppression under English rule."[43] Through the remaining months of the war, he continued to support the Austrian government.

Redlich took a view less steeped in Habsburg patriotism. Vienna, he maintained, was responsible, if not for the outbreak of war itself, then certainly for the atrocities committed thereafter.[44] He also saw the war as laying bare the severe administrative and political shortcomings of the Austrian government: "Even in this relatively brief period that has passed since the outbreak of the war, one can easily see the major failures of the Austrian economy; the lack of leadership, administrative inefficiency, the overall indifference, and so on and so forth."[45] As a solution to these problems, he advocated the administrative reorganization of the empire by increasing the degree of autonomy and granting more leverage to regional administrations.[46]

If Lammasch blamed nationalists for ruining the empire's reputation, Redlich came to ascribe their radicalization to the government's own decisions in the run-up to and conduct of the war. The gravest threat to the empire, as he saw it, was not the nationalist agitation of minorities, but rather the radicalization of German nationalism. Austrian German nationalists, with their grandiose aspirations of German greatness, he insisted, were no less a danger to the empire than Poles plotting independence.[47] In a January 1917 letter to the poet and dramatist Hermann Bahr, Redlich declared the (nationalist) German Liberal Alliance to be the empire's greatest menace.[48] The belief that German nationalism was "a political weapon to destroy the Habsburg Empire" became a key theme in Redlich's post-1918 writings.[49]

Redlich's break with German nationalists coincided with the rediscovery of his Jewish roots. In the summer of 1917, while still technically belonging to the German Liberal Alliance, he accepted an invitation to become the honorary head of a Jewish organization, which outraged his nationalist colleagues. He described intraparty conflict in an August 1917 letter to Bahr: "The radicals are extremely angry with me. They go so far as to claim that I have the pretentious ambition of becoming prime minister."[50] Later the same year, he was expelled from the party. Redlich's romance with nationalism was, as previously mentioned, not untypical for the cohort of former liberals. But while many of his colleagues became radicalized still further during the war, he took the opposite path: the war in effect dispelled his nationalism. It was German nationalism and Austrian administrative failures, he argued, that fueled the unrest of ethnic minorities and contributed to the empire's decline; in this view, the war's mismanagement made national independence not only possible but desirable.[51]

Redlich's argument about administrative failures exacerbated by the war as the major reason for the empire's collapse has recently received much traction in the literature. The newest research on the administration of the Habsburg Empire sheds light not only on the causes of its collapse but also on various nuances of its institutional structures before and during the war. Several scholars have argued that despite the crisis in the late imperial period, until 1914 the Habsburg state showed no sign of imminent collapse. It was only the war—and specifically the Austrian government's war policies, including administrative failures, inefficient management, and repressive measures against ethnic minorities—that opened the way for the downfall.[52]

Federation, Confederation, and Internationalism

It was during the war that Lammasch tied his international initiatives to domestic transformations of the Habsburg Empire. The empire, as he and others argued, could only survive by effectively addressing its nationalities issues and the dissent that had been on the rise since the beginning of the war. Having resisted further federalization before 1914, Habsburg statesmen and ministers in the later stages of the war came to look upon this possibility as a potential means to stabilize the empire.

The 1867 federal union between Austria and Hungary set a precedent not only for such discussions, but also for nationally based political dissent among different ethnic groups and provinces, most notably the Poles in Galicia, the Czechs in Bohemia, and the Italians on the Adriatic. Representatives of all these groups demanded a Hungary-like status, but although most, especially the Poles in Galicia, did secure major autonomy concessions, Vienna resisted further federalization. It was only during the later stages of the war that even Francis Joseph and his senior ministers began to consider federalization necessary for the preservation of the empire's territorial integrity.

Several scholars have recently drawn attention to the importance of federative and confederative thinking in the empire, especially during the last decades of its existence. Jana Osterkamp has demonstrated the importance of federative debates in the empire after 1868.[53] Helmut Rumpler has explained that federalism was "the core issue of the monarchy's existence" in its final decades.[54] These federative discussions traveled across 1918 into postwar Europe, where they would remain as relevant as they had been during the last years of the empire.

Lammasch was at the forefront of these debates and took practical steps meant to steer Austria out of the war and guide its internal reconstruction. In early February 1918, together with Julius Meinl, he held a secret meeting in Bern with the American pacifist clergyman-turned-diplomat George Herron. Hoping to use Herron's contacts and status in Europe, the Woodrow Wilson administration arranged an office for him in Geneva, where he began to work as an attaché of the US State Department.[55] Lammasch's encounter with Herron took place at a critical juncture in the history of the empire and of Europe generally. Only weeks before, President Wilson had announced his Fourteen Points on the transition to peace and the reconstruction of Europe. Wilson denounced secret treaties that, he claimed, led to war, advocated peaceful conflict resolution, and promoted national self-determination and the rights of ethnic minorities.[56] Lammasch was keen to secure US support because he believed that Wilson's thinking was similar to his own vision for the Habsburg Empire and European security. As he saw it, the Western powers would surely recognize the danger to Europe should the Habsburg polity be lost, and would not allow this to happen. In his conversation with Herron, Lammasch expressed his fascination with the Swiss political system, believing that it could serve as a "golden bridge" or model for the Habsburg Empire. Bereft of such a multiethnic federative power, lamented Lammasch, Europe seemed fated to devolve into a confrontation between "Bolshevism and extreme capitalism."[57]

Lammasch was part of a larger cohort of intellectuals and statesmen in the Habsburg Empire who advocated territorial reorganization, but he took this idea one step further. In lieu of a Habsburg federation, Lammasch proposed a Danubian confederation. Also formed from the territories of the Habsburg empire, this entity, he argued, would serve as a guarantor of European security and would thus be in the interest not only of the empire's various nationalities, but also of other countries in Europe.[58] In some ways, Lammasch's proposal was a sign of desperation, a last-minute effort to preserve the Habsburg polity even if in a modified form. The idea of confederative transformations received no significant support among the Habsburg political establishment, but it would gain traction and live on beyond the empire's collapse.

In the meantime, the news of Lammasch's meeting with Herron, when leaked to the public, provoked heated debate in the Austrian senate. Such freelance diplomacy not only defied Austria's alliance with Germany, it also brought to light a confederative model that had no current support within the Austrian political establishment. Lammasch's calculations as to the Entente powers' support of the Habsburg Empire as a polity were misplaced as well; at some point during the way, the governments of these countries had in fact begun to anticipate its collapse. Having accepted the likelihood of this outcome, President Wilson began to make references to ethnic oppression under the Habsburgs, and to describe the empire as a prison of nations.[59]

Wilson's famous Fourteen Points have received much credit in historiography as having laid the groundwork for the post-1918 League of Nations and providing a road map for the transition to the postimperial period. In their focus on Wilson as an advocate of peace, however, many studies have obscured the president's vagueness regarding the fate of East Central Europe and the convoluted nature of his conception of self-determination. As Larry Wolff has recently explained, Wilson long struggled to make up his mind about the Habsburg Empire. In his initial declaration of the Fourteen Points in January 1918, he insisted on self-determination without specifying its nuances or the nature of the state—Habsburg or otherwise—within which such self-determination was to be accomplished. It was only later in the war that Wilson accepted and eventually endorsed the possibility of the empire's breakup, thereby revising or even transforming his own notion of self-determination to imply not just autonomy but also nationhood and independence.[60] Wilson's vision, of course, differed considerably from that of Lammasch.

As late as October 1918, meanwhile, both Emperor Francis Joseph and Lammasch believed that the empire could be saved. On the fourteenth of the month, Prime Minister Max Hussarek issued a manifesto promising the federalization of the empire along national lines. Hussarek resigned on October 25, and Lammasch agreed to step in, officially assuming on October 27 the office of prime minister, with Redlich serving as finance minister.[61] This cabinet would oversee the transition from empire to republic.[62]

The changeover to the postimperial space that Lammasch supervised was complex. Even the chronology of the empire's end remains a matter of controversy.[63] Czechoslovakia declared its independence on October 28, and the first meeting of the constitutional assembly of the Republic of Austria took place on October 30. The emperor, however, abdicated only on November 11.[64] For nearly two weeks, Lammasch's imperial government cooperated with the Austrian republican parliament—the two entities consisting of statesmen and politicians who came from the very same circles.

Versailles, Saint-Germain, and the League of Nations

The last years of the war marked the culmination of Lammasch's intellectual and political career. In 1917 he published what scholars have since regarded as the most important work of his career, *The Laws of Nations after the War*, which addressed wartime breaches of international law and methods to resolve them. Immediately after the war, he wrote and edited several works on a related topic; one was an edited collection of the writings of Woodrow Wilson in German translation, with an introduction by Lammasch.[65] His final book, *League of*

Nations or the Death of Nations (*Völkerbund oder Völkermord*), published post-humously in 1920, presented a more nuanced analysis of international media-tion. Here, for example, Lammasch acknowledged the potential hurdles in implementing such mediation. An international organization, he conceded, would inevitably interfere with state sovereignty and could prove a hindrance to the usual way of doing things. "The axiom of absolute unlimited state sov-ereignty," Lammasch explained, "has become embedded in the European political and intellectual imagination since the seventeenth century; and any interference with an individual state's affairs could become problematic for some." Still, he argued, an international organization with some degree of lever-age over particular states was a necessary vehicle for peace—the only way to prevent war, which must be seen as an "absolute evil" in human history.[66]

This last work was likely based on his experience participating in the post-1918 negotiations in Paris and then Saint-Germain, as well as the early days of the League of Nations. He traveled to Versailles as part of the Austrian delega-tion. Several of Lammasch's contemporaries, including George Herron, com-mented on the disappointment, even trauma, that Lammasch experienced in his last years. He had been preparing for peace, observed Herron, but in Paris the Entente powers treated him like an enemy prisoner.[67]

Austria signed the final Saint-Germain postwar settlements in Septem-ber 1919. The Republic of Austria was a shadow of the empire. Once one of the largest states in Europe, Austria was now severely truncated, having lost not only its various provinces but also territories with significant German-speaking population—lands that most Austrians considered to be their own. It ceded South Tyrol to Italy; part of the Carniola region to the Kingdom of Serbs, Croats, and Slovenes; and the Sudeten areas to Czechoslovakia. In eco-nomic terms as well, the impact of the postwar settlements on Austria was dire. Designated as one of the countries responsible for unleashing the war, it was obligated to pay reparations, and though these were not as steep as for Germany, this financial burden contributed to a major crisis in the Austrian economy long before the Great Depression hit in 1929. As a way of preventing future wars, the victorious allies also precluded the possibility of Anschluss: Austria was prohibited from entering a union with Germany.[68]

If imperial Vienna had shown signs of devastation in the last years of the war, its republican counterpart fared no better. In a development that most of its residents had never before—even in the early war chaos—experienced, the city was hit by crippling food shortages. Saint-Germain, meanwhile, came as a further shock, in particular to Lammasch. He withdrew from the confer-

Heinrich Lammasch (center back, in a dark suit) at Saint-Germain, 1919. Austrian National Library, Pictures (Bildarchiv Austria).

ence, disillusioned with the Entente powers' treatment of Austria. Contemporaries attested that he wept as the conditions of the Treaty of Saint-Germain were announced. Redlich later commented: "No one experienced the trauma of the collapse of the Habsburg monarchy and . . . Saint-Germain as severely [as did Lammasch]."[69]

The territorial and political reorganization of the empire that Lammasch had envisioned never came to pass; but his ideas about international mediation lived on, materializing in the League of Nations—another product of Wilsonian diplomacy and the post-1918 settlements. The League, founded in 1919, represented the culmination of long-standing efforts at international arbitration, dating back at least to the first conference in The Hague. As such it carried on the mission of the Court of Arbitration, of which Lammasch had been a member. The League also marked the climax of Wilson's efforts for international peace and conflict resolution: an institution to facilitate mediation and promote the rights of national minorities.

We know from the abundant research that the League did help forge internationalism of a new kind, offering a venue for regular discussion of, for example, the issue of national minorities, and creating an extensive network of experts and a concomitantly unprecedented international dialogue.[70] We also know that the League's limitations would outweigh its accomplishments. Just as Lammasch suggested in his final book, national sovereignty remained sacred for many in post-1918 Europe, and international intervention would remain of a limited nature. The League was also a cumbersome institution, with complicated administrative procedures. While it could and did hear complaints about minority rights violations, it had no leverage to enforce its rulings on particular states.[71]

Lammasch did not live to see the League's failures during the 1920s and 1930s. But he had sufficient time to be disappointed both with Wilson's concept of self-determination and with the League. Several of Lammasch's colleagues at Saint-Germain and afterward argued that the conditions imposed on Austria violated Austrian Germans' rights of self-determination: the Sudetenland and Trentino, as well as part of Carniola, had a large proportion of Germanophone Austrians, who now found themselves outside their former state.

After Saint-Germain, Lammasch retired to Salzburg. His mission had been the preservation of the Habsburg monarchy and of peace. The first, indeed, was a total failure, and the second came at a price too steep for him to accept. Amid the shock of the treaties' aftermath, he retreated from politics, dying in January 1920, a mere three months after his return from the negotiations.

Redlich between Empire, Republican Austria, and Czechoslovakia

Lammasch's friend and colleague from the empire's last government, Joseph Redlich, evinced a different kind of continuity across the 1918 divide. Similarly to Lammasch, he stepped up his academic research in the last years of the war and after the empire's collapse. He channeled his frustration with the empire's fate into a two-volume *History of the Imperial Problem*. The first and second volumes were published in 1920 and 1926.[72] Why, this study proposed to interrogate, did the ancient monarchy experience a crisis and ultimately fall? Redlich examined the failures of Austria's central bureaucracy; the lack of coordination between its different branches; and the flaws of particular institutions, as well as of many individual bureaucrats employed therein.[73] As Frederick Lindström observes, Redlich's scholarship was intertwined with his political career: "One might say that Redlich was writing himself and his political activities into Austrian history."[74] His self-identification with the empire, moreover, would make it difficult for him to adjust to a new world after its demise.

As compared with Lammasch's experience, the trauma of collapse and transition was different for Redlich in essence but of a similar intensity. While the family of the former was based around Vienna, the Redlichs were divided between what became Austria and Czechoslovakia (which annexed Redlich's native Moravia). Redlich became one of many to face the most immediate dilemma of citizenship—something none had ever encountered under the empire. "An authentic Viennese who in his own person exemplified the racial gallimaufry of the Habsburg realm," Redlich now became torn between two different states—Austria and Czechoslovakia.[75] On November 30, 1918, he traveled aboard an overcrowded third-class train to Moravia, the means of transport and the very landscape, he noted, reflecting the wreckage inflicted by the war and the end of the region's stability.[76] The Czechoslovak government, moreover, linked property ownership to citizenship, thereby dispossessing many of those who either found themselves or chose to live in a different state.[77] The mere decision of where to *attempt* to settle could thus prove catastrophic for many of those who owned land or businesses across borders, including some of our protagonists.

The choice of home became harder for Redlich when he received two competing offers of ministerial positions from the two countries. In 1920 he was again considered for the position of Austrian finance minister. In 1917 German nationalists had blocked his nomination as prime minister, and they blackballed him again now, especially outraged by his rejection of the Anschluss option.[78] But this was not the end of Redlich's involvement with Austrian politics. His networks and experience were too valuable to the new state. In late 1920 the Austrian government, headed by Michael Mayer, undertook to use some of Redlich's international networks to secure economic assistance. In early 1921 he traveled to France, Britain, and the United States, holding unofficial talks in Paris and London and official meetings in Washington. Everywhere the discussions revolved around the same issues: food supply and loans to Austria. In 1922 he made several additional visits to the United States to negotiate Austrian-American trade agreements, making use of his former connections.[79] But these endeavors likewise fell through. The new Austria remained alien to him, and his sense of estrangement would only grow stronger in subsequent years.

In November 1918 an alternative ministerial offer had come from Tomáš Masaryk, now president of Czechoslovakia, who invited Redlich to serve in the Czech government.[80] When Redlich hesitated, Masaryk appealed to Germany's ambassador in Prague, asking for his personal intervention.[81] Masaryk's invitation was unprecedented. Like the other Habsburg successor states, Czechoslovakia fashioned itself as a nation-state, and despite being in reality a small replica of the old multiethnic empire, it carried out monoethnic policies. Czech dominance became evident as early as 1919: over 70 percent of the parliamentary coalition were Czechs. The administrative staff was still less diverse, with Germans excluded entirely and only two Slovak ministers; all other officers were Czechs.[82] Had he accepted Masaryk's offer, Redlich might have affected the outlook of Czechoslovakia's government and its political system for years to come. The very possibility of Redlich's involvement in the Czechoslovak government was another by-product of the imperial past, and of the personal and professional relationships that he and Masaryk had forged long before.

Redlich continued to define himself as an Austrian, but his official ties to republican Austria would never be as firm as in the imperial era. In the early 1920s he retreated from politics and government, shifted back to academia, and relocated to the United States in 1926 after securing an academic appointment at Harvard University.

Conclusion

"I've just returned from Lammasch's funeral," wrote Zweig in a letter to Rolland on October 1, 1920. It was a gloomy picture, he commented. "Never before have I seen such a funeral, so sad, so heartbreaking. Not a single member of the government, no party colleagues showed up; all of them fearing to seem like monarchists by attending the funeral of the last faithful of the unlucky Emperor Karl."[83] Lammasch had become a symbol of the empire in the last days of its existence, and would be posthumously banished from Austrian political discourse for the very commitments that many of his contemporaries had treasured before 1918.

Austria now became one of several states in post-1918 Europe that claimed to build a republic by eliminating remnants of the defunct empire. Despite having supported the monarchy before 1918, thereafter most Austrians renounced any possible Habsburg restoration as something that would threaten the existing political and international order. In April 1919 the Austrian parliament adopted the so-called Habsburg Law, nationalizing the properties of the former imperial family in Austria and banning its members from residence in the new republic.[84] Eliminating the imperial past also implied maintaining distance from those like Lammasch who had been most prominent for their service to the Habsburgs and their devotion to the empire.

Yet despite the official rhetoric of the republic's break with the empire, post-Habsburg Austria became a paradigm of continuity rather than rupture with the imperial past. Austria was the only state in the post-Habsburg space to implement the federal state concept that had been under discussion in the empire long before 1918. According to the structure now adopted, the federal republic became composed of different lands with a certain degree of autonomy from the central government, and the city of Vienna was defined as a distinct administrative unit within the republic. Minsters from the empire, meanwhile, continued to occupy their same or similar positions in the republican government.[85] The new country's political dynamics, including the practice of coalition building, was likewise reminiscent of the empire—a phenomenon facilitated by the many statesmen and politicians who, like Redlich, had held offices in the empire and then transferred to the republic after 1918.

Lammasch and Redlich were part of a large cohort of Austrian statesmen to partake in this transition, and the two of them epitomized the numerous controversies surrounding 1918 and its aftermath. Redlich came of age in the empire and held the same ministerial post in its successor state, returning to government in Austria again in 1931. Lammasch's involvement in postimperial government and politics was brief, but in some ways—in particular, in his emphasis on federalism, confederalism, and internationalism—it was more consequential than that of Redlich or the many other post-Habsburgians who continued in politics through the 1920s and 1930s. His vision of a Danubian confederation as a reformed version of the Habsburg Empire gradually gained traction between the wars as a possible solution to the post-1918 European crisis. It never materialized, and yet the conception of Europe as a potential confederation lived on through the Second World War and beyond, to be eventually incarnated in the European Union. Neither Lammasch nor Redlich lived to see these developments. But other protagonists of this book did see it through, not just as passive observers but as active participants in the new, post-1945 Europe. In doing so, they continued to follow Habsburg imperial models.

2. Conservatives in the East

Poland, Ukraine, and Romania, 1848–1924

In the late fall of 1918, while Heinrich Lammasch and Joseph Redlich were navigating the empire's end from Vienna, their acquaintance and a longtime fellow minister, Leon Biliński, was organizing his new life between Vienna, Lwów, and Warsaw. Born in 1846 in Galicia, an Austrian province on the border with the Russian Empire, he had become one of the most accomplished of Habsburg statesmen, having served in various offices in Vienna from the 1880s to 1916. In 1918, however, he found himself on the margins of politics—no longer trusted by the emperor, who preferred to fill government positions with Germanophone Austrians such as Lammasch and Redlich.

Biliński's story is emblematic of the late empire. Raised in a family of assimilated Jews in the ethnically mixed area of Eastern Galicia, he spoke Polish as his native language, married an ethnic German, but identified as Austrian—a combination of national-minority affiliation with pan-imperial loyalty that was common in the late empire but became increasingly untenable during the war.[1] Too Polish to participate in the imperial government, he became too Austrian for many of his Polish peers, who increasingly aspired to independence. His political career appeared to be over, and relationships with many of his friends and colleagues from the empire seemed damaged beyond repair.

One such relationship was particularly important in Biliński's life and career. Nicolaus (Mykola) Wassilko was Biliński's longtime colleague and—for some years—friend. Wassilko was born in 1868 in Bukovina, a mixed Romanian-German-Ukrainian-Jewish region then bordering a segment of the Ottoman Empire that after 1877 became part of independent Romania. Although raised in an aristocratic Romanian family and educated in Germanophone institutions, Wassilko as an adult chose to identify as Ukrainian. Biliński and Wassilko had known each other for decades, and in Viennese political circles they gained a reputation for reciprocal support. The war became a turning point for them: while Lammasch and Redlich drew closer together, Biliński and Wassilko shifted apart. Despite both preferring empire over any unitary nation-state, by late 1918 they supported two competing national camps: Polish and Ukrainian, both of which had claims on Galicia. During these years and thereafter, a cohort of former imperial statesmen fought for and tried to preserve Polish and Ukrainian independence by building on imperial-era networks and practices.

While continuities between the empire and republican Austria and Czechoslovakia have received some attention in the literature, the empire's afterlife in Poland is a less familiar topic. In Ukraine it is less familiar still, perhaps partly owing to the counterintuitiveness of the connection.[2] The Republic of Austria was, after all, a direct successor of the empire, and Czechoslovakia was formed mostly of former Habsburg territories. Galicia, meanwhile, constituted only about a third of the new Poland, the other parts coming from the Russian and German Empires. The case of Ukraine is even more complicated: while two independent Ukrainian states appeared on maps in late 1918—on the ruins of the Russian and Habsburg Empires, respectively— neither survived past 1921. But the empire's legacy in its former eastern borderland was as important as in its center (Austria) and its German-Slavic frontier (Czechoslovakia).

This chapter deals with two statesmen from the empire's east who, like Lammasch and Redlich, belonged to the older generation, defined themselves as conservatives, and continued in politics after 1918—only now in the politics of Poland and Ukraine. In the empire, Lammasch, Redlich, Biliński, and Wassilko belonged to the same political and intellectual circles: German-speaking professionals who most often started their careers in law and later shifted to politics. They crossed paths in the hallways of the Austrian parliament, senate, and government, where all of them were present at different points of their lives. Their stories illustrate parallel developments with different outcomes; by shifting focus to the east, I explore how the same ideologies and political landmarks in the empire's history (for example, liberalism, conservatism, and the revolutions and political realignments of 1848 and 1867) had different repercussions for territories outside of Vienna. This chapter thus represents an analysis of the ways in which the empire's conservatives incorporated imperial practices in their new states (or under conditions of statelessness) in Europe's east, after the dust and borders had settled.

Galicia and Bukovina: The Habsburg Eastern Periphery

Galicia and Bukovina were both annexed by the Habsburgs in the late eighteenth century. Formerly part of the Polish-Lithuanian Commonwealth, Galicia became a Habsburg possession as a result of the three partitions of Poland between 1772 and 1795, when Austria, Prussia, and Russia each took parts of Polish territory. The partitions caused one of the largest states in Europe to disappear, and it also created, for the first time in history, a direct border between the Russian and Habsburg Empires, with repercussions for centuries to come.[3] Bukovina, formerly part of the Moldavian territories in the Ottoman Empire, was annexed in 1774 as a result of the Austro-Turkish War. The two regions were historically different but shared certain commonalities. Both were economically backward compared to other Habsburg territories. They also shared a border. Until 1848 both regions were administered together as a single entity from Galicia's capital, Lemberg/Lwów.[4] After 1848 they became separate provinces.

Even within the highly diverse Habsburg Empire, Galicia and Bukovina stood out for their ethnic compositions. Poles and Ukrainians each constituted roughly 45 percent of Galicia's inhabitants;[5] but its large contingent of Jews—about 10 percent of the overall population—also set it apart from other Habsburg provinces. The Jewish minority was indeed a majority in some areas of Galicia, constituting as much as 70 percent of some towns' population.[6] Bukovina was more diverse still. In the mid-nineteenth century, Romanians made up about half its population, with Ukrainians—approximately 37 percent—taking the second spot. Germans and Jews, around 7 percent and 3 percent, respectively, represented small minorities, but they dominated the urban space, notably the largest city, Czernowitz (now Chernivtsi, Ukraine).[7]

The twenty years between 1848 and 1867 affected the eastern borderland differently than the empire's core. In 1867 Galician Poles demanded a status for their province similar to that of Hungary. But Vienna refused further federalization, instead offering administrative autonomy in return for the Poles' endorsement of the 1867 agreements with Hungary. Post-1867 Galicia then became an important example of territorial autonomy within the Habsburg Empire.[8] Unlike anywhere else in the Austrian part of the monarchy, where the German language remained dominant, Galician administration and education, including the two universities in Lemberg/Lwów and Cracow/Kraków, operated largely in Polish.[9] Post-1867 concessions to Galicia were more extensive than to any other province outside of Hungary.[10]

Even given these political arrangements, however, Poles considered themselves "losers," insofar as they had failed to secure federative status for Galicia. At the same time, their Ukrainian neighbors, now finding themselves essentially under Polish domination, saw them as winners. The post-1867 Galician autonomy thus unsettled the preexisting balance. Before 1867 the vast majority of Ukrainians had been ultraloyal to the Habsburgs, but the establishment of Polish autonomy in Galicia led many of them to question Austria's intentions and its implicit support of Poles over Ukrainians in Galicia. Just as Poles had earlier resisted Austrian domination, now Ukrainians protested what they perceived as Polish control over Galicia.[11]

Lwów/Lemberg, 1903. Polish National Library, Digital Collection Polona.

The year 1867 became a turning point for Galicians just as much as it did for Austrians. On one hand, many, including Biliński, considered the failure to secure a federal status for Galicia in the wake of the 1867 Austro-Hungarian Compromise as a major loss and even betrayal. But those perceptions were mitigated by concurrent developments in the Russian Empire, where conditions for Poles were becoming progressively worse. This comparative lens affected Poles' attitudes to both empires. In his formative years Biliński and other Galicians watched as the pro-independence revolution in Warsaw (1863–64) was brutally suppressed by the Russian army. The failed uprising forced many to reconsider the efficacy of bold action and to shift their focus toward evolutionary change instead. The failure to achieve a Hungary-like status for Galicia was a disappointment, but it did nothing to change the belief of Biliński and others that, given existing circumstances, the Habsburg Empire was the lesser of two evils by a wide margin.

Conservatism and Its Variants

The belief that the post-1868 Austro-Hungarian Empire provided the best opportunities for Poles fueled, in Galicia, both pro-Habsburg patriotism and Polish conservatism. Unlike the liberals and the nationalists, the conservatives supported the preservation of the existing political and social order, the exclusive political participation of the elites, and a limited access of the lower classes to education and politics. Biliński described his and his fellow conservatives' allegiances as follows: "In my political beliefs, I belong to the conservative camp"—which, in his particular case, meant supporting the existing regime while at the same time favoring pro-Galician reform.[12] "I have become a moderate conservative, a position that does not deprive me of certain aspects of liberalism and support for reforms necessary for the region."[13] The Polish conservatives never formed a party, but they became a leading political force in Galicia and in the Polish caucus in Vienna.[14]

Liberalism and radical nationalism have long dominated discussions of the late Habsburg Empire. Only recently have scholars devoted increased attention to imperial loyalty and its compatibility with nationalism. But even within this new literature, conservatism has remained marginalized. This neglect is unjustified: in Galicia, for example, the Polish conservatives dominated politics through the early years of World War I, losing ground to nationalists only during the later stages of the war. At least several of these conservatives, notably Biliński himself, shaped the politics of post-1918 Poland. The conservatives' impact was sometimes more important than that of their nationalist peers.

Biliński's and other Poles' conservatism was a by-product the Habsburg Empire's politics during the last decades of its existence, both a response to domestic developments as well as to Galicia's geopolitical relationship to Russia. Their preference for Vienna over St. Petersburg or Berlin was also conditioned by the prominent Polish presence in Austrian politics and government. The Austrian parliaments and governments were small microcosms of the empire, regularly including representatives from different regions and nationalities. Ministers from Galicia formed a constant presence in Vienna, at times even constituting a majority, as was the case in the so-called Polish government in office between 1895 and 1897.[15]

Biliński exemplified this trend. Early in his career he excelled as a law professor, quickly rising to dean of the University of Lwów law school, and then the youngest chancellor in that university's history. In the early 1880s he moved from Lwów to Vienna to enter politics. He was first elected to the parliament in 1883 (which meant that some of his political colleagues after 1918 would

Profesor Leon Biliński.   (176)

Leon Biliński, 1883. Polish National Library, Digital Collection Polona.

have been infants when Biliński first rose to prominence). He served as a par-liamentary deputy until 1892, when he was appointed minister of the Austro-Hungarian railways. In 1895–97, he was Austria's finance minister; from 1900 to 1909, a governor of the Austro-Hungarian Bank; in 1909–11, again finance minister; and from 1912 to 1915, head of the combined Austro-Hungarian Finance Ministry. He also served twice as head of the Polish caucus in the Austrian parliament.

Conservative Variants: Wassilko

Wassilko too identified as a conservative, supporting the preservation of the empire and the existing social order that favored the wealthy and the elites. He himself was one of them: a scion of an aristocratic Romanian family raised in wealth and privilege. He was born in Lukawetz, a village in Bukovina that his family had owned since at least the early fifteenth century.[16] At one time predominantly Romanian, Lukawetz had become increasingly Slavic, with Ukrainian peasants forming a majority in the nineteenth century. Wassilko was educated in Germanophone institutions, Vienna's prestigious Theresianum Academy. Returning to Bukovina after graduation, he entered politics by join-ing the Romanian conservative camp.[17] Failing to secure important positions in Romanian organizations, he eventually transitioned to the Ukrainian poli-tics.[18] He became a classic example of what Tara Zahra describes as national indifference: overreaching loyalty imposed upon a national identification that was defined primarily by practical choices.[19]

Wassilko's particular role as a representative of Bukovina and Galicia might help explain his political weight in the imperial capital. He became a deputy to the Bukovina diet in 1898 and to the Austrian parliament in 1899 as a member of the Galicia-based Ukrainian National Democratic Party. After 1907 he served as a leader of the joint Ukrainian representation from Galicia and Bukovina.[20] In 1904 he was elected a member of the Austrian Senate; in this office, which had a lifetime tenure, he was the only Bukovina representa-tive. In 1906 he became the only Ukrainian representative to serve on the electoral reform commission.[21] He never became a minister and never occu-pied high-level positions like those of Biliński. Yet his political leverage in Vienna was similar to that wielded by Biliński and outweighed that of most Ukrainian contemporaries.[22]

Mykola Wassilko, 1916. Austrian
National Library, Pictures
(Bildarchiv Austria).

The Politics of Compromise

It was in their capacities as prominent Austrian statesmen that Biliński and
Wassilko encountered each other in Vienna. They became politically close early
on. Wassilko was the only deputy from the Ukrainian camp to support Biliński's candidacy in government.[23] Outweighing their differences prior to 1914
were their similarities: trust in institutions and rejection of violence; national
fluidity and support of minority rights; and an abiding belief that the empire
must and would survive. Both also shared a vision of compromise and cooperation, a style of politics they would advocate through the years of war and
beyond the empire's collapse.

Compromise was integral to Vienna's Galicia policies early on, conditioned by the proximity of the Russian Empire. In the late 1880s the Austrian
government initiated Polish-Ukrainian negotiations in Galicia to address

Ukrainians' resentment of Polish dominance and thus decrease their potential receptiveness to Russian influence. The nearly four-year effort resulted in the signing of an 1894 agreement that became known as the "New Era"; this provided, among other things, for an increase in the number of Ukrainian deputies in the Galician diet and the establishment of a chair in Ukrainian studies at the University of Lwów, whose main language of instruction had been Polish.[24] But the long-term impact of this hard-won accord was limited: with the exception of the Ukrainian chair, most other provisions never materialized.

The next effort to forge a Polish-Ukrainian agreement would come in 1908, after the Polish governor of Galicia had been assassinated by a Ukrainian student. This 1907 political murder marked a peak in Polish-Ukrainian antagonism, and it was followed by another round of negotiations, this time with the direct involvement of our two protagonists. Biliński organized a meeting with leading Ukrainian deputies including Wassilko. Held in his office at the Austro-Hungarian Bank in Vienna, the meeting aimed to resolve the escalating crisis.[25] The 1908 agreement built on the 1894 precedent: the Polish caucus in the Austrian parliament pledged to coordinate efforts with Ukrainian deputies. The Ukrainians also secured a number of key political posts, including vice president of the provincial administration. Polish deputies pledged to support Ukrainian candidates for ministerial positions in Vienna. The 1908 accord thus bore even more promises than its 1894 predecessor, but these too went mostly unrealized.

Negotiations and compromises remained part of late imperial politics. While post-1867 Galicia represented a case of territorial autonomy, several agreements in the late empire created a basis for extra-territorial *personal* autonomy: a combination of practices that would be imprinted on many of those who came of age politically under the Habsburgs. In 1905, 1909, and 1914, the government proceeded with the implementation of the Moravian, Bukovina, and Galician compromises. These were all motivated by the same goal—to regulate national relations in specific provinces—but operated on different principles. Unlike, for example, the New Era agreements of 1894, which addressed the Ukrainian minority as a collective, the 1905, 1909, and 1914 compromises were designed to provide proportional representation to different national groups in local diets in their respective provinces: all residents of a particular province would be assigned a nationality and only allowed to vote (or attend schools, as was the case in Moravia) accordingly.[26]

These agreements thus imposed national categories on many individuals who might otherwise have identified differently. But in the Habsburg milieu, such compromises signaled the imperial government's willingness to accommodate the various national minorities under its rule. These efforts continued in the empire through 1914, the Galician compromise that year marking the final attempt. This agreement at last yielded significant results: for the first time ever, Ukrainians secured a large representation in the local diet.[27] But this was a case of fatal lateness: the compromise was shattered by the war. These compromises nevertheless shaped politics in several successor states, most notably Czechoslovakia, after 1918. The mandatory attribution of nationality—at the core of, particularly, the Moravian compromise—set a precedent for the forcible national stratification of post-1918 Czechoslovakia.[28]

1914: Serbia, Bosnia, Galicia, and Beyond

Galicia was where Austrian forces engaged in their first fighting of the Great War in the summer of 1914, and when that conflict finally ended, civil wars continued there through 1921. No other region of the empire save the Adriatic was affected as severely as Galicia. As recent research shows, paramilitary violence in post-1918 Europe was more widespread than formerly thought; its duration, and the degree of destruction it wrought, varied significantly from place to place, with the situation more parlous in the east than west.[29] To analyze the impact of the First World War on the eastern borderland thus requires extending the usual chronology in both directions. For the Habsburg realm, that is, the Great War should be seen as rooted in the two preceding Balkan wars, and concluding in the civil wars that followed after 1918.[30]

In his governmental and ministerial capacities and his pre-1914 engagement with the Balkans, Biliński would bear his share of responsibility both for the war and for the fateful choices that the empire and later the new Polish state would take after 1918. In 1908, while serving as head of the combined Austro-Hungarian Finance Ministry, he was appointed governor of Bosnia—a former Ottoman holding that had been placed under Austrian administration in 1882 and formally annexed in 1908. At this point Bosnia came under the jurisdiction of the Finance Ministry—one of only two ministries (the other being that of defense) that Austria and Hungary shared within the federative state. As head of this ministry, Biliński also became governor of the new province. Combining his different offices in Vienna and the Bosnian provincial capital of Sarajevo, Biliński encouraged autonomy as a way to forge loyalty.[31] At the same time, he warned of Serbia's geopolitical ambitions in the Balkans as a potential threat to the Habsburg Empire: an independent state since 1882, Serbia had long shown a great interest in what was now Habsburg Bosnia.

Unlike Lammasch and Redlich, who watched the war unfold from an intellectual and physical distance, Biliński found himself at its very epicenter. In 1914, as a minister, he supported the decision to go to war with Serbia. His militarism followed from several of his political convictions: that Serbia posed a genuine threat to the empire; that the empire could benefit from a war; and that a war could also positively influence a potential restructuring of the Polish territories under different partitions. In particular, Biliński's dream of a united Kingdom of Poland under a Habsburg monarch could only materialize as a result of war. "We decided on the war early on," he stated later.[32] Biliński was not alone in his support of the war, but he was one of the few responsible for its actual outbreak.

Domestic crisis in the Habsburg Empire was a by-product of the war, particularly of Austrian defeats. Yet the situation in Galicia differed from that in the empire's core or its western provinces: the proximity to Russia made Austria's eastern borderland more explosive than other Habsburg regions. Russian forces occupied Galicia and took over its administration twice during the war, first from August 1914 to June 1915, and then again in 1916.[33] The Russian occupation initially encouraged some pro-Russian elements, especially Ukrainians. But in the long run it antagonized many more Galicians, who now encountered a kind of brutality they had never experienced under the Habsburgs. The Russian occupation only consolidated the perception of Austria as the more benevolent of the two empires.[34]

Russian forces were forced out of Galicia in 1915, but domestic developments in the Russian Empire continued to affect the province, with the October Revolution in particular transforming its political dynamics. Upon coming to power in the fall of 1917, the Bolsheviks quickly began armistice negotiations with the Central Powers, signing preliminary agreements on December 15, 1917. In February 1918 the sides met again at Brest-Litovsk. The negotiations were crucial for the Bolsheviks. Not only did they result in Russia's exit from the war, but the very talks themselves helped legitimize the new Soviet regime. Lenin and his compatriots were now accepted as international partners in lieu of the defunct monarchy or provisional government.

In return for armistice and international recognition, the Bolsheviks were forced to give up large swaths of territory, including much of the former Russian Empire's western borderlands. They also recognized several newly independent states: Poland, Ukraine, Belarus, and the Baltic republics. The regions having secured independence de jure now fell under German and Austrian control, with Ukraine being the most illustrative case. Seen by Berlin as a major supplier of food, especially grain, Ukraine was considered vital to repairing Germany's faltering economy. The government of the Ukrainian People's Republic, organized in Kyiv several months earlier when the region was still under Russian control, signed separate agreements with Germany, pledging to supply grain in return for a guarantee of security and independence from Russia. Berlin then proceeded to install a puppet government in Kyiv.[35] The Brest-Litovsk treaty implied an end to Biliński's plan of a Kingdom of Poland that would include all of Galicia. Any Ukrainian state to emerge from the former Russian Empire would necessarily include certain territories contested by Poles and Ukrainians.

To add insult to injury, before and during Brest-Litovsk Austrian ministers cooperated with Ukrainian representatives behind the backs of their Polish colleagues. This marked a rethinking of hierarchies prompted by the unexpected events of the war: given Ukrainians' cross-border connections, Vienna prioritized their cause at Brest-Litovsk over that of the Poles. The Austrian Foreign Ministry negotiated with the Russians in secret; Biliński learned of the meeting and the agreements reached at it only because of his friendship with Wassilko, who was a member of the Ukrainian delegation.[36]

The Brest-Litovsk agreements shook Biliński's faith in Vienna, but not his conviction that the empire should and would survive. Biliński's contemporaries would long remember that even as the new Republic of Poland was being established, Biliński described himself as "an inveterate Austrian."[37] The black mark of his clinging to the expiring empire would endure beyond 1918.

Civil War: Poland, Ukraine, Soviet Russia

The end of the empire—the Habsburgs signed the armistice on November 4, 1918—caused the collapse of existing institutions and hierarchies in Galicia. As Vienna withdrew its forces from Galicia, an outright conflict commenced over the territory between Ukrainians and Poles. On November 1 the Austrians evacuated Galicia's capital. Ukrainian soldiers formerly belonging to imperial units remained behind to take power in what they called L'viv (known to their Polish rivals as Lwów), and the Western Ukrainian People's Republic was now proclaimed. Somewhat shocked by the sheer speed of these political transformations in Galicia, Poles quickly mobilized their forces against the Ukrainians, resulting in what would be one of the most brutal military campaigns in early post-Habsburg Europe.

Wilsonian self-determination, as recent studies have demonstrated, came with a set of problems, especially in Eastern Europe.[38] The discourse of self-determination, Steven Seegle has argued, was essentially all talk; the great powers were motivated by Realpolitik.[39] As Volker Prott has explained, attempts to implement self-determination at the local level all too often resulted in violence, as would be particularly evident in the Polish-Ukrainian war over Galicia.[40]

In political/ideological terms, the fighting prompted soul-searching among those Poles who had earlier advocated cooperation with Ukrainians; it also exacerbated the conflict between Polish moderates and nationalists. At this point Biliński reconsidered his earlier support of Ukrainians: "Who knows if the blood of our [Polish] brothers that was spilled was not due to the mistakes of 1908; if not for 1908, would [the Ukrainians] have ever felt so confident, would they have achieved the positions in Austrian politics and government that they did?"[41] His opponents were unforgiving. During the fighting over Galicia, the nationalist Stanisław Głąbiński attributed Polish problems in the region partly to Biliński's earlier Polish-Ukrainian initiatives.[42] Stanisław Skarbek, another Polish nationalist from Galicia, declared that Biliński might as well admit that he was, in fact, a Ukrainian.[43] His *austriacismo,* and his record of support for Ukrainians, became major obstacles in his subsequent career in Poland.

The war created a further dilemma for Biliński, an assimilated Jew who identified as Polish. In the imperial era, Polish-Jewish relations in Galicia had been occasionally strained, but violence—such as, for example, during the 1898 and 1911 electoral campaigns—was uncommon. The war changed this pattern. The first major upheaval occurred during the Russian occupation of the province in 1915, when many Jews fled Galicia to Vienna and Austria's interior. The Polish-Ukrainian civil war set a further dreadful precedent, not just for Galicia but for Europe in general: on November 22–23, 1918, Polish forces in Galicia engaged in anti-Jewish violence.[44] The aggressors justified their actions with reference to Jewish neutrality in the Polish-Ukrainian conflict: when the fighting first broke out in early November 1918, Jews generally had remained neutral but implicitly supported the Ukrainians, who promised autonomy, as opposed to the Poles, who held to their rigid centralism. Having anticipated Jewish support, Poles now attacked their Jewish neighbors in the city of Lwów.[45] Biliński too had expected Jews to take an active pro-Polish stance, insofar as so many of them, himself included, had chosen the path of Polish assimilation. When these hopes did not materialize, he turned his back on Galicia's Jews, blaming them for their passivity.[46] Under the empire, his Polishness and Jewishness had been compatible, just as he had combined Polish national identification with Habsburg loyalty; but these all became mutually exclusive after November 1918.

It was the postimperial civil wars, and not the First World War, that decided the fates of territories and countries in the former Austrian-Russian borderlands. It was civil war that secured Poland's independence and that removed Ukraine from the map of Europe for decades to come. And it was civil war that led Biliński to revise his views of Poland's neighbors and its national minorities, which would have lasting implications for Polish politics in the post-1918 era.[47]

The War's Aftermath: Poland

Along with families, the war destroyed professional relationships, but not necessarily the networks on which they were based. Even during nonamicable phases, Wassilko and Biliński remained in touch, and their experience of reciprocal negotiations would come in handy after 1918. Neither did the war erase their connection to the now departed empire: particular institutions and policies may have come in for denunciation after 1918, but our protagonists, at least, would still put their faith in the Habsburg-era practices they remembered fondly from peacetime.

Poland emerged like a phoenix from the First World War, regaining territory from the Austrian, Russian, and German Empires.[48] A parliamentary republic with its capital in Warsaw, formerly part of Russia, it faced territorial and political frictions held over from imperial times. Its political elites, who had all matured under different empires, were now designing a new state in opposition to the political models of the previous epoch. In particular, Poland would emphatically be a republic—an about-face from imperial-era monarchical rule—with a strong parliament imposing supervision over the country's executive authorities.

The trauma of imperial collapse affected Biliński much as it did Lammasch and Redlich, but the practical consequences were even more severe for people on the empire's periphery rather than its center. For Biliński, 1919 seemed like a fitting time to "call it a career." As with Redlich, it now fell to him to decide where "home" was in the new Europe. Warsaw was alien to him. By contrast, Vienna was home for many Galicians, as it was for others from different parts of the empire. Moreover, Biliński's ailing wife, an ethnic German, preferred a Germanophone environment to Poland. And despite having supported her husband throughout his career and having learned Polish, there was a strong possibility that she would not be fully accepted in a national Poland—the same concern Redlich had regarding a national Czechoslovakia. In early 1919 the couple moved to the vicinity of Vienna, expecting to spend the rest of their lives there.[49]

The year 1919, however, proved a new beginning, not an end. With their wealth of political and professional experience, people like Biliński, technocrats with extensive networks, were in great demand. His post-1918 political trajectory in Poland in some ways resembled that of Redlich in Austria; their statecraft was similarly prized in both new polities. In joining the governments of the new republics, such statesmen brought with them a vision of politics they had

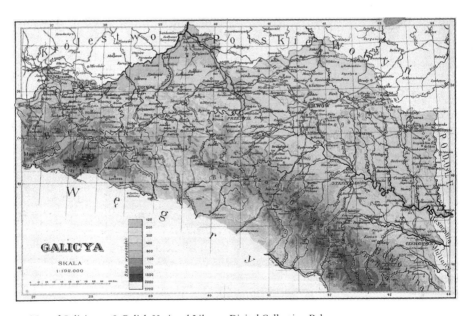

Map of Galicia, 1918. Polish National Library, Digital Collection Polona.

inherited from the empire, so that Habsburg-era practices became embedded in all the successor states.

In July 1919 Józef Piłsudski, Poland's new head of state, invited Biliński to join his government as finance minister. The two had known each other for years and worked together during the war. Piłsudski came from the Russian part of Poland, and though he had spent some of the war in Galicia, he was of a different mindset than those who had come of age in the Habsburg Empire. In private, Piłsudski explained to Biliński the difficulties the latter was bound to face in his new job: Biliński's candidacy was controversial. He was known for his outspoken support of the Habsburgs, for which he, like many other Galicians, seemed suspect by Poles who had matured in Russian Poland.

The proportion of Galicians in the Polish parliament was only half that of their overall share of the population (forty-four out of 432 delegates, or 10 percent of the Sejm), but the perception that Galicians were overrepresented in Warsaw shaped politics in post-1918 Poland.[50] Poland's radical right had long been hostile to Germany and German speakers generally. So when formerly Austrian Poles came to formerly Russian Warsaw, the right readily invented a new adversary, viewing Galicians as interlopers.

Biliński embodied these tensions between different regions of Poland. Poland's right fundamentally opposed his political involvement. Polish nationalists from Galicia still resented his support of the Habsburgs and his attempts to compromise with Ukrainians in the last months of the empire's existence.[51] Then there was the issue of Biliński's mixed family and German ties—a norm in the empire that now became a liability in independent Poland. His German wife, Jósefa Seichs, faced the additional hardship of seeing her family divided by the Austro-Czech border. But Jósefa, who had learned Polish and moved to Warsaw with her husband, did not allow idle talk about their "Germanness" to intimidate her. She encouraged Biliński's participation in the government and held doggedly to her routine of traveling between Warsaw and Vienna with a German maid.[52]

Galicians indeed stood out among the crowd in Warsaw. They held to a different understanding of politics, had a different demeanor, and even looked different. Conversant in German, accustomed to Vienna's coffeehouse culture, and featuring particular dress and manners, they seemed like strangers in Warsaw, which in turn was strange to them. Their arrival touched off a political confrontation. In March 1919 the right-wing Polish periodical *Kurier Warszawski* published an article titled "The Galician Import," decrying the influx to

Warsaw of masses of "procrastinators, illiterates, and idlers" from Vienna, Lwów, and Kraków. Of course, granted the *Kurier* writer, some of these people were qualified, potentially valuable officials; but most were incompetent laggards who would not be up the challenge of the new Poland.[53] But Biliński had qualifications that other Poles did not, and networks stretching across Europe and beyond that might be of great service.[54]

In February 1919, during the first parliamentary sessions in Warsaw, the underlying tensions between deputies from different parts of Poland were already apparent. As the Polish historian Adam Pragier observed, "socialist deputies from Małopolska [formerly in Habsburg Empire] could easily find consensus with the *stanczyky* and *podoliaky* [branches of Galician conservatives] because all of them used to meet in the Pucher coffeehouse in Vienna."[55] But Warsaw had no such coffeehouse political tradition, and Poles from the Russian partition generally had little experience of parliamentary politics. Russian Warsaw, German Poznań, and Austrian Lwów more closely resembled St. Petersburg, Berlin, and Vienna, respectively, than they did each other.

Everything that made Biliński's renewed political career possible, meanwhile—his Austrian imperial past, his experience, and his networks—at the same time hindered that very career. In his capacity as finance minister, Biliński replicated some of the practices he had employed in the empire. In principle, every major decision in the empire had required a vote from the parliament. But that body had become increasingly dysfunctional after the mid-1890s, when, in the wake of the German-Czech conflict, German deputies resorted to obstructive tactics; holding prolonged speeches and even physically blocking access to the parliament, they undermined the very purpose of parliamentary work. Other national-minority deputies followed suit, and obstruction became a common drawback of the imperial parliament. In the resulting crisis of 1897, a majority in the parliament granted the Habsburg government the right to rule without parliamentary vote.[56] The provision was meant to be an exception to the norm, with the parliament maintaining its institutional function of governmental oversight. In reality, however, this so-called emergency legislation became common practice, although it did not entirely undermine imperial institutional structures, as local diets remained intact and functioning. Biliński, who spent decades in different ministerial offices while the imperial parliament remained dysfunctional, pushed numerous important legislative packages through without its approval.

In Poland Biliński insisted, on pragmatic grounds, that instead of introducing some new legal tender, the German mark should be retained—eliciting outrage from the radical right.[57] Cash disbursements unauthorized by parliament caused further conflict. In line with his prior experience from the empire, Biliński circumvented the Warsaw legislature by unilaterally implementing several major changes in Poland's finances. He justified his decisions with economic considerations, but his opponents viewed them as holdovers from the Habsburg Empire's political model, where such economic initiatives did not always require parliamentary ratification.[58]

This pattern of imperial continuities was not exclusive to Poland. As Dominique Kirchner Reill has recently demonstrated, politics in interwar Fiume (now Rijeka, Croatia)—formerly part of the Hungarian half of the monarchy, later contested by Italy and Yugoslavia after 1918—evinced remarkable continuities of imperial practices and a proliferation of currencies similar to those of Poland (with its German marks and Austrian crowns).[59] Gábor Egry has explored the survival of personnel, institutions, and administrative and social practices in territories that formerly belonged to the Hungarian part of the empire.[60] Biliński's approach in Poland was thus a manifestation of a broader trend in the Habsburg successor states.

Biliński was dismissed in November 1919, after the parliament rejected his taxation program. But his brief stint as finance minister was ordinary in the new Poland and in Europe in general, where the spinning wheel of governments was the norm, with none able to hold on for more than a few months. Biliński's successors, their different regional origins notwithstanding, faced similar hurdles.

Postimperial Vienna

Biliński's dismissal did not bring an end to his career in Poland: professional rotations including removals and resignations were common in his vocation. He soon accepted the government's nomination of him as a special envoy to Vienna. This assignment stemmed from the complex international situation in Eastern Europe. In the summer of 1920, Soviet forces were nearing Warsaw, and those who could were leaving the city in anticipation of defeat. But the Bolsheviks were only one of several forces with the potential to jeopardize Poland's stability and alter its borders. The November 1918 anti-Jewish pogroms,

and violence against civilians during the civil war in Galicia, had brought Poland negative publicity across Europe. President Woodrow Wilson himself
condemned Polish violence in Galicia.[61] Warsaw responded by organizing propaganda offices in European capitals, and Biliński landed in its Vienna
branch.[62]

Former Austrians were more likely to be assigned to Vienna: familiarity
with the city and its politics would facilitate their work there. Biliński's nomination, moreover, came from yet another former Austrian, the socialist Ignacy
Daszyński, then serving as Poland's vice premier. As the Russian forces approached Warsaw, many remembered the tsarist army's deplorable treatment
of Jews during the Russian occupation of Galicia in 1914 and 1916. Biliński
himself identified as Polish, but his Jewish heritage remained and presented
certain challenges; assimilated Jews never quite blended in seamlessly in Poland. His post in Vienna would provide not just a new professional opportunity but physical refuge as well. With the imperial era being, after all, not so
far in the past, Vienna represented a second home and safe haven for many of
those who could not find it elsewhere.

Biliński's task was to employ his networks in Vienna to help improve
Poland's international image; in particular, claims regarding Warsaw's cruelty
against Ukrainians were to be countered and refuted. There was a practical
urgency to this: while Warsaw sought to focus international attention on de-
terring the Bolshevik threat, the effort met with a certain amount of diplomatic
distraction, as European political and intellectual circles decried Poland's military engagement with Ukrainians in Galicia. In Austria Biliński arranged
various meetings with deputies and journalists. He would later recall that the
great majority of Austrians he spoke with voiced sympathy for Poland. He
retained particularly warm memories of meeting with his old acquaintance
Karl Renner, who, upon the empire's demise, become the first chancellor of
independent Austria. It was precisely this familiarity with political figures beyond Poland that made Biliński so valuable to his new state.

The propaganda office itself, however, existed only briefly, soon dissolving under pressure from Polish nationalists who maintained that attempting
to justify the country's territorial claims only played into the hands of those
seeking to delegitimize them. Biliński's activity in this office revealed his ambivalent status among Poles; Vice Premier Daszyński did not conceal his
displeasure with his envoy's conduct in Vienna, believing he had shown excessive favor to the Austrians.[63]

Biliński's Austrian connections then led to another assignment in Vienna—but this one would destroy his relationships with many of his old Austrian friends. In 1919 Poland's finance ministry invited him to participate in the international commission overseeing the liquidation of the Austro-Hungarian Bank. This institution was still in operation even after the empire's fall, and its directors in Vienna and Budapest continued to issue loans; the new cash flowing to successor states caused financial complications.[64] On January 1, 1920, the Austro-Hungarian Bank began the process of liquidation; and in subsequent negotiations Biliński represented Poland, just as several of his former subordinates from the imperial finance ministry were in attendance on behalf of their respective new homelands: Austria, Romania, Yugoslavia, Czechoslovakia, and Italy.[65] Such an encounter of erstwhile colleagues was bound to cause tension, but relations were particularly strained between the Austrians and the representatives of the successor states. The bank's director, Alexander Spitzmüller, later recalled that Biliński "outdid his colleagues in the other delegations in showing hostility toward the institution for the sole purpose of currying favor with his government."[66] Biliński was also involved in the dividing up of the empire's gold reserves, which would prove economically detrimental to Austria.[67] None of the previous agreements had mentioned apportioning the gold among the successor states, and the decision to do so was adopted ad hoc by (unsurprisingly) the liquidation commission's non-Austrian members.[68]

The emotional impact of this redistribution was as devastating to the former imperial center as its practical consequences. Who were these people, Spitzmüller demanded to know in his memoir, who took it upon themselves to rob Austria and Hungary of their gold reserves? Renner and Biliński had just recently held amicable conversations as part of Biliński's propaganda assignment. But Renner was now indignant: "These measures were enforced by members of the nation-states, such as Mr. Luxardo, who had earlier worked in our finance ministry. Another of these people is the interesting and distinctive individual Herr Leon Biliński, at one time the finance minister himself."[69] The irony was not lost on those involved. Biliński had hardly been a bystander in the run-up to the war. After 1918 the fact that Biliński, a Pole, had helped steer Austria into that disaster was still bitterly fresh in the minds of his colleagues and contemporaries in the other successor states. In a scenario that none could have predicted in 1914, Poland became a winner, and Austria, a loser, in the Great War.

Biliński's involvement with the liquidation commission destroyed his reputation in Vienna, but it had the opposite effect back in Poland, where, for the first time, he received the acclaim of the country's right wing.[70] His earlier allegiance to the Habsburgs was not forgotten but could now be forgiven, as could certain of his other alleged transgressions, such as his currency and tax reforms. This domestic acceptance came at the price of inflicting major financial damage on the direct heir of the country Biliński had once considered home.

Wassilko between Austria, Poland, and Ukraine

The First World War and the civil war had different consequences, and a different ending, for Galician Ukrainians. For one thing, the years of military slog helped turn Habsburg ultraloyalists into Ukrainian nationalists. The civil war moreover shattered the imperial-era tradition of Polish-Ukrainian negotiation. But neither the Great War nor the civil war that followed could erase the trust in imperial models and networks that had consolidated for decades prior to 1914.

The relations between Biliński and Wassilko, and Wassilko's ideological transformations between 1914 and 1921, illustrate these trends. In 1916 Wassilko informed Biliński that if the Poles insisted on keeping all of Galicia for themselves, Ukrainians would resort to force—an early sign of the enmity that would fester for years, with Galicia indeed soon engulfed in violence.[71] Wassilko had long promoted Ukrainian interests in the empire but at the same time continually affirmed his imperial allegiance.[72] Yet the choice to affiliate with Ukraine and not some other postimperial polity was hardly a foregone conclusion. Wassilko never mastered the Ukrainian language with any fluency. Ukraine's chances for independence, for that matter, were ever unclear.

The story of post-1918 Ukrainian statehood is that of failure, the only national minority from the Habsburg Empire to gain, then lose, independence after the civil war. Two Ukrainian states initially emerged in the territory of the former Russian and Habsburg Empires. The Ukrainian People's Republic, centering on the formerly Russian-controlled Kyiv, secured a guarantee of independence at Brest-Litovsk. At the time, an independent Ukrainian republic was integral to the Austro-German war effort. But arrangements were flawed on both sides: amid military defeats, Germany could neither properly supervise food procurement from Ukraine nor provide any proper military assistance.

In the fall of 1918 German forces withdrew from Ukraine. The Ukrainian People's Republic would live (briefly) on, albeit now left to its own devices.

Another Ukrainian state—the West Ukrainian People's Republic—was founded in L'viv in early November 1918 and immediately found itself at war with the Poles. Whereas Ukrainians from the former Russian Empire were fighting primarily against the Bolsheviks, the struggle of their conationals in Galicia was with Poland. Both also faced the remains of the Russian imperial army and a variety of different military formations that emerged in what used to be the Russian-Austrian borderland. In January 1919 the two Ukraines signed a unification pact, forming a single state and combining the military effort against common enemies.

It was thought that conjoining the two Ukrainian states would boost the chance to secure independence, but from late 1918 on this prospect began to progressively dim. By the summer of the following year, Polish forces had occupied most of Galicia. The chaos was particularly dramatic and tragic in Eastern Ukraine. Memorialized famously in Mikhail Bulgakov's 1925 novel *The White Guard,* Ukraine's capital of Kyiv became prey to different armies and changed regimes over a dozen times in the brief span of 1918–20. Even amid the tumult and brutality of the civil war, however, Ukrainians' hopes for independence remained alive until 1921.

In this period, Wassilko lived and worked in different countries, serving in diplomatic offices in Vienna, Berlin, and Bern. Here he represented different Ukrainian states—first, the West Ukrainian People's Republic, then the Kyiv-based Ukrainian People's Republic. His networks and the languages in which he was fluent were an important asset for the Ukrainian states, just as Poland valued Biliński's experience and networks. But while Biliński eventually settled for an internationally recognized state, Wassilko's cause was for a polity whose chances of survival shrank with each passing year.

Wassilko was yet another example of a politics and personal life intrinsically intertwined. For people like him, moreover—statesmen attempting to choose between different states, potentially affiliated with several at a time, or with none—such ties were particularly consequential. His family facilitated these geopolitical connections. Like Biliński, Wassilko had a Germanophone wife; after the death of his first wife Olga (with whom he had four children), he married Gerda Walde, an Austrian artist and operetta singer well known in Vienna's cultural circles. She was indeed a familiar face in the city, and she appeared in Karl Kraus's famous satire *The Last Days of Mankind.*[73] Gerda Wassilko was a social butterfly and a somewhat exotic figure—a "petite lady with brightly-dyed hair and diamonds. . . . She was a chanson singer and a former mistress of the Shah of Persia, and is now the wife of the Ukrainian ambassador to Berlin and Bern," according to Henry Kessler, a German diplomat who attended some of the same events. "At first I thought she was the wife of a Soviet ambassador, and was carrying on her person all the jewelry the Soviets had confiscated from the Ukrainian nobility," recalled Kessler.[74] This jocular imagery was incongruous to the point of being symbolic: not only did Gerda have no ties to the Soviets, she was the wife of a diplomat laboring to preserve his country's independence *from* Soviet Russia.

In a Europe of new nation-states, Wassilko used his old professional and personal networks toward securing Ukrainian independence. In early 1919, he allegedly tried to procure weapons for Ukrainians fighting Poles in Galicia, part of a larger effort to secure military assistance to Ukraine.[75] He became known as a master of political intrigue, with the American ambassador to Austria, for instance, describing him as "a shrewd, unreliable man."[76] Polish and Austrian diplomats, and even some of his Ukrainian colleagues, regarded him with a similar distrust.[77]

Wassilko's hopes for Ukrainian independence and his continual cooperation with Germany, including in the military sphere, were also contingent on ongoing Habsburg restoration attempts focused not on Austria or Hungary, but rather on Ukraine. In early 1919 the Habsburgs became personae non gratae in Austria, banned from the country and stripped of their titles and property. The last Emperor Charles I's two attempts to reclaim the throne in Hungary in 1921 resulted in failure. But Ukraine was a different story: its statehood was transient during these difficult years, and part of its political establishment looked to the Habsburgs as potential saviors from the Poles and the Bolsheviks. The idea of a Habsburg Kingdom of Ukraine also received some support in political circles in Germany and Poland inclined to create a buffer state between Soviet Russia and the rest of Europe. The potential Habsburg restoration in Ukraine hinged on military assistance from Germany; a tradition of German-Ukrainian cooperation had consolidated for years before the empire's collapse, and Wassilko was now doing his part to carry it on.

One of the Habsburgs, Archduke Wilhelm, spoke Ukrainian and had a good reputation among Galicians. Thus, even if Habsburgs could no longer reside in Vienna or Budapest, Wilhelm could have become a Habsburg king of Ukraine, a Ukraine that would then have marked a direct line of continuity between the Habsburg Empire and post-1918 Europe.[78] Restoration failed here as elsewhere, but the very existence of such schemes far from Vienna and Budapest stands as yet another manifestation of the Habsburg legacy in post-1918 Europe, especially its east.

With a new throne and German military support receding as possibilities, Wassilko turned to Poland, soliciting help from his former colleagues and friends. In private, Wassilko argued that the prudent course would be for the Ukrainian People's Republic (in Kyiv) to make a pact with Poland and Romania against Soviet Russia.[79] Toward this end, he renewed contact with Biliński in an effort to negotiate with Poland. Ievhen Onatskyi, a Ukrainian diplomat working under Wassilko in Italy, later recalled that "Baron Wassilko, my current boss as head of the Ukrainian mission in Italy, when serving as the first ambassador of Ukraine to Germany, played a very important role in the reconciliation between the Ukrainian People's Republic and Poland that resulted in the surrender of Galicia [to the latter]."[80] Wassilko offered to make an incognito trip to Poland, but upon Biliński's consultation with Piłsudski, Wassilko's initiatives and his potential arrival in Warsaw were deemed too great a risk to Poland's security.[81]

The idea of a Polish-Ukrainian rapprochement, however, lived on. In April 1920 the president of the Ukrainian People's Republic, Symon Petliura, arrived in Warsaw for a new round of talks with Piłsudski, Poland's head of state. Like Wassilko, Petliura believed that Ukraine could not afford to wage a war on two fronts—against Poland and Soviet Russia. At the time, it was losing to both: Poland controlled Galicia, and Eastern Ukraine had become a Soviet republic (until 1922 nominally independent from Soviet Russia, but in reality controlled by the same Communist Party headquartered in Moscow). Petliura and Piłsudski ultimately concluded a military alliance against Soviet Russia. In return for assistance in fighting off the Bolsheviks, Petliura renounced Kyiv's claim to Western Ukraine (which largely coincided with Galicia).[82] In the summer of 1920, the combined Polish-Ukrainian force managed to oust the Bolsheviks from Kyiv. But within days, due to a catastrophic miscommunication with their Ukrainian allies, the Poles withdrew, and Soviet forces soon retook Ukraine's capital.

Poland in the meantime was fighting for its survival, and the Polish–Soviet confrontation near Warsaw in August 1920 became a turning point. The Polish army's decisive victory there would have repercussions for all of Europe. In 1917 Lenin had anticipated that, the Bolsheviks having set an example, a communist revolution would naturally break out in Germany as well. When it did not, he aimed to remedy the situation by bringing revolution to Germany by military means. It should be emphasized that at this point, in 1920, Bolshevik thinking was still dominated by the idea of worldwide revolution. After the Battle of Warsaw, Lenin had to adjust his plans; moreover, the domestic ideological struggle between supporters of permanent global revolution, most notably Leon Trotsky, and proponents of socialism in one country, notably Joseph Stalin, would be a by-product of the Soviets' defeat.

The Polish government opted for peace, and in early 1921 Piłsudski entered into negotiations with Soviet Russia. Territorial settlements between the two countries were finalized in the Treaty of Riga, according to which Poland retained most of Eastern Galicia.[83] The Kyiv-centered territory that had been the Ukrainian People's Republic became part of the Soviet Union in 1922. The Riga agreements ended any hopes for an independent Ukraine. By 1922 Galicia and Volhynia (formerly part of the Russian Empire) were secured by Poland. Eastern Ukraine became a formal founding member of the Union of Soviet Socialist Republics. The end of independent Ukraine brought an end to Wassilko's career as well. By the summer of 1921, all of Ukraine's diplomatic positions abroad were abolished. Wassilko announced his resignation in July.[84]

Conclusions

Biliński and Wassilko died in 1923 and 1924, respectively, by which point Poland had secured its place among the independent states of Europe, its borders internationally recognized, including by the Soviet Union. Independent Ukraine, however, disappeared from the map in 1921. The departures of Biliński and Wassilko coincided with and emblematized a new beginning in the European system. In 1918 borders were still in flux, as was the political order, with many of the extant regimes unstable and seemingly reversible. The civil war raging in Galicia could easily have undone some of the postwar territorial settlements. But by 1924 all major boundaries were internationally recognized, and while the Habsburgs still had numerous sympathizers, the chances of a restoration seemed more remote than ever. New nation-states were firmly in place, as was the Soviet Union, now asserting its control over most of the former territory of the Russian Empire. Those states and their boundaries remained intact until 1938.

The transition from empire to post-1918 Europe was different for Biliński and Wassilko than it was for Lammasch and Redlich, but the durability of the Austrian imperial legacy on the empire's former eastern periphery was at least as significant as it was in its center in Austria and the German-Slavic frontier of Moravia and Bohemia that became part of post-1918 Czechoslovakia. This continuity was a by-product of a specific political tradition in the late empire whereby individuals from different provinces and of different nationalities were as involved in government and parliament as were their contemporary peers from the Austrian core. Austrian imperial practices lived on in Poland through the 1920s and the 1930s—with Biliński and many others—despite the charges of *austriacismo* and in defiance of the new state's claims to build from scratch by eliminating any traces of imperial past. And the same was true in Ukraine during its short existence as an independent state (or states) between 1918 and 1921, carried on by Wassilko and the others who also came of age under the Habsburgs and continued in post-1918 Europe. It is not by accident that memories of the late Habsburgs still thrive in today's Ukraine and Poland to the same or even stronger degree than in Austria itself, invoking the "world of yesterday," in Stefan Zweig's phrase, that represented an order and stability that Eastern Europe would never experience again during the twentieth century.

3. Empire, Catholicism, and the Nation, 1880s–1920s

On the evening of September 30, 1918, Heinrich Lammasch, Joseph Redlich, and several colleagues from their Salzburg circle attended a meeting at the home of Viennese coffee magnate Julius Meinl to discuss the political crisis in the empire. That evening they were joined by Ignaz Seipel, a priest and a doctor of theology. He had befriended Lammasch, Redlich, and Meinl in Salzburg during the war, in a time when he served as a professor of theology at the university there. It was during this meeting that Redlich persuaded Seipel to consider the possibility of joining the government.[1] Within weeks of these talks, in late October, Lammasch, Redlich, and Seipel came together in what would be the Habsburg Empire's final governing cabinet, with Seipel becoming minister of social welfare. The bond these men formed during this crisis would influence Austrian and European politics for years after the empire's collapse.

If Lammasch and Redlich made unusual additions to the imperial government—having had no such prior experience—Seipel's background was even more improbable. Born in 1876 and raised in Vienna, he had dedicated his prewar life to theology and the church. Not only his career but even his appearance—to the end of his life, in government service and out, he would wear a priestly cassock and serve liturgies daily—set him apart from most of those who had been involved in the empire's parliament and government. For Seipel, the period of the Great War was as life-changing politically and professionally as it was for Lammasch and Redlich. An adamant supporter of the empire, known for his opposition to the concept of the nation-state, he not only accepted post-1918 Austria upon the empire's passing but helped shape European politics through most of the 1920s. In 1921 he became head of Austria's Christian Social (CS) Party. He also served two terms as chancellor of the Republic of Austria (1922–24 and 1926–29). A onetime monarchist and, per his biographer Klemens von Klemperer, the "most famous priest after the Pope," Seipel became, in John Deak's description, "the father of the first Austrian republic."[2]

If Seipel indeed steered republican Austria, his clerical counterpart from the empire's Trentino region, Alcide De Gasperi, became in the 1920s one of the cofounders of Christian Democracy, Italy's leading political party, and decades later one of the founders of the European Union. Born in 1881, he came of age under the reciprocal influences of Vienna and Rome, absorbing the two different visions of political Catholicism that existed in the Habsburg Empire and the Kingdom of Italy. Spending most of his life, especially after 1918, away from Vienna, De Gasperi was nevertheless an Austrian in the full, Habsburgian sense of the word. He carried certain of the vanished country's patterns with him through the years of fascism, another war, and into the 1950s, when he became an advocate of European integration, an initiative inspired by his early Habsburg experience.

This chapter offers an analysis of two Christian Social parties—the Austrian and the Italian—and their leading personalities Ignaz Seipel and Alcide De Gasperi, respectively. Both of them, and in particular De Gasperi, carried on the tradition of federalist internationalism leading up to the foundation of the European Union in the 1950s. Their contributions to post-Habsburg Europe and eventual European unification cannot be overestimated.

They also were part of the broader cohort that consolidated in the empire, each building upon the networks and experiences that they inherited from the pre-1918 period. Seipel and De Gasperi have both attracted much attention from scholars, but most often in separate contexts and narratives. The two men are rarely if ever discussed in relation to one another, a circumstance that has tended to obscure the important common legacy of Austrian political Catholicism that both carried on from the empire and developed in different directions after 1918.

The Christian Social ideology was one of the most important to emerge in the empire, and it had a lasting effect on Europe in the twentieth century.

Parties based on the Christian Social worldview proliferated in Europe beyond the empire. It was not unique in its impact and longevity—social democracy was at least equally influential. What was, however, significant was that the Habsburg Empire gave rise to several CS parties, each carrying on into several successor states. The continuity is most obvious in Austria itself, where Christian democracy has remained a dominant ideology to the present day. In post-1918 Italy, the CS cause united Italians from the old empire as well as the kingdom, but it was in particular the former who, drawing on a more durable CS tradition, were most significant in the movement.

Political Catholicism has been marginalized in broader European narratives of the twentieth century that trend toward discussion of the radical right, the radical left, or the juxtaposition between the two. But they defined the history of Europe in a similar way as did nationalism and Marxism, fascism and communism. The Christian Social legacy is so lasting, and at the same time so controversial, that any discussion of the empire and post-1918 Europe would be incomplete without considering it.[3]

Austrian Christian Social Ideology and the Empire

Christian Social parties in the Habsburg Empire operated separately from one another and appealed to specific national groups. Yet across different provinces, several clerically influenced parties were bound by the same ideology, and their members came of age under the influence of the same movement leaders in Vienna. In Austria, specifically Vienna, political Catholicism emerged from the ruins of imperial liberalism. Beginning in the 1860s, the movement coalesced around Viennese clergymen who opposed liberals' emphasis on religious equality and ecumenicalism. It consolidated into the Christian Social Party in 1891 under the leadership of Karl Lueger. Though Lueger himself died in 1910—well before the empire's collapse—it was Lueger's party, shaped by his vision of politics and mass organization, that Seipel would inherit in 1921.

Lueger was also mayor of Vienna from 1897 onward. In his dual capacity as a party and municipal leader, Lueger transformed the imperial capital's sociopolitical and even architectural profile, effecting what John Boyer describes as a "city revolution" based on Christian socialist ideology.[4] Dominating local and communal politics, he redesigned the city's architectural and societal landscape, launching major construction projects and augmenting the social safety net and welfare support.[5] In all possible ways, Vienna emerged from Lueger's tenure an entirely different city. With its greatest support in Vienna and a solid base in the countryside, the Christian Social Party became one of the most successful center-right organizations in pre-1914 Europe.[6]

Lueger's organization was based on his vision of the Habsburg Empire as a bastion of Catholicism; antiliberalism, anti-Marxism, and anti-Semitism all combined with an overarching loyalty to the empire. Lueger himself was a former liberal. He thus stood as an important example of the liberal lineage of late imperial clericals, and of the political and ideological contiguities between political Catholicism, pan-Germanism, and social democracy—what Carl Schorske describes as the country's fin-de-siècle political triangle.[7] The succession from liberals to clericals, in particular, might appear somewhat counterintuitive. Clericals rejected many of the basic principles of Austrian liberalism, especially the idea of religious tolerance and equality. Late imperial clericals did, however, inherit and endorse certain premises of liberalism, for instance the institutional integration of the lower classes in politics, and the idea of society's autonomy from the state, a key liberal doctrine.[8]

The three sides of this postliberal triangle also shared certain aspects of each other's ideology while decisively rejecting others. Both the Social Democrats (SDs) and the Christian Socials (CSs) pledged to defend labor from exploitation at the hands of the imperial bourgeoisie. The Marxist-based socialism of the SDs thus confronted a Christian socialism of their clerical counterparts. In the late imperial period, well before the war, the Christian Social and Social Democratic parties became embroiled in a fierce rivalry. Some of their programmatic principles, such as advocacy on behalf of the lower classes, overlapped; but the methods of achieving them differed so drastically that compromise or alliances between the two seemed nearly impossible. The CSs opposed capitalism and internationalism, which they considered inextricably linked: capitalism was essentially international. Border-traversing capital, they argued, was one of the main causes of the exploitation and immiseration of Austrian workers and peasants. Adherents of Austrian social democracy agreed, of course, that capitalism was the root of societal problems and exploitation. But their proposed solution was quite different: the international workers' unity foregrounded by socialists contrasted starkly with the CSs' preoccupation solely with Austrian workers. Also key in this divide was the SDs' intellectual inspiration from Marxism, and their concomitantly Marxist attitude toward religion. It was also in the imperial period that the socialists came to endorse anticlericalism as part of their program—another aspect of Habsburg-era politics that would have strong effects on interwar Austria.

Three major issues—nationalism, and attitudes toward Jews and toward the empire—separated the Christian Social ideology from pan-Germanism. For decades before 1918, the CSs used anti-Semitic rhetoric as a political tool to exploit the widespread anti-Jewish sentiment among Viennese artisans and the middle class, but it never promoted "racial" exclusion. For Lueger, anti-Semitism was a matter of political strategy, a calculation as to how to manipulate public opinion at a time when grassroots anti-Jewish sentiment was common in Austrian society.[9] Lueger was a practical politician; by contrast, the pan-German leader Karl Schönerer was "a nationalist dogmatic."[10] For Schönerer, anti-Semitism was a matter of faith.[11] The Christian Social Party's "anti-Semitic façade" diminished after 1905.[12] Unlike pan-Germans, CSs were loyal to the Habsburg Empire, sharing such patriotism with the SDs. The fact that these movements overlapped—especially during their formative stages—affected their adherents' political choices, with many moving from one party to another as enabled by their complementarity.

It was only with the passage of time that these different ideologies became mutually exclusive, in direct confrontation with one another. Under the slogan "Away from Rome," German nationalists in the Habsburg Empire accused the Christian Social Party of diluting the purity of German culture.[13] This schism spilled over into the postimperial era, when Austrian nationalists' endorsement of pan-German culture threatened the very existence of the Republic of Austria. In the interwar period, the CSs and SDs likewise moved further apart. Their electorates became increasingly differentiated, as did their territorial and demographic bases, and the two parties appealed to different segments of the population.

Lueger thus not just shaped Christian socialism as a movement and a party, but he also defined patterns of interactions among Christian Socials, nationalists, and Marxists well beyond his own life span into the 1930s. Many political alliances and nonalliances in Austria and beyond during the interwar years would be formed in Lueger's shadow by his direct and indirect successors, who had learned politics under the empire.

In Lueger's Footsteps: Ignaz Seipel

Seipel missed the formative stages of political Catholicism in Austria, and his early life was nothing like that of most of our other protagonists. But his later career was emblematic of the development of the Christian Social Party, as empire gave way to interwar Europe.[14] Seipel was a native of Vienna, his family having resided in the city for several generations. Unlike Lueger, who was a career politician, Seipel followed a theological path for much of his life before the war. Serving as a chaplain in different churches in Vienna from 1899 on, in 1903 he began studying for his doctorate in theology. His choice to become a theologian, however, caused him to trade his native Vienna for Salzburg, where in 1909 he received the chair in moral theology (Christian ethics).

In Salzburg Seipel first encountered the confrontation between secularism and clericalism—an experience that would guide his personal and political choices through the 1930s. He became an adamant supporter of the Catholic legacy of the University of Salzburg, resisting any transition on its part to secularism. At the same time, his involvement in discussions surrounding the university revealed the fluidity of politics in the late empire. In 1909 he coordinated an alliance with pan-Germans, who offered to support Catholics over secularists—an alliance reminiscent of the earlier interaction between CSs and pan-Germans in the postliberal period.[15]

Seipel's rejection of secularism and the particular alliances he struck set an important precedent that he would replicate years after the empire's collapse; such was his formative political experience, even before his full-fledged immersion into politics proper and government during the war. Interparty negotiations of this sort became a norm in interwar Austria, the conflicts and alliances serving as another sign of the continuity and transfer of practices from empire to republic.

Seipel, the Salzburg Circle, and the War

Seipel first encountered Lammasch, Redlich, and Meinl during the war. With many Viennese leaving the capital upon the outbreak of hostilities, Salzburg gained prominence as a center of intellectual and political debates, home to what would be referred to as the "Meinl circles." Seipel became part of these intellectual and political networks.

It was also during the war that he tied his academic and religious work to politics. The year 1916 became the culmination of Seipel's academic career. That year, while still in Salzburg, he published his most important scholarly study, *Nation and State,* which laid out his vision of statehood and nationalism. Sharing an almost identical title with a similarly programmatic work by Karl Renner, the empire's leading socialist and one of the cofounders of Austro-Marxism, Seipel's *Nation and State* represented a manifesto in support of the multiethnic empire and against the unitary nation-state. Linking the existence of the Habsburg Empire to the survival of the universal Catholic Church, Seipel argued that its dissolution would be harmful, not just to the particular entities emerging from its ruins but to Catholicism as well. "A [multiethnic] state is necessary," he argued, "to build bridges among different nationalities, forging mutual understanding and respect."[16]

His wartime espousal of multinationalism and rejection of centralism was a radical change from how he had conceived the empire prior to 1914. Before the Great War, he had supported a uniform state. He traced the beginning of federalism in the Habsburg Empire to Emperor Francis Joseph's October Diploma in 1860, which reopened provincial assemblies after a decade of neo-absolutism, and prior to the outbreak of war he saw this development as overall detrimental to the Habsburg polity.[17] National autonomy, he claimed, "contradicted the democratic developments of the time," and thus all the peoples of the Habsburg lands should instead "seek valuable unity" under the auspices of the monarchy.[18] But he changed his views during the war, when national dissent became a threat to the empire. By the fall of 1918, Seipel's views on autonomy and federation aligned largely with Lammasch's and Redlich's. These similarities made it possible for him to participate in the last imperial government, a platform that provided the ground for his career in the post-1918 Austrian Republic.

Between Vienna and Rome: Alcide De Gasperi

The years lived under the empire were similarly formative for Alcide De Gasperi. Born in the mixed Italian-German-Slavic area of Trentino, he was raised in a middle-class Italian family, with his father serving as head of the local police.[19] Politically, however, he came of age under the influence of Karl Lueger, and like Seipel shared Lueger's ideology of political Catholicism.

The Alpine region of Trentino became part of the Habsburg Empire only in the early nineteenth century as a result of the Napoleonic wars. Italians predominated in Trentino, accounting, per the 1910 census, for over 90 percent of the population. Germans represented the largest minority, but their numbers in the overall population were relatively marginal (13,456, compared to 350,847 Italians).[20] These numbers, however, conceal important nuances of national dynamics in the region. Precisely because Italian predominance here was so overwhelming, the Trentino area became the second strongest base of the German nationalist movement in the empire (after Austria proper), as a sort of counterreaction. Germans were, moreover, particularly prominent in the region's urban areas, most notably the city of Trento itself. Interethnic relations in Trentino were thus different from anywhere else in the empire, because of the recentness of its annexation and its particular Italian-German dynamic.

The clericalist movement here emerged later than in Austria proper. Having arisen in the 1870s, it was not until 1904 that it consolidated into a party, the People's Political Union of Trentino (l'Unione Politica Popolare del Trentino); the People's Party of Trentino was founded the following year, fifteen years after its Austrian counterpart. It borrowed the Austrian model and imitated its tactics.[21] Catholicism, Habsburg loyalty, anti-Semitism, and resistance to Marxism were as important for Italian clericals as for their Austrian counterparts.

De Gasperi's Austrian experience was conditioned by his stay in Vienna during his student years, his personal exposure to Lueger's policies there, and his involvement in Austrian politics. Following a path common among the empire's Italian elites, he finished high school close to home but moved to Vienna to complete his studies. Also like many of our other protagonists, he served as a deputy of the Austrian imperial parliament. Elected in 1911 at the age of thirty, he was one of this body's youngest members, and his firsthand exposure to Austrian parliamentarianism would critically shape his understanding of politics, in the pre-1918 empire as well as in post-1918 Italy.

De Gasperi came to Vienna in 1900, when Lueger's career in that city was at its peak. These years in the empire's capital defined both his Austrianness and his Italianness—a national dilemma unexperienced, for example, by Seipel. It was in Vienna that De Gasperi observed not just Lueger's practical work in transforming the city, but also the escalation in tensions between Italians and the Austrian government. Like Seipel, De Gasperi was inspired by

Lueger's practical and political achievements, and drawn to the combination of socialism and Catholicism he embodied.[22] Religion in particular conditioned De Gasperi's commitment to the empire. Describing Habsburg Central Europe as a "Christian republic" and a "Catholic commonwealth," he saw it, much as did Seipel, as key to the church's survival.[23] But the *catholicity* of this commonwealth also entailed the encompassing of different nationalities, an ability De Gasperi particularly cherished and which he realized would be hard to re-create in a nation-state. His vision of the empire and the church, his Habsburg patriotism and Catholicism, thus aligned him with many of Lueger's followers in Austria, including Seipel.

Vienna represented one model for De Gasperi, and Rome another. It was during his student years in Vienna that he made his first trip to Italy. These experiences conditioned his political present and future, reaffirming his belief in the empire's indispensability and the pitfalls of a nation-state. The first consideration had to do with religion. Italy was the seat of world Catholicism, but relations between Rome and the Vatican left much to be desired, marred by the still-unresolved "Roman question." At the time of Italian unification in 1861, the Vatican had refused to join Italy, maintaining its separateness as a state within the state. The Vatican's insistence on retaining its independent status complicated not only church-state relations in Italy, but also the views of committed Catholics (including ethnic Italians) beyond its borders. In the late nineteenth century, Italian politics was furthermore taking a turn to the left: liberals formed majorities in the kingdom's governments, and socialism was on the rise. Whereas Italian governments and the Vatican looked askance at one another, the Habsburgs were devout Catholics. What seemed only too natural in Austria—the existence of a Catholic political party—proved highly problematic in Italy, where the church, keen to maintain a monopoly on influence over believers, for years opposed the founding of any Catholic-based party.[24]

De Gasperi is remembered in the annals of history not so much for his support of religion but rather for his political stance in support of autonomy and federation. Even though federative thinking became increasingly popular during the last years of the empire, De Gasperi was in some ways ahead of his time, and ahead of many other protagonists who embraced federalization as an answer for the preservation of the empire. His federative thinking and his early support of autonomy set him apart from Seipel and even Lammasch; it became a definitive factor in his political career not just under the Habsburgs but primarily after the empire's collapse.

Years before Seipel and Lammasch would come to do so, De Gasperi envisioned the Habsburg Empire as a federation of nations and a model for the restructuring of Europe as a whole. A Catholic federative empire, he argued, would not only help support the Catholic Church but could also serve as a guarantor of stability on the continent in general. Taking his federative concepts a step further, at the turn of the century he advocated the reformation of the monarchy on the federalist model of the United States.[25] The year 1918 would mark a continuation, not an end, of imperial-era federative thinking, and De Gasperi's later conception of European integration—decades after the empire's collapse—represents one of the most vivid examples of the Habsburg Empire's legacy in post-1918 Europe.

De Gasperi on Nationalism, Socialism, and Jews

Albeit supportive of the empire, De Gasperi was never entirely complacent toward its government. Whereas Seipel until 1914 considered cultural and administrative autonomy a threat to the Habsburg state, De Gasperi regarded it as beneficial.[26] Like many of his peers, he advocated for the right of ethnic Italians to be educated in their native language. De Gasperi's involvement in a conflict over an educational institution—an Italian national university in Trieste—marked, if not the first, then definitely one of the formative experiences in his engagement in the politics of the Habsburg Empire.

Campaigns to align universities with their national milieu became an important aspect of post-1868 imperial politics. Universities in Galicia set the precedent: not only did the province gain autonomy, but two of its universities—in Lemberg/Lwów and Cracow—switched from German- to Polish-language instruction in the 1870s. Then in 1882 the University of Prague was divided into two: a German and a Czech institution. Courses in Italian had been offered for years at the University of Innsbruck, a center of Tyrol, which also had an Italian minority. Facing continual pressure from Italian students, the Austrian government agreed to establish a chair in Italian history and literature at Innsbruck, but not, as the students demanded, a separate university in Trieste. In 1904 violence exploded in Innsbruck: when the government attempted to fulfill its promise regarding the chair in Italian, German students responded with protests. Police made arrests among both groups, and the Italian chair at Innsbruck was postponed indefinitely.[27]

De Gasperi's stance on the university question reflected his overall view of politics, particularly his support of institutional solutions and eschewal of direct action and force. He endorsed the idea of an Italian institution but rejected the confrontational means employed by some of his conationals, pleading instead for cooperation with the government. He viewed the conflict over an Italian university from a pan-imperial as opposed to ethnic Italian standpoint: for Vienna, the question of national universities was becoming ubiquitous, with Czechs, Poles, Slovenes, and Ukrainians pressing the same demands almost concurrently. De Gasperi further explained that confrontation was harmful to both sides: the government, he insisted, would not yield to the demand of an Italian university in Trieste, and Italian protestors might in fact jeopardize their chances of securing other concessions, including chairs in Italian studies at German-language institutions. Moderation distinguished De Gasperi's politics in the imperial period, one of the indications of his belief that, however imperfect, the interests of Italians were best served by the Habsburg state.

Like Seipel and Lueger before him, De Gasperi rejected radical nationalism. Notably, he was as critical of Italian as of German nationalist extremes. Both, he claimed, were a menace to the empire. He faulted the Austrian government for supporting Trentino's German People's Union (Volksbund), which constituted, in his view, an instrument of German nationalist agitation in the region. At the same time, he faulted those conationals who refused to accommodate other ethnic groups—Slavs on the Adriatic and Germans in the Trentino area. His attitude toward nationalism, more so than that of Seipel, would be exceedingly consequential for the shape of his career.

For clericals, however—both Austrian and Italian—nationalism was a lesser evil than socialism. The ideological standoff of clericalism versus Marxist socialism consolidated under the empire and influenced political coalitions, or the lack thereof, in the post-1918 era. As in the case of Seipel, De Gasperi's attitude toward socialism was bound up with his view of Jews, particularly his assessment of socialism and Marxism as nefarious attributes of world Jewry. Never attacking Jews as a "race" per se, De Gasperi did make reference to the alleged Jewish economic exploitation of Catholic workers: "strangers without a motherland," as he put it, looting the common people's resources.[28] Or consider De Gasperi's homage to the figure who had had such an influence on his political development: "Karl Lueger," he wrote upon the party founder's passing, "was a man of providence who ensured the victory of the anti-liberal movement." Without him, De Gasperi argued, Austrian politics would have been overtaken by pan-German nationalists or by Jews.[29] Unlike Lueger, De Gasperi would have occasion to adjust his stance, avoiding such provocative expressions later in life, especially when anti-Semitism became officially unacceptable in the postwar period.

Italian Clericals and the War

The war came to the empire's Italian-inhabited lands with some delay in 1915, but its effects there would be more severe than in Austria proper. The Kingdom of Italy was part of the Triple Alliance with Germany and Austro-Hungary, but in 1914 it remained neutral, with the Italian government justifying its refusal to join the hostilities because of financial constraints. But despite Trentino's initial distance from the major theaters of the war, its outbreak affected Trentini profoundly.

De Gasperi dreaded the conflict and made efforts to keep Italy out of it. In the fall of 1914, having observed the brutality of warfare and casualties on the eastern borderland in Galicia, he traveled to Rome to meet with Italian politicians.[30] Italy was still neutral, and Berlin and Vienna were striving to ensure that it would not take sides against them. In 1915 he made a second trip to Rome, this time for talks with Pope Benedict XV, in an effort to enlist the Vatican in maintaining Italian neutrality.[31] De Gasperi's motives were practical: he was well aware that, with Rome having recently begun negotiations with the Entente powers, Italy's potential joining of them would turn the Austro-Italian frontier into an active war zone, and Italians from either side of the border would be pressed into two rival armies to fight one another.

De Gasperi wrestled with the same dilemma facing many of the empire's ethnic minorities, who, despite their long-standing Habsburg loyalty, were now subjected to Austrian political persecutions. His allegiances were tested, and his career and even physical safety were in jeopardy. Austrian Italians, regarded as too complacent by nationalists in the Kingdom of Italy, were potential nationalist saboteurs in the eyes of Austrian officials.

Upon signing the Treaty of London in April 1915, Italy did join the war on the side of the Entente. In switching alliances, Rome was driven primarily by territorial promises; it was anticipated that, upon victory, Italy would annex the Italian-inhabited Habsburg lands of the Littoral, Tyrol, and Trentino, thereby completing the unification that Italian nationalists had initiated in the nineteenth century. In 1915 Trieste and Trento indeed became a theater of combat, and many residents were forced to flee. Some left for Italy, while others were evacuated to inner Austria. Vienna ordered the closure of all Italian-language newspapers in the region, and many area residents, classified as "politically unreliable," were expelled. Families became separated even before Trentino saw real war, with a flow of refugees both abroad to Italy and to the imperial interior.[32]

Early in the conflict, De Gasperi began to use his Austrian and Italian connections for two main purposes: to try to influence Austrian officials not to further persecute their own Italian subjects in territories now riven by war; and to plead with the Italian government to consider the voices of the local population in deciding the fate of the regions in question. In Vienna he helped coordinate refugee relief and organize assistance to Italian prisoners of war in Austrian camps.[33] He also negotiated with Italian officials, urging them not to unilaterally annex his native territories to Italy. De Gasperi held that Trentino's fate should be decided by popular plebiscite. In 1915, as he knew, most of its inhabitants would have supported Austrian over Italian rule.[34]

The war did not shake De Gasperi's commitment to Vienna; if anything, it hardened his belief that the empire should survive. It was one thing to criticize the government and its policies, and something else entirely to question the existence of a state. Even the horrors of modern warfare and Austrian cruelty to Italian civilians did not cause him to reconsider his understanding of the empire as an indispensable polity. This mindset guided his decisions through to the late 1940s and the early 1950s. Post-1945 reconstruction of Italy was thus intrinsically tied to the experience that De Gasperi as well as many of his contemporaries inherited from the empire.

Trentino became yet another symbol of the problematic nature of self-determination in the post-Habsburg space. From early on, De Gasperi maintained that most Trentini would prefer the empire over independent Italy. In 1918 Trentino became one of the areas contested between Italy and the new Republic of Austria. In June 1920 De Gasperi led a delegation of Trentino Popolari (members of the clerical People's Party of Italy or PPI) in a meeting with government officials in Rome. Here he insisted that the annexation of Trentino was in violation of democratic norms, as it had been effected without a plebiscite or local participation.[35]

De Gasperi's commitment to the empire would be a predicament for his career in Italy; Italian nationalists would not forget it, and would see him as more Austrian than Italian, much as nationalists in Poland viewed his peer Leon Biliński as more Austrian than Polish. The parallels between De Gasperi and Biliński, and post-1918 Poland and Italy, are important for understanding the legacy of the empire, the role of former Habsburg functionaries in successor states, and the historical trajectories of states as different as Poland and Italy. While important in their own rights, Biliński and De Gasperi foreground these important political contingencies across post-1918 Europe.

Christian Socialism and 1918

The end of the empire was in no way the end of Christian Social politics in Austria or Europe at large, with the continuity most noticeable in Austria proper. Ignaz Seipel, who rose to prominence as a statesman in the empire's final year, continued his career in republican Austria. He would have occasion to reflect on the controversy surrounding his own political path: a minister in the last imperial government, famously loyal to the empire and dynasty, now building a new Austrian republic in defiance of the charge of *austriacismo.* In 1919 he was elected to the Austrian parliament. His political fortunes matched those of his party, of which he was no longer just a member, but after 1921 its head.

Seipel became a symbol of the political and ideological contradictions of the post-Habsburg space, and of republican Austria in particular. As he himself put it in one of his speeches, his imperial heritage presented certain challenges: "It is likely that the possibility of a former imperial minister becoming a chancellor of the republic would raise some questions."[36] Indeed, as he acknowledged, he had been one of the empire's most committed supporters, although he specified, as if to emphasize his own distance from the particular policies of 1914–17, that he "had done much to reform it into a democratic federative state and lead it out of the war." It was with this goal in mind that he had "entered Lammasch's government and worked toward reforming an old disintegrating state while preserving its tradition."[37] Individuals such as Seipel, who had distinguished themselves before 1918 as ultraloyal, ultraconservative, and ultramonarchist, defied the narrative that connected state building with the radical elimination of empire.[38]

In republican Austria, Seipel became the most important heir to Karl Lueger.[39] The Christian Socials never recovered the electoral ground they had lost after the mayor's passing in 1910, and their standing in Vienna in

particular had been dwindling ever since. Yet the party became more successful in the countryside. Anti-Marxism had become a central doctrine of the
Christian Social Party under Lueger, but Seipel would take it to an extreme in
the first republic; likewise extreme would be the polarization between "red"
socialist-dominated Vienna and the "black" clericalist countryside.

Imperial inheritance also affected coalition building and coalition failures after 1918. The coalitions of 1919 and 1920 resembled the immediate
postliberal period in the empire, with a range of new political movements,
all descended from liberalism and sharing with one another some elements
but decidedly not others. The Christian Socials came in second to the Social
Democrats in the 1919 elections but won the next round in 1920. Despite
decades of political opposition, the two parties formed a coalition in 1919, but
in 1920 the SDs withdrew, refusing to serve as a junior partner. Seipel, by
now the CS leader, entered into a coalition with the former pan-Germans,
now reorganized as the Greater German Party. The breakdown of the 1919
alliance also reflected a continuation of the imperial-era antagonism between
the CSs and SDs, with rigid anti-Marxism confronting rigid anticlericalism,
all compounded by personal animosity between the party leaders—earlier,
Karl Lueger and Victor Adler; after 1918, Ignaz Seipel and Otto Bauer.[40] These
relationships were rooted in imperial precedents and had repercussions for
European politics outside of Austria.

The 1922 Geneva Accords

Seipel became Austria's chancellor in 1922 and spent the first months of his
term touring Europe in an effort to secure financial assistance for the fledgling
republic. Indeed, his deal making in this period was so much a part of his profile that opponents accused him of "selling Austria out"; but from Seipel's
point of view, something had to be done.[41] The country had already been on
the verge of financial collapse since the end of the war, but in 1921 hyperinfla-
tion struck.[42] Without aid, Seipel implied in his meetings in European capitals, the country would be bound to move closer to Germany. The early
agreements between the Entente powers and Austria signed at Saint-Germain
expressly prohibited Anschluss. Seipel himself was ambivalent on this score:
he did not rule out the possibility, but neither did he ever endorse it publicly.[43]
And while many other European states gradually recovered from the shock of
the war and postwar reconstruction, Austria experienced a continual decline,

the severity of its economic crisis in the first years of its republican existence being unmatched by any of its neighbors.

As the political and economic situation worsened, Austrian sympathies toward Germany grew stronger, and the idea of Anschluss more popular. For Europe at large, such a development would be seen as opening the door to another war. The fear of Anschluss was as real in the 1920s as it would be in the 1930s; the memory of the Great War was still quite fresh, as was the impression that the German-Austrian alliance had greatly contributed to its outbreak. European security, argued Seipel, depended on a stable Austria, as the country's collapse could have ramifications well beyond its borders.[44]

The conversations that Seipel held in different European capitals in 1921 and early 1922 revealed the resilience of old political and intellectual networks, as well as the continuity of imperial-era federative thinking. During his state visit to Prague, Seipel held meetings with Edvard Beneš, Czechoslovakia's foreign minister, the two discussing the possibility of increased economic cooperation among successor states. A customs union with Italy was seen as another ameliorative possibility.[45] Beneš continued to advocate cooperation among various successor states throughout the 1920s, suggesting the possibility of a Danubian federation as a solution to Europe's political and economic crisis, an idea that had been popular among many post-Habsburgs, including Seipel's friend Heinrich Lammasch, and to which Seipel was receptive.[46] Federation as a concept remained relevant through the 1920s. After 1918 Seipel became a staunch internationalist, revealing, as did many other protagonists, the compatibility of nationalism and internationalism, and the persistence of federalist internationalism from the empire through the post-1918 era.

Seipel and the League of Nations

Seipel's negotiations with the Entente powers on financial assistance for Austria ultimately failed, but his efforts were not entirely in vain. While individual countries rejected Seipel's pleas for help, the League of Nations stepped in with unprecedented financial initiatives. Initially the League had no mechanism or plans to facilitate the economic reconstruction of particular nation-states, but as Patricia Clavin observes, "the ideology of non-intervention was profoundly challenged by the context of peace."[47] The crisis in Austria, as well as in several other countries, was so severe that action was patently called for.

Negotiations with the League resulted in what became officially titled the "Protocol for the Reconstruction of Austria," part of the so-called Geneva accords signed by the Austrian government in October 1922. According to these agreements, Great Britain, France, Czechoslovakia, and Italy provided loans to Austria under the auspices of the League of Nations. The agreements guaranteed Austrian independence and established a road map for financial and economic reform. They came, however, with strict conditions, requiring, for example, extensive layoffs of civil servants as a way to balance Austria's budget. The League also created a special commission to be based in Vienna, meant to oversee Austria's reforms of its public and private sectors; this body would be tasked not just with facilitating Austria's recovery but also ensuring its ability to repay the loans.

The intervention in Austria represented one of the most important aspects of the League's activity in the interwar period. The League's limitations, especially in the protection of minority rights, became obvious immediately after its founding and have been well discussed in the literature. But it had an

Ignaz Seipel (left) in Geneva, 1922. Austrian National Library, Pictures (Bildarchiv Austria).

important economic role to play as well, both beyond Europe (for example, in regulating relations between Germany and Britain and their former colonies) and at the continent's very heart. In Austria these aspects of the League's profile became intertwined, part of the same political development: as the "custodian" of post-Habsburg successor states, with a "special relationship" to countries in Eastern and Central Europe, the League was responsible not just for the defense of their minority populations but for these states' very viability.[48]

The Geneva protocols proved a success: by 1924 Austria showed signs of recovery, for which Seipel could—and, being a politician, did—take credit.[49] The economic turnaround then became a foundational myth among Christian Socials and interwar Austria at large—the idea of Ignaz Seipel as, in effect, father of the first republic.[50] The paradox was glaring: a monarchist and Habsburg loyalist now was viewed as the most important statesman of the republic. "The Geneva agreements have laid the foundation for economic reconstruction," announced the chancellor in a speech on March 27, 1923.[51] Seipel would later credit both the CS/SD alliance of 1919 and the League-facilitated economic recovery with preventing the rise of Bolshevism in Austria.[52]

Somewhat punningly, Seipel moreover described Austrian cooperation with the League as the country's "annexation [*Anschluss*] to Europe."[53] Christian Social ideology had long been generally skeptical of international capitalism; Lueger himself designed his party as primarily Austrian and Germanophone. But it was Chancellor Seipel who accomplished a quite particular Anschluss—a European-integrationist one—under the auspices of the League of Nations.

Seipel and Internationalism

For Seipel, the League's role and even its physical presence in Austria were crucial: the League facilitated the ratification of agreements in the Austrian parliament despite opposition and shifted the burden of responsibility from Seipel himself to the international community. As Seipel's friend Heinrich Lammasch had earlier predicted, many states, wary of risking their sovereignty, would resist any international intervention, even under the direst circumstances, as was the case in Austria immediately following the war.

Seipel now became, however inadvertently, a symbol of a new type of internationalism in post-1918 Europe. Before 1916 he had rejected autonomy, federation, and internationalism. But he adjusted his views after 1918, not only continuing Lammasch's role in promoting internationalism but also becoming one of its major advocates in postwar Austria. As the chancellor saw it, European internationalism could be traced to the first Hague Convention of 1899, at which Lammasch had represented the Habsburg Empire; in this spirit, Seipel emphasized the value of international mediation and described the League of Nations as a culmination of such efforts. The League, he insisted, did not just help rescue newly republican Austria from financial collapse; it had also, in doing so, contributed to peace and stability throughout Europe.[54]

The Geneva accords, however, and the very presence of League officials in Austria caused severe political tensions, especially between the Seipel-led conservative government and the SDs. From the socialist perspective of the latter, the conditions especially burdened the already vulnerable Austrian working classes. The agreements also caused dissent within the Christian Social Party itself. Beyond Vienna, which per the 1920 constitution formed an autonomous unit within the federal state, various CS-controlled *Länder* (states or federal subdivisions of Austria) struggled to comply with the League's demand that the bureaucracy be reduced and that spending be cut in particular by forcing at least some administrative personnel into retirement.[55]

This paradox was also conditioned by political developments dating back to the imperial era. The long-entrenched opposition between red socialist Vienna and the black Christian Social countryside became increasingly pronounced and politically consequential after 1919. Vienna, with its separate administrative status, resembled a socialist island within an otherwise conservative sea. Yet although the socialists were vociferous in their opposition to the Geneva accords, it was in fact resistance from "black" Austria, and not "red" Vienna that undermined Seipel's position within his own party.

Nationalism and Anti-Semitism

Seipel's internationalism should be taken with a grain (or several) of salt, particularly when seen against the backdrop of his vision of international, and Jewish-sourced, capital as a menace to Austria. Seipel's anti-Semitism was remarkably similar to that of Lueger: political-cultural rather than "racial." Like Lueger, Seipel saw Jews as the underwriters of international capitalism, and himself as defending Austrian workers from them. His stance was also a byproduct of the imperial past and his imperial upbringing, and another mark of continuity between the early Christian socialism of Lueger in the Habsburg Empire and its successor in the Austrian Republic.

The Christian Social Party would gradually radicalize over the 1920s, both reflecting and catalyzing the similarly steady polarization of Austrian politics in general. The rightward shift would be most pronounced among members of the Greater German Party, who remained part of the government coalition through the early 1930s. But a number of CSs too would adopt a more radical anti-Jewish stance, one closer to pan-Germanist anti-Semitism than to imperial-era Christian Social ideology.

In 1924 Seipel's government experienced a new crisis, touched off in particular by the postwar economic crash and the Geneva agreements that Seipel himself prized so highly. He resigned in November in the midst of railway strikes. He was most likely forced to leave as a result of internal pressure from party colleagues, who faulted him for not preventing or suppressing these strikes. His resignation, however, did not mark the end of his political career.[56] He spent most of the next two years on trips to other European countries and the United States, and would be elected chancellor again in 1926, when the Austria he governed would be a different one—a republic on the brink of civil war, slowly slipping into authoritarianism.

Conclusions

Despite the various ruptures and upheavals caused by the war and its aftermath, the clerical parties that emerged in the empire not only survived beyond 1918 but in some cases became even more prominent than they had been. The persistence of political Catholicism across geographical and chronological divides is striking, especially for an ideology that, in the twentieth century, was hardly universal and even somewhat outdated, with religion's appeal gradually dwindling. Driven by their commitment to the Habsburgs as defenders of world Catholicism, clericals had remained loyal to the empire to the last. A fair number of them came to occupy important positions in their new states immediately after the empire's collapse. There was little in the way of open reflection on the difficulty of this transition; most tried to distance themselves from their imperial past, muting the memory of their long-standing commitment to the dynasty, even if they did in fact tend to employ the old empire's models in their latest policymaking.

In terms of longevity and geographical scope, the clericals were rivaled only by Social Democrats, the two movements sharing a commitment to socioeconomic issues but diverging in their attitude toward religion and certain other questions. These latter disagreements ultimately outweighed any philosophical overlap, and the competition between the two ideologies would prevent alliances between parties in the nineteenth and twentieth centuries, with tensions migrating from one epoch to the next.

The post-1918 Christian Social legacy implied a certain understanding of religious-oriented politics, the endorsement of the Vatican, and a concomitant denunciation of Marxism—factors that defined left/right alignments in the politics of several countries after 1918. Habsburg institutions per se had little to do with the mutual antagonism between the Marxists and the clericals, but the political climate of the late empire facilitated the standoff between the sides, making compromise before and after 1918 increasingly difficult. Indeed, while disinterest in cooperation was a product of the imperial past, its consequences would prove more dire for republican Austria than anything seen in the imperial era.[57] Understanding the dynamic between the right and left in interwar Europe is impossible without examining the alliances and practices that Christian Socials and Social Democrats adopted as the empire waned.

PART TWO

Nationalism and Fascism

4. Empire and Nationalism, 1860s–1920s

When commenting on the empire's downfall in the fall of 1918, Heinrich Lammasch, the empire's last prime minister, put the main blame on "Czech and Polish renegades," who, he argued, had conspired against their state.[1] The term "renegade" had by then become part of the empire's political discourse. Used by radical nationalists, it referred to those alleged to be insufficiently true to their national identity. Imperial loyalists, for their part, used it as did Lammasch, to refer to the Habsburg polity's supposed underminers.[2] By late 1918, most conservatives, moderates, and nationalists would in any case concur with Lammasch's assessment of nationalists as having played a crucial role in the empire's collapse.[3] These "renegades" would appear in a different light after 1918 as their nations' saviors, emphasizing precisely the point Lammasch had been making: they had allegedly spent their lifetimes fighting against the Habsburgs and played a major role in the destruction of the empire.

But as Ferdinand Peroutka, a writer affiliated with President Tomáš Masaryk in interwar Czechoslovakia, asked with regard to the Czech case: was this a revolution or not?[4] Unlike the fall of communism in 1989, the year 1918 saw no major military confrontations. Several states, including Poland and Czechoslovakia, declared independence peacefully in late October 1918. The 1918 transition, as Peroutka noted in the 1920s, and several historians have recently argued, was an evolutionary and peaceful one.[5] The renegades that Lammasch and others were referring to actually played little or no role in the empire's downfall.

Prague, October 28, 1918. From *28. říjen a první dny svobody. Když zlomeny okovy. Dějiny naší revoluce slovem i obrazem* (Prague: E. Šolc, 1919).

Yet the perception that radical nationalism was decisive in the empire's collapse, and that the coup de grace was delivered by national revolutions in 1918, became embedded in Europe's political and intellectual imagination. After 1918 a slew of publications, by former Habsburg subjects as well as intellectuals and historians from elsewhere, promoted the idea that national tensions were so grave in the empire that collapse had been inevitable.

Some of the nationalists alluded to in the previously cited 1918 comment by Lammasch took part in creating this narrative. Consider, for example, Stanisław Głąbiński and Karel Kramář, respectively, of Galicia and Bohemia, later Poland and Czechoslovakia. Born in 1862 and 1860, they belonged to the same cohort as Heinrich Lammasch, Joseph Redlich, Leon Biliński, and Mykola Wassilko. Głąbiński and Biliński started off in politics as friends, a personal bond that was not uncommon among the empire's political elites. Even though they came from different provinces, these protagonists belonged to the same political circles, received similar education, spoke similar or the same languages, and negotiated politics in the same coffeehouses. Well into the 1890s, they also shared similar views of politics and espoused the same values of nationalism, loyalty, and internationalism that distinguished our other pro-

tagonists as well. Only the war marked the beginning of outward animosity between the nationalists, the moderates, and the conservatives. It was also the
war that created the preconditions for a radical nationalism of a kind that had
not existed in the empire before, as well as the myth of the radical nationalist
opposition that led to the empire's end.

This chapter offers an analysis of radical nationalists in the empire, and
of how they incorporated imperial models and practices in different successor
states. Its focus is on two self-defined nationalists—Głąbiński and Kramář—
and their transition from empire to Poland and Czechoslovakia. Building on
the rich body of recent literature on nationalism, national radicalization, and
"national indifference" in the late empire, I examine how certain nationalists'
long acceptance of the empire conditioned the political choices they made after
its end, and what the consequences were of these choices for their careers and
for the political life of the countries they represented as well as Europe at large.
Juxtaposing different aspects in the creation of the myth of radical nationalist
resistance to the Habsburgs—the discourse not just of nationalists in the
Habsburg Empire but also of their supporters among the Allies abroad—and
tracing these beyond 1918, this analysis sheds new light on the evolution and
different understanding of nationalism, as well as the continuity of national
politics across the epochal divide and on the role this myth played in several
interwar states.

This chapter and the next also elaborate on generational differences
between former imperial subjects, especially those who identified as nationalists. Their younger peers born between the 1890s and the early 1900s
could indeed be radical, more likely to fight and die for the nationalist cause.
They could be prone to commit or at least condone political assassination
and to endorse fascism after 1919.[6] The vast majority of figures covered in
this study, however—the elder (if only by a few years) peers—were exposed
to a specific mode of politics in the Habsburg Empire, and tended to support
autonomy rather than irredentism before 1914. Having been loyal to the
empire as a polity, they acted as moderates after 1918.[7] Their contemporaries from the Habsburg Empire's former neighbor states—especially Poles in
the Russian Empire and Italians in the Kingdom of Italy—could and did
develop a different tradition of nationalism, which was at times radically
pro-irredentist and even violent. Despite the nationalists' own harping on
1918 as a radical break, the continuity in their politics between the empire
and its successor states is impossible to ignore.

From Conservatism to Nationalism

This continuity was the result of a late Habsburg-era politics that created the conditions for pan-imperial loyalty even among nationalists. It was also the product of a particular line of succession from conservatives to liberals, moderates, and nationalists. Głąbiński was, like Biliński, a product of the Galician Austro-Russian borderland. Born in 1862 in the mountain village of Skole (now part of Ukraine), he was raised in the mixed Polish-Ukrainian area near the border with Russia. The proximity between the Habsburg and Russian Empires affected Głąbiński quite personally. In 1863 his father, Jan Głąbiński, went to Warsaw to join the Polish revolutionaries fighting there for independence from the Russian Empire. In a surge of youthful enthusiasm, Jan risked his life and his family's well-being; Stanisław was at the time just one year old. But Jan did make it home alive, even though many of his fellow Poles, encountering far superior Russian forces on the battlefield, did not. The Austrians imposed political repressions of their own. Jan, scion of a noble family, was barred from university enrollment and never received a higher education.[8] Głąbiński the junior would never repeat his father's mistakes, eschewing choices that might jeopardize his status or career.

Głąbiński began his career under Biliński's mentorship—a connection that reflected the importance of interpersonal relationships in Habsburg-era and interwar politics. Studying political economy at the University of Lwów, Głąbiński became a professor at that institution. In 1889 he was appointed dean of its law school, and in 1908–9 served as the university's rector. Politically, Głąbiński was initially drawn to the Galician conservatives who were accepting of both the government and other nationalities in Galicia—these choices "back in the imperial day" clearly at odds with the nationalistic self-image he would project years after the empire's collapse.

Like many other protagonists of this book, Głąbiński traded academia for politics and would end up occupying some of the same positions previously held by Biliński himself. From 1902 to 1918 he served as a deputy to the imperial parliament, heading, as had Biliński before him, the Polish caucus (1907–11); and he was briefly (1909–10) minister of railways. In 1910 he replaced his former mentor (after contributing to the latter's dismissal from the government).[9] Głąbiński himself shifted to the right at the turn of the century, eventually becoming one of the leading Polish nationalists in Galicia; but the two continued to work together through the 1900s, and he also participated in the round of Polish-Ukrainian negotiations that Biliński initiated in 1909. Głąbiński's involvement with and endorsement of these agreements are important for understanding conservative, moderate, and nationalist politics, and their points of contact in the late Habsburg Empire. He matured in an environment where compromises and negotiations were a norm and violence an exception, and this formative experience would influence his choices for years after 1918, despite his right-wing political shift.

Cross-Border Nationalism

Radical nationalism and conservativism in Galicia had similar political roots. Both represented responses to domestic and international developments in and around the Habsburg Empire: the post-1867 federalization and Galician autonomy, as well as concurrent policies in the Russian Empire. Polish nationalists first organized in the Russian Empire and only later expanded their activities into Galicia. The National League, formed in Warsaw in 1893, was reorganized as a political party in 1897. Prohibited by the tsarist authorities from publishing pro-independence materials, Polish nationalists propagandized over the border, exerting a greater influence in Galicia than in the Russian Empire itself.[10] The National Democratic League was founded in Galicia in 1905, and it operated legally.[11] Insofar as the Russian government would tolerate no Polish political initiatives whatsoever, Austrian Galicia became the crucial staging ground for nationalist mobilization.

Głąbiński joined the ranks of Polish nationalists during the 1890s. He became increasingly critical of Galician conservatism, which he saw as too compliant with the Austrian authorities, too meek in defending Polish interests. Differing understandings of national interests and imperial politics provoked an even sharper conflict between Biliński and Głąbiński. In many ways, however, Głąbiński remained ideologically closer to the conservative Biliński than to his ostensible fellow thinkers among Polish nationalists in the Russian Empire. The latter were irredentists, espousing complete independence and the liberation of Polish territories from Russian rule. Polish nationalists under the Habsburgs, for their part, supported their brethren's aspirations to throw off the Russian yoke—but they hardly saw *Habsburg* rule in the same light. Polish nationalists in Russia considered the use of force an acceptable instrument of achieving their political goals; their counterparts to the west believed in working within existing institutions.

Relations between Głąbiński and Roman Dmowski, the leading Polish nationalist in the Russian Empire, were characteristic of these trends. The two became acquainted before the war, but their affinity was of a limited nature. Polish nationalists in the Russian Empire staged no uprising after 1864, but neither did they cooperate with the government. Głąbiński was a product of the more tolerant Habsburg Empire, which afforded him and others in his milieu numerous professional opportunities.[12] He helped organize Galicia's National Democratic League but became a member only in 1916, at a point when the war had made nationalism particularly fashionable. While Dmowski aspired to Polish independence, Głąbiński remained loyal to the Habsburgs well into the war, at least until 1916.

The two had different visions of whom their struggle was against. Dmowski saw Russia as economically and politically underdeveloped, far behind the might of Germany; Russia, he reckoned, might expand eastward, but not west—it was too weak for that—leaving Polish territories likely to be overwhelmed amid the German sphere of influence.[13] In 1914 Dmowski thus favored Russia over Germany as the lesser of two evils. But Głąbiński could never support Russia, and these two competing visions clashed with renewed force during the war. Still more incongruous were their views on national minorities. Early on, the Polish National Democrats in the Russian Empire adopted anti-Jewish rhetoric.[14] Anti-Semitism was, meanwhile, never as prominent in the Galician party's program; Głąbiński reserved greater animosity for Ukrainians.[15] These differences were elided somewhat after 1918, but despite years of cooperation, those nationalists who had come of age in different empires continued to operate with different mindsets.

Before 1918 Głąbiński was more radical in word than deed—a fact that he tried to downplay after independence. He evinced radicalism not in his attitude toward the government but rather toward other nationalities, and his worldview never implied irredentism.[16] The image he sought to project after 1918 would hardly correspond with his actual behavior in the imperial era. Despite his many later statements to the contrary, Głąbiński not only did *not* combat the empire, he actively sought to gain political prominence in it, working for and alongside its political establishment. Unlike their nationalist peers from the Russian Empire, the Polish nationalists in Galicia endorsed their state.

Głąbiński: Ambitious Loner

Głąbiński's imperial career was somewhat erratic. He became minister of railways in 1909, but his time there was brief; his tenures as head of the Polish caucus and minister, and his accomplishments generally, fell short of Biliński's. The year 1909 marked the pinnacle of Biliński's extraordinary career as a statesman; for Głąbiński, it was a beginning that soon went awry. While Biliński had navigated the corridors of power in Vienna with remarkable ease, Głąbiński felt isolated. In each case, the new position entailed personal adjustments. Biliński's wife Jozefa accompanied her husband to Vienna, and so did Głąbiński's spouse, Maria. But while Biliński's family felt at home in Vienna, the Głąbiński household had been dysfunctional in Lwów, and moving to Vienna brought no improvement.

As a couple, the Głąbińskis were alienated from one another, and the husband's published reminiscences of his wife are limited to the nuances of her erratic, overly emotional behavior. They long remained childless, and Maria developed a particular affection for her many dogs. Głąbiński's tenure as railway minister afforded his wife the chance to travel in style in special carriages—which was particularly embarrassing politically when, during a trip from Lwów to Vienna, one of her dogs ran away at a station stop, and the train was forced to wait while staff was deployed to look for a minister's pet.[17] The arrival of children did not brighten this family life. In the early 1900s the Głąbińskis adopted a young girl, Stasia, from an orphanage. But she never quite fit in, and moved to Warsaw upon reaching adulthood. The father came to see her in Warsaw, but she did not reciprocate these visits. Relatively late in their lives, in 1924, the Głąbińskis also had a son, but his birth brought little improvement to the family life. Maria died in 1926, when Stanisław junior was just two years old. The father and son never bonded, and the latter would grew up with a sense of abandonment.[18] Preferring to keep his family life private, Głąbiński rarely commented on it, and for years after his wife's death he led the life of a loner, albeit surrounded by many, and focused on his activism.

This situation at home was complicated, but cause and effect remain unclear: did Głąbiński dedicate himself to work so assiduously because home life was strained, or did this unhappiness result from his excessive commitment to politics? Głąbiński never altered his work patterns; he prioritized career over home life until his death.

Czech Nationalists between Austria, Germany, and Russia

Polish politics and nationalism can only be explained within the broader geographical and historical context of the Polish territories as they evolved following the eighteenth-century partitions of the Polish-Lithuanian Commonwealth. Likewise, Czech politics and nationalism in the late Habsburg Empire should also be understood within the broader history of the Czech lands before and during the Habsburg period. In 1526, as a result of a marital alliance, the Kingdom of Bohemia and Moravia joined with the Habsburg dynasty. This expansion of the initially rather compact Duchy of Austria into hitherto Slavic lands represents one of the most consequential annexations in history. Over the centuries, Austrian policies transformed this initially predominantly Slavic territory into an area of German political and administrative dominance. German became the language of administration, which facilitated the Germanization of local elites in Bohemia; it was not a legally enforced process, but German identification naturally became the preference for the many aristocratic families in the region. The dynamic of ethnic and cultural relations here was different than in other provinces. Ethnic Germans in Bohemia were not just a minority, but part of a larger Germanophone population in the empire with strong ties to Vienna, a type of connection that would fuel German-Czech tensions in the centuries that followed.

Over the centuries, the two cultures—Slavic and German—became increasingly blended. Bohemia, and Prague in particular, came to represent a nationally fluid space, where boundaries between German and Czech were hard to draw.[19] Language rarely served as an equivalent of nationality. Aristocratic families in Bohemia who chose the path of German assimilation were neither Czechs nor Germans, but rather imperial citizens who supported the Habsburgs. Bilingualism was common in Bohemia in the nineteenth century.[20] The choice of national affiliation and self-identification was a pragmatic one: in these matters, as Garry Cohen and Jeremy King have demonstrated, socioeconomic status or class was more important than ethnicity.[21] Even as late as the 1860s–70s, the Czech nobility "showed little interest in the national cause, and were Bohemians and nothing more."[22] National fluidity or even "indifference," as Tara Zahra has defined it, was the norm in Bohemia for much of the second half of the nineteenth century.[23]

This "politics of flux," as Jeremy King has described it, began to show cracks in 1871, upon the failure of the so-called Fundamental Articles agreements.

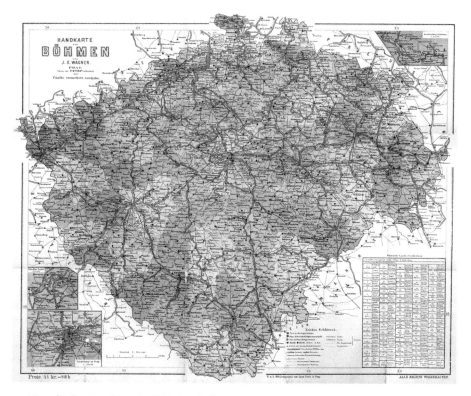

Map of Bohemia, 1860s. Czech National Library, Digital Collection.

In the wake of the 1867 Austro-Hungarian Compromise, Czech politicians had anticipated a transition from dualism to "trialism," by which Bohemia would acquire a status similar to Hungary's. The ethnic Czech population in Bohemia, and particularly in Prague, had been steadily rising, and would continue to do so in the latter half of the nineteenth century. Czechs made up about 60 percent of the population, with Germans ranking under 40 percent.[24] German nevertheless remained the main language of administration and education.[25] Federalization and autonomy could counter this German dominance.

The 1867 compromise and federalization proved a turning point in the relationships not only between the Austrians and the Hungarians but also between the Austrians and the Poles, as well as between the Austrians and the Czechs. Vienna now refused further federalization and, moreover, rejected Czechs' request for the sort of political concessions that Poles had secured in Galicia. Autonomy could disrupt the empire's economy, insofar as shifting decision making from Vienna to Prague might come at the expense of other regions, especially Austria itself, which was economically dependent on industrialized and coal-rich Bohemia.[26]

Czech politics in the late empire were a response to the failure of trialism and autonomy, as well as to perceived German domination in Bohemia. In the early 1870s Czech politicians decided to boycott the imperial government and parliament. They would later revise this decision and renew their participation in imperial institutions, but this early boycott established firm new patterns in the relationship between Vienna and Prague: the involvement of ethnic Czechs in the empire's administration would remain marginal, while their participation in the parliament would be more active but also more confrontational than that of their Polish counterparts.

Reconsidering Czechs' post-1867 boycott of imperial institutions, members of the "Young Czechs" movement that consolidated in 1874 took on a more active political role, now seeing an institutional means to advance their cause.[27] The differences between the "old" boycotters and Young Czechs were ideological rather than generational; the two cohorts moreover blended over time, with members of the former joining the parliament in the late 1870s. Their demands included the opening of a Czech university in Prague and the establishment of Czech-German bilingualism in Bohemia. The 1882 division of the Prague university into two—a German and Czech one—represented a concession by the government to Czech demands. The Czech university, however, was marginal under the empire, and its German counterpart remained more prestigious and able to attract prominent faculty.[28] The Young Czech movement became a springboard for several different parties—both moderate and nationalist ones—that would later play a role in interwar Czechoslovakia. Now working with and within imperial institutions, Czech politicians were fighting for Czech dominance in Bohemia and Moravia.

While the division of the Prague university remained controversial, the 1897 reform to attempt to equalize the status of Czech and German languages in the administration of Bohemia was even more so. According to the decree, all local officials were required to be fluent in both German and Czech; those who did not know Czech were given four years (until 1901) to pass a language exam as a prerequisite for their professional employment.[29] The decree led to German protests in Bohemia and Vienna, resulting in the transformation of Austrian parliamentary culture in ways that would likewise spill over into the postimperial era.[30] That same year of 1897, German deputies staged the first major parliamentary obstruction—a practice that would later be imitated by different groups in different parliaments before and after 1918. The conflict over the university and tensions surrounding bilingualism reflected the evolution of Czech nationalism, as well the dynamic of Czech-German relations in Bohemia. Czech nationalism was essentially directed against Germanophone domination in Bohemia, but not against the Habsburg state as such.

Kramář and Czech Radicalism

Karel Kramář was in effect the Stanisław Głąbiński of Bohemia—the most prominent Czech politician to come of age in the empire and then become a leader of the nationalist camp in Czechoslovakia. Like Głąbiński, he supported autonomy during his considerable imperial-era career but refashioned himself as a pro-independence firebrand during the war, emphasizing especially this aspect of his politics after the empire's collapse.

Born in 1860 to a wealthy industrial family on the German-Slavic frontier some 130 kilometers from Prague, Kramář moved as a teenager to the city to attend a German middle school, most likely on the insistence of his father, who encouraged and financially supported his son's education and travels.[31] German education would open up career paths in the empire beyond Bohemia. He studied in Prague, Strasbourg, Berlin, and Paris; even at home in Prague, he broadened his horizons by learning English.[32]

The internationalism of his academic ventures, paradoxically, would play a role in Kramář's development as a nationalist. He moved from Prague to Vienna to complete his law degree. During his student years, he published in German and French periodicals; upon completing his doctorate in law, he attended classes at German universities.[33] One of these, taken in Berlin in 1884, proved especially influential, affecting his political choices for years to come. This was a summer seminar offered by the prominent German economist Adolph Wagner. Kramář later recalled that "Wagner was a nationalist and, to a certain degree, an anti-Semite, and he showed great interest in politics."[34] That summer in Berlin, Kramář rubbed elbows with men who would go on to be key players in European politics, among them the Austrian journalist Hermann Bahr, several university professors, at least one diplomat, and Michael Hainisch, the future second president of the Republic of Austria.[35]

Kramář thus came to know German nationalism intimately, conversing with its leading proponents on their home turf. Just as Roman Dmowski in Warsaw admired German might and considered imitating German strategies

Karel Krámař, 1916. Austrian
National Library, Pictures
(Bildarchiv Austria).

of national mobilization, so did Kramář learn from German nationalists, returning home with new perspectives. Both Kramář and Dmowski believed that
Germany posed a civilizational threat to Czechs and Poles, respectively. Kramář
perceived Central Europe as teetering between the German and Slavic poles,
with the latter ultimately cast as savior of those threatened by the former. "Germany," Kramář wrote retroactively in 1922, "understands the danger posed by
the rapprochement of the Slavic peoples."[36] Kramář and Dmowski shared similar visions of an enemy and of the means to combat it: to counter German
nationalism, they would imitate it.

Kramář entered politics in the 1880s as a student in Prague, in particular joining the Realist Party—an attempt to find a middle ground between the
Old and Young Czechs and stimulate organizational change in the Czech repre-

sentation in Vienna.[37] Kramář was one of the group's founders, along with Tomáš Masaryk. He remained with the Young Czechs through the early years of the war. Eventually shifting to the right, he became prominent in the radical nationalist wing. For his part, Masaryk critiqued the Young Czechs for their radicalism and left to found a different party; he would remain a moderate.[38] This parting of the ways, relatively early in Kramář's life and career, would define Czech politics for decades after the empire's collapse.[39] The rift between these two figures resembled the concurrent change in the relationship between Głąbiński and Biliński.

Kramář's pre-1914 nationalism was akin to that of Głąbiński: compatible with imperial loyalty. He critiqued the Austrian government's gradual curtailing of Bohemia's privileges within the empire. As he saw it, in 1526 the Kingdom of Bohemia had entered into a union with the Habsburg dynasty as an equal partner, with its own administration and set of privileges. But over time, especially during the centralization drive of the eighteenth century, Bohemia had lost its status, becoming then just another province under Habsburg rule.[40] The nineteenth century only reaffirmed this pattern of gradual absorption into the centralized empire, and the failure of the 1871 agreements proved a major disappointment.[41] Kramář's goals at this time were limited to national autonomy, specifically the rights of education and administration in one's native language, as well as support for the industrial development of Bohemia and Moravia, and semi-independent finances and taxation.[42] The radical wing of the Young Czechs resembled, moreover, its Polish National Democratic equivalent in Galicia. Each opposed aspects of the government without questioning the empire.

Kramář on Germany and Russia

Kramář was nevertheless unusual in the empire in that his anti-German nationalism became contingent on his Russophilism. If Głąbiński's nationalism was conditioned by wariness of Russia, Kramář's was driven by the conflict with the Germans and his perception of Russia as the only real counterweight to German dominance in the Austrian Empire and in Europe in general. By the 1890s many other Czechs shared Kramář's preoccupation with German influence, in particular in Bohemia. Yet no other prominent politician looked to Russia as a solution—to say nothing of translating such a view into action.

For many of his contemporaries, Russophilism was a cultural phenomenon devoid of political content. Attempts to incorporate Russian culture and language into Galician life in the 1870s–80s, for example, in no way implied Galician Russophiles' intention to *join* the Russian Empire.[43] Among Czechs, Masaryk became known for his Russophilia, immersing himself in the study of Russian literature, history, and philosophy.[44] Kramář's Russophilism, however, was different: it also bore a strong political component. In an 1890 letter to his colleague and friend Josef Kaizl, Kramář described Slavic unity as the "ultimate refuge" against German domination.[45] He linked the existence of the Czech nation with the preservation of the Russian Empire.

His personal life too became intertwined with politics. During one of his trips to Russia, he made the acquaintance of Nadezhda Abrikosova, a scion of the Khludovs, a wealthy Russian merchant family. At the time, Abrikosova resided in Odessa with her husband and their children. She eventually left her family to accompany Kramář back to Prague and marry him, after obtaining a divorce.[46] Such personal associations with Russianness may be considered part of the backdrop of Kramář's support for imperial Russia through its last days and beyond, after the Bolshevik takeover.

At the same time, Kramář nurtured political ambitions in Vienna on an even grander scale than did Głąbiński. Rumors circulated that he fancied himself as foreign minister—a position that would enable him to carry out the reorientation of Austria's foreign policy that he advocated.[47] In 1882 the Austrian government concluded a mutual defense treaty with Germany and Italy. Kramář supported, to the contrary, a pact with Russia. He was never offered the position; the foreign ministry was considered too sensitive to be entrusted to politicians with nationalist tendencies. Neither did Kramář seek any lesser post, thus keeping with the tendency of Czech statesmen to generally eschew participation in the central imperial government. Kramář remained similarly ambitious after 1918, in this period seeking nothing less than the Czechoslovak premiership.

Kramář's pro-government stance, meanwhile, outshone even that of Głąbiński; he went so far as to decry the rhetoric of his fellow nationalists as harmful to the Austrian state. In a 1906 publication he cautioned, "We have to cease any flirtations with the radical destruction of centralism."[48] His and Głąbiński's reluctance to endorse radical rhetoric—to say nothing of radical action—was typical of prewar nationalism in the Habsburg Empire, where the vast majority of its citizens, including nationalists, remained loyal to their state and worked within, not against, its institutions.

Militarism and Nationalism

The war, and specifically the Austrian government's policies, forged a nationalism of a new kind, inciting irredentism and the drive to independence. In August 1914 Czechs overwhelmingly supported the Habsburg Empire as a polity that should continue.[49] Czech leaders took time to assess the meaning of the war's outbreak. In that first month of hostilities, Masaryk left for Italy, then settled (after a brief stopover in Switzerland) in London. Together with his younger ally Edvard Beneš, he organized the so-called Maffia, originally envisioned as an intelligence and coordination center for Czech resistance against the Habsburg Empire. By the spring of 1915, Maffia members were openly calling for anti-Habsburg rebellion, and in November of that year, the Czechoslovak Foreign Committee in Paris, headed by Beneš, issued a declaration of war on Austro-Hungary.[50]

It was only during the war that the possibility of replacing the Habsburg Empire with new nation-states actually presented itself.[51] Kramář's irredentism, however, was notably slow to develop. Unlike Masaryk, he believed that the empire would survive the war, and he refused to participate in Masaryk's political enterprises. In 1914 Kramář's position was that radicalism would be ineffective, and that Masaryk's international campaign was akin to the sound of a muffled trumpet.[52] Only by late 1915 did he endorse the independence movement and join the Maffia in Prague.

In line with his previous views, Kramář linked his pro-independence campaign to Russia. For him, the war represented the culmination of the age-old struggle between two civilizations, "a battle between Germandom and Slavdom." Later in the conflict, he supported Masaryk and Beneš's anti-war sentiments but opposed taking any radical steps without Russian assistance.[53] He took advantage of the political opportunities that presented themselves during the war; in 1915, for instance, he made contact with Alexander Borzhenko, a professor at Odessa University. From his base in the southern Russian Empire, Borzhenko provided ideological and moral support for Kramář's plans. There was reason to hope; Russia's leading liberal, Pavel Miliukov, supported an independent Czechoslovakia as a buffer state between Russia and Germany.[54]

Insofar as Kramář's Russian intrigues came to pose a direct threat to the Habsburg state, he was arrested in May 1915.[55] Having confessed to the attempt to make contact with the Russian government, he was sentenced to death but, after awaiting execution for over a year, was amnested in 1917.[56] About a dozen

Czech activists underwent the same experience, with some, like Kramář, shifting rightward toward the end of the war.[57] Kramář would make use of his own and others' wartime experience; their prison terms and death sentences generated political capital, and it was anticipated that their suffering would be rewarded after the war in the form of political offices. In this way Austria's wartime persecution of Czech nationalists had a considerable influence on politics in interwar Czechoslovakia.[58]

But it was not the Austrians but the Bolsheviks who ruined Kramář's plans for a Czech-Russian alliance. The October Revolution came as a shock to Kramář. His entire life and ideology had been built on the critical role that the Russian Empire must play in the international order. He therefore saw the revolution as a catastrophe of historic proportions, a radical change to rival the fall of the Roman Empire. And even that great polity, he remarked ruefully, "did not collapse overnight; it had been slowly disintegrating over centuries of internal crisis."[59] At first Kramář expected the setback to be short-lived; Bolshevik rule would no doubt crumble amid broad resistance from Russian society. Kramář saw his immediate task as mobilizing international assistance to what remained of the tsarist armed forces. Restoring Russia's monarchy was a must.

Bolsheviks, Nationalists, and Galicia across the 1918 Divide

If Kramář had reason to fear the Bolsheviks, still more did Głąbiński: their military forces threatened Poland at large, and his and his family's very safety. The Bolshevik strategy was to establish bases across Russia proper, then move to reconquer territories that had belonged to the Russian Empire. This brought them into clashes with Russian tsarist forces (the Whites) as well as units of other nationalities in territories that by 1918 were seeking independence. Eastern Europe thus became a zone of yet another conflict, nearly as destructive and in some ways even more consequential than the First World War itself. The reception of the October Revolution among Poles—at the time still divided among different empires—was initially mixed. On one hand, the Bolshevik takeover could presage the fall of the Russian Empire as a polity, which could make Polish independence possible. On the other hand, the Bolsheviks immediately laid claim to all territories belonging to the Russian Empire. In any event, the change of regime in Russia transformed Polish politics across the border.

Like Kramář, Głąbiński remained loyal to the Habsburg Empire through the first years of the war, but toward its end (and only then) refashioned himself as an irredentist. The outbreak of hostilities found him in Galicia. He spent the first few months there, but in the fall became part of a group of refugees leaving the province on a special train to Vienna ahead of the arrival of Russian forces. This experience cemented his hostility to everything Russian and deepened the rift between him and other Polish nationalists, who were more ambivalent as to who should be considered the Poles' main enemy.

Austria's military defeats, meanwhile, forced him to reconsider his political tactics. Głąbiński did not discount the possibility of the empire's collapse, and he tried to play a double game. From 1916 on he simultaneously professed imperial loyalty and advocated independence, playing up his nationalism in Polish circles, and his belief in the Habsburg polity in the presence of government officials. In the summer of 1916 he resigned from the parliament's Polish caucus, protesting its support of the monarchy. But as the socialist Ignacy Daszyński would later recall, as late as 1917 Głąbiński was still "making the rounds of various cabinets describing himself as the Habsburgs' most loyal subject."[60] He could only get away with this dual performance because most of his fellow Polish activists were then engaged in more or less the same behavior—a pattern that set them apart from their Czech or Italian counterparts, who endorsed independence early on.

The war marked the end of long-standing cooperation between conservatives and nationalists, and of nationalists' reluctant involvement in interethnic alliances. Polish-Ukrainian violence created new tensions within the empire's Polish political establishment as well. This was the moment when the conservatives, notably Biliński, began to question their earlier decisions, especially regarding the possibility of Polish-Ukrainian cooperation. Polish nationalists such as Głąbiński in turn cast doubt on the whole logic of conservatism, and began to present themselves as having *always* struggled against both imperial domination and any national rivals who might stand in the way of an independent and solidly Polish Poland.

In January 1919, during the civil war in Galicia, Głąbiński was dispatched to Bucharest to negotiate French military assistance to Poland.[61] He traveled on a special train, as he had in 1914, but this time was keen to avoid the "crowds of Ukrainians."[62] The upheaval only reaffirmed Głąbiński's anti-Ukrainian convictions. "There is no denying," he remarked, "that the Ukrainians were also contemplating independence, and the conflict over Galicia caused them to 'hate Poles.'"[63] Thus, Głąbiński became radicalized during the war, yet both during the conflict and in the interwar period he relied on concepts that he had formulated under the empire.

The war also caused new breaches between Polish nationalists in the Habsburg territories, setting precedents for later thorniness in interwar Poland. Dmowski continued to believe that Germany posed a greater threat to an independent Poland than did Russia. For his part, Głąbiński not only remained loyal to Austria but also, like so many others in the Habsburg Empire, could only see Russia as a major political menace. Two different visions of statehood, nationalism, and the use of force would manifest themselves after 1918, when, in their political tactics, if not their "official" ideological designation, nationalists from the former Habsburg Empire would be more akin to their conservative and moderate peers than to nationalists who had matured under the Russian Empire.

Stanisław Głąbiński (on the right). Polish National Library, Karykatury Sejmowe, Zaszyty 1–4, Avtolitografje Zygmunta Skrwirczyńskiego (1922).

National Democratic Parties, 1918–19

Polish and Czech nationalists gained momentum in late 1918 and would build their careers and parties on a projection of their presumed (rather than actual) long-standing nationalist opposition to Habsburg rule. A somewhat specious narrative that was created during the war, as part of the combined efforts of nationalists at home and their allies abroad, thus took root in the new successor states.

The National Democratic Party of Poland was a result of the merger of pre-1918 organizations from the Russian and Habsburg Empires, and it espoused a direct line of continuity between the pre- and post-1918 periods. The history of Czech nationalism between the empire and interwar Europe is more complex. During the war, the Czech Maffia represented the most radical wing of Czech politics; Masaryk and Beneš were more active in promoting Czech independence than Kramář. Yet in interwar Czechoslovakia, they represented a moderate center, while Kramář became the leader of the nationalist right. In late 1918 he established the Czech State Rights Party. In early 1919 it was renamed the Czechoslovak National Democratic Party, now matching its Polish counterpart. Both parties, the Polish and Czechoslovak National Democrats (NDs), built their constituencies and reputation on claims of nationalist political dissent in the empire: it was, they asserted, they and they alone who (in their respective milieus) had resisted Habsburg oppression and established the new states.

The two parties' involvement in government and mainstream politics varied: in Poland the NDs remained a dominant force through the mid-1920s. In Czechoslovakia, by contrast, they would be one of the few parties ousted from the governing coalition, finding themselves politically marginalized as early as 1921.[64] The NDs joined the Czech government as a junior partner the same year, but Kramář himself never occupied a ministerial post. His attitudes to government and politics had been conditioned by political developments in the pre-1918 period and the consolidation of the Czech national camp under the empire.

The first ministerial positions in Czechoslovakia were distributed during negotiations of former Maffia members and their affiliates who had cooperated in achieving Czechoslovak independence late in the war.[65] Masaryk became president and Kramář prime minister. To the latter fell the honor of delivering the opening speech to the first Czech parliament, and he used this momentous occasion to hail the liberation from the centuries-long "barbarism and oppression" under Habsburg rule—a reference point to which he would return constantly in his subsequent political career.[66]

The chaos and violence that ensued upon the war's conclusion affected everyone, and Kramář was no exception. On January 8, 1919, a young Czech left-wing activist tried to assassinate him near his office in Prague as a protest against the government's alleged collusion with big business and capitalism.[67] Kramář survived and continued in politics, now having endured a death sentence, months on death row, and an assassination attempt. His fellow nationalist Alois Rašín, the minister of finance, would be less lucky, falling in 1923 to a leftist assassin likewise motivated by the perception that the government was siding with capitalists to oppress labor. These acts of violence revealed the increased volatility of Czechoslovak politics. Indeed, the severity of the Czechs' governmental crisis was on a different scale than the figures involved would have experienced before 1918.

Versailles, Nationalists, Bolsheviks, and Imperialists

Shortly after the attempt on his life, Kramář departed to Versailles to participate in the peace conference there—an event of critical importance for his life and career as well as for Czechoslovakia. The new republic had not been formally invited, but its delegation participated unofficially, as did a Polish representation. These groups took part in various negotiations over territory, specifically the borderland of Teschen (Cieszyn), which both Poland and Czechoslovakia claimed as their own. Kramář was willing to be flexible, commenting in talks with Głąbiński that Czechoslovakia and Poland should not fight over "a few villages"—remarks received in the Czech press with indignation as national betrayal.[68] The fact that these politicians were able to frame a territorial dispute this way revealed the persistence of a nationally accommodating, Habsburg-imperial mindset, even in ostensible nationalists.

Working through such territorial stumbling blocks was complicated enough by the fact that some of the rival negotiators had belonged to the same state prior to 1918; but conflicts within a single new country's delegation were sometimes even sharper. Kramář and Beneš, for instance, butted heads at Versailles, marking the beginning of a conflict that would linger for over a decade. The two drifted apart during the conference, with Beneš dissatisfied with Kramář's conduct of the negotiations and ultimately his very presence. In a letter to Masaryk he complained, "Kramář is impossible. . . . He only wreaks chaos here," adding that Kramář's temperament rendered him a poor fit for the position of prime minister.[69]

Kramář's agitated state was linked to the situation in Russia and the consequences of the October Revolution there. He still believed that Czech national survival was contingent on a strong Russia—an imperial, not Bolshevik Russia. While in Paris, he made arrangements for a future meeting with General Anton Denikin, commander of the White forces then fighting for the restoration of the Russian Empire, to discuss potential Czechoslovak involvement in the anti-Soviet campaign. Kramář insisted that he was acting in defense of Europe: defeating the Bolsheviks, he argued, was in the interest of the whole continent. For years he would maintain that Czechs and Slovaks owed their independence to pre-Soviet Russia.[70]

Intervening against the Bolsheviks was highly controversial. First, various armies fighting against Lenin became implicated in atrocities against civilians, especially Jews. The Bolsheviks were, by contrast, the only political force in Russia to openly condemn anti-Semitism; indeed, it was official Soviet policy that anti-Semitism be extirpated as counterrevolutionary. For his part, Kramář insisted that anti-Semitism was prevalent among combatants generally, the Whites only revealing an overall trend.[71] As late as 1920, he continued to defend Denikin in his speeches to the Czechoslovak parliament, denying any alleged wrongdoings on the part of the White forces.[72] The major European powers (including Czechoslovakia) eventually adopted a policy of nonintervention toward Soviet Russia; in an effort to keep the communist threat "contained," they would avoid potentially inflammatory interference in Bolshevik domestic politics. Kramář's was a minority view.

Meanwhile, with Kramář in Paris, the first elections took place in Czechoslovakia. The NDs lost seats in parliament, and Kramář was dismissed, replaced by the Social Democrat Vlastimil Tusar.[73] Frustrated with Prague's response to the question of the Russian Civil War, and with his own dismissal, Kramář became an opposition figure, boycotting the government despite the presence of other NDs in numerous coalitions. Members of various governments extended invitations for Kramář to join, but he refused, considering that nothing less than the premiership would be acceptable to him. Kramář's ego and ambition would earn him, from Bohumír Šmeral, the wry sobriquet of "Karel the Giant."[74]

Personal animosities that had begun in the imperial period flared up once more after 1918. Kramář reviled Habsburg-era moderates-turned-Czechoslovak-statesmen, especially his former ally and friend Masaryk, blaming him and others for Kramář's political demise. Kramář later declared in his memoirs that Masaryk was "bereft of any political instinct whatsoever."[75] His bitterness was rooted in the fact that Masaryk had indeed shown nothing in the way of radical tendencies prior to 1914. Kramář, by contrast, had always seen himself as a national leader.[76]

A true believer, Kramář began referring to himself as the "father of the nation," and to Masaryk as having lucked into his position. Ferdinand Peroutka, a journalist close to Masaryk's circle, commented sarcastically in the 1920s that "Kramář claimed that his nationalism, compared to that of Masaryk and Beneš, was like the light of the sun when compared to the light of a candle." This, he added, was in keeping with the general outlook of the NDs, who believed themselves to be "better than anyone else" and dealt with political obstacles by making accusations of Germanophilia.[77] Peroutka, to be sure, was one of several intellectuals who undertook in this period to promote Masaryk's image in Czechoslovakia and Europe generally. Nationalists such as Kramář had no such support.

Pětka, the Castle, and the Nationalists

The conflict among these figures epitomized trends in Czechoslovak politics in the interwar period. The 1919 elections set the stage for the emergence of the coalition of the Pětka ("the Five"): an extraparliamentary body including the five major parties in Czechoslovakia that in 1920 formed a pro-government alliance. The number of parties in subsequent coalitions varied, but the name stuck, as did the institution, serving as an advisory board to President Masaryk. The coalition was hardly ideal, but coordination among different political forces in Czechoslovakia was nevertheless among the smoothest of the successor states.[78]

The narrative of Czechoslovak exceptionalism in interwar Europe is, however, another myth, forged in particular by politicians and intellectuals affiliated with the Masaryk circle. The obvious successes of the Pětka coalitions—the very ability of Czech political culture to bring together several major parties, and do so consistently over more than a decade, into the mid-1930s—concealed many contradictions in the functioning of the Czechoslovak state. Notably, for most of the interwar, the Pětka was exclusively Czech. The Slovak People's Party participated in one of the coalitions, but its status never matched that of its Czech counterparts. Germans remained outside the government until 1926, and their participation thereafter would be marginal even compared to that of Slovaks. The Pětka's power as a mediator was, moreover, limited. The tensions between the Castle—the office of the president and prime minister— and the parliament escalated over the course of the 1920s. The sharing of power between the executive and the parliament was never smooth.

Most of the post-1918 Czech political establishment came from the same milieu that had worked toward independence during the war. But it would be less than a year before Masaryk, Beneš, and Kramář found themselves on opposite sides of the political spectrum, promoting different visions of statehood and nationalism in open opposition with one another. Kramář's thinking changed little across the 1918 epochal divide, and even when hierarchies were transformed—with Czechs now in control, and Germans becoming the underrepresented minority—his vision of the enemy remained the same. "The Germans do not want to and cannot get used to the fact that times have changed," he insisted in a speech to the parliament.[79] He militated, moreover, to get the German language removed from administration, education, and street signs; the Habsburg Empire's accomplishment of German-Czech bilingualism would be obliterated in Czechoslovakia. Kramář here reflected the paradoxes of Czechoslovakia, which, albeit in a sense being a smaller-scale replica of the old empire, defined itself as a nation-state and correspondingly promoted national centralization and assimilation.[80]

The conflict between the Castle and the nationalist right, however, concealed important similarities between the two sides. Both Masaryk and Kramář, for example, shared a commitment to removing Austrian leftovers such as German street names.[81] Most differences between the figures under discussion, then, came down to strategies toward achieving shared goals, with nationalists supporting radical solutions that Masaryk found unacceptable. Kramář and the nationalists went to extremes, attempting to destroy the multiethnic foundation of the new state and reduce its political culture to Czech nationalism. In taking this position, Kramář claimed to be carrying on the radical nationalist tradition of the pre-1918 period. But for years in the new Czechoslovakia, many of those around him, including leading members of the Czech political establishment, would recall no such tradition, at least not as represented by Kramář—who had been a Habsburg loyalist, reluctant to join the pro-irredentist nationalist campaign even during the war. The disconnect between these "two Kramářs" complicated his career and political prospects.

Kramář's defense against charges of pro-Habsburg patriotism (and hypocrisy) was to assert the consistency of his pro-Czech vigilance. "Now we face accusations that our [pro-Habsburg] patriotism was stronger than our [Czech] nationalism. But it would have made no sense for us to ignore our needs, our economy, and our culture," he explained in a speech to students in 1936. Pro-Habsburg loyalty, he argued, had benefited Czechs under the empire.[82] On a different occasion, he insisted that his two tenures in the Austrian parliament had been spent promoting Czech national interests.[83] "Our goal was the destruction of the Habsburg monarchy," he declared in another speech to the Czechoslovak parliament in 1920.[84] Yet he also claimed that to the extent nationalists had worked to build "a strong Habsburg monarchy," they had done so "in the best interests of the Czech population."[85] The speculations about Kramář's conflicted allegiances were grounded in fact: like his Polish counterpart Głąbiński, prior to 1914 Kramář had espoused a peaceful patriotism and showed no sign of irredentism.

Nationalism and Autonomy: Poland

After 1918 Poland was torn by debates much like those raging in Czechoslovakia regarding the nature of the state; in both countries, the National Democrats stood for a unitary model, while their socialist opponents favored federation instead. The nationalists in parliament passed a constitution providing for a weak presidency with only nominal powers. Józef Piłsudski, at the time Poland's leading socialist, then refused to assume the post, becoming "chief of state" instead. The socialists and nationalists held two different conceptions of the state and minority policies, the former advocating autonomy and federation; the latter supporting a unitary state and assimilation. Never patched, these divides contributed greatly to a political crisis that resulted in authoritarianism in Poland.

The rift between Kramář and Masaryk in Czechoslovakia had its counterpart in that between Głąbiński and Piłsudski in Poland. In April 1920 Głąbiński proposed a resolution in the parliament on Poland's war aims in the east: "Recently, there has been some talk that Poland is fighting a war in the east, not to unify all Polish territories, but to create a new independent state at the expense of Polish national interests."[86] This referred to the Piłsudski-Petliura pact, a 1920 Polish-Ukrainian anti-Bolshevik agreement that could be seen as ratifying Ukrainian independence and statehood. But this would-be alliance was obviated by Poland's defeat of the Soviet forces in August 1920. It was not long thereafter, in March 1921, that Poland concluded another agreement, this time with Bolshevik Russia itself, that effectively annulled the 1920 accord with Petliura. Unease over this potential accommodation of Ukraine, and over concomitant attitudes toward Polish nationhood generally, fueled tensions between nationalists and socialists that continued into the 1930s.

Just like Kramář, Głąbiński built on his ideas from the Habsburg Empire but offered more radical solutions after 1918. He became a deputy of the Polish parliament (Sejm), part of a Galician cohort in Warsaw. As early as March 1919, just months after independence, he proposed the founding of a commission on "Jewish issues" to research the status of Jews in Poland.[87] Using rhetoric similar to Kramář's, he elaborated his views on nationality and the nation-state in a speech to the parliament in January 1923: "We now commence the fifth year of the independent Polish Commonwealth. . . . I repeat once more that other nationalities have equal rights. But only Poles, only those who are fully dedicated to the state, can make decisions on matters related to the existence of the state and its fate."[88] Similarly controversial was Głąbiński's take on patriotism: "As some of you may recall, . . . no one in Austria claimed to be an Austrian patriot"—an assertion that elicited a vocal response from Poland's left, specifically, Galician socialists: "But you did! . . . You courted the Habsburgs."[89] Like Kramář, Głąbiński claimed to have always aspired to national statehood. In reality, however, he had gone out of his way to flaunt his support for the Habsburgs.

Głąbiński's attitude toward Ukrainians in this period remained unchanged, but he did grow more markedly anti-Jewish—a reflection of anti-Semitism's generally increased momentum since the Great War. Before 1918, anti-Semitism had been a strong component in the ideology of Polish nationalists under Russian (but not Austrian) rule. Now, as if getting in step with the times, Głąbiński expressed more radical views than he ever had previously. In 1924, during his tenure as minister of religion and education, he went so far as to propose a *numerus clausus* ("fixed number")—quota restrictions on the number of Jewish pupils to be admitted to Polish schools. This initiative, unprecedented in independent Poland, was never formally promulgated and was rescinded by Głąbiński's successor in 1927.[90] That such measures were even being considered, however, attests to the country's ongoing instability, as its governments changed every few months. Głąbiński remained afloat, participating in various coalitions, but never held any post for long.

The nationalists in Poland were part of mainstream politics, just as they had been under the empire. Their initiatives became more radical than in the imperial era, but most went unimplemented or did not last long. In the early 1920s Poland operated as a democracy, with institutions in place that curbed some of the most radical initiatives. Poland would experience a major crisis and descend into semi-authoritarianism, yet it was only the cataclysm of another global war that caused the ultimate destruction of its institutions and democratic tradition.

Radical Nationalists and the Watershed of 1918

The continuity of nationalist politics as represented by Głąbiński and Kramář should prompt us rethink our vision not just of nationalism and its alleged role in the Habsburg Empire's collapse, but also of the founding and functioning of the successor states, especially during the immediate post-1918 years. In their multiethnicity, these states were like small-scale replicas of the empire, but they pursued policies of national centralization, with most statesmen across the political board endorsing new and harsher policies toward minorities. But across the epochal divide of 1918, the self-proclaimed nationalists from the Habsburg Empire had more in common with their Habsburg-grown conservative and moderate peers than with those nationalists who had come of age in Russia or Germany. Despite their myriad of differences, nationalists from the empire employed similar tactics prior to 1918 and thereafter; their actions and decisions likewise followed a comparable pattern across various countries.

They belonged to a political cohort for whom institutional solutions were the norm and violence an exception. Their successors—those born in the early 1880s and after—were more zealous, some willing to put their lives on the line for the national cause. Those who had learned politics under Habsburg rule were, from this standpoint, moderate, and if for a time they seemed radical, it was mainly because of the war or the Austrian government's policies in prosecuting it.

5. Empire and Fascism, 1890s–1928

If liberalism, conservatism, clericalism, and nationalism are all typically associated with the Habsburg Empire, fascism appears to mark a contrast: a variant of nationalism that foregrounded the unity of the nation in a more radical and xenophobic way than any nationalists had done under Habsburg rule. Post-1918 fascism, writes Marco Bresciani, has long been discussed as a Western European phenomenon; such accounts, he argues, efface the intricate connection between the pre-1918 Habsburg state and later Italian fascism: the crucial role that the newly annexed territories from the former Habsburg Empire played in the ascent of fascism.[1]

Italy is rarely seen as a Habsburg successor state, and if included in this category, it indeed stands as an untypical one. The territories Italy annexed from the empire between 1918 and 1920 were geographically small in comparison with the newly emergent successor states. But in symbolic terms, Italy's gains were among the most consequential in all of Europe. Post-1918 Italy became, at least on its northeastern borderlands, a smaller replica of the bygone Habsburg Empire. The former Habsburg component in post-1918 Italian politics was at least as important in such prototypical successor states as in Austria and Czechoslovakia.

The Habsburg experience proved formative most notably for Benito Mussolini, a prewar Italian socialist turned fascist.[2] In 1908–9, Mussolini spent several months in Trentino before being detained by the Austrian police for his political activities and expelled. Albeit brief, Mussolini's Habsburg sojourn enabled him to become acquainted with many Italians in the region. Even in this early period, the sheer lack of nationalist sentiment among his fellow Italians in Trentino appalled him: "It is certain that there are no irredentists [here], and if they do exist, they are not very active. . . . Temperamentally the Trentini are conservative, not radical."[3] He returned home to the Kingdom of Italy puzzled by the fact that his conationals in the Habsburg Empire favored Vienna over Rome. Mussolini transformed his dismay into action after 1918, when, radicalized by the war, he became a nationalist, eager to address the challenges faced by Italy, especially pertaining to the integration of new territories.

Fascism was a response to the crises caused by the war. But its doctrine and practices were also conditioned by Italy's distinctive status after 1918: a multiethnic state acting as if it were a homogeneous one.[4] Fascism became an all-Italian phenomenon, but it had flourished in the former territories of the empire.[5] Significantly, the first *fascio* emerged in Milan in March 1919, but the first incident of fascist squads' violence took place in July 1920 in Trieste, in the territory that Italy had annexed from the empire.[6] In terms especially of national policy, the Habsburg polity had been the furthest thing from the Italian fascist state, but in a convoluted, unintentional consequences manner, the pre-1918 empire was an incubator for the fascism that arose soon after its demise.

This chapter relates a history of fascism and antifascist responses in the territories that belonged to the Habsburg Empire and after 1918 became part of Italy. Unlike the previous chapters, which discussed statesmen of a similar political cohort who after 1918 found themselves in different states, this one focuses on a single country, bringing together two individuals of different political affiliations who after 1918 both lived in Italy.

One of the protagonists, Alcide De Gasperi, has appeared in an earlier chapter on political clericalism. Joining him in this discussion is his Italian nationalist peer, Francesco Salata, who was in many ways similar to the Polish and Czech nationalists Stanisław Głąbiński and Karel Kramář. My analysis of Italian politics also incorporates a discussion of conservatism, clericalism, nationalism, and internationalism from the preceeding chapters, bridging it all to Marxism and internationalism, specifically on the empire's southern borderland.

De Gasperi and Salata were among the most prominent Italian representatives in the Habsburg Empire who also played key roles in post-1918 Italy. The two belonged to a similar generation, born in 1881 and 1876, respectively, and participated in similar institutions in the empire. After 1918 the two found themselves in Rome, living through a turbulent transitional period that was fraught with great political unknowns. This too is another story of the transfer of imperial practices across time and space, in particular an analysis of two political opponents who in fascist Italy found much in common and in different ways carried on the legacy of the defunct empire.

Building upon the recent scholarship on post-1918 transition, nationalism, and fascism in the former territories of the Habsburg Empire, I de-emphasize the year 1922 as a radical break in the history of Italian politics, at least regarding the former territories and citizens of the Habsburg state. This analysis instead reveals a remarkable degree of continuity of national and nationalist politics between pre-1922 Italian liberals and post-1922 Italian fascists. The major political differences in the field of national politics, I argue, were not between Italian liberals and Italian fascists but between Italians from the former kingdom and those from the empire.

Italy as a Habsburg Successor State

Post-1918 Italy was a product of the long history of Italian state building. For hundreds of years, territories in the Italian peninsula had been scattered among different political units, some belonging to the Habsburg Empire. In 1861 the emerging Kingdom of Italy united several independent polities into one in a process that resembled the Berlin-led German unification a decade later. Yet with many Italian-inhabited territories still outside its borders, the kingdom represented a landmark in rather than the end of Italian unification.

Prior to the late 1850s, the Habsburgs had long ruled over Lombardy and Tuscany, including Milan and Florence; the Austrian Littoral—the crown land of the Adriatic coastline, consisting of the Istrian Peninsula, the regions of Gorizia and Gradisca, and the city of Trieste; and the Alpine regions of Tyrol and Trentino. East of the Adriatic coastline lay the landlocked region of Carniola, with its symbolic capital in Laibach (Ljubljana), today's Slovenia. In 1859, after losing a war to the coalition of Piedmont-Sardinia and their French allies, the Habsburgs were forced to cede Lombardy and Tuscany, as well as the city of Venice, to the Kingdom of Piedmont-Sardinia. They nevertheless retained some of the territories most cherished by nationalists as Italian: the Littoral, Tyrol, and Trentino. Moreover, while the city of Venice was part of Italy after 1861, its environs remained under imperial rule. Another key town, the port city of Fiume (now Rijeka, Croatia), was after 1867 incorporated into the Kingdom of Hungary.

All these territories had ethnically mixed populations, among the empire's most diversely complex. On the Adriatic, Italians, Slovenes, Croats, Serbs, Germans, and Jews of varying heritages shared space for centuries. Italians predominated in the urban areas, while Slavs (mainly Slovenes) resided mostly in the countryside. The Slovenian presence was particularly strong in Carniola. By contrast, Tyrol and Trentino represented a mixed German-Italian region; with Germans here having a dominant status, the national dynamic resembled that of Bohemia, with some of the concomitant tensions being remarkably similar. Nationalists in the Kingdom of Italy regarded these areas, especially the Adriatic, as essentially Italian, and the failure to annex them early on generated a sense of loss that fueled Italian nationalism in the kingdom. Without the Adriatic territories, claimed the nationalists, without the regions of Venezia Giulia as well Trentino in the Alps, the unification of Italy was incomplete.[7]

Austrian Trieste

The historical background of Trieste, long the crown jewel of the Habsburg Adriatic, can shed light on the controversies surrounding the annexation and postimperial transition. Trieste acquired a special status within the empire due its location on the Adriatic. Prior to annexing Trieste, the Habsburgs had ruled over a landlocked polity, and the Adriatic coastline represented the empire's only substantive access to the sea and trans-European travel and trade. From the early eighteenth century on, the Habsburgs invested heavily in Trieste, aiming to transform it into a major port. The city was more Austrian than it was Italian: its architectural landscape and cultural scene were reminiscent of other imperial cities such as Vienna and Prague rather than Rome or Florence.

By 1914 Trieste represented the cumulative effects of Austrian imperial efforts over the centuries. It was the empire's largest port and third-largest city, a bastion of cosmopolitanism, internationalism, and autonomism rather than nationalism, "national pluralism" rather than national exclusivity.[8] Later in the century, this culture of pluralism was quite different from the nationalism in

Trieste, 1901. Austrian National Library, Pictures (Bildarchiv Austria).

the Kingdom of Italy, and the furthest thing imaginable from fascism as it developed after the First World War.[9]

Italian nationalism in Trieste, then, resembled Polish and Czech nationalism in Galicia and Bohemia. The city was predominantly Italian: in 1910, Italians constituted over 70 percent of the city's population, with the Slovenes lagging far behind at 18 percent. Germans represented under 10 percent of the population, while a small number of Croats added to the Slavic constituency.[10] In particular, Italian nationalism in Trieste flourished as a response to the Slavic presence, to Slovenes' requests for cultural autonomy in a city that many Italians considered "theirs."[11] Just as elsewhere in the empire, the national sentiment of different groups on the Adriatic fueled each other's radicalization, their nationalisms developing in a constant conflict with one another, even as most of them remained loyal to the multiethnic Habsburg polity.

Francesco Salata between the Empire and the Kingdom of Italy

Francesco Salata was in many ways representative of the Italian variant of nationalism in the empire. Born in 1876 in Istria—part of the Austrian Adriatic, now mostly belonging to Croatia—he was raised in what Vanni d'Alessio describes as an Italian and Slavic "dual society."[12] He moved to Trieste in his youth and later divided his time between that city and Vienna, with occasional trips to Italy.

Salata's path to radicalism was akin to that followed by peers in other parts of the empire. In the 1890s, under the influence of his mentor, the Italian journalist Teodoro Mayer, he became close to the circles of the Italian Liberal National Party—an equivalent of the Polish National Democrats. Salata met Mayer in Vienna, and the two became close. In 1899 Salata began to write for *Il Piccolo,* Trieste's leading Italian nationalist newspaper, of which Mayer was the editor-publisher. But as with Głąbiński and National Democracy, Salata for years declined to join the party, preferring to remain an outside advisor. He never shied away, however, from radical politics, taking part in organizations more nationalistic than the Lega Nazionale (National League); he was a member, for instance, of the Istrian Political Association (Società politica istriana), which promoted irredentism.[13] This involvement did not keep him from participating in other imperial institutions and building a political career in the empire.

As in the cases of Kramář and Głąbiński, Salata's radicalism before 1914 manifested itself in his attitude toward other nationalities rather than through some opposition to the multiethnic empire per se. Notably, he actively resisted any institutional validation of the Slovenian or Croatian languages in mixed areas on the Adriatic, and he favored Italian autonomy within the empire. He advocated for these things, it should be emphasized, through the empire's institutional venues: the parliament and local diet. Institutional experience was an integral part of his early political life. He spent years in Vienna, including several terms as a parliamentary deputy (1897–1907). Such acceptance of Austrian institutions marked an important similarity among nationalists across the empire, and differentiated them from their peers from other states, particularly in the Kingdom of Italy and the Russian Empire.

The First World War, Nationalism, and Fascism

As was the case with many other protagonists of this book, it was only the war that caused Salata to rethink his status and affinities in the empire. Italy's participation in the Great War had mainly to do with the prospect of gaining territory from the Habsburg Empire, and the disappointing post-1918 territorial arrangements would, along with the war's outcome generally, play a key role in the radicalization of Italian politics.[14] In 1914 Vienna was rushing to war, but Rome remained neutral. Although it was part of the Triple Alliance (an agreement concluded in 1882) with Austro-Hungary and Germany, Italy did not, like its cosigners, enter the war in 1914. Members of the Triple Entente, meanwhile, pressured the government in Rome to switch sides, and the mood in the kingdom changed precipitously as nationalist fever took hold, with many particularly enticed by the prospects of expansion. The war, it was thought, could help accomplish the long-cherished dream of gathering all Italophone territories under Rome. That, however, would require a switch of sides, which the Italians did in 1915. By signing the London agreements that year, Italy joined the Entente coalition and secured guarantees of territories to be annexed after the conclusion of the war: all of the Littoral, including Trieste and Istria; Dalmatia; and Tyrol, including Trentino.[15]

The Italian territories of the empire experienced a fate similar to that of Galicia in the empire's far east, the two regions now occupied by foreign armies. For Italians, however, the situation was even more complicated by the fact that here the Italians confronted or were forced to fight against each other: Habsburg Italian subjects pitted against their compatriots from the Kingdom of Italy. Austrian relief efforts, notably evacuation strategies, likewise followed Galician precedents.[16] These efforts were now complicated by rising pro-irredentist sentiment among Italians within the empire—in large part a response to the war and to Austrian policies.

Salata endorsed pro-annexation policies early in the conflict and, in a life-changing decision, relocated to Italy. In March 1915, during the negotiations but before the signing of the London agreements, he met with Sidney Sonnino, Italy's foreign minister, and the two discussed the possibility of Trieste's annexation to the kingdom.[17] In Rome he became a member of the General Secretariat for Civil Affairs, an institution preparing for the incorporation of Austrian territories into Italy. His wartime political involvement laid the groundwork for his political career in post-1918 Italy.

Salata's status during and after the war was also connected with his professional training. He was not only a politician, but also a specialist in historical geography—a subject area that became particularly important during the First World War and in the years immediately following. As Steven Seegel has recently argued, the politicization of geography in Europe began well before the twentieth century, but reached its peak during and in the aftermath of the Great War.[18] Much of Salata's academic work after 1914 involved the study of historical maps, with an eye toward justifying Italy's territorial claims.[19]

Salata's political choices had grave consequences for his family. While he was in Rome, his wife Ilda remained in Trieste with their daughter. Salata knew that returning home would mean his arrest, and so he never went back. Unable to reach their main target, the Habsburg authorities harassed his family. In 1915 Ilda was brought to Trieste police headquarters for interrogation, and in the spring of 1916 she was deported to the village of Mödling, near Vienna, only to be moved again to the town of Mittergrabern in northeastern Austria. She was allowed to return home in the summer of 1917, but the ordeal took its toll on her health: she contracted tuberculosis, which eventually claimed her life in 1922. Such a personal sacrifice for the national cause was not uncommon; activists were prepared to suffer greatly for their convictions, and Salata and his family reflected the trend.[20] Salata remained in Italy until the war's end. In 1918 he briefly returned to Trieste to move his family to Rome. Unlike many of the other figures discussed in this study, who found it difficult to settle on a home and career after 1918, Salata was clear in his preference for the Kingdom of Italy and its politics.

Salata now built on his experience as a scholar and a politician. In early 1919, he traveled to Paris with the Italian delegation as a technical expert on border-related issues.[21] As part of the winning coalition, and having paid a dire price for its involvement in the war, the Italian government demanded all the territories specified in the London treaties plus the *corpus separatum* of Fiume, which had been part of Hungary within the empire.[22] Although Fiume was predominantly Italian (around 60 percent of the population as of 1914), Rome had not included it in the list of its demands in London because at the time it was not deemed sufficiently important.[23] The Italians' claim on the Littoral and Dalmatia, meanwhile, was contested by the newly created Kingdom of Yugoslavia; Tyrol and Trentino were coveted by Austria. The borders took months and years to settle, with some of Rome's hopes dashed: most of Dalmatia, for instance, became part of Yugoslavia, and Fiume was at first made a "free city" under international control.

In 1919 the Allies supported the foundation of Yugoslavia and opposed Italian claims to some of the territories that they had promised to Italy during the 1915 London negotiations. In protest, the Italian delegation walked out of the conference. This delegation itself was wracked by some of the same tensions experienced by their counterparts from Czechoslovakia. They could not produce a unified list of territorial demands.[24] The tensions in Paris generated a political crisis at home: even as the Entente portrayed the Italian delegation's position as too rigid, nationalists in Italy accused the delegation of being complacent.

Italian nationalists took the territorial settlements after 1918 as an unacceptable affront. Many deemed the war a mistake; its steep price, the blood of Italian soldiers and civilians, paid in vain. Of a total population of thirty-eight million, six million men had been drafted into the army in 1915, with four million taking part in combat against Austria, some six hundred thousand killed, over a million wounded, and six hundred thousand more taken prisoner.[25] Such casualties caused widespread outrage. The government pledged assistance to veterans and their families but could hardly deliver on its promises. Technically, Italy was one of the war's victors, but in the public mood it was as if the country had been defeated.

The settlements took years to work out, adding to the general sense of unease and fueling political extremes. The 1920 Treaty of Rapallo finalized borders between Italy and Yugoslavia, with Italy securing large portions of the former Austrian Littoral, a region that after 1918 became known as Venezia Giulia (the Julian March). Tyrol was now divided between Italy and Austria: the former gained South Tyrol (which became known as Alto Adige) and Trentino, the two regions becoming part of one province. Fiume on the Adriatic was finally annexed to Italy in 1924.[26]

The annexation of these territories redefined the Kingdom of Italy as no prior domestic political event had. Italians formed only about 52 percent of the population in Venezia Giulia.[27] But even among ethnic Italians, many had openly favored Vienna over Rome, and expressed misgivings about their new state, fueling tensions between the central government and the new territories.

Particularly affected by the war and annexations was Trieste, whose status as an economic and financial center was irrevocably altered after 1918.[28] The city's railway networks had been destroyed during the war, severing connections between the Adriatic and the empire's core. Moreover, Italy had other ports that Trieste could not compete with. The Mediterranean basin was more important than the Adriatic, and trans-European routes were likewise more efficient than the Danube.[29] The Italian state, as several scholars have demonstrated, showed little interest in the economic upkeep or development of Trieste.[30] The city remained a cultural and architectural jewel, but in terms of commerce and finance, it was now marginalized in comparison with Rome or Milan.[31]

At the local level, however, everyday practices changed little in the transition from the empire to the new states. What Dominique Kirchner Reill describes in her book on postimperial Fiume as "parallel" and "multiple" sovereignties—imperial, local, and national, depending on the situation—and as the persistence of local practices, was characteristic of all the postimperial Adriatic territories now under Italy.[32] Despite the shift of central governance from Vienna to Rome, local administrations in the first years after the war remained packed with cadres who had occupied the same or similar positions under the empire.[33]

Administering the New Territories

Rome's early policies toward the new territories revealed considerable ambivalence. Early on, between late 1918 and 1920, several consecutive prime ministers—Vittorio Emanuele Orlando (October 1917–June 1919), Francesco Nitti (June 1919–June 1920), and Giovanni Giolitti (June 1920–July 1921)—favored some degree of local autonomy.[34] Nitti in particular pledged to support the rights of national minorities, and within months of the annexation, military rule was replaced by civilian governance.

Autonomy and the protection of minority rights increasingly came under scrutiny by a cohort of radical nationalists. In late 1918, Carlo Galli, the Kingdom of Italy's former consul to Habsburg Trieste, predicted that nationalists would oppose any special treatment of the new territories.[35] Indeed, as early as 1919 nationalists began denouncing the liberal government's alleged overindulgence of ethnic minorities.[36] The early fascist organizations on the Adriatic and in Trentino targeted minorities but received "favorable reception" from the government nevertheless.[37] The ethnic component played a key role in the foundation and evolution of fascism. These instances of violence against minorities also highlight the convoluted relationships between Italian liberals (in power) and Italian fascists before 1922: boundaries between the two were more fluid and their minority policies overlapped to a greater degree than many historians have acknowledged in the past.

Antonio Mosconi, the civil commissioner of the province of Venezia Giulia, was emblematic of the divergence in this period between the central government's liberal intentions and politics as practiced in the provinces. Mosconi used the term "aliens" to refer to those who refused to accept Italian as their sole language, and he advocated assimilation or emigration for minorities.[38] Mosconi was not a fascist; he was a pro-government loyalist in the administration of Prime Minister Nitti, a head of state known for his official support of tolerance and autonomy. But non-Italians in the new territories immediately experienced the difference between the old multiethnic empire and the new nation-state, even before fascism arose to make nationalism its centerpiece.[39]

Both Italians and Germans in Trentino experienced major changes in the transition from Austria to Italy. Under Habsburg rule, especially during the war, Italian nationalist irredentism had not been uncommon in the region, but many Italians in Trentino had mixed feelings about the annexation to Italy, preferring the empire instead. Their German counterparts were even more resistant to the idea of the Italian nation-state. Tensions between the Italians and the Germans in Trentino that had been palpable during the empire escalated further after 1918. Even before the onset of fascism, some Italian liberals addressed Germans as a potentially dangerous presence, their requests for autonomy as political defiance. Italian nationalists started referring to the Germans in Trentino as *allogeni*—"neither citizens nor foreigners."[40] New language requirements barred Germans from participating in public services.[41] While the Habsburg Empire in the last decades of its existence had moved progressively toward including different minorities, supporting autonomy and at least partial federalization, the post-1918 Italian state was moving in the opposition direction.

The Office for the New Provinces

Epitomizing the contradictions of prefascist Italian policies was the Central Office for the New Provinces, a unit created in July 1919 to oversee the transition of the newly annexed territories from the empire to Italy.[42] This Rome-based administrative entity had branches in Trieste, Venice, Trentino, and Zara. Answering directly to Prime Minister Nitti, it was staffed primarily with former politicians and functionaries of the Habsburg Empire that now found themselves in Italy. The office's composition reflected the Italian government's willingness to engage the local elites rather than impose policies unilaterally from the capital. As such, the administration of the new territories would constitute a symbiosis of the best of Austrian imperial and Italian national practices—in effect, Austrian models attached to an Italian matrix.[43] The office thus provided continuity between the Habsburg Empire and the Italian nation-state.

The director of the office was Francesco Salata, appointed in recognition of his role in advancing the cause of annexation since 1915, his wartime sacrifices, and, not least, his knowledge of these territories. His activities in this post would reveal the lasting effects that the Habsburg political system had even on radical nationalists, and would likewise highlight the two different visions of nationalism espoused by Italians from the former empire as opposed to those from the Kingdom of Italy. Having supported Italy's territorial claims during the war and in its aftermath, Salata proved never quite as radical as his peers who had come of age in the kingdom. A nationalist by imperial standards, Salata was a moderate in the Italian nation-state.

Salata's career soon went downhill as a result of the clash of the competing visions of nationalism, centralism, and autonomy. In the fall of 1922 Italian Prime Minister Luigi Facta dissolved the Central Office for the New Provinces, signaling the end of an era. Mussolini became prime minister on October 31, 1922. Submitting his letter of resignation from the office, Salata protested the government's shutdown of the last vestiges of regional autonomy.[44] Even before Mussolini's takeover, Rome had begun a program of centralization, and entities such as the Central Office were deemed obsolete.

The involvement of nationalists in transmitting imperial practices across the epochal divide of 1918 was remarkable but not uncommon in the post-Habsburg context. Nationalists from Trieste or Trentino had more in common with their political opponents from the empire than with their nominal allies from the kingdom.

Battles over Civilization

Many of Salata's former colleagues from the empire were vocal in their dissent against Italy's liberal governments. Consider the case, for instance, of Alcide De Gasperi, a native of Trentino and Salata's colleague in the Office for the

New Provinces. He too had made a career in the empire, becoming one of the leading members of the Italian Christian Social Party in Trentino. De Gasperi was one of the most famous representatives of conservative clericalism, part of the Christian socialist tradition in the empire. Unlike Salata, who during the war had shifted rightward and endorsed annexation to Italy, De Gasperi had remained, like most other clericals across the empire, loyal to the Habsburgs to the end.

In considering De Gasperi's post-1918 career, we might note in particular his involvement in the transition from the empire to the Kingdom of Italy and his role in the institutions that oversaw this process. Notably, De Gasperi denounced the annexation itself as needlessly aggressive and antagonistic toward the local population. In true Habsburg style, he used institutional means—the parliament and the Central Office for the New Provinces, as well as Italy's still uncensored press—to voice his concerns regarding what he saw as the appalling corruption accompanying the would-be integration.

In March 1920, De Gasperi published an article titled "Will the Devastated Lands Ever Be Reconstructed?"[45] Here he questioned Rome's strategies of integration and highlighted the economic implications of the process. Financial malfeasance was both a cause and a consequence of the turmoil: the quick turnover of civil and financial administration was generating chaos.[46] Widespread corruption was also enabled by stereotypical perceptions. Some in Rome, that is, considered this former periphery of the Habsburg Empire as steeped in backwardness—an Italian region, yes, but civilizationally inferior to the old kingdom—a view that was based especially on the ethnic makeup of the new territories, with Italian nationalists disparaging the region's minority inhabitants, particularly Slavs.

In June 1920 the Trentino-based *Il Giornale del Popolo* echoed De Gasperi's concerns in an article tellingly titled "The Depredation of the Liberated Territories." Published anonymously, the piece described the particularly creative corruption brazenly perpetrated by Italians from the old kingdom as they moved into the new territories to do business. People who had suffered through years of Austrian "oppression," and then the far more material ruinations of the Great War, could not afford the rising cost of living in their new nation-state, as middlemen from Rome extracted enormous profits for themselves.[47]

The regime that tolerated such goings-on had pledged to carry out a campaign of development and modernization, but it was now, to top it all off, engaging in a political purge. The unnamed editorialist commented, "The people who have spent some two winters in grim circumstances and unprecedented privation are now subjected to an operation of 'purification' and 're-sanitation' by the new regime that began last March. From the beginning of the campaign to deal with the inhabitants of our territories, I had little faith in the work of the magistrate and commissions who carry out their work amid such pomp."[48]

In 1921 De Gasperi initiated a parliamentary inquiry into corruption related to the annexation of the new territories; the case landed with Salata, then head of the Central Office.[49] During meetings of this body on June 7 and 8, 1921, Salata conceded the absence of proper financial record keeping, which made proving incidents of corruption, or even understanding their scale, a virtual impossibility.[50]

De Gasperi meanwhile took up another claim—that of the alleged civilizational inferiority of the new territories vis-à-vis the rest of Italy: "We are supposedly fifty years behind when compared to the old provinces; Trentinos [are said to] lag behind, to be in the previous century. . . . We must ask: compared to what regions? These comparisons are odious. . . . [A] region with the lowest crime rate, a region with no illiteracy, that has had mandatory primary education for fifty years, hardly merits the accusation of lagging behind."[51] In debunking the stereotypical perception of his home region, he rejected the very essence of Rome's civilizing mission. In the process, significantly, he underscored the priority of people over the state. "For us," he wrote around 1925, "the natural rights of individuals, of families and human society, are more important than the state itself, because without them the state is nothing more than a political organization."[52] The Italian government was, from this standpoint, acting ineptly, and showing a selective disregard for the inhabitants of its new territories.

Italy's post-1918 liberal governments thus exposed the limits of tolerance and inclusion: though supposedly an oppressor, the empire, insisted De Gasperi and others, had been more mindful of its citizens than the present kingdom. While Austrian imperial governments had offered limited self-administration, Italian liberals increasingly dismantled such institutions in their new territories. The chaotic integration, moreover, antagonized many of those who might have previously supported Italy over Austria; it provoked a pro-Habsburg nostalgia and *austriacismo* that in turn fueled Italian nationalist backlash and fascism.[53]

Empire and Fascism

If Italy's liberals showed little tolerance of the country's new citizens, the fascists that supplanted them were far worse. Unlike Hitler in the decade that followed, Mussolini came to power as the result of an attempted coup; he then secured concessions from Italy's establishment politicians, many of whom believed he would not survive long in office. Prime Minister Giolitti ascribed the emergence of fascism, which he believed to be a temporary phenomenon, to the initial fumblings of Italy's democracy; the liberals, he thought, would soon absorb the fascists.[54] Giolitti's colleague, the former prime minister Antonio Salandra (in office from 1914 to 1916), was even more indulgent, declaring himself an "honorary fascist."[55] Neither Giolitti nor Salandra fully endorsed fascism; the former, for instance, viewed it primarily as an instrument to stave off socialism and communism.[56] The willingness of such politicians to "go along" opened the door to right-wing radicals, facilitating Mussolini's seizure and eventual monopolization of power.

Italy was one of the first countries in Europe to succumb to right-wing extremism, but early on, Mussolini did reach out to political opponents. His first government, formed in 1922, included members of different parties, with the fascists keeping three portfolios for themselves.[57] Defying those who had thought his government would be short-lived, Mussolini would eventually initiate the repression of (among others) those who had made his coming to power possible. But the regime's crackdowns could have been foreseen as early as 1922, when authorities began to scrutinize even self-proclaimed nationalists from the old empire as *insufficiently* nationalist.

Mussolini's takeover also revealed the growing tensions between different types of nationalists. Insofar as those who matured in the kingdom could be more radical than their ostensible conationalists from the empire by an order of magnitude, it is hardly surprising that the fascists were markedly different from Habsburg-grown nationalists. The latter embraced a conservative political style that maintained continuities with the imperial era. Those sufficiently exposed to the Habsburg system typically remained committed to the mode of politics they had learned in the empire.

Tensions between Mussolini and Francesco Salata exemplified the unresolved differences and increasingly open rupture between the nationalisms that emerged from the two separate political traditions. In 1921, for example, Mussolini expressed concern that Salata was granting too much autonomy to ethnic Germans in Trentino.[58] Before 1918, Salata himself had objected to what he saw as Germanophone domination in the empire, and in Trentino in particular. But after 1918, when the ethnic hierarchy flipped and Germans became an underrepresented minority, he ceded to them some of the same rights to which the Italian minority had been entitled under the Habsburgs.[59] His vision of autonomy came under scrutiny by the Italian governments, including liberal administrations, even before Mussolini's takeover, as reflected in the dissolution of the Office for the New Provinces. But Mussolini would eventually proceed with the elimination not just of autonomy but also of institutional venues for dissent, applying draconian measures to the national-minority questions Italy had inherited from the empire.

Mussolini's coming to power affected Salata directly. After losing his post as head of the Central Office, he remained a senator, but the high political profile he had had immediately after the war was greatly diminished. Known especially for his opposition to the forcible centralization promoted by Italy's governments of the early 1920s, Salata would thus follow the pattern seen among the relatively moderate nationalists from the empire in their various successor states. Their influence spiked after 1918, but, amid a radicalism more extreme than their own, declined shortly thereafter.

Fragmented Opposition

Salata was hardly alone in being perplexed by the rise of the fascists. Many in Italy initially observed Mussolini with caution; some of those who found him ideologically distasteful nevertheless considered it possible to cooperate with him. This early response to fascism was conditioned by the perception of liberals' failure to protect Italy, rather than reflecting any particular achievement of fascism per se. The postwar political crisis had given rise to a radicalization on the left. Prominent among Italy's socialists were Bolshevik sympathizers, and with strikes paralyzing the country in 1919, it was common among conservatives, liberals, and clericals to be warier of the left than of nationalists. Many remembered Mussolini as Italy's leading prewar socialist, whom the years of conflict had remolded into a nationalist—perhaps he could be useful in neutralizing, in turn, the threat posed by his former comrades?

The relationships between Italian clericals and fascists were yet another example of the Habsburg legacy's persistence in post-1918 Italy. Founded in 1919, the Italian People's Party (PPI, or Popolari) united politically active Catholics from the former empire and the kingdom. The party was led by the Sicilian priest Don Luigi Sturzo, with Alcide De Gasperi as one of its cofounders. The tradition of Italian political Catholicism had been stronger in the empire than in the kingdom: the Vatican had explicitly prohibited Catholics in the Kingdom of Italy to participate in any political activities. The PPI thus became an heir to the Italian Christian Social party from the Habsburg Empire.[60]

Like the liberals, the PPI initially endorsed the fascist phenomenon, "looking to Mussolini with some hope."[61] In keeping with his estimation of socialism as a greater threat than right-wing nationalism, De Gasperi saw fascism as a "reaction to the communist internationalism that undermines a nation's liberties."[62] He believed that Mussolini's violence was only temporary and would subside once his government was established in office. De Gasperi even anticipated that the Popolari would make common cause with the nationalists to combat the liberals and socialists, the two major scourges, in his view, of the modern state.[63]

These hopes proved illusory. Meeting with Mussolini on November 3, 1922, De Gasperi anticipated cooperation.[64] But the two men's shared commitment to Catholicism had concealed radical differences in their views on politics, especially concerning De Gasperi's native region. A staunch supporter of autonomy, De Gasperi was suddenly faced with a nationalist leader who would make no concessions to local initiative or self-government. From then on, De Gasperi opposed collaboration: "As Catholics and as Italians, how could we contribute to the negative forces emerging from fascism, to the spirit of skepticism and disgrace . . . that defies all morality?"[65] Disillusioned with Mussolini, he described the fascist government as "the antithesis of freedom" and began the search for new allies.[66]

De Gasperi's subsequent attempts to reach out to different political forces revealed both a growing unease with fascism and, on the other hand, the would-be oppositionists' inability to compromise in forging a potential alliance. He considered forming a united front to oppose the government, seeking allies not just on the right but on the left as well. The liberals and the Popolari, in particular, shared a common fear of communism as Italy's greatest threat; but the two parties could not agree on practical issues related to the economy. The PPI insisted on an agrarian redistribution for the benefit of small landowners, while the liberals refused to include such measures in their agenda—a standoff that had previously revealed itself when the liberals had been in power.[67]

The Vatican was another potential ally. It would take the church some time to clarify relations with the fascists and vice versa. Even before fully endorsing Mussolini, the Vatican was openly skeptical of the Popolari; church dignitaries remained suspicious of the concept of a Catholic political party. When Pope Pius XI took office in 1922, he proved even more confrontational toward the PPI.[68] For that matter, any cooperation with Mussolini's political opponents might provoke fascist reprisals on the Vatican.[69] The church's rapprochement with Rome become more pronounced in the late 1920s, culminating in 1929 in the Lateran Accords. This treaty put an end to "the Roman question" in Italian history: the Vatican officially became a sovereign state, on whose territory the Italian government renounced its claims forever.[70] In return the Vatican gave its endorsement to Mussolini. The 1929 agreements thus foreclosed any possible cooperation between the church and nonfascist forces.

With no hope of coalition building on the right, De Gasperi now turned to the left. The socialists and the Popolari were unlikely allies: before 1918 the clericals and Social Democrats had been political and ideological opposites. Anticlericalism had been, indeed, one of the key principles of Austrian social democracy in the empire and remained part of the doctrine after 1918 as well. Sturzo and De Gasperi were meanwhile aghast at Italian socialists' increasing radicalization following the war; many now openly sympathized with the October Revolution, anticipating a similar scenario for Italy. De Gasperi had formerly looked on socialism as a "sand castle" but was at least willing to reconsider his stance after 1922. The Popolari now gave consideration to an alliance with the non-Bolshevized left. But while both sides were determined to combat fascism, they clashed over practical issues, especially regarding the agrarian question: the Popolari defended private ownership of land, whereas the socialists insisted it must be largely nationalized.[71] Both parties remained in their separate opposition to Mussolini, and both eventually fell victim to repressions.

Italy became one of several countries in the post-1918 Europe where the political tradition from the Habsburg Empire affected coalition building and coalition failures. Notably, the collapse of center-left alliances was a by-product of pre-1918 politics in Italy, just as in Austria. Italy was neither an exception nor a paradox in the post-Habsburg world; the effects of the Habsburg polity on its post-1918 evolution proved as consequential as they were for more typical post-Habsburg successors such as Austria or Czechoslovakia.

Italians and Slovenes

With the antifascist opposition among ethnic Italians in disarray, the Popolari considered making common cause with ethnic minorities who were affected by fascism to an even greater degree than Italians themselves. Specifically, the Popolari joined forces with Slovenes to fight for regional autonomy, an issue the PPI had long foregrounded. Slovenian activists who favored an alliance with the Popolari claimed that "there are some half a million Slovenes and Croats, and forty million Italians. The PPI has a good program."[72] The numbers, indeed, spoke for themselves; without Italian support, Slovenes stood no chance in Italian politics, their situation in the country worsening with every passing month after 1918.

Slovenian liberals faced dilemmas similar to Italian clericals: each group operated from a standpoint shaped under Habsburg rule, envisioning—mistakenly—imperial-era practices and institutions as potentially successful models for the Italian nation-state. Despite their shared interests and the common foe, however, the alliance never materialized. The two sides looked askance at one another. In 1921 De Gasperi had expressed misgivings as to demands for national autonomy on the part of Germans and Slavs: "This is how we differ from our German and Slavic colleagues. . . . In their proposed autonomy, the Germans have asked for what amounts to a nationalities-policy anarchy, with the right to have their own police force, flag, and budget. Such demands jeopardize peace in the country, and the rights of the Italian nationality." The Italian Popolari, he argued, sought a different kind of autonomy, based on local communal administration and a decentralized state.[73] The PPI eventually abandoned the idea of autonomy, so key a concern for Slovenes, which only reinforced the expectations that Italians would never support the autonomy claims of national minorities, and that nothing would come of attempts at interethnic cooperation.

The Italians now acted from a position of dominance, as did their Czech peers in Czechoslovakia vis-à-vis Germans, and the Poles in Poland with regard to Ukrainians. Even those who supported interethnic alliances before and after 1918 changed their stance when ethnic hierarchies changed. The failure of the Italian antifascist opposition to effectively address minority issues was as detrimental to Italy as was the Czechs' inability to properly address the German question in Czechoslovakia.

With their opponents thus splintered, the fascists ramped up operations across the country. Violence, however, did not become the norm until the middle of the decade, with the elections of 1924 standing as a turning point. The fascists would likely have won a majority in any case, but Mussolini was unwilling to chance it, arranging for the pressuring of voters before and during balloting, forcing many to cast their votes for the fascists. When the new parliament met in May 1924, socialist deputy Giacomo Matteotti gave a speech denouncing the electoral violations committed and demanding the expulsion of fascist deputies. Within days he was kidnaped and murdered. Matteotti's assassination caused another crisis, with several of Mussolini's ministers demanding the removal of those responsible for the crime, prompting him to purge such dissenters in turn.[74]

De Gasperi too became a target of repression; now not only his career, but his very life was on the line because of his political views. His support of autonomy and resistance to centralization and Italianization made him vulnerable. The persecution of antifascists was now common, but individuals such as De Gasperi could in particular be singled out for their associations with the Habsburg Empire and their alleged favoring of it over a national Italy.

Charges of *austriacismo*—a perceived loyalty to the Habsburg Empire and questionable allegiance to Italy—increased as Mussolini solidified his grip.[75] In December 1925 the nationalist newspaper *Il Piccolo* described De Gasperi as an *ignobile austriacante*—just as the same publication had branded other former Austrians and as Mussolini had described him years earlier.[76] In 1926 an assassination attempt was made on De Gasperi's brother Augusto. He survived, but Alcide faced continued threats. On March 16, 1927, De Gasperi and his wife Francesca were arrested by police at the Florence train station and jailed.[77] Francesca was soon released, but De Gasperi was tried and sentenced on charges that he had forged documents, supposedly to assist his brother-in-law Pietro Romani (a parliamentary deputy) in his flight from the country.[78]

The same year, a fascist periodical ran an article titled "De Gasperi in Canossa," claiming that De Gasperi had abandoned his former views and come to side with Mussolini.[79] De Gasperi denied this, his defiance hardly disposing the authorities to leniency; he ended up spending nearly two years in prison. Upon his release in July 1928, he was banned from politics. He decided to remain in Rome and secured a job as an archivist at the Vatican, where he worked quietly for many years.

De Gasperi's removal from politics was like that of Salata, albeit more forcible and more strictly "political." He and Salata would cross paths in the Vatican archives, where both ended up for different reasons. Their decisive political break with one another came only in the late 1920s, when Salata moved closer to the Mussolini regime and De Gasperi remained a defiant outsider, keeping to his archival research through the 1930s.

Moderates, Radicals, Fascists

Alcide De Gasperi and Francesco Salata exemplified the difficult transition and paradoxes of integration in post-1918 Italy. Prior to 1918, they had divided their time between Italian-majority territories and Vienna, and each had served as a deputy in the imperial parliament. After 1918 they worked together for a time in institutions charged with integrating the new territories. But even Salata—a nationalist, radicalized by the war—found himself at odds with Italian official-dom, whether of the liberal or fascist variety, his nationalism proving moderate and tepid in comparison with the new regime's program of Italianization and its confrontational style of politics.

The failure to mount an organized opposition to fascism proved fatal to many in Italy. After 1918 these men's careers were threatened in similar ways, as were their lives and families. They faced the same accusation, at times leveled by the very same persons, of *austriacismo,* a cudgel typically wielded by radical nationalists in the successor states to manipulate public opinion. But even amid these perils, faced with ominous personal and professional consequences, they seemed reluctant to reach out to one another—part of the larger picture by which opposition to Mussolini remained fragmented. Their failure to join forces is emblematic of their cohort's tragedy. Those on the extremes, right or left, showed boldness, determination, a willingness to take action. Those standing for the principles of traditional liberal democracy, of moderation, were all too often fearful or unwilling to sacrifice their own ambitions for the greater good.

This is not to suggest that the only ones to oppose the rising fascist regime or be victimized by its repressions were former Habsburg subjects; Italians native to the old kingdom would often suffer similar or worse fates. Some former Austrian subjects, moreover, would make successful political careers under Mussolini. But generational divides matter: activists in the younger cohort, who had had less exposure to imperial political models and who came of age in a time of nationalism and violence (especially the First World War), were more likely to endorse the radical right and its use of force and intimidation. They were also more likely to put their lives on the line for the national cause, unlike many of their predecessors, who preferred institutional options.

PART THREE

Austro-Marxism and Post-Habsburg Successors

6. Democratic Socialism and Left-Wing Radicalism

Austria and Czechoslovakia

In the 1890s the halls of Vienna's Café Central, replete with cigarette smoke and intellectual discussion, became a second home for a group of young Austrian socialists, including Otto Bauer, Rudolf Hilderding, Max Adler, and Karl Renner. There they debated the essence of Marxism, nationalism, internationalism, and statehood, arriving at a distinctive understanding of these concepts that eventually became known as Austro-Marxism.[1] The Austro-Marxist school of thought would have a lasting impact on twentieth-century Europe, its legacy persisting not only though the interwar period but also after the Second World War as a "third way" alternative to Western capitalism and Soviet communism: "socialism with a human face."[2] Their rejection of violence, their support of institutional solutions and national autonomy, and their federative thinking became important parts of the Habsburg imperial legacy in post-1918 Europe. The founders of the Austro-Marxist doctrine and their disciples defined the afterlife of the empire across all of the post-Habsburg space and beyond—from Italy in the west to the Soviet Union in the east.

Their particular vision defied traditional divides between orthodox and revisionist Marxism; ideologically it existed, as Norbert Leser and other scholars have put it, "between reformism and Bolshevism."[3] While employing the

Café Central, 1890s. Austrian National Library, Pictures
(Bildarchiv Austria).

rhetoric of revolution, Austrian Marxists insisted on achieving revolutionary change via democratic means. They regarded the empire as the best venue in which to practice Marxist internationalism, and they addressed the imperial dilemma of nationalism and ethnic tensions by promoting extensive autonomy for national minorities.

The doctrine of Austro-Marxism was formulated in the empire, where it provided the ideological foundation for the Austrian Social Democratic Party. But it first became a practice—a basis for political decisions and policies— after 1918. This chronological disjuncture between theory and practice was one unique characteristic of Austro-Marxism; its geographical profile was another. Under Habsburg rule, the Austrian Social Democratic Party operated as a pan-imperial organization structured on federative principles, with several autonomous national sections. No other state, not even the Russian or Ottoman

Empires, had a Marxist-based party as diverse and geographically far-reaching as did Austria-Hungary.

Despite its chronological and geographical reach, Austro-Marxism has not received its due attention in the literature.[4] Most studies are dated, tied to a specific epoch between the late 1960s and the early 1980s when discussion of Eurocommunism sparked a renewed interest in Austro-Marxism.[5] Much of this research revolves around key protagonists from pre-1914 Vienna, and/or focuses solely on the Austro-Marxist influence on Austria itself (whether pre- or post-1918). This scholarship is overly marked by what Anson Rabinbach describes as the "language of tragic drama," with Austro-Marxism seen primarily through the lens of its defeat in 1930s authoritarian Austria.[6]

This focus on Austria obscures the parallel developments in many socialist and communist parties across Europe that all had their roots in the same empire-born ideology. The constant references to defeat, moreover, seem motivated by a not-so-subtle inclination to marginalize Austro-Marxism within the broader narratives of European histories. Despite Austro-Marxists' status as history's "losers" in the inter- and postwar era, their vision persisted beyond the Second World War in several states, including those under communist rule. A nuanced analysis of Austro-Marxism's failure should also lead to a better understanding of the authoritarian victories in several countries, and of the road to the Second World War in the post-Habsburg space and Europe in general. The so-called losers deserve more attention than we have granted them.

Part III of this book presents a narrative of the chronological and geographical transformations of Austro-Marxism across European space and time. It foregrounds historical and geographical continuities between the empire and several states of post-1918 Europe, explaining how a doctrine formulated before 1918 became a political practice thereafter. This chapter focuses on the Austrian-Czech vector in the history of Austro-Marxism, exploring the ideological and political contingencies between this school of thought and different variations of socialism and communism in post-1918 Austria and Czechoslovakia. Just as Austro-Marxism was intertwined with the empire, its Social Democratic Party reflected the symbiotic relationships between Austria, Bohemia, and Moravia.[7] In particular, several leading Austrian socialists came from the Czech-German frontiers of the empire. The Social Democratic parties in post-1918 Austria and Czechoslovakia not only had some of the same leadership but also were built on the same Austro-Marxist tradition.

This chapter brings together four socialists—Otto Bauer, Wilhelm Ellenbogen, Ludwig Czech, and Bohumír Šmeral—who all emerged from the same Austrian-Czech milieu and who were leading members of imperial social democracy, representing the Austrian and Czech sections. After 1918 the former two ended up in Austria, with the latter two in Czechoslovakia. In this chapter I trace these protagonists' lives and careers from the late 1880s, the period of social democracy's founding in the empire, through the mid-1920s, when democracy in general was, albeit threatened, still intact.

Marxist Variations: Bauer, Ellenbogen, Czech, Šmeral

Our four protagonists reflected the cosmopolitanism of Vienna and the transnational composition of the socialist milieu gathering at Café Central.[8] The crowd there represented a microcosm of the Habsburg Empire. Many of those who defined themselves as *Austrian* Marxists came from different parts of the empire, all of them sharing a commitment to internationalism or multiethnicity. The backgrounds of these four were typical of many socialists across the empire. Born between 1863 and 1881, they came of age in Austria, Bohemia, and Moravia. Some of them are more famous than the others: Bauer is the most prominent, while Ellenbogen, Šmeral, and Czech are little known outside of Austria and the Czech Republic. Yet all of them played important roles not just within their respective parties but also in European politics in general across 1918. As a cohort, they shed light on the significant transformations of Austro-Marxism post-1918 and the different political and ideological trajectories that many of its adherents took after World War I.

Bauer, born in 1881 in Vienna, was raised speaking German in an assimilated Jewish family with roots in Bohemia. He studied law at the University of Vienna, and in 1903 he cofounded a workers' association in that city.[9] He rose through the party ranks, particularly during the war, when Victor Adler—the founder of the Austrian Social Democratic Party—nominated Bauer as his successor. In 1919 Bauer became leader of the party and remained in this post through 1934.

Wilhelm Ellenbogen had a similar family pedigree. The eldest of the four described here, he was born in 1863 in the Moravian town of Lundenburg (Břeclav in Czech), in a German-speaking family of assimilated Jews. Moving to Vienna with his family as a young boy, he was educated at the university there and, in a rarity for socialists in this context (who were typically trained as lawyers), eventually earned a medical degree. Between 1901 and 1918 he was a deputy of the Austrian imperial parliament, Vienna by then becoming his home. A native speaker of German and fluent in Italian, from 1897 on he worked as the central party bureau's representative to Austrian Social Democracy's Adriatic branch.[10] In 1919 he served as head of Austria's Socialization Committee, overseeing the transition from capitalism to socialism in line with the Austro-Marxist vision of the process.

Of the four, Ludwig Czech was the most cosmopolitan. He was born in 1870 in a Germanophone family of assimilated Jews in Galician Lemberg/ Lwów. His family hailed from Moravia, and his father worked as an engineer for the Austrian imperial railway.[11] Educated at the University of Vienna, Czech moved to Moravia after finishing his studies and spent many years practicing law in the Moravian capital of Brno, which would be the locale of most of his pre-1918 life. After the empire's collapse, he distinguished himself as a leader of the German Social Democratic Workers' Party in independent Czechoslovakia.

Another product of the German-Slavic frontier, Bohumír Šmeral was born in 1880 and raised in the western Moravian town of Třebíč. He spent most of his life in Prague, where he first moved for his studies. His father had been a teacher of German at a local school, a reflection of ethnically diverse Moravia.[12] Šmeral came to Marxism as a student of law at the University of Prague. Guided by a political vision much like that of Bauer and Ellenbogen, he has been called the "only true bearer of Austro-Marxism" among Czechs.[13]

Each of these four figures mirrored the national, social, and intellectual base of imperial and European social democracy. With Bauer as one of the cofounders of the Austro-Marxist school, Czech, Ellenbogen, and Šmeral belonged to what Helmut Gruber has described as the "heirs" of Austro-Marxism: the many individuals who were not involved in the initial debates, but who played an important role in the evolution of this worldview.[14] The Jewish roots of three of them reflected the social composition of the empire's Social Democratic parties, as Germanophone assimilated Jews were an important part of this profile. At least some, including Bauer and Ellenbogen, were independently wealthy, living off their family wealth and businesses. They studied in Vienna and Prague; but three of the four (the exception being Czech) never practiced their specializations, devoting themselves instead to writing, political organizing, and eventually governance.

The four protagonists were involved in the many controversies that wracked Austrian Social Democracy and the parties that, postempire, emerged from its ruins. While Karl Renner served as chancellor of the first and then the second (post-1945) Austrian Republic, it was Bauer who played the most important role in shaping the party's policies between the wars.[15] These four figures also had extensive geographical ties—Ellenbogen was influential in Austria, Czechoslovakia, and Italy—and diverse national affiliations: Czech served as a leader of German Social Democracy in Czechoslovakia, and Šmeral was head of the Czechoslovak Communist Party. Friends before 1918, they remained in touch beyond 1918, even after going their divergent geographical and ideological ways.[16] Such shifts in personal relationships are important for our understanding of the continuities and ruptures centering on that fateful year of 1918.

Party: Elusive Unity

Austro-Marxism was a product of debates within the Austrian Social Democratic Party—the only pan-imperial party to be founded as early as 1889 and surviving as a single organization (albeit with different national sections) until 1916. Social democracy, like Christian socialism, emerged in the empire in the wake of the collapse of Austrian liberalism. Each of these two socialisms purported to stand for the rights of "the little people," and both appealed to workers. The Social Democrats proved more effective in organizing labor, eventually securing an almost complete monopoly on the political representation of trade unions.[17] The two parties developed in opposition to one another. In particular, anticlericalism became part of social democratic doctrine early on, rendering a center-left alliance nearly impossible to achieve, and setting a precedent for left-versus-right political conflict in the interwar period.[18]

Both parties emerged in an empire where political opposition was tolerated. The founding of imperial social democracy is a telling example. The first Austrian Social Democratic Party was established in 1874 in Neudorf near Vienna. Targeting Germanophone workers from Austria, it initially operated on an underground basis.[19] In the period of the mid-1870s to the late 1880s, however, it transitioned to legal status.[20] By the late 1880s, the Austrian government relaxed restrictions against socialists enough for them to hold their founding congress in Hainfeld in Lower Austria. The relatively free exercise of political rights was another part of the imperial legacy that all these socialists would inherit and carry with them in their various successor polities.[21]

The party's origins help explain how the same ideology generated different variations of socialism and communism in post-1918 Europe. The 1889 Hainfeld Congress marked the emergence of the Social Democratic Party as a pan-imperial organization. The congress was essentially a German-Czech gathering: over a hundred members came from Austria, and some eighty from Bohemia. Several Slovenes and Ukrainians were also in attendance, but as individuals unaffiliated with any of the parties.[22] At Hainfeld the leading Austrian socialist, Victor Adler, pushed for the foundation of an empire-wide party with a central bureau in Vienna. Imperial social democracy was thus born of a compromise between Austrian and Czech socialists, whereby the latter ceded leadership to the former. Such a compromise was always fraught. Despite bearing the word "Austrian" in its title, the party's roots were in Bohemia—the empire's industrial stronghold—rather than Austria proper. Both before and after Hainfeld, Czech activists raised concerns that cooperation with Germanophone Austrians could lead to the Germanization of Czech labor.[23]

A small microcosm of the empire, mirroring its heterogeneity and the rising national tensions, the Austrian Social Democratic Party also became emblematic of the debates on autonomy and federation in the late empire. During its 1897 congress in Vienna, the party adopted a federative principle, with each national section now becoming an autonomous unit. The central bureau in Vienna operated as an umbrella entity for these several sections: Czech, Italian, Polish, Ukrainian, and South Slavic. Yet just like the empire itself, this federative organization was fraught with many contradictions. Notably, Germanophone Austrians continued to dominate the party. It was only in 1897 that, under Czech pressure, a German section was founded, marking a separation from the Austrian pan-imperial party; even then, the central bureau in Vienna retained its functions, and German remained the official language at party congresses.

Czech socialists also regarded the Austrians' joint party/union "jurisdiction," not just over Austria proper but the whole empire, as highly problematic.[24] A separate faction in Czech social democracy began to take shape almost immediately after the Hainfeld Congress. The term "separatism" was first used in the Czech socialist milieu in 1891.[25] In 1910 the Czech party split into two branches, separatist and centralist. Starting in 1911, the two ran separately in elections and formed separate factions in the imperial parliament.[26]

These internal conflicts within imperial social democracy revealed the limits of Marxist internationalism, nationalism, autonomy, and federation in the late empire. As Jakub Beneš has observed, we typically associate nationalism with nationalists and consider that Marxism, as the bearer of internationalism, should be the opposite.[27] Yet Austrian social democracy at times epitomized precisely the sort of ethnic rancor, even nationalism, that was typical of the movement's nationalist opponents. The Marxists' nationalism was cultural, rather than the "racial" variety of the pan-Germans, but the underlying national sentiments were alike. Indeed, Marxists and nationalists in the empire had much in common.

The national split within imperial social democracy should also be understood in its historical context as a by-product of the continual debates on nationalism and internationalism/multiethnicity in Europe in general. The boundaries between centralists and separatists, moreover, were fluid. Šmeral, for example, vacillated between the two. He endorsed cultural autonomy for national sections, with the preservation of the Austrian executive to oversee finances and the distribution of resources among different national branches.[28] Czech social democratic separatism, that is, was at this time kept internal to the party; its adherents remained loyal to the concept of the Habsburg polity as a unified multiethnic country. They all continued to cooperate on social issues and supported other aspects of the party's program.

Nationalism and Autonomy

The Hainfeld Congress and the subsequent federalization of the party marked the beginning, not the end, of Austro-Marxists' debates on autonomy and federation. The Austrian Social Democratic Party became a major supporter of autonomy and federalization, and this political and intellectual tradition from the empire would influence numerous left-wing parties in post-Habsburg Europe.

Meeting in Brno in 1899 for a yearly congress, Austrian socialists approved a program of national autonomy that implied federalization and the creation of autonomous units within the empire.[29] The Brno program was the result of long-standing debates on multinationalism and ethnic issues. Much like Marxist doctrine in general, however, it suffered from vagueness and a host of loopholes. For example, the mechanisms of its implementation remained unclear, since each of the empire's provinces was home to several nationalities, boundaries between which could be impossible to draw. As an alternative to the territorial principle, Karl Renner and Otto Bauer advocated national autonomy on the *personal* principle. This would target representatives of national/

ethnic communities that lacked territorial cohesion; it rejected the linkage of ethnicity with territory, instead proposing the foundation of national associations that would exercise their particular ethnic rights, such as schooling in one's native language.[30] This program of extraterritorial autonomy became a hallmark of the Austro-Marxist school.

Both programs were also indicative of the socialists' preference not just for autonomy but also for a multinational federation as opposed to a nation-state—a view that would condition their post-1918 political choices. The seeds of such thinking can be found, for example, in Bauer's *The National Question and Social Democracy,* published in 1907, in which he rejected the idea of "the nation-state . . . as the rule, the multinational state as a mere exception."[31] True, he conceded, the proletariat demanded national autonomy; but national liberation could only come through social liberation, the end of the bourgeoisie's exploitation of the working class.[32] This support for federative over exclusively national solutions left a durable legacy that affected politics—socialist and otherwise—in several countries of post-1918 Europe.

Austrians were not the only ones to address the nationalities issue. In a book published just two years after Bauer's, with the identical title of *The National Question and Social Democracy* (1909), Šmeral argued for "absolute autonomy for each of the Habsburg Empire's ethnic communities."[33] Defining the Habsburg Empire as a historical necessity, he questioned the possibility of a Czech nation-state: "Czechs could not survive in a small state without harming their own national interests; in a small state . . . the Czechs could evolve only as an agricultural nation. . . . We need Austria as much as Austria needs us."[34] Such policy statements reflected not only the overreaching support of the empire among the socialists but also their commitment to autonomy and federation. The latter would remain an essential part of their vision long after the empire's collapse.

Between Germany and Russia

Austro-Marxism, with its emphasis on institutional solutions, interethnic dialogue, autonomy, and political tolerance, was markedly different from the social democracy then taking shape in Germany and Russia. Austro-Marxists, and Bauer in particular, endorsed the rhetoric of revolution but insisted on achieving revolutionary change by democratic institutional means.[35] The transition from capitalism to socialism, argued Bauer, could not be enforced; it could only be achieved democratically.[36] At the same time, he rejected Marxist revisionism. Eduard Bernstein, the leader of the revisionist camp in European social democracy, asserted that revolution would not be necessary after all. Insofar as workers' living standards continued to improve under capitalism, he argued, the transition to socialism and communism would occur naturally over time. Bauer rejected this view. Capitalist production, he insisted, was incompatible with the workers' needs, and in their state of constant oppression, "the masses are not aware of the need for a social revolution."[37] As a middle ground, Austro-Marxists espoused revolution via institutional politics—a radical change to be accomplished without violence.

This variant of Marxism, with its singular understanding of revolution, democracy, and nationalism/internationalism, was a product of the Habsburg Empire's particular geographical location and ethnic makeup, and of the specific type of politics waged in the post-1867 federative empire, which operated on the basis of a parliament and regional institutions in the provinces. This Marxism also represented a response to concurrent debates within the European socialist movement, as well as to pressure from the neighboring states of Germany and Russia.

Vienna was a cultural center of Europe, but the workers' movement was stronger in Germany, as was the socialist party there. Austrian socialists were constrained by interethnic divisions, while German socialists, like most socialists in Western Europe, could focus on the proletarian struggle and revolution. Yet the Habsburg monarchy was of crucial importance for European social democracy. Several leading German Social Democrats had biographical ties to the empire. Karl Kautsky, the leader of the "orthodox" camp, spent his childhood in Prague and moved with his family to Vienna at age seven. He later moved to Germany but maintained friendly relations with many of the empire's socialists. And vice versa, several leading Austro-Marxists (for example, Rudolf Hilferding) after 1918 moved to different countries, especially to Germany, after having spent a large portion of their lives in the empire and directly contributing to Austro-Marxism as a doctrine and a practice. Imperial social democracy thus to some extent seeded itself or spun itself off in other lands.

The reciprocity between Germany and Austria affected the composition and strategies of both parties in pre- and post-1918 Germany, the Habsburg Empire, and several successor states. "Kautsky," commented Ellenbogen, "mentored two generations of socialists," including in the Habsburg Empire.[38] Yet despite taking part in the drafting of the Austrian socialist party's program at

Hainfeld, Kautsky regarded his comrades to the east as inferior and decried their incrementalist tactics; he perceived a great disconnect between their bold revolutionary words—for example, in the party program in Brno—and their lack of revolutionary *action*.[39] German Social Democrats dominated the Socialist International—an organization established in 1889 to unite the various socialist parties of Europe.[40] Adler compensated for this alleged inferiority vis-à-vis the Germans by maintaining a party that was larger and more complex; the imperial organization was not just more programmatically multiethnic, it also helped maintain a certain aura of Austrian grandeur. National splits notwithstanding, the ideological unity of pan-imperial social democracy was unparalleled in Europe.

If relations between Austrian and German socialists were of limited affinity, those between Austrian socialists and their ostensible cothinkers in Russia were all the more so. Having come into existence at roughly the same historical moment, Austro-Marxism and Bolshevism were indeed polar opposites. Austrian Marxists insisted on a mass party, on politics via legality and democracy as opposed to force—the furthest vision imaginable from the hierarchical and autocratic ruling party espoused and later practiced by Russian Bolsheviks.[41]

Several leading Bolsheviks spent time in the Habsburg Empire. Facing persecution at home before the war, many Russian activists chose exile in Europe, often choosing Switzerland and Austria. In 1913 Leon Trotsky and Joseph Stalin shared tables at Café Central with their Austrian counterparts. For Trotsky, Vienna represented the site of a temporary exile; but Stalin, then a relatively young and still unknown Bolshevik, was deployed to the city by party leader Vladimir Lenin to research the nationalities issue and Austrian socialists' responses to it.[42]

It was, in fact, because of Lenin that Stalin found himself in Vienna in 1913—a telling choice of a research destination for the author of what would become one of the Bolsheviks' main treatises on the nationalities issue. As Lenin saw it, the task of writing such a work was better suited to a Georgian than a Russian, who might easily lapse into Russocentrism and national chauvinism.[43] On Lenin's instructions, Stalin interviewed various leading Austrian socialists, including Bauer himself.[44] Stalin's stay in Vienna resulted in the publication of *Marxism and the National Question*. Ostensibly similar to books by leading European socialists, including Bauer and Šmeral, Stalin's work instead represented the outright rejection of the Austro-Marxist concept of national cultural autonomy.[45] Positing an essential connection between nation and territory, he critiqued Renner and Bauer's concept of extraterritorial autonomy, and denounced federalization as harmful to proletarian unity.

Another leading pre-1914 Bolshevik, Trotsky likewise had an opportunity to study Austro-Marxism firsthand. He spent years in political exile in Vienna before 1917, and would later criticize the Austrian socialists as hopelessly questing after compromise, indeed failing to be revolutionaries as he understood the term:

> They were well-educated people whose knowledge of different subjects was superior to mine. I listened with intense, and, one might almost say, respectful interest to their conversation in the Café Central. But very soon I grew puzzled. These people were not revolutionaries. Moreover, they represented the type that was furthest from that of the revolutionary. This expressed itself in everything—in their approach to subjects, in their political remarks and psychological appreciations, in their self-satisfaction—not self-assurance, but self-satisfaction. I even thought I sensed philistinism in the quality of their voice.[46]

Trotsky followed developments in the Habsburg Empire closely. Commenting on the conflicts within the Czech socialist party, he detected in the Czech separatists a Marxist revolutionism that, he claimed, was lacking among their Austrian Germanophone peers:

> I of course could have nothing in common with the deplorable national narrowness of such men as Němec, Soukup, or Šmeral, who tried hard to convince me of the justice of the Czech case. At the same time, I had watched the inner life of the Austrian labor movement too closely to throw all or even the principal blame upon the Czechs. There was plenty of evidence that the rank and file of the Czech party was more radical than the Austro-German party, and that the legitimate dissatisfaction of the Czech workers with the opportunist leadership in Vienna would be cleverly utilized by Czech chauvinists like Němec.[47]

Trotsky's observations on the radicalism of the Czech separatists were almost prophetic. The nation-based Marxist dissenters would radicalize even more during the war. The Vienna experience, in any event, proved transformative for the Bolsheviks, who, despite their mocking and rejection of Austro-Marxist tactics early on, would experiment with some of the very same tactics in the Soviet Union during the 1920s.

Parliament, Government, Intransigence

Ideological differences between German, Austrian, and Russian socialists were partly a by-product of their different political experiences. Socialist party unity in the Habsburg Empire was elusive, yet imperial social democracy as a single entity survived officially until 1916. Unlike the German party, which became torn between orthodox and revisionist camps, and the Russian socialists' 1903 schism between Bolshevik and Menshevik factions, the Austrian Social Democratic Party remained relatively united ideologically through the late years of the war. The institutional experience of socialists in the empire also differed from that of their German and Russian counterparts. The parliament in Austria first convened in 1848 and operated regularly from 1868 on, despite internal disruptions; it was therefore an institution that had a much longer history than its German and Russian counterparts.

Bauer's and Ellenbogen's reflections on the Austrian parliament affirmed the importance of the empire's institutional structures as pillars of democracy. To be sure, Bauer disdained parliamentary procedure itself as "idiotic"; his focus was on party-specific work.[48] But he also recognized the inherent value of parliamentarism as such. In 1909, for example, he emphasized the role of parliamentary work "in the whole of our political activity," explaining that the parliament offered a venue in which socialists could discuss their politics and their attitude toward the nationalities issue.[49] "We should not underestimate parliamentarism," he noted again in 1913.[50] Ellenbogen held similar views. Parliamentary obstructions, he wrote, harbored elements of a revolution—a revolution against the form and composition of this particular parliament, dominated as it was by the bourgeoisie.[51] But nowhere did he or any of his party comrades advocate the wholesale destruction of the parliament or any other imperial political entities. The Austro-Marxists' attitude toward revolution and institutions contrasted markedly with the Bolsheviks' and German socialists' conceptions, a difference that would carry into the post-1918 period.

It was during the late empire that Austro-Marxists built their trust in institutions. Socialists were first elected to the parliament in 1897. It was also the parliament that introduced universal male suffrage in 1907: a political development that first and foremost benefited the socialists, enabling them to garner their largest vote share ever. Universal suffrage was part of the socialists' long-standing agenda, and the very fact that it was accomplished by institutional politics rather than force further inculcated the idea of Austrian institutions as inviolable. Before 1914, despite internal splits, the party adhered to a single electoral list and coordinated its parliamentary politics. Internationally, the different ethnic sections maintained a degree of autonomy: each sent its own delegation to congresses of the Second Socialist International—an umbrella institution without any centralizing functions, which united socialist parties from different countries. Several of our protagonists, including Bauer, Ellenbogen, and Šmeral, became deputies in 1907. Ludwig Czech ran for parliament in 1901 and 1907. He lost both times, but his campaigns provided significant exposure to the imperial political culture that he, too, would incorporate in his activities after 1918, when he would head the German Social Democratic Workers' Party in Czechoslovakia.

While participating in the parliament, the socialists remained adamant in their refusal to cooperate with bourgeois parties. This rejection of bourgeois alliances became another key principle of the Austro-Marxist school of thought, and it circumscribed socialists' involvement in government both before and after 1918. No socialists served as ministers under the empire. Several would hold ministerial positions in different countries after 1918, but the contradiction between an active involvement in parliaments and the refusal to join any coalition governments would be particularly consequential for post-1918 Austria and Czechoslovakia.

Nevertheless, the essential trust in parliamentary and institutional mechanisms carried on to the post-1918 period. The Austrian Republic, as John Boyer has observed, reflected a continuity of parliamentary crisis, with imperial-era obstructions becoming the norm in the republic as well.[52] Yet this continuity was not solely negative. Parliamentary obstructions remained part of a constitutional process that would only be destroyed in the 1930s by a type of political violence that had no precedent in the empire.

Pacifists Turned Militarists

Before 1918, none of the figures under discussion were prepared for the empire's collapse. Their belief in the indispensability of the empire was partly a matter of practicality: Ellenbogen, Bauer, and Czech as Germanophone assimilated Jews would not easily fit into a unitary national state. Šmeral considered the empire the best guarantor of Czech national interests in a world where, he believed, a Czech nation-state could not be sustainable. Commitment to the empire as a geographic polity was the socialist norm, among centralists and separatists alike.

The war ultimately destroyed the pan-imperial party, just as it did the Second Socialist International. In the abstract, Austrian Social Democrats opposed war on ideological grounds, insofar as the burden of fighting would be borne mainly by workers. In 1911, for instance, Bauer had published a pamphlet titled *Big Capital and Militarism,* in which he argued that any modern war would invariably profit big business but bring only misery to the proletariat, who would constitute the majority of combatants. Meeting for their congress in Basel in 1912, members of the Second International collectively denounced militarism. But the fateful year of 1914 saw a striking change, not just among Austro-Marxists but all across Europe, in many socialists' analysis of war and their rhetoric concerning it. All over the map (except, notably, in Serbia and Russia), socialists adopted a "patriotic" line and endorsed their governments' policies. International socialist unity thus faltered under the pressure of war and militarism. Several international socialist gatherings took place after the war broke out, but 1914 marked the end of the Second Socialist International.[53]

The central bureau of the Austrian Social Democratic Party lent its support to the Habsburg dynasty at war, with Bauer, Ellenbogen, and Šmeral all endorsing this party line. On July 28, 1918, Bauer issued a memorandum full of militaristic rhetoric.[54] Ellenbogen would later describe his support as the "greatest shame of [my] life."[55] Šmeral had no reservations; as late as 1915, he praised Germany's military potential, confident in the ultimate success of modern (German) technology.[56]

This new militarism of 1914 caused new splits within the Austrian party. In particular, antiwar opposition among Austrian socialists consolidated around Friedrich Adler—the party leader's son, now his father's most outspoken opponent. In 1916 Friedrich assassinated Karl Stürghk, Austria's sitting prime minister. Tried and sentenced to death (later commuted to eighteen years in prison), he was pardoned in 1918. The war, the split with his son, and the latter's going to such extremes as assassination must have hit the elder Adler hard. He would die in 1919 after a prolonged illness.[57] The socialist faction in the parliament also disintegrated, and by 1916 its former members had joined their respective national representations. Not only did the war destroy the Austrian imperial party, it also left behind a bitter aftertaste, leading to acrimony between former friends and colleagues. These conflicts would never be fully patched up, and some leading socialists would turn to communism.

Bauer at War

Among high-profile Social Democrats, Otto Bauer was one of the few to see war firsthand. The official war announcement coincided with the inauguration of the Austrian draft, in which Bauer, a reserve officer, was immediately called up. The fall of 1914 saw him deployed to the Carpathian Mountains on the Russian-Austrian border in Galicia. His first letters from the front were full of enthusiasm, but several weeks into the war his tone began to shift, the approach of winter taking a physical and emotional toll. "I am tired and depressed," Bauer wrote to Victor Adler. "There is nothing pretty about being here: up in the mountains, we subsist in sub-zero temperatures. . . . The optimism of October has all but vanished."[58]

Things took an even worse turn on November 23, 1914, when Bauer was captured by Russian forces. The Austrian prisoners were made to march for a week, until December 3, when they were loaded onto trains bound for Smolensk. The train journey, at least, must have come as a relief: complying with the Hague conventions on prisoners of war, the Russians treated officers with respect, allowing them to ride comfortably. In January 1915 Bauer wrote again to Adler, describing his situation: he had been brought to Siberia, one of some twenty-eight thousand interned in a camp east of Lake Baikal. The conditions under which he spent the next three years in Siberia were difficult but never desperate; officers were not required to work and were under relatively few restrictions. He complained of a lack of information but was able to request books and newspapers.[59] In Siberia he began work on his *Das Weltbild des Kapitalismus* (The Worldview of Capitalism) and first heard news of Russia's February Revolution, which—scarcely able to contain his enthusiasm—he expected to presage a cycle of worldwide transformations.[60]

Meanwhile, Bauer's colleagues back in Vienna were faced with a series of crises. Victor Adler struggled personally and professionally. The party he had created was now in shambles. In 1917 he undertook a new campaign to secure the release of Bauer, who had been one of his closest allies. A team of Austrian socialists negotiated with Russian counterparts in St. Petersburg and in Stockholm, and in the summer of 1917 Bauer was released and transported to the Russian capital.[61]

His experience as an Austrian POW in Russian Siberia, and in particular his exposure to the Russian revolutions of 1917, proved transformative not just for Bauer personally, but for the party and Austrian socialism and communism through 1938. He had shifted to the left, now questioning the inevitability of the war. While in prison in Siberia, he made sympathetic comments about the Bolsheviks, despite not believing they would last in power.[62] By late August 1917 he was back in Vienna. His interest in the Russian revolutions led to speculation that he himself had become a Bolshevik, but Bauer denied it. In a letter to Karl Kautsky (October 28, 1917), he described the Bolsheviks as "Jacobins who believe in the power of the guillotine."[63] He also opposed the importation of Bolshevik practices into Austria, and observed moreover that the Bolsheviks represented only a small minority of the Russian population.[64] He reaffirmed his anti-Bolshevik views in several publications after 1918, notably, in his *Bolschewismus oder Sozialdemokratie?* (Bolshevism or Social Democracy?). Here he explained that Bolshevik radicalism, while applicable to Russia, was unsuited to countries that had a long-standing tradition of democratic institutionalism.[65] Such references to Austria's however flawed legacy of parliamentarism, and the complete lack thereof in the Russian Empire, were emblematic of how Bauer would continue to view the relationship between democratic and nondemocratic or violent politics in post-1918 Europe.

Bauer's ideological evolution was at least partly responsible for the perseverance of democratic socialism: several leading socialists, including Bauer himself, had shifted to the left during the war, yet after 1917 they rejected communism or Bolshevism. This leftist faction declared itself part of the Socialist International and thus remained part of mainstream socialist politics.[66] The Austrian Communist Party was founded in December 1918 as a response to the wartime crisis in Austrian social democracy.[67] The communists, however, failed to secure the support of even the most left-leaning socialists, and the communist party would remain weak in interwar Austria. Meanwhile, Victor Adler nominated Bauer to succeed him as leader of the Austrian Social Democratic Party, a position the latter would hold through 1934.

Away from the Front Lines

The war proved equally transformative for Bauer's colleagues, including those who did not see the fighting firsthand. Ellenbogen, for example, spent most of the war years safely in Vienna. But he did undergo a personal crisis in this period, due at least in part to his long-standing involvement in Italian politics. By late October 1918, he was willing to give up on the "old Austria." Pointing to the de facto breakup of the different nationalities and the near capitulation of Austrian troops, Ellenbogen claimed that most of the monarchy's citizens had "lost faith in the old Austria."[68] Remarkable in this context is not the fact that Ellenbogen accepted the dissolution of the Habsburg polity on October 30, just days after the proclamation of independent Czechoslovakia and Poland, but that so many of his peers did not, clinging to the empire even after it had, for all intents and purposes, collapsed.

Czech socialists experienced transformations similar to their Austrian colleagues. Despite the long-standing tradition of the party's separatism, it was only late in the war that most endorsed independence. The similarities in the political evolution of Social Democrats from different national parties were notable. But even late in the war, Šmeral continued to support the empire as a geopolitical necessity; in his assessment, it represented the best venue for internationalism and workers' cooperation, and a better alternative to any nation-state. His enduring support of multiethnic solutions underlay his political and ideological choices after the empire's downfall, notably his difficulty in accepting a nationality-based Czechoslovakia and his continued opposition to nationally determined social democratic parties in post-1918 Europe.

In late 1918 Šmeral was not oblivious to the changing political scene in Bohemia and the empire in general. Not unlike his nationalist peers, he espoused nationalism and imperial loyalty at the same time. For example, he initiated contacts with pro-independence Czechs associated with Tomáš Masaryk. At the same time, he attended meetings with Austrian ministers and continued to endorse the Habsburgs, arguing that the imperial polity best served the interests of the smaller nations of Central Europe, including the Czechs.[69]

In trying to navigate between nationalists and imperial loyalists, Šmeral found himself in a politically impossible position: Austrian colleagues accused him of betraying the socialist cause, while Czech nonsocialists (and even some socialists) saw him as acquiescing to an Austrocentric imperial government.[70] Both sides accused him of opportunism.[71] His dedication to the dynasty became the subject of rumor and derision: when the empire's collapse seemed imminent to all but Šmeral, Ferdinand Peroutka commented that "being an imperial opportunist in October 1918 is like breaking ice that is in any case about to melt."[72] The actual melting would hit Šmeral hard; he had a career after the war but would never quite feel as at home as he had in the empire.

Bauer and Ellenbogen in a New Europe

Surviving the war was one thing, but *living* after it was another. The empire's collapse caused practical difficulties for many of our protagonists, whose families were divided among different Habsburg provinces. Boundaries between different parts of the empire had been porous, but suddenly there were new borders. Bauer's family, for instance, owned a business in Bohemia, as had the Ellenbogens in Moravia, but now these regions were part of Czechoslovakia. After 1918, former citizens of the empire could only join one state.[73] The Czechoslovak government quickly nationalized the property of those who became citizens of the Austrian Republic, with Bauer, Ellenbogen, and Joseph Redlich among those affected.

The shock of collapse and the difficulty of accepting a greatly reduced Austria were aggravated by the emotional aspects of the peace negotiations. Bauer was present at the Versailles conference as part of the Austrian delegation, and he described the dealings of the Western allies there as barbarous; the *Arbeiter-Zeitung,* with Bauer as a staff member, denounced the Treaty of Saint-Germain between the Allies and Austria as "a crime against humanity."[74]

In the republic, the Social Democratic Party, and Bauer in particular, supported Anschluss as the only way for Austria to survive the economic and territorial destruction wrought by the war. Even if Austria was partly responsible for the war, its collapse as a multiethnic polity was interpreted as a lamentable result of the forces conspiring against it. Bauer, similarly to Heinrich Lammasch, blamed minority nationalism for causing the empire's downfall. He elaborated his views in *The Austrian Revolution* (first published in 1923). "In essence and origin the Austrian revolution was a revolution of the Jugo-Slav, the Czech and the Polish bourgeoisie," wrote Bauer.[75] But unlike Lammasch, Bauer also viewed events from a Marxist standpoint, describing all that transpired between 1914 and 1918 as a bourgeois victory over the dynasty. Here Bauer sounded like a Marxist and a Habsburg loyalist wrapped up in one.[76]

If Slavic nationalism had destroyed the empire, Bauer argued, thereby depriving Austria of its resources essential for survival, then Austrians should join the ethnically and culturally similar Germany. This would afford little Austria a chance of economic survival. The Slavs had wrecked the old Austrian entity (and taken with them some key industrial centers), Bauer continued, and

Austrian foreign minister Otto Bauer (standing at far left) with Austrian colleagues boarding a train to Weimar to discuss Austria's possible annexation by Germany. *Wiener Bilder,* March 2, 1919.

the new one was stillborn, bereft of key resources. Its only opportunity for economic and political viability lay in unification with Germany: "Our most important aim in the peace negotiations had to be the assertion of our rights to union with Germany."[77] His vision of the empire's collapse thus explains his support for Austria's annexation to Germany, a view that he shared with most other socialists during the 1920s.

In the republic the socialists fortified some of the principles they had adopted under the empire. In 1919 the Social Democratic Workers' Party of Austria became proportionally the strongest social democratic party in the world.[78] Their combination of electoral success and inexperience in actual governance created a precarious situation. On one hand, several Social Democrats occupied major ministerial posts: in 1919 Bauer became Austria's foreign minister; Ellenbogen minister of social welfare and later undersecretary of trade; and several other socialists occupied key positions, including Karl Renner as the first chancellor.[79] Their entry into government might seem counterintuitive, given their long-standing previous rejection of ministerial positions. Bauer himself recognized the dilemma and the potential breaches of socialist policy, but he justified the party's government participation and its 1919 coalition with the Christian Socials as a "historical necessity"—a way to prevent a coup from the right or left. This coalition, formed from a position of power insofar as the socialists had the most votes, was conditioned on the other side's agreement to carry out socialist policies.[80]

In the postwar experience of Bauer and his colleagues in government we can find additional continuities between empire and republic; in particular, an attempt to translate Austro-Marxist models from the former period into policy practices in the latter. Notable in this regard was Bauer's and Ellenbogen's work on socialization—a process that Ellenbogen described as a transition from capitalism to socialism.[81] In early 1919 Ellenbogen became head of the Socialization Committee in the Austrian parliament, as the Social Democrats now commenced taking practical steps toward the economic changes they had long envisioned. Among the resulting achievements were the nationalization of major industries, including Austria's energy sector.[82] The commission was soon disbanded, however, with its final meeting taking place in September 1919. It went into oblivion after the socialists had resigned from the government.

By 1920 the socialists had retreated from their experiment with government service; Austria would not have another socialist minister until after 1945. Bauer himself resigned in 1919 after serving only eight months, and the other socialist ministers would be gone in 1920.[83] When, in the election of that year, the socialists came in second and were relegated to junior status, Bauer refused to form another alliance, describing his opposition thereto as a "historical necessity."[84] His viewpoint can be understood: socialism remained a popular force, particularly in Vienna. Insofar as the Social Democrats seemed ever poised to win a national election, Bauer believed that remaining oppositionist, outside of possibly compromising coalitions, would be essential to their viability as a unified party. Applying the Marxist framework of historical development, he cited the will of the workers, who "regarded a purely bourgeois government as a lesser evil than a new coalition. Thus the working class abandoned the government to the bourgeoisie and the peasantry."[85]

Even after coming in second in the 1920 national elections, the Social Democrats remained a dominant force in Vienna. For many in Austria and in Europe, "Red Vienna," with its multitude of socialist initiatives, was a symbol of democratic socialism, what Anson Rabinbach described as "a third way between communism and Bolshevism."[86] Social democracy's prominence in Vienna also sustained the hope of success in the country in general. But the countryside voted primarily for the Christian Socials, and Bauer's hope of socialists' reconquering all of Austria never materialized. The polarization between "red," socialist-dominated Vienna and the "black," Christian Social countryside plagued Austrian interwar politics, becoming a source of constant tensions and fueling the reciprocal radicalization of both parties and their respective constituencies.

Bauer's refusal to cooperate with the Christian Socials was a by-product of his rigid support of intransigency—an ideological principle that Austro-Marxists had first adopted in the empire. The practical implications of this stance in republican Austria were more consequential than they had been before.[87] It marginalized the socialists and facilitated the rightward shift in Austrian politics. The Christian Social Party was eventually forced to look for a coalition partner on the right. These were some of the larger political consequences of Bauer's blaming the empire's breakup on Slavic nationalism, and his insistence that it benefited only the bourgeoisie rather than workers; of his party's intransigence vis-à-vis coalitions; and of his disavowal of revolutionary struggle as opposed to incrementalism.

Šmeral: Ideological Elephant

While the major political divisions in Austria were ideological in nature, in Czechoslovakia, ethnicity added still more fuel to the contentiousness. Social democracy in Czechoslovakia grappled with the same nationality issues as did the Czechoslovak government in general. Socialists here too enjoyed major early electoral success, gaining close to 30 percent of the votes in the 1919 elections.[88] But all traces of unity had vanished, with divisions between parties of different nationalities far more pronounced than they had been in the empire.

Bohumír Šmeral did not conceal his disappointment with the empire's collapse. However, he was able initially to look on the bright side, hailing the opportunities afforded by the founding of the new republic. The Czechoslovak state opened new horizons for socialists to realize goals left unaccomplished before 1918. While plans to reform national minorities policy and to institute real federalism had never materialized in the empire, the republic, Šmeral believed, could offer better prospects. Czechoslovakia's ethnic heterogeneity was akin to that of the Habsburg Empire, but as a new state it could be organized on an entirely different basis.[89] "We recognize the existence of the independent Czechoslovak Republic not only as a simple fact, but as a great historical progress against the former state," he declared in early 1921.[90]

Šmeral's early hopes soon turned into disillusionment. From his point of view, the "private-capitalist regime" that had "mobilized the entire apparatus of the Austro-Hungarian reactionary regime" was fully operational in Czechoslovakia as well.[91] The new state, he continued, was based on principles of militarism and capitalism, and as such was unacceptable for the working classes in Czechoslovakia. Social democracy in the empire had provided at least a semblance of internationalism and proletarian unity. The several Social Democratic parties in Czechoslovakia, by contrast, were organized on the national principle: the Czechoslovak Social Democratic Workers' Party, for example, brought together Czechs and Slovaks, while other minorities—Germans, Hungarians, and Ukrainians—had their own separate socialist parties. In defiance of imperial-era standards of intransigence, moreover, Czechoslovak socialists had joined the ruling Pětka coalition together with bourgeois parties. Šmeral could not reconcile himself to this break with the policies of internationalism and ideological purity. As he saw it, there was no point in having socialist ministers if they refused or were unable to carry out genuine socialist policies. His adherence to Austro-Marxist models was as rigid as Bauer's and was similarly consequential.[92]

Šmeral's career in early Czechoslovakia resembled that of many who, formerly committed to the empire as a multiethnic polity, had difficulty resigning themselves to the concept of their new nation-states. He joined the Czechoslovak parliament but refused to take an oath of allegiance to Czechoslovakia.[93] His experience and his networks, however, were valuable assets for the new republic. Prime Minister Vlastimil Tusar tried to lure Šmeral back into the government, but to no avail; Tusar saw the defiant Šmeral as "an elephant who will no longer turn around."[94] Šmeral was reelected in 1925 and served as a deputy until 1929. Yet much like Bauer in the same decade, he would in this period focus mainly on party work.

Šmeral and Soviet Russia

Disappointed with the crisis of mainstream democratic socialism in Czechoslovakia, Šmeral began to seek solutions elsewhere. Communism, with its emphasis on internationalism and interethnic unity, had a strong, seemingly salvific appeal for him. The Bolshevik brand of communism, he argued, was a more appropriate heir to Austro-Marxism than the ethnically divisive socialism playing out in the new Czechoslovakia.

The combination of circumstances—Bolshevik successes and his disappointment with Czechoslovakia—determined his shift to the left. Before the war Šmeral had shown little interest in Russia, nor had he believed in the viability or advisability of forcible revolution. But after 1918 he became fascinated with the Bolsheviks and began to speak of their "world-wide vision."[95] Šmeral visited Moscow and Petrograd in early 1920, keeping detailed diaries of his impressions. He recorded the hopes, the lofty ideals, and the new reality: "I'm back from Soviet Russia, and everyone I bump into asks me what's happening there, what I saw and experienced. My answer will be brief: I returned from another world as a different person. Something huge, almost incomprehensible is taking place in Russia. Many new things are being born there."[96]

His fascination with Bolshevism, however, had its limits. He argued that Bolshevik tactics, while applicable for Russia, were not suitable for Czechoslovakia—a perspective reminiscent of Bauer's: "When I went to Russia in the spring of 1920, I explained to Lenin that we ardently pursued revolutionary aims but that we could not follow a tactic derived from a Russian theory."[97] He would continue for years to see Czechoslovakia as unripe for a radical revolution, and in particular to doubt the applicability, in that country, of Soviet-style monopolization of power within a single communist party.

Communism and Czechoslovakia

In Czechoslovakia, just like in Austria, the leftward shift among socialists represented a response to the crisis of the war and postwar adjustments. The history of Czechoslovak communism also resembles political developments in other successor states, notably Yugoslavia and Italy. This was a matter of competing parallel paths toward communism: one homegrown, the other imported from or imposed by Soviet Russia. The dueling visions of communism pertained especially to the different means of achieving it: evolution versus revolution; democratic membership versus centralization and strict hierarchies.

The first branches of what would become the Communist Party of Czechoslovakia were formed in Kyiv and Petrograd in the wake of the October Revolution. Both were founded by former Czech recruits to the Austrian army (Alois Muna and Josef Hais, respectively) who became prisoners of war and encountered the Bolshevik victory in the Russian Empire firsthand.[98] The Kyiv and Petrograd groups formed the core of the radical left faction in the Communist Party of Czechoslovakia through the 1920s.[99] By contrast, Šmeral represented a homegrown type of communism that, albeit inspired by the October Revolution, differed from the Soviet project, evincing the legacy of Austro-Marxism rather than Bolshevism.[100] Šmeral regarded communism as a stage in the development of social democracy from the pre-1914 period.[101] Communists, he hoped, could overcome divisions among socialists and shift the focus from allying with the bourgeoisie to defending the proletariat.

In May 1921 Šmeral presided, as one of the cofounders, over the first congress of the Communist Party of Czechoslovakia, which included Czechs, Slovaks, Hungarians, and Ukrainians.[102] In October 1921 the German left joined as well, so that now communists of all Czechoslovakia's national groups were represented by a single party.[103] The party, however, was fraught with some of the same problems as its socialist counterpart, in particular, the same Czech predominance: even after the October merger, Czechs made up about 70 percent of members.[104] The new republic's Social Democrats and communists thus inherited some of the same difficulties that Austrian socialists had faced in the empire, except now the ethnic hierarchy changed: while Czechs had struggled against German domination in the imperial party, they now imposed their authority upon their peers in the left-wing parties of Czechoslovakia.

Despite bearing "communist" in its title, the party was not a Bolshevik one. Šmeral rejected the ideas of a radical, October-style revolution and of the dictatorship of the proletariat so central to Bolshevik doctrine. Czechoslovak communists followed a "special path of development" that differed from "international templates."[105] Relations with the Communist International (Comintern) were complicated as well. This body was founded in 1919 by Russian Bolsheviks who claimed it to be a continuation of the Second Socialist International, dissolved during the war. Yet it differed structurally from its predecessor. The Socialist International had been rather loose, with no centralized control; the Comintern would be centrally directed from Moscow.[106] Even after joining the Comintern later in 1921, Šmeral held out hope that the tradition of democratic socialism could be preserved. Joining the Comintern, moreover, did not yet imply the endorsement of Bolshevik tactics. In the early 1920s communist parties within the Comintern still had the privilege of openly debating varying strategies and approaches.

Early Soviet political culture itself afforded considerable latitude, and concomitant hope for progress both at home and abroad. In 1922 the Bolsheviks under Lenin adopted a relatively mild economic course and tolerant national policies. The first years of the Soviet Union carried much promise of achievement and improvement. But Stalin's increased political profile after Lenin's death affected not just Soviet politics but the international left, in particular jump-starting the Bolshevization of communist parties in Europe, including Czechoslovakia. To a certain extent this represented the completion of Lenin's original design, with the Comintern consolidating its control over hitherto independent-minded communists.

The Bolshevization of the Communist Party of Czechoslovakia (1924–25) coincided with a similar process in Yugoslavia and Italy. In January 1925, in a speech at a meeting of the Czechoslovak Commission of the Communist International, Stalin accused Šmeral of right-wing deviations, of tactics that "lead to adapting oneself to the bourgeoisie."[107] This militant Bolshevization under pressure from without also coincided with the increased persecutions communists faced within their own country: in 1925 thousands were arrested in a second wave of anticommunist crackdowns in Czechoslovakia.[108] The Czechoslovak party also experienced a crisis within its own ranks, with some members supporting the Austrophile democratic tradition represented by Šmeral; others favoring a leftward turn toward Bolshevization; and still others pushing the party toward the right and cooperation with bourgeois parties.[109]

The Bolshevization of the Czechoslovak Communist Party marked a turning point in Šmeral's career. Starting in 1925, he was assigned to work on Comintern assignments abroad—activity that was marginal in comparison with his former role in the movement. The party he had helped pioneer, meanwhile, became Moscow's puppet. In 1929 Klement Gottwald, Moscow's favored candidate, became the new party leader.[110] Šmeral nevertheless remained a communist for the rest of his life.

Despite these domestic and international pressures, communists in Czechoslovakia secured a large following and enjoyed considerable electoral success. During the 1920s the Communist Party was one of the largest in

Czechoslovakia and per capita the largest communist party in Europe.[111] Particularly in regions of the country where Ukrainians and Slovaks predominated, the communists siphoned off much of the Social Democrats' former electorate. This, however, was a different party from the one that Šmeral had envisioned in the early 1920s. His notion of "a communist party [that] would enjoy . . . freedom of movement . . . in the domestic and international situation in the early 1920s" proved an illusion in Czechoslovakia.[112]

Ludwig Czech and German Socialism

If Šmeral was disappointed with the ethnic fragmentation of social democracy in Czechoslovakia, his German socialist peers were even more so, now finding themselves at the outskirts of politics, marginalized and even antagonized by the new government of independent Czechoslovakia and by their many colleagues from the former pan-imperial party. Yet they too continued to follow imperial-era models in post-1918 Europe, applying earlier precedents to the politics of Czechoslovakia and remaining committed to the Austro-Marxist tradition. The political and ideological continuity among German socialists in Czechoslovakia was as pronounced as it was among their Czech peers.

Ludwig Czech epitomized the difficulties Bohemia's and Moravia's German socialists faced during the transition from empire to nation-state. A native of Brno, Czech had after the war decided to remain in the new Czechoslovakia. He became a member of the German Socialist Party of Bohemia, Moravia, and Silesia that was originally formed in September 1917 in Brno. In 1919 it was renamed as the German Social Democratic Workers' Party of Czechoslovakia. Czech became head of the party in 1920 and remained in this position until its dissolution in 1935.

Having lost several bids to the imperial parliament before 1918, Czech was now elected to its Czechoslovak counterpart and in 1921 became vice speaker. His career in Czechoslovakia, and his party's fortunes, reflected the complicated relations between Czechs and Germans in the new state in general and within social democracy in particular. In 1918 the German Social Democrats refused to acknowledge Czechoslovakia's borders as established by international treaties.[113] In the course of the early 1920s, German socialists moved from outright rejection of Czechoslovakia to conditional acceptance, shifting their priority to ethnic autonomy within the new republic. Both sides took certain steps of rapprochement, but the conflict was never fully resolved.

Czech's personal and political dilemma in this period was not unlike that of Šmeral; both were disappointed by the complacency of the Czechoslovak Social Democratic Party, its cooperation with the government, and its national exclusiveness. After joining the parliament, Czech, for example, anticipated cooperation between Czech and German socialists. When this alliance failed to materialize, he blamed Czech socialists for not reaching out to national minorities. It would take years for German socialists to formalize their cooperation with non-German parties, and relations between Czech and German socialists would remain tense.

Similarly to Bauer, Czech remained committed to Austro-Marxism, especially the old imperial socialists' program of ethnic autonomy. In 1922 his party sought parliamentary approval for the creation of a multiethnic commission to implement national autonomy.[114] The initiative was based on a Habsburg-era precedent: the 1909 attempt to create a similar council as part of autonomy-related initiatives throughout the empire. In both epochs, the proposed legislation failed. In 1909 the proposal did not get enough votes to pass. In 1922 German socialists in the Czechoslovak parliament secured the support of the Hungarian caucus, but were unable to bring other parties on board. In some ways Czechoslovakia and other successor states demonstrated a reversal of policies from the late empire. Autonomy had been receiving increasing support across the political board in the late empire, but it became mostly unpopular in the successor states, even and especially among those who had earlier pleaded to adhere to the Wilsonian principles of self-determination.

Relations between Czechs and Germans, however, warmed up in the mid-1920s as a result of reciprocal efforts. In 1926, on the government's initiative, two ethnic Germans became ministers. This did not, however, secure the cooperation of German socialists; Ludwig Czech still denounced the "reactionary capitalist government."[115] It would be three more years before a German Social Democrat would accept a ministerial position, when Czech in 1929 became minister of social welfare, continuing the work he had begun under the empire.

Austro-Marxism between Empire and Nation-States

While German socialists thus scored certain advances in Czechoslovak politics, many of their fellow Social Democrats in other countries remained outsiders, further marginalized over time. Such was the case with the Austrian

Social Democrats under Bauer, who found themselves outside of government coalitions. Communists in Czechoslovakia too eventually abandoned their Austro-Marxist roots, their organization becoming effectively a puppet of Moscow. The Austro-Marxist legacy, then, fell victim to two fraught phenomena in these two successor states: the rigid intransigence pursued by Bauer in Austria, and the fragmentation of social democracy in Czechoslovakia. In the long term, these developments were equally consequential, both eventually facilitating the consolidation and prominence of radical extremes in Austrian and Czechoslovak politics.

Our four protagonists and the parties they represented are important in their own rights. But it is the parallels between their lives on one hand and political developments across Europe on the other that, it seems to me, are most telling. After 1918 these figures found themselves citizens of different countries and members of different parties, but they all tethered their choices to their imperial-era experience, to the Austro-Marxist tradition. The façade of differences—between Bauer and Ellenbogen within Austrian social democracy; between Šmeral and Czech as representatives of Czechoslovak communism and German social democracy, respectively; and among all the socialists separated in 1918 by the Austrian-Czechoslovak border—conceals the underlying similarities all rooted in the same ideology of Habsburg-era Austro-Marxism. This is, as well, a remarkable testament to the afterlife of political practices from that imperial polity, persisting through the interwar era until the Nazi takeover in the late 1930s.

Ideological intransigence and national fragmentation contributed to the eventual downfall of the Austro-Marxist tradition in various countries. Yet even in its capacity as one of history's "losers," Austro-Marxism remained a key factor in European politics in the 1920s and 1930s, and then, in a resurrected form, again after the Second World War. The Austro-Marxists' defeat and the authoritarians' victory were neither final nor inevitable, and examining the dynamic between them, not just in one country but across Europe, helps us to understand the radicalization of interwar Europe, and the sense of a lost legacy that so many in this period experienced.

7. From Promise to Terror

Poland and Ukraine

The socialist encounters at the pre-1914 Café Central were as important for Europe's East as for Austria proper. During their 1913 Vienna sojourn, Russia's prominent Bolsheviks Joseph Stalin and Leon Trotsky shared tables, drank coffee with Austrian socialists, and learned the nuances of Austro-Marxism firsthand. As described in the previous chapter, they disdained the Austrians' lack of revolutionary thinking and saw their federative solutions vis-à-vis national minorities as misguided. A few short years later, however, the Bolsheviks would begin to borrow Austrian models, endorsing federalism and extensive territorial autonomy for minorities first in Soviet Russia and, after 1922, in the Union of Soviet Socialist Republics. Soviet nationalities policy, indeed, became a modified version of the Austro-Marxist solution to minority issues.

This transfer of models from the Habsburg Empire to post-1918 Soviet Russia and later the Soviet Union was facilitated by another cohort of coffee-house politicians, those who matured in the Habsburg Empire and moved to the USSR in the 1920s to help build communism there. This cooperation between the Bolsheviks and socialists from the former Habsburg Empire was somewhat counterintuitive, given the Austro-Marxists' rejection of Bolshevism and the growing animosity between the two camps especially after 1917. But this development had a certain logic: it was a by-product of the imperial past and particularly of Marxist and socialist trajectories specific to the Habsburg Empire's eastern borderlands. Far removed from Café Central, many socialists in Galicia made the acquaintance of peers from the Russian Empire during the early days of socialist movements beginning in the 1870s. Before 1918 the vast majority of socialists in Galicia rejected Bolshevik methods. But the two empires' collapse and the resulting interregional civil strife affected the former Habsburg eastern periphery dramatically, and its frustrated residents began to seek solutions elsewhere than just in Vienna. At least some found their answers in Bolshevism.

This chapter tells the story of socialism and Marxism in Galicia, and their chronological and geographical transformations across the epochal divide of 1918, involving the Habsburg and Russian Empires, Poland, Ukraine, and the Soviet Union. It brings together four protagonists who stood at the roots of Galician, Polish, and Ukrainian Social Democratic parties, whose membership and models set the tone for leftist politics in interwar Poland and the Soviet Ukraine. Ignacy Daszyński, Herman Diamand, Mykola Hankevych, and Semen Vityk were born in the 1860s and 1870s and died in the 1930s. They represented different generations but belonged to the same circle—one bound by shared ideas on Marxism, nationalism, and multiethnic politics. Living in Austria, Poland, and Ukraine (and then Soviet Ukraine) after 1918, they all carried imperial-era models and practices into postimperial Europe.

Discussions of the continuities of the Austro-Marxist tradition in territories well to the east of Vienna are sparse.[1] Several accounts exist of socialism and Marxism in Galicia, focusing especially on Polish-Ukrainian-Jewish relations both in Galicia in general and in the socialist movement, with some reference to the Austrian imperial context; but these halt in 1914 or 1918, as if the empire's end necessarily meant also the end of this political tradition.[2] The brand of Marxism as it developed in the Russian Empire, in particular in the Polish and Ukrainian territories, has drawn more attention. And quite naturally so: it was indeed Russian Marxism, or at least one of its variants, that led to Bolshevism; and Polish Marxism in the Russian Empire, or at least one of its variants, contributed to Polish communism. By contrast, Galician socialism and Marxism are all but forgotten in most narratives of European history.

Yet the development of Galician socialism is crucial for understanding the post-1918 trajectory of socialism and communism east of Vienna, including in the Soviet Union. Here too, Habsburg-era socialism lived on, in the form of its former practitioners who found themselves in Soviet territory, and even in the policies of the Russian Bolsheviks, who for reasons of their own opted to imitate Austrian socialist models in the Soviet state.

These Eastern European heirs of Austro-Marxism would, like the bearers of this tradition generally, be numbered among history's "losers," eventually sacrificing their political careers, and often their lives, to right-wing authoritarianism in Poland and Stalinism in the Soviet Union. Yet their very attempt to implement the Austro-Marxist legacy in post-1918 Europe stands as another remarkable testament to the extended afterlife of the Habsburg Empire and its political practices.

Between Vienna, Warsaw, and Kyiv

Cross-border ties between the two empires played a defining role in the history of socialism and Marxism in Galicia. Cross-border cooperation also helps explain how the Habsburg Empire became a de facto role model for Soviet nationalities policy. Marxism was first brought to Galicia by activists from the Russian Empire as a result of geographical proximity, as well as of the different levels of industrialization in the border regions of the two empires. Galicia was industrially underdeveloped, not only in comparison with other areas of Austro-Hungary but also with the neighboring territories in the Russian Empire. The workers' movement was stronger in Russian-held Warsaw than in the Habsburgs' Lemberg/Lwów, and Marxism had a correspondingly stronger base in the Russian Empire than it did in Galicia.

The first meeting of Galician socialists took place in Bolesław Limanowski's home in Lemberg/Lwów in 1878.[3] Limanowski had moved to this capital of Austrian Galicia from Warsaw in 1870 to flee police persecutions in Russian Poland.[4] In the 1870s socialist activity was illegal in the Habsburg Empire as well, but political persecution was less severe than in Russia. The wave of socialist political exiles from the Russian Empire that spread across Europe, it should be kept in mind, included a Polish cohort.[5] Galicia became a microcosm of this internationalism and cosmopolitanism, a meeting point and melting pot of ideas from all over Europe, including from St. Petersburg, Warsaw, Kyiv, Vienna, and Geneva.

Socialist Variants: Daszyński, Diamand, Vityk, Hankevych

Coming of age in the same intellectual and political circles organized by Limanowski and other socialists, our protagonists were relatively close to one another in age, received similar educations, and were friends for good portions of their lives. In terms of national background, this was a quite mixed cohort, with the boundaries between Poles, Ukrainians, and Jews at times difficult to draw. Internationalism became a guiding principle of these encounters, and it remained imprinted on generations of Galician socialists. The socialists who gathered in Limanowski's home during the 1870s all conversed in Polish, but for them this was a socialist lingua franca: all held the viewpoint that workers' interests were more important than national affiliations. Their stories, at the same time, were different from many of their socialist peers in other regions of the monarchy because of their political and geographical peregrinations within the Habsburg polity and beyond it, in part due to cross-border ties with imperial Russia, Soviet Russia, and later the Soviet Union.

Ignacy Daszyński's early involvement with socialism was formative. He was born in the town of Zbaraż in Western Galicia in 1866. His family later moved to Drohobych—an ethnically mixed coal-mining town in Eastern Galicia. Engaging in socialist activity in high school under the influence of his elder brother Felix, he was arrested, expelled from school, and settled in Lemberg/Lwów. Before finishing high school, he moved to Paris. His university experience replicated that of high school: barred from the University of Lwów, he would graduate from it only years later as an external student.[6] While many of the empire's socialists traveled, studied, and worked throughout Europe, few—including none of the other figures discussed here—faced the sort of harsh political restrictions the Austrian authorities subjected Daszyński to; in some ways, his early life was more like that of a socialist in the Russian rather than Habsburg Empire.

Herman Diamand represented the same generation as Daszyński, but he took a different path to Marxism. Born in 1860 in Lemberg/Lwów, he was raised in an assimilated Jewish family speaking German. He received a Germanophone education, studied law at the University of Czernowitz—in the hometown of Mykola Wassilko, another protagonist of this book. Diamand too began to engage in socialist activity as a student, but because of his different upbringing, education, and career path, his entry into Austrian socialism was smoother and more immediate than Daszyński's. He came to Vienna in

1895 for a law internship. By now immersed in socialist circles, he built close ties with Victor Adler.[7]

In some ways, Daszyński was closer to Mykola Hankevych than he was to Diamand. Born in 1869 in the town of Sniatyn in Eastern Galicia, Hankevych followed a path to socialism similar to that of Daszyński. The product of an aristocratic family that had earlier split into two separate branches, Ukrainian and Polish, Mykola represented the former but never broke ties with his Polish roots—a connection that would be reflected in his relationships with his political comrades. He spent his adolescence in the city of Przemyśl in Western Galicia and attended the University of Lwów. He became a socialist during his student years, part of the same circles as the other figures discussed here.[8]

Semen Vityk was born in 1876 near Drohobych in Eastern Galicia, raised in the family of a railroad worker. His family later moved to Western Galicia, and like Hankevych he attended high school in Przemyśl and later studied at the University of Lwów. He would become the only Ukrainian socialist to serve as a deputy in the Austrian imperial parliament (between 1907 and 1918). From 1918 to 1925, he divided his residence and activities between Austria, the several Ukrainian states, and Poland, and eventually settled in the Soviet Union.[9]

These four not only stood at the roots of socialism and Marxism in Galicia, but also continued the tradition beyond 1918, keeping in touch despite their ideological and political disagreements and new borders. In the Habsburg era, their lives ran parallel to those of their Austrian and Czech peers, but their destinies were later contingent on political developments unique to Eastern Europe.

The Parties

The four figures under discussion played key roles in the founding of several socialist parties in Galicia. Cross-border influences were critical to Galician socialists' particular ideological features. While Austrians in general supported internationalism and the preservation of the Habsburg Empire, Polish socialists from the Russian Empire promoted Polish independence early on as a means of liberation from Russian oppression. The two contrasting visions of Marxism and statehood gave rise to certain dilemmas for Galician socialists, marking important differences between them and their colleagues and peers elsewhere in the Habsburg Empire.

The first program of Galician socialists was drafted in 1880 in Geneva. Designed primarily by Polish exiles from the Russian Empire, it reflected the political realities of the Romanov rather than Habsburg polity, in particular including Polish independence as an ultimate goal. The Geneva program also revealed early tensions between Polish and Ukrainian socialists. The 1880 document was initially titled the "Program of Galician Polish and Ruthenian Socialists," but the word Ruthenian was dropped at the time of publication. "Galician" socialism thus became synonymous with "Polish": not only did it operate in the Polish language, but its program referred solely to Poles. Some left-wing Ukrainian activists raised concerns about Polish-Ukrainian cooperation, which in their view could hamper the development of the Ukrainian workers' movement—a sentiment reminiscent of Austrian-Czech relations in the pan-imperial party, both in the run-up to its founding and throughout its existence.[10]

Cross-border influences played a similarly important role in the development of Ukrainian socialism and Marxism in Galicia. Notably, when Czechs agreed to join pan-imperial Austrian social democracy, their Ukrainian peers took a different path. Defying the pattern of early Polish-Ukrainian cooperation, they proceeded with the founding of a nationally based socialist party. The Ruthenian-Ukrainian Radical Party (URP), formed in 1890 under the influence of Ukrainian exiles from the Russian Empire, promoted social liberation of the toiling classes and national independence as a long-term goal. The party was socialist but not Marxist, its focus being on peasants rather than workers—a reflection of the social makeup of Galicia, where agriculture still predominated. Some of the most prominent activists of the Ukrainian left, including Hankevych and Vityk, became URP members.

Whereas the URP eventually became a hotbed of Ukrainian nationalist sentiment, Hankevych and Vityk gradually shifted toward Marxism. But their early affiliations with both the Limanowski circle and the Ruthenian-Ukrainian Radical Party shed light on important developments in pan-imperial, Ukrainian, and Polish social democracy in the late imperial era. Ideological boundaries— between nationalism and socialism, nationalism and Marxism, and "ecumenical" socialism as opposed to the Marxist variety—were not as strict in the late empire as they would be after its collapse.[11]

The first Marxist party in Galicia too was a by-product of conversations within the Limanowksi circle. The Workers' Party of Galicia (later renamed the Galician Social Democratic Party, Galicyjska Partia Socjaldemokratyczna in

Polish, the GPSD) was formed in 1890, with all our protagonists joining. The dynamic within this party would be reminiscent of earlier alliances and conflicts; the GPSD participated in international socialist congresses as a Polish organization, together with colleagues from the Russian Empire.

The cross-border, transimperial ties so seminal to Marxist and socialist development in Galicia resulted in correspondingly significant rifts among socialists in Galicia, and between them and their Austrian peers. The projected resurrection of the Polish state militated against Ukrainian national interests, as the former would include territories with a large Ukrainian population.[12] A Polish independent state would also require the cooperation of socialists from different empires—a task incompatible with the varying programmatic principles within Galician social democracy. This conjuncture resulted in the creation of separate Polish and Ukrainian parties. In 1897 Daszyński and Diamand cofounded the Polish Social Democratic Party of Galicia and Silesia (PPSD). Two years later Hankevych and Vityk formed the Ukrainian Social Democratic Party of Galicia (USDP).[13] The parties became autonomous sections of the Austrian Social Democratic Party.

The unique dynamic of these two parties' relations is crucial for understanding the evolution of socialism and Marxism in post-1918 Eastern Europe. Notably, in the prewar period Hankevych and Vityk endorsed the goal of Polish independence, and Daszyński and Diamand, that of Ukrainian independence—for their conationals in the *Russian* but not the *Habsburg* Empire.

Relations between the parties' leaders would long remain amicable. Even after Galician social democracy split into two parties, Hankevych and Vityk, leaders of the Ukrainian left, continued to serve as members of the Polish Social Democratic Party's executive bureau—a situation unparalleled in the empire, where national Social Democratic sections did not otherwise thus share personnel.[14] The compatibility of nationalism with internationalism, of nationalism with Marxism, was even stronger here than in Bohemia and Austria: the transition from a national party to a Marxist one was seamless, as was the concurrent belonging to several Marxist parties organized on national principles.

By the 1890s, however, Galician socialists began to shift away from their Russia-based peers. While Limanowski had moved from Galicia, Daszyński, Diamand, Vityk, and Hankevych became more present in Vienna—not just physically, but also in terms of political and ideological influence through their participation in congresses of the Austrian Social Democratic Party and, later, their involvement in the Austrian parliament and other institutions in the capital. Both Daszyński and Diamand were frequent guests in Adler's home. Adler's understanding of Marxism was different from that of Limanowski; despite their shared support of internationalism, their ideas of how it should be implemented varied greatly. While Limanowski and other Polish socialists from the Russian Empire saw Lemberg/Lwów as a platform where they could realize political ideas that they had developed in Warsaw or in exile in Western Europe, Galician socialists themselves would increasingly look to Vienna for models and direction.

Unlike their peers from the Russian Empire, moreover, Galician socialists were increasingly exposed to Austrian institutionalism. Several of our protagonists served as deputies. Daszyński was elected in 1897, becoming at thirty the parliament's youngest member, and immediately distinguished himself as one of its most charismatic and sophisticated voices. Diamand was elected in 1907 and became one of the parliament's most prominent specialists in economics. Vityk too secured a mandate in 1907. In the late Habsburg era the parliament suffered from organizational chaos, but the experience it afforded nevertheless mattered; for example, the very mobilization required for election campaigns and the alliances one had to form (or not form) to wage them were part of the imperial institutional upbringing.

It became clear early on that socialism and Marxism in the Habsburg and Russian Empires had divergent developmental patterns and aims. For those mentored by Adler, incremental political action was the norm, and force a deviation; whereas it was typical for activists in the Russian Empire to view the state as primarily an incarnation of violence, one that could only be combated by similar means. Despite close and prolonged cooperation, cross-border ties between the Habsburg and Russian Empires fueled rather than undermined Austrian patriotism. The Russian Empire, for many, epitomized violence and repression and was seen as a breeding ground for the same; the Habsburg Empire, by contrast, seemed a haven for internationalism of the sort no succeeding unitary nation-state would be likely to match. "If Poles in Russia had as much freedom as Czechs have in Austria," Daszyński noted in a conversation with the Czech socialist Bohumír Šmeral, "there would not be this deadly animosity between Poles and Russians."[15] In a speech to the parliament in 1912, Vityk decried the Russian Empire's "suppression of a nation of twenty-eight million . . . sending the sons thereof to prison and Siberia."[16] Daszyński opposed the idea of importing tactics used by socialists in the Russian Empire to Galicia.[17] The Lemberg/Lwów–Vienna vector became gradually more important than the Lemberg/Lwów–Warsaw or –Geneva connections.

On Nationalism and Internationalism

The late 1890s and early 1900s also revealed unresolved tensions between the PPSD and USDP, as the two sought to secure their influence in Galicia. Because of the structures of pan-imperial social democracy, the split in the Galician wing was to the advantage of the Polish over the Ukrainian party. Though recognized as an autonomous member of the Austrian Social Democratic Party in the empire, the USDP struggled for corresponding status at international congresses. In 1907 in Amsterdam, for instance, Ukrainian socialists were only granted permission to attend as part of the Polish delegation.[18] Nothing encapsulated better the tensions between Polish and Ukrainian socialists than the Galician election campaigns: otherwise amicable relationships would fray, despite the outward commitment to a single electoral list that was to benefit socialism as a whole.

Just as elsewhere in the empire, the most contentious disagreements flared up not between but rather within ethnic-based parties. In particular, the separatist tendencies of Czech Social Democrats inspired the younger generation of Ukrainian activists. Tensions within the USDP escalated in 1910, during Limanowski's seventy-fifth birthday celebration. Convening in the Skarbek Theater—a landmark of the Galician capital, and a center of local cultural life—the crowd was as diverse as the Limanowksi-hosted gatherings of the 1870s.[19] Both Hankevych and Vityk were in attendance, the former toasting the guest of honor and expressing the hope that he would "live to see an independent Warsaw."[20] This amicable exchange, as well as Hankevych and Vityk's long-standing dual positions within the PPSD and USDP, provoked a strong reaction among younger Ukrainian socialists, resulting in a split of the USDP along the lines of the Czech Social Democrats.

In February 1911, Julian Bachynskyi, a onetime Ukrainian socialist turned nationalist, offered some rather snide advice to his former associates in an article titled "The Reciprocal Relationships between the Polish and Ukrainian Social Democratic Parties in Galicia." "The party," he wrote, "should once and for all put an end to the duality manifested in the hermaphroditism of its official representatives, comrades Mykola Hankevych and Semen Vityk."[21]

The political provocativeness of the term "hermaphroditism" and Hankevych and Vityk's particular double duty notwithstanding, the ideological backdrop of this situation was nothing out of the ordinary; Marxists in particular prioritized multiethnic politics over nationalism.

The conflict Bachynskyi referred to, moreover, was emblematic of the general trends in Austrian social democracy: tensions between internationalism and nationalism, centralism and autonomy, and cross-border influences. Around the time of his article, the schism within the Czechoslovak Social Democratic Party influenced similar nationalist tendencies within other national sections of the party, including in Galicia. The conflict within the USDP, however, cannot be attributed solely to the example set by separatist Czech Social Democrats. The origins of Galician social democracy and the region's particular status as a borderland accounted for the specific pattern of relations among Galician socialists. In 1911 Hankevych and Vityk both left the USDP, a break that inaugurated a long period of soul-searching for the two.

Hankevych's family epitomized both the national fluidity of this region and the ethnic tensions that even Marxists and socialists could be subject to. Whereas Mykola Hankevych supported Polish-Ukrainian alliances, his younger brother Lev was opposed.[22] For the Hankevych brothers, the debate of nationalism versus internationalism was a personal one that went unresolved to the end of their lives. Under the empire, the two cooperated within the same party, and even after the split in the USDP adhered to some of the same values. But the empire's collapse would bring on a crisis of different proportions that affected them both more severely.

Vityk's political peregrinations in the wake of the 1911 USDP split likewise help explain his personal and political choices after 1918. In 1911 he tried to join the PPSD but encountered Polish opposition on ethnic grounds, with various PPSD members protesting the inclusion of a Ukrainian.[23] He then joined the German section of the Austrian Social Democratic Party as a corresponding member, but he was forced to leave within two years, expelled on charges of financial corruption linked to ethnic-based politics.[24] The accusations against Vityk were never confirmed, but the rumors damaged his reputation: he was alleged not only to have misappropriated funds but also to have jeopardized the socialists' electoral chances. Vityk's exclusion from multiple branches of the party followed from certain of his choices, but it also reflected the gradual "ethnicizing" of socialism in the empire. He remained unaffiliated until 1914, when the USDP united its former ranks, bringing the centralists and separatists back together.[25]

Jewishness, Nationalism, Marxism

National conflicts within Galician social democracy did not cease with the founding of separate Polish and Ukrainian parties. In 1905 a cohort of socialists in Galicia organized the Jewish Social Democratic Party—the only one of its kind in the Habsburg Empire. It was not uncommon for socialists of Jewish descent to face national dilemmas in the empire; but the founding of a Jewish Social Democratic Party in Galicia—and not anywhere else in the realm—was yet another reflection of the region's particular ethnic makeup. More numerous than elsewhere in the Habsburg Empire, the Jews of Galicia were also different. In particular, while assimilationism was prominent in Galician society in the latter half of the nineteenth century, so too were traditional and orthodox Judaism. Cross-border ties with the Russian Empire affected the socialism of Jews as well. The Polish Socialist Party in Russia (PPS) had a Jewish section, and a separate Jewish socialist party, the Bund, was established in the Russian Empire in 1897, with many members of the PPS joining in.[26]

By contrast, Austrian Social Democrats, and in particular members of the PPSD, looked askance at the idea of a separate, Jewish socialism. Herman Diamand of the PPSD, for example, reflected the awkward position of Galician Jews who wavered between assimilation, tradition, nationalism, internationalism, and the two empires. In his youth he had experimented with Zionism; contemporaries even described him as "a true national Jew."[27] Later in life he endorsed assimilation and internationalism, and denounced the founding of a separate Jewish party.[28] The Jewish Social Democratic Party never took root, mainly because of such opposition on the part of assimilated Jewish Social Democrats in Galicia and Austria. Barred from participating in the general party convention, the organization soon dissolved.[29]

But this marked the beginning, not the end, of debates on Jewishness, nationalism, and Marxism in Austrian social democracy. In 1907, two years after the Jewish Social Democratic Party's abortive founding, Otto Bauer addressed the issue of Jewish national identity and socialism in his groundbreaking *The Question of Nationalities and Social Democracy*. Did Jews, in fact, constitute a nation? Where did assimilated Jews fit in the modern world? For Bauer, Jewishness was only one aspect of his identity, hardly predominant.[30]

The Jews had "given up their [separate] culture," he argued.[31] In Vienna the central committee of the Social Democratic Workers' Party of Austria refused to recognize an autonomous Jewish section; most Jewish members likewise preferred to remain in non-Jewish parties.

Bauer's stance on the subject reflected his personal views and those of many of his colleagues in the empire-wide party who had similar Jewish family backgrounds. But the political urgency of Jewish national concerns meant that Jewish socialism would develop differently in Galicia than elsewhere in the empire. This represents a subset of the trend by which nationalism impinged on Galician socialism more aggressively than in other Habsburg lands: the legacy of eighteenth-century Polish statehood; cross-border ties with the Russian Empire; and the particular experience of the region's Jewish population—these all played their part.

War: The Eastern Front and Socialists

In Galicia especially, it was the war that ultimately destroyed socialist internationalism. None of the figures discussed in this chapter fought in the war, but the conflict did make an immediate and lasting impact on their lives. Their experience was more like that of their friends and colleagues on the Adriatic coast, that other liminal zone, than in the Austrian interior; the conflagration unleashed by decisions made in European capitals affected, above all, the people of the borderlands.

The news of the war came as a shock. Diamand's notes from the early days reveal the emotional unpreparedness that many experienced in the summer of 1914: "After reading the news of the ultimatum I felt stunned; could not sleep the entire night."[32] He largely kept away from Galicia, relocating his family to inner Austria. In July 1915 he visited Lemberg/Lwów, probably for the first time since the war had begun, and reported back to his wife: "I am in a strange state; walking around Lwów as if nothing had happened; there are a lot of military personnel, a lot of commotion, but the buildings, the alleys, and the shops are all there as before. But the heart senses immediately that the Russians had been here, they plagued the city, destroyed morals, placed themselves above people."[33]

The experience of Galician socialists would be conditioned by the politics of the Russian as well as Habsburg Empires. Having predicted in 1912 that there would be war over Galicia, Daszyński now declared that all socialists should join forces against Russia and make common cause with Austria, "their natural ally."[34] Like most other socialists under the Habsburgs, in 1914 Daszyński supported the preservation of the empire.

Initially, both Daszyński and Diamand aspired to a Polish autonomous unit within the Habsburg monarchy. In the summer of 1915 in Lemberg/Lwów, Diamand joined the Polish Supreme National Committee, which promoted autonomy within the Habsburg Empire. He also attended meetings of Galician Jewish organizations, promoting Polish-Jewish cooperation.[35] In 1916, however, the PPSD added independence to its platform.[36] Daszyński now endorsed Polish statehood, on equal terms with Austria: "Our geographic, historical, national, and political situation is such that it poses no threat to the Austrian state," he declared in a speech to the Austrian parliament in January 1917.[37] Poles, he continued, would like to maintain friendly relations with Austria; as for other nationalities, it was up to them to decide whether to remain in the monarchy or to proceed with independence.[38] For Daszyński, and Diamand as well, independence was an option that presented itself as a result of the war.[39]

The pro-independence shift came even more gradually among Ukrainian socialists. In 1915 Hankevych joined the Main Ukrainian Council, which, analogous to the Polish Council of which Diamand was a member, promoted Ukrainian autonomy in Galicia within a politically limited scope.[40] His colleague Vityk decried Austrian military defeats, but still believed the empire might last. Only in mid-October 1918 did he finally admit that the country "could no longer exist in its present form."[41] Indeed, the commitment to the empire on the part of these Ukrainian socialists was not unlike that shown by Polish conservatives, notably Leon Biliński; all supported the Habsburgs even after the empire had collapsed.

Daszyński and Diamand between Vienna, Lwów, and Warsaw

Poland emerged victorious from the war but had to struggle to retain its independence and territory through the four subsequent years of what has come to be known as the "Russian Civil War" but might more accurately be called the "War of Russian Imperial Succession." This civil war affected territories outside of Russia and their non-Russian inhabitants to an even greater degree than most of Russia's interior. It was this prolonged conflict that determined the fate of Polish statehood.

Despite the brutality of Polish-Ukrainian violence in Galicia, the civil war evinced the survival of the multiethnic socialist legacy of the Limanowski circle of the 1870s. In 1919, for example, during the Polish-Ukrainian stage of the conflict, Daszyński opposed the incorporation of Ukrainian and Belorussian territories into Poland, arguing instead for the creation of an independent Ukraine as a buffer state between Poland and Soviet Russia—in effect the latest instance of the support he had shown for Ukrainian autonomy since the late nineteenth century.[42] He changed his mind within a few years and in 1921 endorsed Warsaw's negotiations with Soviet Russia in Riga.[43] Yet across the years, the socialists defended federalism and national autonomy against Poland's nationalists, who sought to enforce centralism instead.[44]

Independence caused a great deal of practical difficulties. For Daszyński and Diamand, it entailed a move from Vienna—their first or second home—to Warsaw, a place they had known only indirectly, and which seemed alien to many Galicians. Warsaw had been part of a different political and intellectual space; the movement of Galician socialists between the Russian and Habsburg Empires had been largely unilateral—from Warsaw to Lemberg/Lwów, but not the other way around. Warsaw lacked the coffeehouse culture that had long been so crucial to the interactions of Austrian socialists and their practice of politics. The Polish capital also lacked many of the institutions long a norm in Vienna and Lemberg/Lwów. Parliamentarism had been nonexistent in the Russian Empire for most of its history, and the sort of local governance and autonomy that had played such a crucial role in Galicia had barely taken root.

Each of the new states faced economic difficulties on an almost unprecedented scale, and each of our protagonists was affected in various ways. "My apartment [in Warsaw] gets heat only every other day," wrote Diamand in February 1920 to his wife in Lwów.[45] Yet Vienna was now worse off than Warsaw: "It is so cold in my apartment that I cannot stay home," Diamand commented during a brief sojourn in the Austrian capital in October 1920.[46] Deprived of the empire's former industrial stronghold that was now part of Czechoslovakia, Austria suffered a severe economic crisis in the first postwar years.

Both Diamand and Daszyński shuttled between Vienna and Warsaw immediately after the war. This was to become, figuratively, an ever-longer journey as the two countries and their political establishments drifted further apart amid contentious territorial and financial settlements. Only then did Warsaw become a new home—not only because of personal choices, but also under the pressure of political contingencies in the new Europe.

As in Austria and Czechoslovakia, in post-1918 Poland the Social Democrats, incarnate in the Polish Socialist Party (PPS), consisting of different sections from the three former empires, became a major political force. The PPS built on imperial precedents and cross-border cooperation from the pre-war period. Several leading members of the party, including Józef Piłsudski himself, Poland's head of state, had resided in Galicia before 1918. Former members of the PPSD advanced politically as well. Daszyński in 1919 became vice premier. Diamand was elected to the parliament, where he became involved in financial and economic reforms as a member of numerous commissions, just as he had done under the empire.

Daszyński's career hinged on imperial precedents, and his choices invariably reflected his imperial experience. Well known under Habsburg rule as a spellbinding speaker, he carried this reputation with him into the new Republic of Poland. "The Sejm and the entire gallery anticipated Daszyński's first speech in the parliament as if he were a great celebrity," commented his contemporary, the journalist and writer Bernard Singer. Part of his charm lay in his physical presence; Singer recalls him as "a tall man, dressed in black, with grey hair and long arms."[47] Daszyński's profile as a lion of Polish politics endured into the 1930s.[48]

PPS club in the Polish parliament, 1919–20. Polish National Library, Digital Collection Polona.

The legacy of the Habsburg Empire loomed over Polish politics for decades, revealed in various personal and political flare-ups in Warsaw after 1918. Polish nationalists accused Daszyński of having supported Austro-Hungary's former foreign minister Ottokar Czernin, "the minister of peace," in 1918.[49] If Daszyński was too Austrian, Diamand was, according to the Polish nationalist press, too German or too Jewish. From 1919 to 1927 he divided his time between Warsaw and Berlin, preparing trade agreements between the two countries. Attending international socialist congresses, he would later fondly recall his meetings with Austrian and German colleagues.[50] But as an assimilated Jew and a German-speaking Polonophile, he was after 1918 considered "not Polish enough." Despite their ideological disagreements, then, similarities among Galicians were hard to ignore; they seemed to share the same demeanor and even attire, and most important the same "coffeehouse politics"—all of which set them apart from their colleagues from the other parts of Poland.

Just as conservatives and nationalists from Galicia came to play an important role in post-1918 Poland, so did their socialist peers, who collaborated with associates and friends from the former Russian Empire. Daszyński's role in the politics of the new Poland, especially before 1926, was every bit as important as Piłsudski's. The Austrian models of incrementalist and democratic socialism, federalism and autonomy, and multiethnic politics became integral to the post-1918 Polish Socialist Party.

Hankevych in Post-1918 Lwów

Whereas Poland survived the civil wars of 1917–21, Ukraine in this period lost its chance for independence. Two Ukrainian states had appeared on maps by November 1918: the Ukrainian People's Republic in Kyiv, formerly under Russian rule, and the Western Ukrainian People's Republic in Lwów/L'viv—an attempt to transform Eastern Galicia, with its Ukrainian majority, into an independent Ukrainian state. But neither of these polities survived past 1921. That year all of Galicia was annexed by Poland, the acquisition officially acknowledged by the Allies in 1923. Eastern Ukraine became Sovietized and in December 1922 joined the newly founded USSR.

Vityk and Hankevych now faced choices of a different magnitude than did their Polish peers, the Ukrainians being the only ethnoterritorial group discussed here to not have a nation-state of their own in interwar Europe.

Galician Ukrainians dispersed all over Europe. Some emigrated to Austria, Germany, or Switzerland; others stayed in what was now Poland. But some Galician Ukrainians found themselves in the Soviet Union. This de facto diaspora represents an underappreciated repercussion of the empire's collapse: the geographic redistribution of this particular cohort in post-1918 Europe was broader and more diverse than almost any other group from the former empire.

Galician Ukrainians' ideological trajectories in the interwar period often reflected a continuity across the epochal divide of 1918, but some members of this cohort would experience a particularly novel desperation, feeling truly lost in the new Europe. And though they chose different solutions and paths, the roots of their decisions can be traced to the pre-1918 period.

Mykola Hankevych's family illustrated some of this national discord, now particularly aggravated by the civil war. In 1889 he had had a love affair and a son with a Jewish fellow socialist, Róża Vorzimmer (neé Altenberg). The two later separated, and the boy, Henryk, was raised by Róża and her husband, Jakub Vorzimmer. After this marriage fell apart in 1907, Róża raised three children, Henryk and his two older siblings, by herself. Róża, an assimilated Jew, was a Polonophile, and she raised her children to identify as Poles. In November 1918 Henryk enlisted in the Polish army, serving to demonstrate that Polishness and Ukrainianness were no longer compatible.[51]

Dreading the looming outbreak of a Polish-Ukrainian civil war, Mykola Hankevych used his connections to contact Daszyński, then head of Poland's temporary government, in a desperate attempt to head off this interethnic violence.[52] On November 25, 1918, he was the only Ukrainian to attend a meeting of the Polish magistrate in the city of Lwów/L'viv, using the occasion to condemn Polish-Ukrainian fighting as well as Polish and Ukrainian involvement in anti-Jewish pogroms.[53]

The war and the brutality of Polish-Ukrainian violence did not shake Hankevych's commitment to Polish-Ukrainian amity. In December 1920 he took part in the fifth congress of the Ukrainian Social Democratic Party, which had renewed its activities after a long pause. There he delivered an address that echoed and reaffirmed the principle on which he had founded the USDP back in 1899: an insistence on "an independent Ukraine and an independent Poland." That same year of 1920, he expressed great respect for Piłsudski.[54] In September 1921, months after the conclusion of the Riga treaties that assigned Galicia to Poland, Hankevych shared his views on the Ukraine/Poland issue in an article for a socialist periodical: "It is true that the fate of today's Ukraine is not the same as the fate of Poland. Yet the historical process in Eastern Europe has just begun, and is not yet complete. . . . History shows how dangerous wars between Poland and Ukraine can be. . . . A necessary condition of Polish democracy and Polish independence is an alliance with all the peoples of the [former] Russian Empire—from Finland to the Caucasus—and a free and independent Ukrainian republic."[55]

Just as he had in the empire, Hankevych still believed after 1918 that the fates of independent Poland and Ukraine were intertwined, and that both polities could be secured through interethnic (and now, in the common sense, international) cooperation. In early 1921 he insisted that European stability was contingent on Ukrainian independence. "Peace and stability in Europe," he wrote, "can only be achieved under conditions of freedom and independence for the peoples who, after long centuries of oppression, have received a historic chance for same."[56]

But it was one thing to promote such cooperation under the Habsburg Empire, and something else entirely to do so after 1918, after Poland had taken territories many Ukrainians considered their own. Hankevych's consistent support of Polish-Ukrainian cooperation caused further rifts between him and his colleagues from the USDP in Galicia. He now faced accusations of national betrayal, of prioritizing Polish over Ukrainian interests. The USDP published an official condemnation in the party's major periodical *Vpered* (*Onward*):

> Polish comrades dreamt of seeing a people's Poland, . . . a democratic Poland in alliance with other democratic states. Hankevych became excited by this idea. . . . He became its major advocate. He concluded almost every speech with the slogan: "Long live independent Poland and independent Ukraine." This slogan became his political faith, his "blood and bones." . . . Hankevych stood at the head of the Ukrainian party, but he had never severed ties with Polish social democracy. Instead, he became the "viceroy of the PPS."[57]

This post-1918 criticism of Hankevych was based on imperial precedents, on the reputation he had secured in the empire and the practices he carried on after its collapse. His reluctance to adjust to the new political realities and his continual endorsement of Polish socialists resulted in his expulsion from the USDP in December 1921.

Poster of Mykola Hankevych's invitation for a talk at a meeting of Polish socialists in the early 1920s. Polish National Library, Digital Collection Polona.

Vityk in Post-1918 Vienna

Like Hankevych, Semen Vityk struggled to find his political way in the new Europe. But while Hankevych remained in Poland, Vityk chose a different path. In late 1919, after Lwów had fallen to Polish forces, Vityk moved back to Vienna and spent several decisive years there. At the time, the capital of the new Republic of Austria played host to a large contingent of émigrés from Eastern Europe and Russia, persons who, like Vityk himself, had fled Poland, Bolshevism, or both. In coming to Vienna, Vityk was in a way returning home. He blended into his German-speaking surroundings with an ease rare among members of the city's Eastern European émigré community.

Vienna's considerable Ukrainian contingent included some who had formerly lived under Habsburg rule, and others who had emigrated from the

Ukrainian territory that had been part of the Russian Empire. In the latter category was Nadia Surovtsova, a former official of the Ukrainian People's Republic who had left Kyiv in 1918 upon the Bolsheviks' coming to power there. In Vienna she became active in Ukrainian émigré circles and rented rooms in her apartment to people from all over. In 1924 Vityk showed up at Surovtsova's door, having probably been referred to her by a mutual acquaintance. They shared an apartment for about a year and eventually came to endorse a similar ideology. Surovtsova, who had come of age in the Russian Empire, was struck by Vityk's Austrianness. "Vityk," she wrote, "had something in him that was typical of a 'Mr. Deputy.'[58] . . . A former deputy of the Austrian parliament, he retained some of their features. Even in his shabby overcoat and old suit, he still had what they called 'the look.'"[59]

Years after the collapse of the Habsburg dynasty, former Austrian deputies such as Vityk stood out in a crowd, even literally, on the streets of their new or old cities and in the new institutions that sprang up in the post-1918 successor states. As Surovtsova put it:

> It is funny how other Galicians . . . who did not like [Vityk], or who even hated him, had exactly the same features as he did. . . . They were very different from our Dnieper Ukrainians [from the former Russian Empire], but I cannot really define this difference. Perhaps it was because ours were in a completely foreign land, while the Galicians, even after the revolution, felt at home in Austria; and perhaps because in their education and manners, even in the way they looked, they were European, while the vast majority of Ukrainians from the east had features of provincials, lost in someone's else market.[60]

The intellectual and political culture of Café Central continued to define Galician socialists for years after the empire's collapse. These people, in the formulation of another contemporary, were the "coffeehouse socialists"—a designation alluding to their Austrian past: in Austria, politics indeed was often conducted *at* cafés.[61] Vityk, widely known as "Mr. Semko," was "an elegant figure who frequented coffeehouses."[62] This type of politics was utterly alien to those from elsewhere, and these patterns would mark divides between Austrian and Russian Poles as well as Austrian and Russian Ukrainians for the rest of their lives.

Like many of his socialist peers, Vityk evinced a progressive and internationalist spirit in his personal life as well. Late in life, he married Ruża

Lonska, an "exalted lonely woman" of Jewish-Polish heritage. He treated her "with irony" but did put her to work for the Ukrainian cause. She followed him, if "rather loudly," participating in politics and supporting her husband in his Ukrainian aspirations.[63] Lonska shared her husband's peregrinations and his fate.

It was in Vienna, a city incarnating a spirit of impoverished cosmopolitanism and seemingly living on the memory of imperial might, that Vityk became a communist. His choice represented a response to the personal and professional crises he had experienced after 1918. Like his Czech comrade Bohumír Šmeral, he was aghast at the post-Habsburg national fragmentation of social democracy. Additionally burdened by the failure of Ukrainian national aspirations, he became one of several socialists to shift leftward after 1918. Like the others, he saw communism as a continuation of Austro-Marxism; the multiethnic Soviet Union became for him the best venue for translating Austro-Marxist ideas into praxis.

Imperial-era Social Democrats who turned to communism after 1918 were most likely to be national minorities—especially Slovenes and Ukrainians—either trapped in a nation-state dominated by an ethnic group not their own, or having no state at all. Activists who evolved in this direction were all driven by disillusionment with traditional socialism, whose adherents had divided along national lines and were reluctant to offer assistance to minorities—who had deprioritized, that is, their proclaimed principle of interethnic tolerance and in effect left their national-minority comrades to their own devices. Chaos and frustration, of course, were pervasive in the postwar years, and national-majority socialists had their own ideological and political crises to weather. But minorities, particularly Slovenes and Ukrainians, were affected more severely than others, and were more likely to endorse radical solutions.

In Vienna Vityk became part of a larger cohort increasingly sympathetic to the Bolsheviks and Soviet Ukraine as an alternative to Poland. In 1921 he became the editor of a periodical titled *Nova hromada* (New society), which was alleged to be funded by the Soviet consulate in Vienna.[64] "Our journal," Vityk wrote in a letter to a friend, "is designed to provide an analysis of the political, social, and economic conditions in Soviet Ukraine, as well as in the territories annexed to Poland."[65] But the primary aim of the journal was not just to survey the existing situation but also "to awaken criticism in the minds of our citizens, to unite Ukrainian forces toward the revival of a Ukrainian state, based on the power of the working classes of Ukraine."[66] Unlike Šmeral,

Vityk expressed no reservations about the Soviet version of communism. He claimed that the Bolsheviks had succeeded where all previous regimes failed by granting national and social liberation to the working masses. In Soviet Ukraine, that is, he believed his dream had come true.

Much like Šmeral, Vityk believed that communism would be a continuation of pre-1914 socialism. In his view, Austro-Marxist models could be planted on Soviet soil: the Soviet Union would thus build on the Austrian experience. This belief was not a product of starry-eyedness, but rather reflected the realities of the early Soviet Union. The ethnic autonomy projects that had been debated but never implemented under the Habsburg Empire finally found their realization under Soviet rule.

Soviet Ukraine and National Autonomy

Ukraine became Soviet as a result of the civil war and Bolshevik military expansion into Ukrainian territories between late 1917 and early 1921. The Bolsheviks had a strong base among Ukrainians in the Russian Empire, with the party having a considerable Ukrainian membership even before 1917.[67] The Ukrainian Soviet Socialist Republic (USSR), first established in late 1917 with its capital in Kharkiv, was nominally independent from Soviet Russia, but both polities were headed by the same Communist Party with its central bureau in Moscow.[68] By early 1921 the Bolsheviks had occupied most of the Ukrainian territories of the former Russian Empire. The year 1922 marked the ultimate merger, as the USSR became the second largest republic in the newly founded Union of Soviet Socialist Republics.

The October Revolution and the Bolsheviks' efforts to extend their power over all territories of the former Russian Empire brought a new urgency to the nationalities question. The Bolsheviks' thinking on this issue evolved over the years but had its roots in the pre-1914 period; their national program, as Francine Hirsch has explained, was designed in virtual dialogue with Austrian Social Democrats.[69] As mentioned in the previous chapter, Stalin's Vienna-based research had led him to reject Austro-Marxist national solutions; in his view, federalism would foster interethnic conflict and potentially threaten class unity.[70] For his part, in his capacity as a revolutionary, Lenin initially promoted self-determination of the oppressed national minorities of the Russian Empire, and in 1914 argued for their right to secede.[71] But by 1918 he insisted that the goal of ethnic autonomy must not be allowed to weaken the interethnic unity of the workers now under Soviet power; secession, he argued, would only benefit the bourgeoisie, not the toiling masses. Independence would thus not be allowed.

The Bolsheviks' insistence that national self-determination must be accomplished *within* the Soviet state led them, in the course of their post-1918 establishment of control over most of the former Russian Empire, to become what Stephen Kotkin has described as "accidental federalists."[72] In 1918, Stalin, then serving as head of the Soviet Commissariat on Nationalities, insisted on federation as a model for the Soviet state—part of an effort to appeal to national minorities, especially Ukrainians. In 1921, acting on his promises of self-determination, Lenin proposed solving the "nationalities question" by granting a form of nationhood to ethnic minorities within the Soviet state.

While Wilsonian self-determination, or the "Wilson moment," has received its due attention in scholarship, the Bolshevik alternative has, outside of Russia, been marginalized in general studies on Europe.[73] Lenin's emphasis on self-determination, however, indeed had a broad appeal and contributed to the Bolshevik consolidation of control over territories of the former Russian Empire in the first years of Soviet power.

In 1923, after the founding of the Soviet Union, the Bolsheviks undertook a program of extensive national autonomy of a kind that was unprecedented in Europe. Both Lenin and Stalin continued to oppose the concept of extraterritorial *personal* autonomy but endorsed the creation of multiple ethnoterritorial units for different minorities within the Soviet Union. The Bolsheviks thus implemented a modified version of the national autonomy that Austro-Marxists had theorized under Habsburg rule. This Soviet "nativization" (*korenizatsiia*) campaign supported schooling in the native language of national minorities, and promoted local ethnic cadres over Russians. In 1923 in Soviet Ukraine, the Ukrainian language was made mandatory in education systems and administration. The Soviet Union thus became, in Terry Martin's definition, the "affirmative action empire," the first state to promote underrepresented minorities over the majority.[74]

Vityk between Vienna and Kharkiv

For activists such as Vityk, these early Bolshevik policies gave much cause for optimism. In the early 1920s Vityk became part of a large cohort of statesmen and intellectuals who increasingly signaled a fascination with the Soviet Union. Most of these now endorsed Soviet rule, having initially opposed the Bolshevik takeover. This "change of signposts" movement included a large number of Ukrainians who saw Soviet Ukraine as the only form of Ukrainian statehood available at the time. This polity was part of the Soviet Union but had its own government, parliament, and, during the 1920s, Ukrainian-language schooling and administration. "The Union of Soviet Socialist Republics is a grand international player, and Ukraine occupies the second position in it," wrote Vityk in 1924.[75]

Having endorsed the Soviet Union, Vityk decided to relocate there in 1925, moving his family from Vienna to Kharkiv, at the time the capital of Soviet Ukraine.[76] There he joined the Club of Political Immigrants and the International Bureau of Assistance to Fighters for Revolution, and became head of the history section of the Politburo of the Ukrainian SSR.[77] He and Surovtsova were moreover employed in the Foreign Ministry's commission on Ukrainian émigrés.[78]

This commission's task was in effect to keep tabs on Ukrainians outside of the Soviet Union, with an eye toward identifying "bourgeois" elements potentially hostile to Soviet power.[79] Men such as Vityk, long immersed in Ukrainian politics and with deep ties to Ukrainians in Galicia and émigrés in Western Europe, made perfect candidates for such an assignment. Vityk threw himself into this work with a passion, like many other Soviet operatives at the time who truly believed in the proclaimed ideals of communism and national and social liberation. Whether Vityk fully comprehended the implications of this activity for other people's lives is unclear. In retrospect, Surovtsova commented, "Slaves to the socialist and national camps, we were committed to the party, the Fatherland, and the communist idea. . . . This database would later be used by those who unscrupulously destroyed the communists and noncommunists of Ukraine. That is the story of my last joint work with Semen Vityk."[80] As Surovtsova notes, some of those appearing in the database were later persecuted by the Stalinist authorities. In any case, Vityk must have known that by joining the Commissariat of Foreign Affairs he was agreeing to work for the Soviet security services.[81]

Come and See: Cross-Border Propaganda

Ideological differences hardly meant the end of friendships first formed under the Habsburg Empire. For example, even during the postwar period of heightened tensions, while living between Vienna, Kharkiv, and Lwów/L'viv, Vityk and Hankevych exchanged information about mutual friends and shared their views on politics. They stayed in touch through at least the late 1920s, even as they drifted further apart politically.

While Vityk considered communism a continuation of Austro-Marxism, Hankevych, like most of the socialists who had come of age in the Habsburg Empire, still regarded it as a deviation, a far cry from properly democratic socialism. What Vityk enthusiastically hailed as the "dictatorship of the proletariat," Hankevych mocked as the "dictatorship over the proletariat."[82] Vityk, however, continue to impress his enthusiasm upon his friend. In a January 1926 letter to Hankevych, he wrote, "As you may know, for the last four months I have been living in Kharkiv. During this time, I have familiarized myself with the local situation here, and learned it from inside. The most important fact is that there are no oppressors here. The dreams we could only dare to dream during our meetings in 1895 and 1897, ideals we set for the future, all the things for which we were mocked by the others . . . here it has come true."[83] In the same letter, following the best tradition of Soviet propaganda, Vityk invited Hankevych to come to Soviet Ukraine: "Come and see it for yourself." Vityk must have known that at least some of those who came would decide to stay, granting additional legitimacy to the Soviet system.

Socialism and Communism in Galicia

Vityk's message would fall on fertile ground among many Ukrainian socialists in Galicia who, unlike Hankevych, rejected a Polish-Ukrainian alliance and looked for solutions elsewhere. The year 1921 marked the beginning of a leftward shift among Galician Ukrainian socialists, as they responded to the civil war and the annexation of Galicia to Poland. The Hankevych family epitomized the relevant divisions. In Galicia, Lev Hankevych, Mykola's younger brother and a prominent proponent of separatism under the empire, initiated a pro-Soviet faction among Ukrainian socialists.[84] This leftist faction openly boycotted the Polish government and increasingly supported Soviet Russia.

The year 1923, when the international community officially recognized Poland's annexation of Galicia, saw a further radicalization within the USDP. The Allies' ratification of Poland's move had come with the proviso of ethnic autonomy, specifically for Ukrainians. The Polish government, however, proceeded to eliminate any traces of such autonomy that had remained since the Habsburg period. Polish-ruled Galicia thus became a sharp contrast to the Soviet Ukraine next door, where extensive national autonomy was the norm.

At its 1923 annual congress, the USDP adopted a resolution in favor of Soviet power: "The Ukrainian Socialist Republic is the only representation of Ukrainian statehood. Contemporary Soviet Ukraine, despite not fully reflecting our aspirations and slogans, is not a fiction, but is the only possible form of statehood capable of fulfilling all the national and social needs of the Ukrainian working classes."[85] Despite its shift to the left, the USDP retained its name and claimed continuity with the pre-1918 party.

While the USDP's evolution followed from domestic developments in pre- and post-1918 Galicia, a more radical faction of leftist activists eventually did consolidate into a communist party. The Communist Party of Eastern Galicia, founded in 1919, was renamed the Communist Party of Western Ukraine (KPZU) in 1923 and eventually split into two factions. One group endorsed cooperation with Polish communists; the other worked with the Communist Party of [Soviet] Ukraine to target its outreach to the Ukrainian population, especially "the USDP, which became ever more infiltrated by [the communists]."[86] This KPZU posed a greater threat to Poland as currently constituted than did the Polish Communist Party itself: national minorities, particularly Ukrainians, were more prone than Poles to militate against the government in Warsaw. Moreover, the KPZU included a large contingent of non-Galicians: émigrés from Eastern Ukraine who had come to Galicia to help build communism there. The party thus became a beachhead of Soviet influence in Poland. Equally alarming to the Warsaw authorities was the USDP's gradual convergence with it; in 1924, therefore, both parties were banned.[87]

The communization of socialist parties in post-Habsburg successor states across Europe had some of the same causes; in particular, national-minority socialists reacted to the post-1918 crises in remarkably similar ways in both Galicia and on the Adriatic. Antagonized by their governments, and with little or no support from Polish and Italian socialists respectively, they shifted to the left, finding refuge in communism—the only doctrine and movement that adhered to internationalism and offered protection to minorities.

Russian intervention nevertheless made the Galician case different from the rest of Europe. In this region Soviet propagandists acted like missionaries, spreading—with the assistance of local Ukrainian fellow thinkers—the perception that Poland and socialism equaled national and social oppression, while the Soviet Union and communism offered salvation. The communization of Ukrainian Social Democrats was a product of Poland's nationalities policy in Galicia, Soviet nationalities policy in the Ukrainian SSR, and Soviet outreach in Galicia.

Conclusions

By the late 1920s our four protagonists had shifted far apart geographically and ideologically. Ignacy Daszyński and Herman Diamand remained in a Poland that, from 1926 on, would slip into authoritarianism, but they stayed active in politics. Their Ukrainian imperial-era colleagues were still more displaced in every sense. While Semen Vityk enjoyed the peak of his political career in Kharkiv, Mykola Hankevych became increasingly isolated. In 1928 he made efforts to revive the USDP on the Austrian noncommunist model. The party did come back to life, but only as a faint echo of its predecessor. Hankevych died in Shklo (near Lwów) on July 31, 1931. Vityk outlived him, but the late 1920s marked a new phase in his life and career: a turn in Soviet policies would affect him personally—a story that continues in the last chapter of this book.

It was Austrian social democracy that inspired many of the ideas of Daszyński, Diamand, Vityk, and Hankevych, and they carried that inheritance with them well beyond 1918. Their different interpretations of the imperial legacy took them in different directions, both geographically and ideologically, but the continuity of the tradition revealed itself in their personal and professional decisions after 1918, including what country to choose as their home; how, or whether, to engage in politics; and their general outlook and daily routines. Austro-Marxist practices lived on not only in Poland, which was at least partly a Habsburg successor state, but most remarkably also in the Soviet Union, which ostensibly represented a "clean break" with the politics of the pre-1918 empires.

These continuities should prompt us to rethink not just the Habsburg Empire, and particularly Austro-Marxism as one of its lasting legacies, but also the ways in which cross-border ties between the Habsburg and Russian Empires affected politics in Europe after 1918. The Bolsheviks not only borrowed Austro-Marxist models, but in their implementation relied on a cohort of Galicians who had come of age under the reciprocal influences of the two empires, and for whom neither Russia nor its different variants of socialism and Marxism were foreign. Socialist and communist trajectories in these territories can thus only be fully understood within the broader chronological and geographical context of the pre-1918 period—the context of the two empires whose territories later became part of Poland and the Soviet Union.

8. Nationalism, Marxism, and Communism

Italy and the Kingdom of Serbs, Croats, and Slovenes

The encounters at Café Central were equally important for socialists on the Habsburg Empire's southwestern and northwestern borderlands, territories that after 1918 became divided between Italy, the Kingdom of Serbs, Croats, and Slovenes (KSCS), and Austria. Yet just as Ukrainians and Poles are usually missing from accounts of those encounters, so do Italians and South Slavs rarely appear in discussions of Austro-Marxism and its post-1918 legacy.[1] This topic's neglect calls for remedy, as the Austro-Marxist tradition left its mark on these territories too, influencing left-wing politics and political dynamics in both Italy and the KSCS.

This chapter examines Italian and Slovenian socialism and Marxism in the late empire, with a focus on two areas: the city of Trieste, a major center of the Habsburg Littoral, a region that became known as Venezia Giulia in post-1918 Italy, and Alpine Trentino on the Austrian-Italian borderland. The socialism of the empire's Italian subjects was distinctive in the way it generated two sharply differing variants of Marxism. Italian socialists in Trieste developed a durable tradition of internationalism that was even stronger there than in Austria.[2] Italian socialists in Trentino, however, preferred a nationality-based party and rejected interethnic alliances; the compatibility of Marxism and nationalism there was even more evident than in Bohemia or Galicia. Socialism was weaker among the Slovenes, but just as Marxism and socialism developed in conversation among Poles and Ukrainians in Galicia, the Italian-Slovene socialist encounters in the empire affected politics in Italy and KSCS after 1918.

Italian and Slovene socialism in the empire developed under the auspices of Austro-Marxism: its legacy would persist through the war and then gradually recede in the 1920s, losing ground to different variants of right- and left-wing extremism and authoritarianism in both states. The year 1918, however, did not constitute a radical break: the political traditions of tolerance, nonviolence, and support for autonomy and federation would be as important for Italian and Slovene Marxists as it was for their peers from Austria proper. Here too the federative ideas from the empire influenced the two countries and their left-wing parties for the next two decades. In political and ideological terms, Austro-Marxism had nothing in common with communism or fascism, but imperial-era developments can help explain how some socialists who matured under Austro-Marxism could come to endorse communism, while others shifted to nationalism or even fascism.

This chapter brings together four socialists—two Italians, Valentino Pittoni and Cesare Battisti, from Trieste and Trento; and two Slovenes, Ivan Regent and Henrik Tuma, from Trieste and Ljubljana—and describes their paths to socialism and their lives and careers during the transition from empire to successor states. Born between 1858 and 1885, our protagonists belonged to different generations but were part of the same political cohort of protagonists discussed throughout this book. Pittoni and Battisti were the most prominent Italian socialists in Trieste and Trentino, respectively. Tuma and Regent played similar roles in the empire's South Slavic Social Democratic Party, and were the only Slovenian socialists to serve as deputies in the imperial parliament. All of them are familiar figures in their respective national historiographies, but insofar as these fields have developed separately from one another, they rarely have appeared in the same comparative narratives.[3]

Several of these protagonists were friends across 1918: Pittoni in particular maintained close personal and professional connections with several leading Austrian Marxists, including Otto Bauer and Wilhelm Ellenbogen, as well as Slovenes Regent and Tuma. Any discussion of Austro-Marxism and its legacy would be incomplete without a nuanced understanding of these personal connections among socialists from all over the empire and the ways they evolved across 1918, not just in Austria but in Europe more broadly.

Building on the discussions of post-1918 Italian politics and of Austro-Marxism in Austria and Czechoslovakia in previous chapters, here I trace parallel developments within imperial social democracy between the empire and interwar Italy and the KSCS. This is also a story of loyalty to the Habsburgs, at least, until 1914, after which some of the four subscribed to nationalism while others remained true to the tradition of Austro-Marxism. Battisti died during the war, but the three others lived beyond 1918 to confront both left-wing radicalism and fascism, losing their battles with these movements in the course of the 1920s.

Marxism, Socialism, Nationalism

Marxism had a late start in the empire's southwest—a reflection of its demography and social composition. Apart from Trieste, a major industrial hub, this was a more agricultural region than Bohemia and Austria. These territories, however, did produce a range of socialist parties, crystalizing, naturally, in cities: Trieste, Trento, Pola (alternatively known as Pula or Puji) in Istria, Ljubljana, and Gorizia. Several of these, notably Trieste and Trento, boasted at least two socialist parties—an Italian and a Slovenian one in the former, a German and an Italian one in the latter.[4] Trieste became the most important center for Italian and Slovenian socialists, despite the fact that Slovenes constituted a minority in the city.[5]

Boundaries between different nationalities in the imperial southwest were hard to draw, and yet early socialist leaders in the region insisted on ethnic-based politics. Italians, Germans, and South Slavs, in particular Slovenes, competed for the same electorate and faced some of the same dilemmas as did their Czech and Germanophone counterparts in Bohemia. Between Italian and Slovenian socialism, the former was the stronger, a reflection of the largely agricultural nature of Slovenian-inhabited territory, with its lower percentage of workers. Relations between Italian and Slovenian socialists on the Adriatic were reminiscent of those between their Austrian and Czech peers in Austria and Bohemia, and between Poles and Ukrainians in Galicia; the literature has largely lost sight of such parallel developments within imperial social democracy.

During the 1860s and 1870s, workers' and socialist organizations on the Adriatic were based on the national principle, operating separately. In 1869 Italian socialists in Trieste established the Italian Workers' Society, which focused its outreach on Italian laborers. The Workers' Confederation of Trieste, founded in 1888, initially consisted of three sections, one each for Italians,

Slovenes, and Germans.[6] Although designed as a multiethnic organization, it was dominated by Italians; its Slovenian section was eventually absorbed by the German one, which likewise took a backseat to the Italian.[7] In 1894 the Italian socialist leader Carlo Ucekar formed the Social Democratic League to represent Italian-speaking workers in the Habsburg Empire; Slovenes, too, established their own organization in Trieste, and the two operated separately.[8]

Several socialist parties that emerged in the 1890s revealed a similar dynamic. In 1896 a South Slavic Social Democratic Party was founded in Ljubljana; the following year, in an effort to extend its coverage in the Littoral, this party opened a branch in Trieste.[9] Also in 1897, following the federalization of pan-imperial social democracy, Italian socialists in Trieste voted to reorganize the Social Democratic League as the Adriatic section of the Social Democratic Workers' Party of Austria.[10] Established after the Hainfeld Congress, these bodies were generally less effective than their sister organizations in Bohemia and Austria.[11]

The belatedness and relative weakness of Marxism and socialism on the Adriatic, and the fact that Italians and Slovenes formed separate, nationally based parties in the region, has led to the perception that their roles within Austrian social democracy and Austro-Marxism was minor. But the contribution of Adriatic socialism to the development of pan-imperial social democracy and the evolution of Austro-Marxism should not be underestimated. The decade prior to the introduction of universal suffrage in 1907 and the period thereafter would see socialists in Trieste set on a new trajectory, their leaders endorsing an Austro-Marxist vision that would remain influential through the war and beyond.

Trieste and Internationalism

Valentino Pittoni, an Italian socialist from Trieste, played a key role in the development of Austro-Marxism as a doctrine and practice, and in the seeding of its models in the empire's southern borderlands.[12] Coming of age under the influence of the leading Austro-Marxists in the late empire, Pittoni became a staunch supporter of autonomy and federation, a vision that he would carry into post-1918 Italy.

In the empire Pittoni became known as an "Adler man," a reference to his closeness to the founder of imperial social democracy, and his implementation of its models and practices in Italian territory before and after 1918. Born in 1872 in the mountain region of Bolzano, he moved to Trieste as a child, re-locating to Vienna in the late 1880s to study law at the university there. Adler and Pittoni became personally acquainted in 1896, when Pittoni served as a translator from German to Italian during Adler's visit to Trieste. Adler invited Pittoni to join the pan-imperial Social Democrats, and he agreed. Pittoni quickly progressed through the party ranks, becoming by the early 1900s the undisputed leader of Italian socialists in Trieste. A member of the editorial board of *Il Lavoratore,* the major Italian socialist periodical in Trieste, he was also elected to parliament in 1907 and reelected in 1911, serving for years as head of the pan-imperial socialist caucus there.[13]

Was Pittoni indeed an "Adler man?" asks the historian Elio Apih. "In a certain sense, yes; if it means that in their development, workers' institutions in Trieste imitated Viennese models; an Adler man in the sense of being a man of the new socialist politics in Austria."[14] It was Pittoni, the argument goes, who imprinted on Italian socialism of the Littoral the importance of international-ism and multiethnic politics, and the idea of the pan-imperial Social Demo-cratic Party as a mechanism to fulfill and maintain this worldview. Pittoni saw no conflict between his national affiliation and his commitment to Vienna, writing in 1905, "We want to ensure the development of all nations toward their liberation. . . . Politically, we live in Austria, but culturally we live with our friends from Italy."[15] He consistently endorsed the Italian-Slovene socialist al-liances and supported Slovene socialist candidates in Trieste as part of the Aus-trian Social Democratic policy of a single electoral list. He saw no inherent tension between Austrianness and Italianness; this was a view that Pittoni would maintain through the end of the empire and that would affect his tran-sition to post-1918 Europe.

If Pittoni was an Adler man, by the early twentieth century many of his party colleagues were the opposite: separatists akin to their Czech peers in Bohemia, who rejected Adler's commitment to a unified party and centralized control over trade unions throughout the empire. On July 30, 1909, a group of Italian socialists formed a "Trieste autonomous group of the International Socialist Party."[16] These dissidents accused the party leadership, Pittoni in par-ticular, of "Austrianism" and "Slavism."[17] Charged with betraying the Italian cause, Pittoni became a black sheep in the party, just as Hankevych and Vityk did within the Ukrainian section. Unlike their Czech counterparts, however, Italian socialists overcame their divisions, at a moment (early 1911) when dif-ferences between Czech Social Democrat separatists and centralists, as well as between Czech and Austrian Social Democrats generally, seemed irreconcilable.[18] The tradition of internationalism and multiethnic alliances that Austrian Marxists elaborated in their writings took actual root among Italian socialists in Trieste.

Pittoni's support of the pan-imperial party reflected his conceptions of the empire, statehood, and nationality. In particular, the federalization of the Social Democrats at the 1897 congress in Vienna—a party plank as historically significant as the endorsement of national autonomy at the Brno congress two years later—set an important precedent for Pittoni. "The program of Austrian Social Democracy presents an example of how a federation of nations may be achieved," he remarked.[19] His support of federalism also reflected his vision of Trieste, which, because of its ethnic composition, he saw as scarcely assignable to any one nation-state. For him, federation was the norm, the nation-state an oxymoron.

His endorsement of the party was contingent on its efforts in addressing the nationalities issue. The 1899 Brno program raised considerable concern among socialists on the Adriatic—even more so than among their peers in Austria, Bohemia, and Galicia. Territorial autonomy, Pittoni argued, would be prohibitively complex in the empire's southwestern borderland, where, he explained, disentangling national groups would be as difficult as separating "Siamese twins."[20] Neither the Austrian censuses nor the various national autonomy projects accounted for these crucial variables. The concept of *personal* national autonomy developed by Karl Renner and Otto Bauer thus became even more important for Pittoni than for many other socialists across the empire, including in Austria. Pittoni's support for extraterritorial ethnic autonomy would significantly shape his vision of statehood, nationalism, and internationalism for years after the empire's collapse.

Trento and Nationalism

While Pittoni is practically unknown in European historiography outside of Italy, his socialist peer from Trentino, Cesare Battisti, often appears in different narratives alongside Italian nationalists. During his 1909 trip to Trentino, Mussolini described Battisti as the only advocate of the Italian national cause in the entire Habsburg Empire, and this labeling of Battisti as a nationalist would live on.[21] Battisti's fame is also bound up with his violent end: in the course of the war, he joined the Italian army and was executed in 1916 by the

Austrians on charges of treason. Even in the context of the war and the brutality it wrought, Battisti's execution generated much international dismay.

Unlike Pittoni, who matured intellectually and politically between Habsburg Trieste and Vienna, Battisti came of age under concurrent influences from Italy and the Habsburg Empire. Born in 1875 in Trento, he began his university training in Graz; making the rounds in Italian student circles in Austria, he befriended Alcide De Gasperi, a fellow Italian from Trentino who was prominent in the Christian Social Party. In 1897 Battisti became one of the cofounders of the Italian Trentino branch of the Social Democratic Workers' Party of Austria. Advancing quickly through both party and professional hierarchies, in 1900 he organized *Il Popolo,* which would become Trento's leading socialist periodical.

By the turn of the century, Battisti was Trentino's most prominent Italian socialist, the equivalent of Pittoni in Trieste. But his vision for the party differed from that of the latter, and Italian socialism in Trieste and Trentino developed in different patterns. The strategic and tactical divergence between the Trieste and Trentino movements was conditioned by these territories' differing statuses within the empire, and their particular ethnic compositions and patterns of interethnic relations. Trieste had been a Habsburg possession since the fourteenth century, whereas Trentino was annexed only in the early nineteenth century as a result of the Napoleonic Wars. Habsburg loyalty was the norm in Trieste, but memories of semi-independent statehood in the long-lived Bishopric of Trent (from 1027 to 1802) were still fresh among many in Trentino.

The fact that Italian socialists in Trentino, particularly Battisti, could be seen as nationalists is indicative of the convoluted nature of internationalism and nationalism in imperial-era Marxism. In the post-1918 Italian political and intellectual discourse, Battisti became a hero and a radical nationalist who had allegedly long fought for Trentino's independence from the Habsburgs. This myth, however, was based on misinterpretations and was in itself a product of the radical nationalist discourse in post-1918 Italy. Before 1914 Battisti espoused no signs of radical nationalism or irredentism. He described the empire as "a clerical, feudal, and militarist state" and denounced its alleged neglect of national minorities.[22] It was the Austrian government itself, he argued, with its repressive policies toward Italians, that was fueling irredentism.[23]

However, despite the fact that Italian socialism on the Littoral and in Trentino came to represent two different models (internationalism and nationalism, respectively), until 1914 the similarities between Pittoni and Battisti outweighed their differences. Both supported autonomy rather than irredentism, and endorsed the Austro-Marxist vision of socialism via democratic means and participatory institutions. For all his later reputation as a firebrand, before 1914 Battisti limited himself to demanding autonomy, not independence, of the imperial government. The idea that Italian socialists harbored any irredentism to speak of was a fiction created and promoted by Italian nationalists in the kingdom before 1918 and into the interwar period.

Henrik Tuma: Anarchism, Nationalism, Slavophilism, Socialism

While Italian socialists from Trieste and Trentino were gradually shifting apart, Italian and Slovenian socialists in Trieste found much in common. Their relations were collegial, in part because their respective leaders shared similar values. The opening of the South Slavic Social Democratic branch in Trieste not only expanded outreach but also facilitated cooperation between Italian and Slovenian comrades—a tradition formed under the empire that would have a lasting effect in interwar Europe. A change in leadership among Slovenian socialists similar to that among their Italian peers also helped in building alliances. Early Slovenian socialist leaders espoused strong national views, but the generation that followed them supported, much like Pittoni, internationalism within the imperial party and multiethnic alliances on the regional level.[24]

Henrik Tuma, Ivan Regent, and Pittoni were part of what Sabine Rutar refers to as Trieste's ethnically mixed "socialist milieu."[25] Pittoni was thus closer to Tuma and Regent than he would ever be to Battisti—a pattern that helps explain the divergent developments in socialism in post-1918 Italy. Tuma, who was almost fifty years old in 1907, was one of the empire's elder statesmen, while Regent was one of its youngest. Each had missed the party's founding; after joining the Social Democrats in the early twentieth century, they rose through the leadership ranks. Their paths to Marxism had twists and turns, by way of other parties and movements that initially had a stronger base in the region. And despite coming to share, in the late imperial era, the same ideology of Austro-Marxism, Tuma and Regent would diverge in post-1918 Europe, representing two distinct visions of Marxism.

Like his path to Marxism, Tuma's family background was notably complex, a feature essential for understanding his politics across the 1918 epochal divide: his support of the empire and, later on, of federalism over a nation-state.[26] The product of a multiethnic family, he grew up trilingual, speaking Slovenian, Italian, and German. Born and raised in Ljubljana, he studied at a gymnasium there and later at the law school of the University of Vienna, at the same time working as a schoolteacher and private tutor of French and Italian. Spending years of his life in Trieste, his own family would epitomize cosmopolitanism. His wife Maria was born and raised in Egyptian Alexandria in a family of Slovenian entrepreneurs. The couple would have ten children together, all born in Gorizia. Eight survived into adulthood.

Similarly multifaceted was Tuma's road to Marxism. As he would later recall, his father, a shoemaker, had wandered all over Austria and read much, including Marx and Ferdinand Lassalle. "My anarchist brother, Ferdinand, moved to Vienna early in life. . . . I learned a lot about socialism by listening to debates between my father and brother."[27] It was by way of following in his brother's footsteps that in 1883 Tuma came to Vienna, where, aside from studying law, he joined the city's anarchist circles. His eventual ideological shift was conditioned by political developments in the Russian as opposed to Austrian Empire. In the years following 1881, anarchism in Europe came to be associated in particular with the assassination of Russia's tsar Alexander II (known as "the Liberator" following his 1861 emancipation of the serfs). The radicalism of the opposition in the Russian Empire was alien to most in Austria, including Tuma, who would support moderation and reject extremism through the rest of his life.

But it would still be years until Tuma began to identify as a socialist. Like several other figures discussed in this study, he came to Marxism via national politics. In 1901, for example, he ran successfully for parliament as a member of the Slovenian cultural organization Edinost (Unity).[28] But as a deputy in Vienna, he became increasingly disappointed with the narrowly national focus of most Slovenian parties. Seeking alternatives, he contemplated creating his own party around the principle of Slavic unity under Vienna.[29] But his Slavophile ideas remained theoretical constructs, and in the course of seeking an ideology and politics beyond ethnicity he discovered Marxism.

Tuma's disappointment with national politics had especially to do with its adherents' claims on multiethnic towns as somehow Slovenian national domains; this was something he could never accept. His view of Trieste was emblematic and remained unchanged by the events of 1918. Like Pittoni, he saw it as an archetypically pan-imperial city, one that could not be assigned to any particular nationality nor belong to any nation-state. This vison was part of the reason for his attraction to Marxism, and it remained his guiding principle through the last years of the empire and beyond its collapse.

Ivan Regent, another leading Slovenian socialist who differed significantly from Tuma, represented a younger generation. Born in 1884 in the countryside near Trieste, he became a socialist early in life but relatively late in the context of this narrative. The most junior protagonist of this book, he died the latest of all in 1967. Regent came to socialism in Trieste at a time when Pittoni had already arisen to prominence within the Italian Social Democrats there. During his student years he began attending sessions of the South Slavic Social Democratic Party in Trieste, and soon joined. He became close with Pittoni: both shared a similar ideology and endorsed Slovenian-Italian socialist cooperation.[30] In 1914 he became head of the South Slavic Social Democrats in Trieste.

Tuma and Regent initially expressed similar concerns about Slovenian national politics. The clerical Slovene People's Party dominated Slovenian politics during much of the late empire, which attested to the relatively parochial nature of the mainly agricultural population. The Social Democrats, who were weaker among Slovenes, represented the polar opposite of clerical ideology. In their view, clericalism and religion generally meant benightedness; Marxist doctrine represented progress. Allying with the Christian Social Party, or any other non–Social Democratic entity, would by definition be antithetical to progress. Regent's insistence on socialist political purity was, in its rigor and consistency over time, second perhaps only to the famous intransigence of Otto Bauer.

Slovenian socialists, meanwhile, were not immune to the separatist currents roiling other imperial Social Democrats. Inspired by Czech and Italian separatists and provoked by initiatives of Italian-Slovenian socialist alliances, in August 1912 activists split from the South Slavic Social Democratic Party to form the socialist Omladina group. This cadre prioritized national interests over joint socialist outreach, which meant resisting perceived Italian inroads in particular.[31] Slovenian socialist separatists, however, were never the force in their own milieu that their Czech peers were in Bohemia. And despite internal tensions, until the war the worldview of internationalism and interethnic alliances remained viable, with supporters of centralism still dominant in the party.

The socialist politics practiced by these Italians and Slovenes, and the tradition of cooperation set by Pittoni, Tuma, and Regent before 1914, outlived

the Great War and the empire's collapse. The resilience of this internationalism is especially notable given the national origins of the socialist movement
on the Adriatic, and the early divisions between Italian and Slovenian labor
organizations there.

Socialists at War: The Southern Borderland

On the southern borderland too, it was the war and not nationalism that ultimately shattered socialist unity. In the summer of 1914 the southern borderland quickly became one of the empire's most tumultuous regions. With Austria
now finding itself at war against a South Slavic nation-state, Vienna's treatment
of its southern borderlands and its population was even more brutal than in
Galicia. Political persecutions commenced here even before 1914: during the
1912–13 Balkan wars, the Austrian government had arrested many on the
charge of Serbophilism.[32] Many were forced to flee, their careers in ruins and
lives endangered. The glaring political dichotomy of this period—between
those in Vienna who supported the government's decision to go to war, on one
hand, and those in the borderlands who most suffered from it, on the other—
caused new breaches in personal relationships among the erstwhile comrades
of imperial social democracy.

As attested by the experience of Wilhelm Ellenbogen, relations between
colleagues and friends began to fray even before the first shots were fired. An
Austrian liaison to the Italian party, Ellenbogen had been long acquainted with
Italian socialist politics, having taken part in Italian socialist congresses before 1918. Ellenbogen would later recall that his Italian colleagues "fanatically
opposed the war."[33] Ellenbogen himself had earlier endorsed the decisions of
his government and party—something he would come to regret as he sought
to help Italian friends and colleagues deal with their new troubles. Pittoni was
particularly frustrated with the support that many Austrian socialists, including Victor Adler and Otto Bauer, lent the Habsburg dynasty at war.

The war became a transformative point for Battisti: like the empire's nationalists, he shifted to outright separatism only after 1914. Battisti denounced the "total impotence" of Austrian socialists, whom he accused of
"immediately justifying the war."[34] In August 1914 he relocated to Italy with
his family.[35] Citing what he characterized as Austria's barbaric treatment of
Italians, he called upon Rome to enter a war of liberation against the Habsburg
Empire.[36] Battisti's involvement with Italian nationalism and the war soon

resulted in a violent end. When in 1915 Italy signed the London treaties, he enrolled in the Italian army. From the front lines he sent letters to his wife full of enthusiasm for the war on Habsburg rule. Now more than ever, Battisti believed that the war against Germanism was justified.[37] His commitment to the Italian cause, however, would prove fatal. Captured by Austrian forces, he was deported back to the empire, tried on charges of treason, and executed in July 1916.[38] Although a traitor to Austrians, he became a national hero for many Italians.[39]

The beginning of the Austro-Italian war affected other Italian socialists too, and to a greater and more personal extent than was typical among their Austrian comrades, except for those directly engaged in combat. Even ultraloyalists such as Pittoni fell under suspicion and faced persecution. He was in Trieste in August 1914, but after the beginning of the Italian campaign in May 1915 he became a refugee; forced to flee the city, he went to Vienna.[40] Austrian socialists failed to intervene on behalf of their Italian colleagues.

Pittoni's experience epitomized the failures of Austrian wartime policies that eventually led to the empire's collapse. Austrians themselves had to concede that Pittoni's editorship of the pro-Vienna *Il Lavoratore* made the strongest counterforce against the nationalist and irredentist *Il Piccolo;* as such, Pittoni represented Vienna's interests in Trieste. The Austrian government, however, was reluctant to support Pittoni's publication owing to its socialist editorial stance; the same fear of socialism would help fuel right-wing extremism in interwar Europe, particularly Austria and Italy.[41] As a result, despite Pittoni's abiding belief in the integrity of the Habsburg polity, his own government treated him much as it did the irredentists now becoming rampant on the Adriatic.

Echoing Joseph Redlich and Heinrich Lammasch, Pittoni argued that the crisis of the war was laying bare all the flaws of imperial governance: "The worst calamity results from the uncontrollable and arbitrary actions of the bureaucracy."[42] His correspondence from the years 1915 through 1918 reveals a sense of despair. He kept in contact with Victor Adler, and the two corresponded regularly during 1914–15, but later he became closer to Friedrich, the junior Adler, who unlike his father ardently opposed the war—a shift of priorities perhaps reflecting Pittoni's own view of his Austrian colleagues and their role in instigating the military disaster. Yet Pittoni continued to support the Habsburg state. Until 1918 he believed that the empire would survive the war intact, to include Trieste. As he had written in 1916, "All of my projects are predicated on the belief that the course of the war will not affect the political status of Trieste."[43] Even amid personal tragedy (including the loss of his brother to a fatal nervous collapse), Pittoni stayed his political course, never breaking ties with Austrian socialists.[44]

Even more traumatic was the experience of Pittoni's Slovenian peers. Likewise finding themselves in the midst of a war zone, they were distrusted by the Austrian government but driven into the Austrian army nevertheless. Regent was among those drafted, and he served until mid-1918—the second, after Bauer, of this book's protagonists with firsthand experience of the war.[45] The outbreak of war found Tuma in Gorizia, whose territory would come under heavy fire in the summer of 1915. The family sought to move from Trieste, but Tuma was apprehended by the Austrian police; as a politically engaged Slovene, he was categorized as hostile, hence prohibited from entry into Austria's interior.[46] This category did not, however, prevent the Austrian government from drafting two of the Tuma sons, who eventually found themselves fighting against forces of the Kingdom of Italy.[47] Both would meet the end of the war as Austrian soldiers.

Nationalism, Statehood, Federation

Alienated from Vienna, Pittoni, Regent, and Tuma now discovered they had much in common, and during the war Pittoni revived his idea of an Italian-Slovenian socialist alliance. In April 1915 he organized a combined congress of the South Slavic and Italian Social Democratic parties in Trieste, including Tuma; in 1916 he attempted to launch a Slovenian socialist periodical in that city.[48] The personal and professional setbacks that Pittoni and Tuma experienced during the war did not, however, turn them into nationalists.

Other socialists were not immune to the nationalist sentiments that Vienna's wartime policies were provoking among Slovenes and Italians. "A new separatist group, similar to that existing among the Czechs, has begun taking shape in our party," wrote Tuma in a collective letter to leading socialists across the empire in December 1917.[49] The split in Slovenian socialism had occurred earlier, but it was only during the war that the separatist faction gained momentum among Slovene socialists.

Yet even in the midst of the war, a cohort of Italian and Slovene socialists reasserted their commitment to cooperation and autonomy. As the war progressed and independence became an option, Pittoni and Tuma voiced their preference for federations over nation-states. They advocated extraterritorial autonomy for Trieste along the lines of the program developed by their Austrian colleagues Karl Renner and Otto Bauer. The Kingdom of Italy organized its economy around other port cities, so while Trieste was important in cultural terms, it was almost redundant to Italian commerce, and Pittoni predicted (correctly) that annexation would mean the decline of the city's economy. In his view, Trieste could be part of a new political configuration emerging after the war, and he supported the creation (or restoration) of a Republic of Venice, with Trieste incorporated therein as an autonomous city under the aegis of the League of Nations.[50] Such federative thinking remained a cornerstone of his political beliefs across 1918.

Tuma too supported a nonnational and extraterritorial reorganization of Trieste, but for different reasons. His vision for the city had to do with his assessment of Slovenian politics. Slovenes, he hoped, would gradually expand along the Adriatic. But in his view this could only be accomplished under the Habsburgs: outside the empire, Slovenes would either be absorbed by Italy or fall further behind economically—Tuma here thinking as a Marxist rather than a nationalist.[51] Doubting that Trieste could ever belong solely to Slovenes, Tuma calculated that their best chance for prosperity would be to secure autonomy in Trieste as a city under international control but unassigned to any particular nationality.[52]

These figures' political projects, however, ran up against a dilemma in the late fall of 1918, when it became clear that the Habsburg Empire would not survive the war. In defending their vision of Trieste as a nonnational city, they found themselves at odds with other Italians and Slovenians, most of whom by late 1918 advocated the city's annexation to their respective state—Italy or the Kingdom of Serbs, Croats, and Slovenes. While support of federative nonnational solutions had been common before 1918 among the empire's elites, and particularly among socialist politicians, the continued endorsement by Italian and Slovenian socialists from Trieste of federation over nation-state would be an anomaly in post-1918 Europe.

Italian Socialism across 1918

After 1918 Italian socialists from the empire became drawn into the Italian Socialist Party from the former Kingdom of Italy (the Partito Socialista Italiano, or PSI). The party had been founded in 1892 and had followed a different path than Austrian social democracy. Even before World War I, the PSI had espoused radicalism of the kinds that had never been endorsed by Austro-Marxists. The PSI's maximalists or revolutionaries, a radical faction that initially included Mussolini, consolidated before the war and gained momentum after 1914. The maximalists endorsed the use of force as a method of revolutionary struggle. The outbreak of war brought new challenges to the PSI, worsening its extant divisions. While the party's reformists supported Italian neutrality, the maximalists promoted Italy's military intervention against Austria. The Great War thus marked a point of radicalization for socialists in the Kingdom of Italy, but the roots of revolutionary maximalism, and the eventual transition from socialism to fascism, should be traced to the pre-1914 period.

In 1919 the PSI became the basis for a new expanded organization in interwar Italy, a result of the merger between socialist parties and their members from the Kingdom of Italy and the Habsburg Empire. Holding 156 seats in the kingdom's parliament, the PSI emerged in 1919 as one of the nation's strongest political forces and one of the largest per capita socialist parties in Europe. Yet ideological, political, and personal differences between socialists from the kingdom and their colleagues from the defunct empire persisted well beyond 1918. The Triestini, for example, who had come of age in the tradition of Austro-Marxism, maintained a separate section within the PSI. In September 1919, almost a year into independence and acknowledging the inevitability of Trieste's annexation to Italy, Slovenian socialists from the city agreed to a merger between the PSI and the South Slavic Social Democratic Party in Trieste.[53]

Internal ideological splits within the PSI also resulted in the formation of the Communist Party of Italy. The leftward shift in Austria helped prevent the consolidation of communism there. In Italy, to the contrary, it helped usher in that movement. In 1917 only a fraction of Italian socialists had endorsed the Bolsheviks' October Revolution, but by 1919 the communist faction of the party became dominant.[54] The split was formalized during the 1921 Livorno congress of the PSI, which also marked the official founding of the Communist Party of Italy.[55] But even in 1921, most of the Italian left—both socialists and communists alike—opposed the Bolsheviks' tactics in Russia. Italian communists in particular refused to succumb to Moscow-style centralization and insisted on maintaining autonomy from Soviet Russia. Like its counterpart in Czechoslovakia, the Communist Party of Italy was organized on principles different from those guiding the Bolsheviks. It was an early paradigm of non-Bolshevik methods, aiming to chart a different path to communism.[56]

The story of the Communist Party of Italy is thus reminiscent of its counterparts elsewhere in post-Habsburg Europe. Several of these parties and their leaders who had come of age under the influence of Austro-Marxism began with a local autonomous initiative by individuals who, albeit encouraged by the Bolsheviks' coming to power in Russia, did not necessarily believe in the applicability of Bolshevik methods in their own respective countries.[57] Each of these communist parties, however, soon split between local-minded moderates and Russia-backed maximalists who endorsed Soviet methods and models. By the mid-1920s, under relentless pressure from Moscow, all of them—in Italy, in the Kingdom of Serbs, Croats, and Slovenes, and in Czechoslovakia—would succumb to Bolshevization. Italian communists grew more receptive to Moscow's influence after experiencing persecutions at home. Mussolini began anticommunist crackdowns in 1923 and banned the party altogether in 1926. Operating underground, the Communist Party of Italy became increasingly dependent on financial support from Moscow.[58]

Pittoni between Trieste, Rome, and Vienna

Despite the war, new forms of statehood, and the radicalization of the left and right, the post-1918 period in Italian politics was characterized by certain continuities with prewar tradition—not just that of the Kingdom of Italy, but also of the Habsburg Empire. In the war's immediate aftermath, few entertained a Bolshevik scenario in Italy. The possibility of a communist revolution in the country was discussed in a 1918 conversation between the Italian socialist Giuseppe Borgese and Aldo Oberdorfer, a socialist friend of Pittoni's from Trieste.[59] Initially Oberdorfer believed that a radical scenario was unlikely in Italy; Bolshevik-style hierarchy, centralized control, and revolutionary violence, he argued, were alien to Italian political culture.[60]

As the public mood in the country changed, however, Oberdorfer soon adjusted his views. In early 1919 he noted the demise of the democratic socialism that had been the cornerstone of Austro-Marxism: "The integral socialism of Valentino Pittoni that had been practiced in Venezia Giulia no longer has a place in the Kingdom of Italy. . . . Authentic socialism, without revolutionary slogans, without boasting, without exuberance, based on parliamentary institutions, and always committed to the affirmation of its principles," no longer existed in Italy.[61] In 1921 he estimated that many in Italy would be in favor of a Bolshevik-style change of course.

The concurrent radicalization of Italy's right and left particularly affected those who, having come of age under the Habsburgs, eschewed political extremism. While the historiography of twentieth-century Italy abounds with discussions of fascism, the simultaneous leftward shift of the 1920s has remained somewhat marginalized. Yet it was the latter rather than the former that had the most immediate impact on many of the country's socialists, especially those from the former Habsburg Empire.

Meeting the end of the war in Trieste, Pittoni found himself at a crossroads, facing a dilemma much like those of his former colleagues and friends across Europe—Bohumír Šmeral and Ludwig Czech in Czechoslovakia, and Mykola Hankevych and Semen Vityk in Poland, Austria, and Ukraine. In January 1921 communists occupied the offices of *Il Lavoratore,* the leading periodical of Trieste's Italian socialists; Pittoni was sacked from its editorial board not long after.[62] The leftward shift within the Italian Socialist Party was more damaging to Pittoni's personal life and professional career than the immediate postwar radicalization of the right.

Pittoni never endorsed left-wing maximalism and, in a development reminiscent of his Ukrainian colleague Hankevych, gradually drifted away from mainstream politics. In 1920–23 he worked in the cooperative movement. Unemployed for some months and generally marginalized, he soon became physically ill and emotionally exhausted. In late 1922 his daughter Marina suggested soliciting help from socialist colleagues in Prague, an idea that struck Pittoni as a dismal one:

> Your letter from the 13th [November 1922] found me very depressed. . . . I thought about the thing you asked me—you know yourself all too well—and I found it humiliating and depressing, especially in my current situation. Also, I was never as intimately friendly with colleagues in Prague as I was with those in Vienna. I do know Bechyna well enough. I have never had friendly relations with Haberman; we rather disagreed in our views of politics. The only one I had a positive rapport with is Němec, who in the meantime has become less influential. He is the only one to whom I can write a confidential letter with private requests.[63]

The socialists Pittoni refers to here had represented the Czech separatist faction within imperial social democracy. They had militated against the unity of the pan-imperial party and its trade unions, the same unity Pittoni himself had spent much of his career preserving and later seeking to revive. Thus, while he knew all the relevant political figures, their relations had been strained.

He found refuge in Vienna, a city that in the immediate postwar years hosted many of those who could not find a more suitable place for themselves on the turbulent continent. His sister Cecilia resided there after 1918, her husband working in journalism. Pittoni made the move in 1923. The decision to leave Italy must have been heartbreaking, not least because the rest of his family—his wife, his daughter Marina, and son Alfredo—remained in Trieste. But professional prospects seemed brighter for him in the Austrian capital than anywhere in Italy. Wilhelm Ellenbogen helped with the relocation and supplied contacts to Italian antifascists.[64] Pittoni founded a new periodical, *Vienna Rossa* (Red Vienna), and spent the rest of his life in Austria.

Republican Vienna was not the same as its imperial-era incarnation, but it still appealed to many who had the urge to come "home" to Austria, where there would be no precipitous radicalization of the kinds they were witnessing elsewhere. To be sure, Austria and the Marxists trying to make their way there faced difficulties of their own, but the Austro-Marxist tradition and the country's democratic institutions remained very much alive during the 1920s.

Left-Wing Radicalization: Slovenes

The leftward shift among Slovenian socialists in Italy was even more pronounced than among Italians. Even before Mussolini's takeover, Italy's liberal government imposed restrictions on minorities, limiting the institutional representation of non-Italians and closing their schools. The same Oberdorfer who had earlier noted the radicalization of the Italian left now observed the effects of Rome's policies on minorities. Italy's Slavs were being ousted from political participation, their schools were being shut, their language marginalized or forbidden. The liberals' assimilationist policy, Oberdorfer argued, would further poison relations between Italians and minorities by undermining the state loyalty of the latter. Neglect of minority rights could harm the prospects of Italian socialists, who did not technically endorse assimilation but did little to stop it: "We need to sincerely support the use of the Slovenian and Croatian languages in public institutions and in citizens' interaction with the government and courts; we need to respect any local institutions that are not openly anti-Italian or pro-Austrian."[65] Refusal to cooperate with minorities could turn Venezia Giulia into an ethnic and ideological battlefield, he warned.[66]

Relations between Italian and Slovenian socialists after the war were rocky. In 1919 Italian socialists began to accuse their Slovenian counterparts of national separatism—charges similar to developments in the former Habsburg Empire and its socialist parties.[67] In 1920 a group of Slovenian socialists approached their Italian comrades requesting that the PSI propose parliamentary consideration of a plebiscite to decide the status of Venezia Giulia. The Italians, who viewed that region as an integral part of the Italian state, refused, and the episode caused an irrevocable rift. By the early 1920s, such traces of cooperation as had existed among the former comrades began to evaporate. Slovenes formed a separate commission within the PSI where all business was conducted in Slovenian, and in September 1921 they attempted to form a separate organization: the Socialist Party of Slovenes and Croats of Venezia Giulia.[68] The party, however, never caught on, and its members remained within the Italian organization.[69]

Alienated from the government and rebuffed by their ostensible Italian comrades, Slovenian socialists shifted to the left in large numbers, a trend marked by Oberdorfer: "I no longer have trust in our Slovenian colleagues. Before the war, the Slavs were with us, disciplined and well-versed in socialism; and our old colleagues remained the same. But the new ones, acting on the general discontent of recent years, and mindful of their many co-nationals outside the country's borders, have incorporated many elements foreign to socialism; and many of them are extremely dangerous."[70] The government responded with more pressure and further restrictions. Ivan Regent would later recall Italy's post-1918 policies in this regard as motivated by stereotypes, by the idea that Slovenes "had to be subjugated lest they become revolutionaries."[71] Official Rome looked on them with suspicion, as a potential fifth column for the Kingdom of Serbs, Croats, and Slovenes, or for Soviet Russia and world communism.

Tuma and Regent on Socialism and Communism

Torn between different ideologies (nationalism, socialism, and communism) and countries (Italy and the KSCS) Slovenian socialists faced a sharper dilemma than their Austrian or even Italian counterparts. Put on the defensive, like national minorities elsewhere, they were more likely to endorse political extremes, whether of the left or right. Both Henrik Tuma and Ivan Regent reflected this trend. Their relationships after 1918 were reminiscent of the complex dynamics between their Ukrainian comrades Mykola Hankevych and Semen Vityk.

Tuma's story was marked by a series of traumatic transitions. He brought his family back to Gorizia in 1916, but February 1919 found him traversing government offices in Rome, making inquiries of various ministers regarding one of his sons: Yaroslav Tuma had wound up in Italian captivity, and remained there even after the armistice. His mission proved successful: Yaroslav was released, and returned to Trieste.[72] Tuma's professional network came in handy, but he received little support from those who had once stood closest to him. Italian socialists in particular remained uninvolved, for various reasons; some, like Pittoni, were distracted by personal problems of their own. Others had become embroiled in the political infighting that beset the PSI after 1918. This falling out of former colleagues would have political consequences for each individual and for their several states.

Tuma's views of socialism, nationalism, internationalism, and communism in post-1918 Italy were similar to those of Hankevych in post-1918 Poland. He too was disappointed with the failure of multiethnic politics, with repressive government policies compounded by a lack of support from Italian peers. He defined himself as a "stubborn internationalist."[73] Yet having also fallen under the communist spell early on, his vision of it, he insisted, was a particular one: "My communism was not a negative-revolutionary concept. My Bolshevism was not based on pure demagoguery. . . . I regarded socialism above all in economic terms as a project of positive transformations."[74]

Initially he supported the 1917 October Revolution and faulted his socialist colleagues in Italy for their "lack of political will," that is, their reluctance to follow the Bolsheviks' example and undertake a revolution of their own. But he quickly became disappointed with Soviet methods. Tuma favored international revolution on the Marxist model, just as Trotsky and Lenin had until 1920, when the latter was forced to adjust his course after the Soviet military defeat at the approaches to Warsaw.[75] Like Trotsky, Tuma would continue to oppose the idea of revolution in a single country. Indeed, the Soviet Union threatened to become a continental corruptor: "Russian Bolsheviks are paid agents in Europe," he wrote in 1924. "I condemn the leaders of the Russian Bolsheviks, for they have no idea what a socialist system is."[76] He came to see Bolshevism—as certain other adherents of Austro-Marxism were quicker to see it—as an aberration of Marxism.

While Tuma was gradually rejecting communism, his colleague and friend Ivan Regent, much like Bohumír Šmeral and Semen Vityk, embraced it. The worldview of the latter three was affected by the concurrent radicalization of the left and right, and by their abiding support of Austro-Marxist models, particularly the core principles of internationalism and intransigence. Like Šmeral, Regent witnessed the fragmentation of the socialist movement with dismay; the solution seemed to lie in communism. And like Šmeral and Vityk, Regent considered the transition from socialism to communism a natural one: "The socialist movement of Slovenes and Croats in Venezia Giulia has grown into a communist movement."[77] In 1920 in Trieste, he discussed with a friend the idea of establishing a communist party.[78]

Equally important for Regent was the communists' commitment to unity and multiethnic cooperation. Italian communists were notably more amenable than socialists to cooperation with Slovenes. In one of the writings he produced after siding with communism, Regent pinned his hopes on the progressive radicalization of Italian and South Slavic socialists, who leaned toward the "establishment of a communist order in Venezja Giulija."[79] Not only did his communism evince continuities with his imperial-era thinking, but his vision of Trieste and the surrounding area as virtually unassignable to any one nation-state was also part of the inheritance from the empire and its socialist tradition.

Despite their ideological disagreements, and even during periods of heightened tensions, Tuma and Regent remained in touch and corresponded prolifically through the 1920s and 1930s, just as did Vityk and Hankevych. The two likewise refrained from public attacks on one another. But Tuma did ridicule the communist ideology. In the spring of 1920 he published an article rather catchily titled "Extremists—Hey, Communists!" that sparked polemics between former comrades. Regent was quick to deny the equation of communists and extremists: the former, he said, were simply those who "accept Marx's doctrine of revolution, and educate the proletariat about possible ways to implement this teaching. That is to say, they strive to guide the proletariat in the right direction."[80] As Tuma well understood, however, while the concept of proletarian revolution was certainly a Marxist one, Regent's emphasis on "guidance" smacked more specifically of Leninism, of Lenin's insistence on conflating Marx's temporary "dictatorship of the proletariat" with an institutionalized and politically monopolistic party.

Tuma after 1920 followed a path similar to Pittoni's. With communists gaining the upper hand in the Slovenian left, Tuma simply no longer fit in. Shunted aside as he was by his radicalized Italian and Slovenian peers, he withdrew from active politics. Like Pittoni, he left Italy before the period of the crackdown on the country's left; it was not that he faced imminent persecution,

Building in Laibach/Ljubljana, 1890–1900. Slovenian National Library, Digital Database.

but that Italy no longer felt like home. In 1924 he left Gorizia and moved to Ljubljana. Nearing his seventieth birthday, he rediscovered his passion for geography and would publish several pamphlets on the toponymy of the southern Alps. But having regained these interests, he had, in every sense possible, lost both his home and the cause to which he'd devoted so much of his life.

For his part, Regent remained a politically engaged communist, reflecting yet again the many different trajectories of Austro-Marxism in post-1918 Europe. Like many of his comrades, he was increasingly constrained in post-1922 Italy. After 1925, when Mussolini stepped up his suppression of the left, Regent was, like many other communists and socialists, imprisoned on multiple occasions, held for days and sometimes weeks on end. After months of this ordeal, he made the decision to emigrate, leaving Trieste in 1927 for Ljubljana by way of Paris and Brussels. He spent the rest of his life abroad and would never return to Italy.

Socialism, Communism, Fascism

The story of Italian and Slovenian socialists in transition from empire to post-1918 (or even post-1914) Europe is that of tragedy, the gradual loss of home, profession, and faith in democratic socialism—felt even more poignantly here than in the empire's former core and its Czech-German frontier. Particularly dramatic was the fate of Battisti, the only socialist figure discussed in this book to have volunteered for military service, and moreover to have fought against, not on the side of, the Habsburgs. Nor was any other of our protagonists executed by his own state. Battisti's socialist peers from the Littoral fared better, surviving the war, but would all be cast out of active politics, with some opting or forced to emigrate in the 1920s.

The story of this loss is important for understanding broader political trends in different states across the epochal divide of 1918. The heavy focus on fascism in studies of post-1918 Italy, while perhaps understandable, can serve to efface the long-term, pre-1914 crisis of democratic socialism, not just in the Kingdom of Italy but also the Habsburg Empire. Pittoni, Tuma, and Regent experienced an initial decline in their political activism years before Mussolini came to power, a downturn having little to do with Italian nationalism or fascism per se. The crisis of the left, including the disintegration of Austrian social democracy during the war, affected Italian and Slovenian socialists in post-1918 Italy more immediately and crucially than did radical nationalism and fascism.

Given the great contestedness of Italian territories in 1918–19 and the continual political crises of interwar Italy, it is remarkable that Austro-Marxism did not vanish from the empire's former southwestern borderlands in late 1918. Its practices instead became embedded in a variety of left-wing parties to emerge in postwar Italy and the Kingdom of Serbs, Croats, and Slovenes, and would only fade away gradually in the 1920s. By then our three surviving protagonists found themselves on the margins of politics. Regent, however, would continue with his political involvement in several states, including the Soviet Union, an episode to be discussed in the following chapter.

PART FOUR

Post-Habsburg Succession and the 1930s

9. Radical Politics, Conservative Responses

Europe in the 1930s

In 1933 Ludwig Czech, head of the German Social Democratic Party in Czechoslovakia and minister of social welfare in its government, met in Prague with his Austrian socialist colleague Julius Deutsch. Back in 1918 they had parted ways, transitioning from imperial Vienna to republican Austria and Czechoslovakia and finding themselves amid a myriad of unknowns. In 1933 Deutsch traveled from Vienna to Prague on a critical mission: facing an authoritarian onslaught in his native land, he was hoping to secure Czechoslovak assistance—possibly including the military variety—against Austrian fascism. Czech and Deutsch, who had known each other since the days of the empire, were now trying to use their old networks to address a new crisis fast engulfing Europe.[1]

The year 1933 was in some ways even more unsettling than 1918. Hitler had just become chancellor in Germany, and Austria was on the brink of civil war. The fifteen years of constant tensions since 1918 had left many on the edge of emotional exhaustion. For many socialist leaders, the 1920s had been full of hopes and expectations. In the early part of the decade, when the shock of the empire's collapse had barely set in, some of these hopes were nurtured by discussions of institutional solutions that would replicate models from the defunct Habsburg polity without technically reviving it. A Habsburg restoration would hardly be welcome, but Habsburg institutional models and political practices remained relevant. Different federative and confederative concepts were designed, both for international cooperation as well as for minority protections within specific states.[2] One such model was the Danubian Federation—an attempt to reproduce the empire's old economic unity in the Danubian space now divided between different nation-states. The League of Nations as a form of supranational institution continued to be significant. Its authority was limited at best—restricted to policy suggestions without any leverage to enforce them—but it retained its value as a venue for policy discussion and political pressure.[3] Legal and judicial systems in several successor states, meanwhile, borrowed heavily from the Habsburg predecessor. Parties, ideologies, and individuals that had matured politically under the empire continued to influence politics in several states for years after 1918.

The year 1918, then, saw the beginning of new states but not the end of the empire's political tradition. The 1930s, however, represented another epoch. None of the federative solutions discussed in the 1920s came to fruition. Europe was becoming inhospitable to those who refused to endorse the extremes, whether of the right or left. Such was the position many of our protagonists were facing: still holding out hope that stability might return, but finding themselves in increasing precarity, with ever fewer options for refuge or rescue.

The year 1933 thus marked the beginning of an end. Hitler's coming to power in Germany affected the post-Habsburg space directly, facilitating the political and eventually military escalation in Austria. By 1933 Austria, and Vienna in particular, was in the midst of a civil war. The city that had served as the first or second home for so many of those who came of age under the Habsburgs no longer offered a refuge for those forced to flee persecutions in Italy, Poland, Yugoslavia, and other new states. Czechoslovakia seemed like an island of relative calm in the sea of storm; its capital, Prague, became a place of accidental and nonaccidental encounters for many of those who either fled their own homes or, as Deutsch did, arranged meetings there to discuss possible solutions to the crisis in their home countries.

This chapter explains the gradual radicalization in the post-Habsburg space and the ways it affected the people who lived through it. The story of Europe during the "age of extremes" is a familiar one, but it is usually told from the top-down perspective: the imposition of authoritarianism in individual countries and its effects on their citizens. Here I explore how the gradual onset of authoritarianism in Europe between Italy and the Soviet Union affected those who supported the Habsburg Empire's institutional and political models through the 1930s. My particular focus is upon Austria, whose descent into authoritarianism affected not just Austrians themselves but also many of those elsewhere in Europe who had come of age under the Habsburgs.

The Austrian Civil War: Socialists, Catholics, Fascists, Nazis

The crisis in Austria that brought Julius Deutsch to Prague had escalated gradually since 1918. In some ways it represented a continuation of the prewar tensions in late imperial politics, themselves rooted in the earlier collapse of liberalism. Just as Austrian imperial practices outlived the empire, so did the crises of imperial politics travel, unresolved, beyond the epochal divide, influencing republican Austria and several other states.

Austria's first republican parliament in particular marked a political continuity from the pre-1918 empire. At the core of this body was a coalition of the two major Austrian parties, the Social Democrats (SDs) and Christian Socials (CSs), who came first and second, respectively, in the 1919 elections. Not only did the parties feature some of the same membership and leadership across the 1918 divide, but their ideologies and programmatic principles were virtually unchanged. Remaining in charge of the parties were Otto Bauer (the SDs) and Ignaz Seipel (the CSs), with the latter, a Catholic priest, moreover leading the country for much of the 1920s, serving two terms as chancellor (1921–24 and 1926–29). Both defined not only their parties' politics through much of the interwar period, but also fueled the conflict between these organizations—another legacy of the imperial era that manifested itself with new force after 1918.

Another legacy of the empire, and a by-product of its postliberal politics, was the failure of center-left coalition politics in post-1920 Austria. The differences between the Social Democrats and Christian Socials were rooted in the parties' Habsburg-era political traditions. The Austro-Marxist worldview, as formulated under the empire with the direct involvement of Otto Bauer, emphasized democratic institutional transitions to socialism, and also intransigence—the rejection of allegedly distracting or confusing alliances with bourgeois parties. Bauer's party did form an alliance with the Christian Socials in 1919 after gaining the majority of parliamentary votes. But in 1920 he refused to become a minor partner in what would now be a new coalition dominated by the CSs. In doing so, he inadvertently forced the CSs to look for allies on the right. These two parties' failure to ally resulted in a rightward shift in Austrian politics as early as 1920. It was at this point that the Christian Socials entered into a co-alition with the Greater German People's Party (Großdeutsche Volkspartei, or GDVP), a successor of the pan-Germans from the empire. In the 1920s the GDVP was radically nationalist, but not fascist or Nazi. In the early 1930s, however, they would shift further right, becoming Hitler's main base of support in Austria.

Several of these parties and the movements that formed the basis for them had previously emerged in the empire. But they were transformed not just by late imperial politics but also by the war and the postwar crisis that affected Austria more than most other successor states. Part of this change implied militarization that was unprecedented in the imperial era. In the 1920s and 1930s, political tensions in Austria were particularly exacerbated by the existence of several paramilitary forces, also divided along party lines. The first of these to take shape, the Heimwehr (Home Army), emerged during the last years of the war as a volunteer entity initially meant to protect contested borders. Officially a nonpartisan institution, it received support from the Christian Social Party. In 1923 the Social Democrats established their own military force, the Schutzbund (Defense Union). This was organized on a nonprofessional basis but received army training.[4] The existence of military units with party affiliations, a phenomenon unheard of in the empire, represented a stark novelty of the new epoch.

The Christian Socials and Social Democrats, however, used their respective military units differently, and their tactics reflected their particular legacies from the imperial era. The Christian Socials turned the Heimwehr into an instrument of political struggle; for their part, true to their unyielding moderateness, the Social Democrats never deployed the Schutzbund.[5] The uneven approach to force not only disadvantaged the socialists, it created a situation in the country whereby the Christian Socials held an exclusive monopoly on violence. This followed a certain historical logic: while the CSs had never resorted to outright violence in the empire, they had acted, even before 1918, with a notable aggressiveness, never concealing their antiminority and antisocialist stances.

The renunciation of violence, meanwhile, was codified in the Social Democrats' official party program adopted at the congress in Linz in 1926.[6] Drafted by Bauer himself, this program was reminiscent of the general principles that Austro-Marxists had adopted under the empire.[7] The Linz program likewise featured the particular SD combination of revolutionary rhetoric with the rejection of force, in keeping with Austrian socialists' long-standing insistence that socialism must be achieved solely by democratic means. Bauer himself explained the continuities across 1918: "The Austro-Marxist school was destroyed during the war and revolution," he wrote, "but the concept remained, and it found its reflection in the Linz program."[8] Bauer's commitment to Austro-Marxist pacifism backfired after 1918. As Anson Rabinbach notes, "The paradox of Austrian socialism"—the rejection of the use of force, and at the same time a reluctance to form alliances with conservatives or centrists—"clearly resulted from the legacy of the pre-1914 period."[9] The socialists' refusal to engage in a more aggressive response opened the door to right-wing extremists, who would not be contained by institutional means.

Otto Bauer, Ignaz Seipel, 1927–1932

The Linz program was first put to the test in 1927. In January of that year the Schutzbund organized a peaceful demonstration in the region of Schattendorf in Austrian Burgenland, near Hungary. Right-wing nationalists not only staged a counterprotest, they opened fire, the confrontation resulting in the death of two Schutzbund supporters, including a child. The trial of the nationalists responsible for the killings took place in July 1927 and resulted in acquittal. Outraged by the verdict, workers staged a new demonstration on Vienna's Justizplatz, the seat of Austria's Ministry of Justice. The ensuing chaos resulted in further violence and dozens of casualties as government forces fired on demonstrators. Socialist leaders convened to discuss the situation, and decided to abide by the Linz program. The Schutzbund stood by.

If Bauer was primarily responsible for keeping socialist actions nonviolent, his Christian Social peer, Seipel, facilitated the right-wing (and government-condoned) violence that eventually paved the way for Austrian authoritarianism. Having led the CSs since 1921, Seipel began his second term as chancellor in 1926, and it was he who the following year gave orders to disperse the demonstrations by force.

The year 1927 marked the beginning of the confrontations—military and political—that would plague the Austrian republic for the next decade. Seipel himself cannot be held accountable for all the problems in Austrian interwar history, but he certainly created preconditions for authoritarianism and the end of democracy. As Anton Pelinka has recently argued, Seipel's response to the 1927 crisis was consistent with the overall view of statehood and democracy he had harbored since before 1918. Seipel, writes Pelinka, "was not a democrat himself, but he did not oppose democracy."[10] Having supported the empire, he never fully endorsed the republic, even when serving as chancellor. But neither did he actively oppose it, demonstrating a remarkable political flexibility reminiscent of his imperial-era mentor and predecessor Karl Lueger.[11] Interpreting the crisis as insoluble by democratic means, Seipel then shifted toward what Pelinka describes as the chancellor's vision of "true democracy"—in plain language, authoritarianism.[12]

While creating the preconditions for authoritarianism, Seipel, however, did not directly benefit from it. The economic and political repercussions of the Great Depression were even more severe than the immediate post-1918 crises. In 1929 Seipel and the SDs became deadlocked in an ongoing confrontation over social welfare. The chancellor submitted his letter of resignation, somewhat unexpectedly, on April 3, 1929, in the process also dismissing the entire government.[13] He remained active in political and intellectual circles in Austria and abroad, but would never return to government. He died in 1932.

The end of Seipel's career was as controversial as its beginning in the late empire. A unique figure in Austrian politics, reflected even in his priestly attire and the religious duties he continued to execute through the years of his chancellorship, Seipel was always a divisive personality. As John Deak has demonstrated, his posthumous perception has likewise been polarized. Biographers have tended to cast him as either a hero or villain, often discussing him not as an autonomous individual but rather in terms of the binary he formed with either his SD counterpart Otto Bauer, or with his CS successors, notably the openly authoritarian Engelbert Dollfuss. Many of these accounts are either openly sympathetic or antagonistic. This binary perception and the unconcealed bias only reaffirm the critical role Seipel played in Austrian history, not just as the founder of the first republic, but also—as Deak has argued—a precursor to its authoritarianism and "a spiritual father of clerical fascism."[14]

Austria between Authoritarianism, Fascism, and Nazism

With Seipel's departure, the Christian Socials' Johannes Schober became the new chancellor. He built on the political decisions Seipel had made before him and carried out some of the same policies. In particular, Schober endorsed the

Heimwehr as uniquely capable of fending off the "red menace"; in 1930 members of the Heimwehr—an entity that was initially designed for military purposes only—became ministers.[15] Heimwehr never defined itself as a fascist organization, but as John T. Lauridsen has argued, it imitated fascism in everything except for the latter's imperial aspirations.[16]

The Austrian government's cooperation with the Heimwehr was based on certain shared interests. Fending off communism was one of these; but more important, and ever more urgent in the early 1930s, was the question of Austria's independence. Italian fascists had imperial aspirations, but their Austrian followers did not, focusing solely on Austria and its fate in a Europe increasingly torn between different extremes. The rise of Nazism in neighboring Germany created new geopolitical challenges for the country. Hitler made no secret of his territorial ambitions, and the annexation of Austria was one of his primary goals. The Christian Socials never endorsed Nazism; their priorities shifted considerably over the 1920s and the 1930s. Right after 1918, they had endorsed Anschluss, sharing this view with many other political forces in Austria, including the Social Democrats. But they reconsidered their support of Anschluss as early as the 1920s, fearing that the Social Democrats who had become strong in Germany's mainstream politics could extend their influence to Austria as well. They were even more adamant in their opposition to the Nazis, who could pose a direct threat to Austrian independence.

Other right-wing groups in Austria, however, did support the Nazis. Notably, the Greater German People's Party, a member of the government coalition since 1920, shifted even further to the right in the late 1920s and early 1930s.[17] In 1922 Wilhelm Ellenbogen, a leading Austrian socialist, could comment dismissively of the GDVP as a marginal phenomenon, a "fifth wheel" in the governmental carriage.[18] The party's very entry into mainstream politics, however, presaged developments that Ellenbogen could not have foreseen at the time. In the 1930s the GDVP became Hitler's bastion in Austria. Not all GDVP members wound up becoming Austrian Nazis. But many did, and thus did the radical, "racial" nationalism of imperial-era pan-Germanism acquire an ominous new form and vigor in the 1930s.[19]

The GDVP's endorsement of Hitler ruptured the coalition that had been in effect since 1920. To replace a departed ally, the Christian Socials turned to the Heimwehr. In 1930 the Heimatblock—a political party based on the Heimwehr—entered the government. In 1932 it became part of a majority in a coalition government formed with the Christian Socials.[20] While the GDVP suppprted the Nazis, the Heimwehr adopted a fascist ideology. Outright Nazis in government were thus replaced by fascists.

This development was also a consequence of the tensions between the Christian Socials and Social Democrats dating back to the empire. In 1931 the CSs again sought a counterforce to the radical right by trying to form an alliance with the left, reaching out to the SDs. While the leadership of the Christian Social Party and the government now featured new faces, Austria's Social Democrats were still led by Otto Bauer. And, just as he had done in the 1920s, in 1931 Bauer rejected an alliance with the Christian Socials. Capitalism, he argued, was nearing its death, and allying with the bourgeoisie at this precise moment would muddy the waters of the workers' cause. As he saw it, socialists should remain in opposition through the ultimate collapse of capitalism, standing ready to win the people's mandate for the transition to socialism thereafter. This was the vision that Bauer had nurtured since the imperial era, and not even the violence of 1927 had altered his belief that the transition from capitalism to socialism must be achieved solely by democratic and institutional means.

Capitalism was indeed crumbling in Austria and elsewhere under the pressure of the worldwide financial crisis, but its downfall would precipitate the onset of authoritarianism rather than democratic socialism. In 1932 the CS chancellor Engelbert Dollfuss put an end to Austria's parliamentary system and its post-1918 democracy. In part, he can be said to have been motivated by not entirely antidemocratic considerations: facing the threats of an increasingly aggressive Germany and of homegrown Nazi sympathizers eager to advance Germany's ambitions with regard to Austria, Dollfuss sought to preserve his country's independence by outlawing the Nazis and establishing a fascist dictatorship. He initially kept the door open to political compromise with other parties, negotiating with Social Democrats regarding a potential new coalition in early 1933. But these talks went nowhere, and the chancellor proceeded with his own radical solutions, dissolving parliament and organizing the Fatherland Front, an ostensibly nonpartisan organization that included supporters of the regime, with all parties beside the Christian Socials banned.

At this point, Dollfuss's main opposition was that voiced by his own CS colleagues. He then proceeded to liquidate the Christian Social Party and its affiliated workers' associations, absorbing both into the pro-government Fatherland Front. By late 1933 Austria was ruled by an authoritarian government, but this authoritarianism differed from that of its Italian and German neighbors; neither a completely fascist nor Nazi state, this was rather a unique variant of corporate authoritarianism that limited the participation of existing institutions without entirely demolishing them. Austria was now a corporate state, governed by sector-based chambers that replaced the parliament.[21]

The history of the Austrian right is thus one of the most complicated episodes of interwar Europe. While Germany and Italy saw democracies collapse under the pressure of right-wing radicalism, in Austria democracy came to an end amid the confrontation of two variants of the radical right: fascists and Nazis. Both were homegrown, and both traced their roots to the empire. Both, however, radicalized only in the late 1920s and early 1930s, and the confrontation between them resulted in the establishment of a fascist-like authoritarian regime. Fascism in Austria, that is, resulted from the vexed politics of the Republic of Austria; as a movement it consisted especially of Christian Social activists who had shifted rightward during the 1920s.

This Austria torn by internal tensions became also an object of international attention. Both Nazi Germany and fascist Italy followed political developments in Austria closely. Benito Mussolini had reason to fear the potential rise of Nazis in Austria: as Hitler's fifth column in the country, they could facilitate Germany's annexation of Austria. Attempting to head off this outcome, Mussolini actively supported Austria's homegrown and pro-independence fascists. Providing military and financial assistance, he bolstered Chancellor Dollfuss's efforts to preserve Austria's independence, on the condition that Vienna would help to combat the red menace that, Mussolini feared, could spread to Italy.[22]

In February 1934, in compliance with their Italian partners, the Austrian police conducted a search of the Social Democratic Party's headquarters in Linz. On the thirteenth of that month, socialists in Vienna had convened at a private home, where Otto Bauer allegedly first endorsed the use of force against the government but later retracted his statements, pleading for a peaceful resolution.[23] Workers did go on strike, but with no leadership or agenda. The government carried out arrests among socialists and demonstrators. On February 15, two days after the beginning of the would-be revolt, several organizers fled Austria.

The crisis deepened in July 1934 with an attempted putsch in Vienna, as Austrian Nazis supported by Germany tried to overthrow the country's existing regime.[24] The government's national defense units fought back and held their positions, although Chancellor Dollfuss himself was shot and killed. Kurt

Schuschnigg, minister of justice in Dollfuss's government, took over as chancellor and, following his predecessor's course, intensified Austria's reliance on Italy and Hungary. He also stepped up political repressions against the socialists. Indeed, it was the socialists who suffered graver consequences of this attempted coup than did the Nazis who had staged it.[25] The Social Democratic Party and its associations having already been outlawed, many former members were imprisoned.

It was in the wake of this grave crisis that the Habsburgs reappeared in the political arena. In 1919 the Austrian government had issued the so-called Habsburg Law, which forced members of the royal family into exile, confiscated their property, and barred them from political office. But after the 1934 putsch, facing imminent German aggression, Chancellor Schuschnigg revoked the Habsburg Law and began to make references to the "rebuilding of the monarchy," without mentioning actual restoration. The Austrian constitution was revised such that the federal state was no longer defined specifically as a republic.[26] Monarchy seemed back on the table. The Habsburg restoration, or as Schuschnigg termed it, the "rebuilding," never came to fruition, but it was only with Germany's annexation of Austria in 1938 that the idea received its final burial. Even after 1934, democracy was splintered but not yet entirely destroyed, and as several of our protagonists observed, conditions in Austria remained freer than in Germany or Italy.

1934: Otto Bauer

Those believing the 1934 Austrian crisis would be short-lived included the socialist leader Otto Bauer. He was primarily responsible for the party's decisions during the fateful 1920s and 1930s, notably for the Social Democrats' commitment to nonviolence and refusal to join coalitions. But in 1934 he was among the first to flee Austria, moving to Brno, Czechoslovakia, about an hour from Vienna by train.[27]

The escape and emigration hit Bauer hard emotionally. After arriving in Brno, he experienced pangs of conscience: how would his comrades react to his flight?[28] He also took responsibility for the Austrian crisis, admitting that his rigid adherence to imperial-era models—his insistence that socialists continue, in the republic, to employ the same tactics they had under Habsburg rule—had been catastrophic. Days after arriving in Brno, he published a fifty-page pamphlet explaining what had happened and why: "Undoubtedly, we made mistakes. . . . It is all the easier for me personally to confess our mistakes, for I can do so without throwing the blame on anyone else; since I am more responsible than anyone else for the mistakes we committed."[29] He characterized his choices as a political miscalculation: he had believed that "the maintenance of a frankly opposition policy could prevent the masses, impoverished and embittered by the economic crisis, from flocking over to the National Socialists."[30] He had believed that restraint might stem the tide of violence, but what transpired was just the opposite.

What had happened in Vienna, Bauer emphasized in his 1934 analysis, could presage utter disaster: "The overthrow of Social Democracy in Austria has opened both of these paths: the path to Hitler and the path to the Habsburgs." To Bauer, these were equally dangerous, as both could lead to war: "Europe has yet to learn by experience what a key position for European peace has been destroyed by the defeat of Austrian Social Democracy."[31] Bauer believed that right-wing radicalism in Europe could be deterred by a strong and united socialist movement, and he tried in Brno to revive international socialist cooperation: "What we need and can build up today in Austria and beyond is a democratic mass organization with hundreds of thousands of members."[32] He worked to do exactly that, collaborating with other Austrian refugees and émigrés to attempt to revive the party and give a new shape to the socialist movement. He and other socialists clung to the hope of a worldwide socialist revolution that would bring down Nazism in Germany and elsewhere in Europe.[33]

1934: Wilhelm Ellenbogen

In the 1930s, several of Bauer's colleagues rejected his tactics of passivity and noncooperation as dangerous to the party and the country. This opposition within the party was represented notably by Wilhelm Ellenbogen, one of the leading Austrian Social Democrats since the empire. He criticized both the Schutzbund's passivity and the socialists' failure to coordinate during critical moments. After July 1927 Ellenbogen urged that the tactic of noncooperation be abandoned, in particular calling for an alliance with Christian Socials.[34] In 1933 he declared that the crisis required an appropriate response—if necessary, a military one.[35]

Yet internal dissent among the socialists was largely as muted as that among the Christian Socials. Though Ellenbogen had long belonged to the leadership of Austrian social democracy, his voice was not enough to reverse Bauer's policies. And just as Dollfuss's authoritarian vision prevailed in Austria's "black" party, so did Bauer's views remain dominant in its "red" one. Both parties were for many years inherently democratic in their composition and programs, but their failure to reach compromise both within their own ranks and between them doomed Austria's democracy.

The weakness of their opposition was not only detrimental to both parties, it jeopardized particular individuals' freedom. Unlike Bauer, Ellenbogen remained in Vienna after 1934. He was arrested during the clashes in February of that year. His prison term was relatively brief; in May, socialists were released on the condition that they refrain from politics.[36] Pre-1938 fascist Austria would never be as oppressive as fascist Italy or Nazi Germany; the socialists' early release from prison was one indication. And in this period Austria's governmental policies, though politically oppressive, posed no direct threat to individual lives.

Social democracy in Austria thus collapsed not just under the onslaught of the radical right, but also because of specific ideological and political choices made by party leaders who had come of age under the empire. Bauer's insistence on continuing Austro-Marxist practices after 1918 backfired, his rigid intransigence and his renunciation of the use of force having tragic consequences not only for himself personally, but for Austria and Europe at large.

Joseph Redlich: Lost between Continents

Despite the initial reservations both Bauer and Ellenbogen had regarding the prospects of the Republic of Austria, they did accept it after 1918. This was not a foregone conclusion; both had property and family ties to territories that after 1918 became part of Czechoslovakia. But having spent most of their imperial-era lives in Vienna, they sailed through the transition to republican Austria without much rockiness. The choice of where home was, and the road to accepting it, proved less smooth for some of their contemporaries. Ultimately, the crisis in Austria that began in the 1920s and escalated in the following decade bore out the adage that "you can't go home again."

Joseph Redlich, the empire's last finance minister, belonged to the latter category. A native of Moravia, a Germanophone assimilated Jew, he had spent much of his adult life in Vienna—a member of the elite both before and after 1918. Acquainted with many in the empire's political circles, he was close to

Tomáš Masaryk. Like Bauer, he had grown up in a territory that after 1918 became part of Czechoslovakia; but unlike Bauer, he struggled to decide between that country and the new Republic of Austria. After his nomination as finance minister was scuttled in 1920 by opposition from German nationalists, he shifted back to academia. In 1926 he moved to the United States to take a visiting professorship at Harvard University. He spent the late 1920s between the continents—academic semesters in Cambridge and summers in London, Paris, Vienna, and Vulpera-Tarasp in Switzerland.[37] Redlich would wander between various countries for the rest of his life.

Redlich's trajectory was not uncommon among the statesmen of his political and intellectual circles, for whom this sense of unbelonging and alienation was a typical post-Habsburg mood. Letters to his friend the poet Hermann Bahr revealed the onset of depression in the mid-1920s. Redlich complained of an overwhelming sense of rootlessness pursuing him wherever he went. In the summer of 1928, at the time residing in the United States, he vented his frustration to another friend, the poet and dramatist Hugo von Hofmannsthal: "We once had a Fatherland, a mission, and a history. Now . . . we have to face the remarkable decline of culture in the new Austria."[38]

Yet the fatherland maintained its pull on him, and in the early 1930s he gave in. In the summer of 1931, in the midst of the worldwide Great Depression, the largest Austrian bank, Creditanstalt, collapsed.[39] The same year, Redlich returned to Austria to serve—yet again—as minister of finance. He took the post on June 20, 1931, at the height of the Creditanstalt crisis, but stayed in government for just over three months. Upon resigning in October, Redlich cited the lack of support he had received from the parliament and the anti-Semitic smears he had faced, including even from fellow cabinet members.[40] He also fell ill in the summer of 1931, hit hard by the strain of government work amid the overall Austrian crisis.[41] This time Redlich remained in Europe to serve as a deputy judge in the Court of International Justice in The Hague.

In the early 1930s Redlich observed the ascendancy of right-wing movements across Europe, especially in Germany, with grave concern. He traced the roots of Nazism to the Habsburg Empire, explaining how Hitler had appropriated the pan-German doctrine of the Austrian politician and parliament member Georg Schönerer. Pan-Germanism, in Redlich's view, had initially been conceived as a tool to bring down the Habsburg Empire as a multiethnic polity. It had failed in that particular mission, but did not die entirely and was revived after 1918 by Hitler: "Nothing prevented the young Adolf Hitler from adopting the doctrine of Schönerer, whose weekly reviews he had avidly read and whose speeches he had listened to fervently while he was living as a youth in Vienna. Indeed, in his famous autobiography Hitler recites how in his teens he had been an ardent disciple and follower of Schönerer."[42]

In the 1930s Redlich vacillated between hope and despair. He had come to believe that the German annexation of Austria was inevitable, that it could be postponed but not prevented. This was a conviction he shared with Mussolini, whose intervention in Austrian politics constituted precisely a response to Hitler's anticipated move on Austria. Remembering the devastation of the Great War, Redlich commented with dismay in a note to a friend, "History teaches us very little. Not even to those who lived through it."[43] But like many others of his generation, he held out some hope, believing even in the 1930s that Austria's problems were solvable, and that democracy in Europe could be restored.

Redlich did not live to see the most gruesome outcomes of the developments he observed: he passed away in Vienna in November 1936.[44] He did not see the crowds that welcomed Hitler with great enthusiasm when Nazi forces marched into Vienna's central Heldenplatz. Generations of Austrians after Redlich would, in a similar vein, absolve Austrians of their responsibility in supporting Nazism; significantly, one of the first to emphasize this image of Austria as the first victim of Hitler's aggression was none other than Otto von Habsburg, the empire's last crown prince.[45]

Between Vienna and Rome: Post-Habsburg Italians

For some former inhabitants of Vienna such as Redlich, Austria became inhospitable. Still, throughout the 1920s and even in the 1930s, it continued to attract a large number of émigrés from countries where the political situation was worse than in Vienna. Some of the early émigrés included the Italian socialist Valentino Pittoni, who experienced the crisis in Italy and then Austria firsthand. One of Trieste's most prominent socialists before 1918, Pittoni had been marginalized within his party, his life and career crushed between the ascent and collision of radical left and radical right. After losing his editorship of the leading Italian socialist periodical, *Il Lavoratore,* he became an outlier. In 1923 his family helped arrange his relocation to Vienna, where he solicited assistance from former colleagues, including Wilhelm Ellenbogen. The emigration was not an easy choice: it entailed separation from his family and in ef-fect the remaking of a career from scratch. But Vienna provided security and professional opportunities no longer available in Trieste. In the Austrian capi-tal, Pittoni began working for the *Arbeiter-Zeitung,* a leading socialist periodi-cal with roots in the empire; but neither this publication nor Pittoni would ever again have the influence they enjoyed prior to 1918. He spent the rest of his life in Vienna, where he died in 1933.

The radicalization of politics in Italy forced some into exile, but opened new doors to others inclined to endorse the new regime, a trend reflected by Francesco Salata. A leading Italian nationalist in the Habsburg Empire, he moved to Rome in 1915, settling there permanently after the war. A radical by imperial standards, he appeared as a moderate in post-1918 Italy in compari-son with kingdom-bred nationalists. Salata only endorsed Il Duce gradually, by the late 1920s, and returned to mainstream politics in the early 1930s. He too, like many of the other figures discussed in this study, felt the pull of Vienna, making his way from Rome back to the capital of his bygone country.

Salata spent most of the 1920s in Italy building his academic career, which became his springboard back to politics. In March 1929 he began work-ing at the archive of the Foreign Ministry, tasked with selecting and preparing its documents for publication, and in 1932 he joined this ministry's historical-diplomatic commission. He had come far from his initial wariness of Mussolini to serving, by the late 1920s, as the regime's key ideologist, a go-to man for na-tionalist propaganda.

His academic work also paved his way back to Vienna when a new job opportunity presented itself, the result of Mussolini's determination to build an Italian presence in Austria as a hedge against Germany. In April 1934, with Mussolini's endorsement, Salata drafted a memorandum in support of the founding of two organizations: an institute of Italian culture in Vienna, and an institute of Austrian culture in Rome. The same year, Salata relocated to Vienna to serve as unofficial liaison between the two capitals. He would soon advance still higher in the diplomatic hierarchy; in August 1936 he was made Italy's new ambassador to Austria.

Salata's support of Austrian independence contradicted Mussolini's for-eign policies. By 1936 Mussolini realized that the Anschluss was inevitable, and that it would be best for him to get on the "right side" of it.[46] Rome's rela-tions with the West correspondingly soured, and the chances of allying with France and Britain appeared more and more remote. In the fall of 1937 Salata was dismissed and recalled to Italy.[47] He was politically irrelevant once again, just as he had been in 1922. Even after accepting Mussolini, Salata remained out of step with his regime; having endorsed fascism, that is, he continued to resist Nazism. While Italian fascism represented the furthest thing from the mode of politics practiced under the Habsburgs, Nazism was even further. Despite these professional disappointments, Salata remained in Italy and supported Mussolini until his death in 1944.

Salata's second chance in politics had been granted only because he endorsed Mussolini. Those who did not were marginalized, imprisoned, or expelled. Alcide De Gasperi after 1918 moved from Vienna to Trieste, and later to Rome. As head of the newly founded Italian People's Party, he initially contemplated cooperation with Mussolini but soon went into opposition. Arrested in March 1927, he was sentenced and imprisoned until July 1928, whereupon he was released on the condition that he refrain from active politics. He spent the following years working at the Vatican Archive. The persecution he had suffered did not break his will, and he wrote and published prolifically, albeit avoiding sensitive political issues.

De Gasperi observed with dismay the concurrent rise of the extreme right and left in much of Europe. In the early 1930s he began to voice concern regarding the political situation in Germany. Even in the winter of 1933, just after Hitler had come to power, De Gasperi still had faith that international diplomacy would be capable of responding to the rising danger.[48] But his optimism dwindled with time. In his view, the hopeless polarization of European politics was a matter of the radical right and left fueling one another. Watching the crisis unfold in Austria, he noted the extent to which the communist threat had enabled the radical right to consolidate. "The fear of Bolshevism," he wrote in August 1935, "induced conservative deputies to give in to the radical [rightists]."[49] Hitler and Stalin imitated one another's tactics, each meanwhile representing themselves as responding to the threats posed by the other.[50]

The year 1918 thus marked a turning point in all of these lives—Pittoni's, Salata's, and De Gasperi's. But in the immediate postwar years, all of them shared some affinities—the socialists, the nationalists, and the clericals supporting similar political models and an institutional tradition that they all had inherited from the empire. They shifted apart gradually over the 1920s and the 1930s. For Salata and De Gasperi, the years 1933–34 represented, in some ways, a more radical turning point than 1918, marking the beginning of the true end of the Habsburg era in European history.

Czechoslovakia: Right-Wing Radicalism and Fascism

By 1933 Vienna and Rome had closed their doors on those who supported democracy over authoritarianism. Some opted to stay home and lie low, retreating to an internal exile from political and intellectual life; others chose emigration. Czechoslovakia's capital of Prague, in the meantime, flourished in what was, at least outwardly, still a democratic state with fully functioning institutions. Indeed, interwar Czechoslovakia would never see the sort of extremes of political hostilities experienced by Italy and Austria.

As governed by the Pětka, the country permitted the existence of opposition groups on the right and left, but the mobilization of the major political parties in a coalition helped prevent radicalization, drawing most voters toward the moderate center. The Czech right wing—the Czech National Democrats headed by Karel Kramář and Alois Rašin—was strong after 1918, but experienced a decline shortly thereafter. In 1935 Kramář tried to unify the nationalist opposition, merging two right-wing groups to form the National Unity organization, which he headed until his death in 1937, but whose role in Czechoslovak politics remained marginal.[51] Czechoslovakia did produce a fascist movement, but it never became part of mainstream politics.

The far left was likewise relatively weak in Czechoslovakia. The country's Communist Party was founded in 1921 by Bohumír Šmeral. Carrying on the tradition of Austro-Marxism of which he'd been a part, he conceived of communism as an heir to this worldview, as reviving the internationalism and interethnic unity it had foregrounded. But he became marginalized within his party in 1925 as a result of his resistance to control from Moscow.[52] He spent the next ten years traveling between Czechoslovakia and Western Europe, working on different assignments on behalf of the Comintern. His disagreements with Moscow notwithstanding, Šmeral remained a devoted communist. The fateful year 1938 saw him, too, put to flight. Upon Germany's annexation of the Sudetenland, he was one of many to leave Czechoslovakia. While most of those fleeing went west, Šmeral chose Moscow instead, arriving there amid the most gruesome political purges then victimizing multitudes of allegedly backslidden communists and "saboteurs."

It was, then, the radical right, not the left, that ultimately drove Šmeral from Czechoslovakia. His politics and worldview were far more complex than that of Stalin (to say nothing of Hitler). But after 1938 Europe no longer had room for political complexity—certainly not for the ideological nuances of a

Habsburg era–raised socialist intellectual. In a world polarized by radical extremes, the East, dominated by Soviet communists, was a safer place for Šmeral than the West, then being overrun by Nazis. At the outbreak of the Second World War, Šmeral was still in the USSR, where he died of natural causes in May 1941, just weeks before Germany's invasion.

Ludwig Czech and "Pure German Culture" in Czechoslovakia

Ethnic Czechs such as Šmeral had many reasons to fear the Nazi ascendancy, but Jews, even assimilated ones, were all the more vulnerable. Several of the figures discussed in this study belonged to this latter category. Before 1938, Austria and Czechoslovakia were, if not ideal for them, at least safe. The year 1938 suddenly confronted them with a precariousness their non-Jewish peers did not experience.

Ludwig Czech was, like several of our protagonists, a representative of Moravia, and a Germanophone assimilated Jew; but unlike Bauer and Ellenbogen, he ended up in Czechoslovakia after 1918. His adjustment to postimperial realities was akin to that of Redlich in its difficulty. With his Jewish roots and imperial upbringing, Czech too found it difficult to accept the new mode of politics in post-1918 Europe. In prewar Brno, he had combated German nationalist tendencies; after 1918, using the Czechoslovak parliament as his venue, he opposed language regulations that limited the rights of the city's German minority.[53] Like Šmeral, he was hit hard by the ethnic schisms plaguing social democracy in post-1918 Czechoslovakia. He became alienated from his Czech colleagues, meanwhile continuing the same friendships with Karl Renner and other Austrians that they had forged in the imperial period.[54]

In 1920 Czech became head of the German Social Democratic Workers' Party. Under his leadership, this organization took an oppositionist stance, for some years refusing to ally with other political forces and thus remaining on the margins of Czechoslovak politics. But the political situation in Austria and Czechoslovakia soon shifted. By the mid-1920s, the ruling coalition in Prague expressed interest in bringing ethnic Germans into the government as part of a program of interethnic reconciliation. Czech joined the government in 1929 as minister of social welfare; in 1934 he became minister of public health.

German Social Democrats in Czechoslovakia were more affected by the rise of Nazism than were German nationalists. In the early years of Czechoslovakia's existence, Marxism was quite popular among the country's ethnic Germans. But toward the late 1920s and especially in the early 1930s, political preferences in this cohort underwent a shift. Radical right-wing organizations in Czechoslovakia received support from Germany, and they succeeded in siphoning off part of the electorate that had formerly supported the German left. Nazism's impact on interwar Czechoslovakia was thus as important as on Austria.

The right-wing ascendancy forced Czech to rethink his stance toward Czechoslovak socialists. The Czechoslovak and German Social Democratic parties began cooperating after 1928, impelled by the need to join forces against the right.[55] This cooperation continued through the mid-1930s. In 1935 Czech decided to stay in government and publicly thanked Czechoslovak socialists for their support.[56] But this alliance had consolidated too late and was too weak to counteract German nationalist dissent in Czechoslovakia and pressure from abroad. In 1938 the German Social Democratic Party of Czechoslovakia dissolved itself.

Despite the semblance of stability, interwar Czechoslovakia was wracked with unresolved tensions that facilitated German aggression in 1938. The German minority was never properly integrated into the new state, and a feeling of alienation persisted even among those who, like Ludwig Czech, were politically prominent and served in government. For Czech and German Social Democrats in Czechoslovakia, 1938 became a major turning point, in some ways more critical than 1918. Such were the contradictions of yet another successor state that, despite compositionally resembling the old multiethnic empire, behaved as if it were a monoethnic state.

Slovenian Socialists: Henrik Tuma and Ivan Regent

When Italy became fascist and authoritarian, and when Austria started its political descent, at least some of the former Habsburg citizens, notably Slovenes from the Adriatic, looked to Yugoslavia as a possible escape route. Yugoslavia was a product of the post-1918 territorial arrangements, an entirely new state built on the ideals and promises of South Slav unity. Yugoslavism became a popular concept in particular during the war. But the immediate post-1918 years revealed many complications of a South Slav unity. Serbia became dominant early on, being the only entity that had been independent since 1882; other parts of the new state had formerly belonged to the Habsburg and the Ottoman Empires. The tensions among nationalities, but primarily between the Serbs on one hand and the Croats and Slovenes on the other, only worsened over the years. Amid a nationwide crisis of interethnic violence, and fearing Yugoslavia's disintegration at the hands of defiant Croats, King Alexander I took emergency measures on January 6, 1929, suspending the constitution, dissolving parliament, and establishing a royal dictatorship—his way to try to restore stability and unity.[57] All parties organized on ethnic or religious principles were banned; elected officials were replaced; and the military was coopted into state administration. Yugoslavia too thus succumbed to authoritarianism.

But for all its problems, Yugoslavia, being a milder dictatorship than Italy or Germany, provided, like Austria in the same period of the 1920s and early 1930s, a refuge for those facing persecution elsewhere. Notably, it hosted a cohort of Slovenian émigrés from territories that became part of Italy after 1918. Some of these Slovenes relocated to Yugoslavia immediately after the First World War, but many others fled Italy as a result of political persecutions in the wake of Mussolini's takeover.

Henrik Tuma and Ivan Regent, Slovenian socialists who had matured in the empire and spent the immediate post-1918 years in Italy, came to Yugoslavia in the 1920s. Tuma found himself in a situation similar to that of Pittoni: a Social Democrat adhering to the tradition of Austro-Marxism after the empire's collapse, he was ousted from politics by radical maximalists. He quit Italy in 1924 at sixty-six years of age and settled in Ljubljana, where he abandoned active politics. Yugoslavia offered little solace. The politics Tuma witnessed there was, in his view, much like what he had experienced in Italy. "The Yugoslav nationalist state presents a miserable image," he wrote in 1925, adding that "[Prime Minister Nikola] Pašić and his colleagues are following in Mussolini's footsteps," an allusion to the Serb-dominated central government's treatment of Slovenia.[58] In a letter to Regent, he described Yugoslavia as a country based on a "nationalist-fascist principle" that he predicted would be short-lived and end catastrophically: "I am sure that the system will destroy itself, but I fear that in the process it will destroy the state as well. I am certain that we might well be faced with the outbreak of a Second World War."[59] He became even more skeptical as to the country's prospects over time. In July 1934, in a letter to Senator Ivan Hribar, Tuma complained about discrimination in the state services in Slovenia. "You know me, I am not a nationalist," he wrote, "you can easily judge it from my work. But I try to work for the benefit of my people."[60] He was particularly alarmed by the rise of radicalism in Europe. "Hitler," Tuma told his son Boris in 1932, "only became possible because of the coming to power of the petite bourgeoisie. Today's state is a petit-bourgeois state."[61] He spent the rest of his life in Ljubljana, dying in 1935.

Tuma's colleague Ivan Regent also left Italy in search of refuge, but for a different reason. After the war he had moved further leftward to become a communist. When Mussolini outlawed the Communist Party of Italy in 1926, Regent decided to emigrate. Leaving his wife and daughter behind in Italy, he moved to Ljubljana.[62] The Communist Party of Yugoslavia had been formed in 1919 but was banned by King Alexander the following year. Yugoslavia would be no safer than Italy: after establishing his dictatorship in 1929, Alexander unleashed political persecution on the regime's opponents, forcing some to flee the country. Amid the mass arrests of this period, Regent was forced to move yet again. He crossed the border from Yugoslavia to Vienna, a move arranged secretly by his friend and colleague Rudolf Golouh, another Slovenian socialist turned communist.

Regent's subsequent peregrinations—at times staying in one place for a few years, other times for mere months—reflected the difficulties his generation experienced after 1918. He was an extreme example, representing as he did a movement that elicited particular trepidation in nearly every European capital; but many noncommunists, forced to move for other reasons, faced similar hurdles. Regent brought his family with him to Vienna, where their sojourn proved brief: communists were soon outlawed here as well, and he was forced to move once more. The family now relocated to France, settling for a time in Paris, only to soon face a situation similar to what they had encountered in Ljubljana and Vienna.

Regent finally found refuge in Moscow, to which he was invited by Italian communist leader Palmiro Togliati. Like Šmeral, Regent had been ousted from his home by the onset of right-wing politics and now saw the Soviet Union as the only safe haven in Europe for someone endorsing the left.[63] In January 1931 he moved to Moscow to serve as secretary of the communist-controlled Organization of International Aid. In the Soviet capital the Regent family occupied a room in the Soiuznaia, "a shabby old residence hotel for foreign communists."[64] Regent began working also in the publishing industry, translating works of major Russian Bolsheviks into Slovenian.

Even in this technically settled period, life was not easy. All these relocations took a toll on Regent's family. His wife, Malka (Amalia Licer) sometimes came along, sometimes not. Their adopted daughter Mara remained in Trieste for some time while her parents were in transit from one country to the next.

In Moscow the family had to subsist on Regent's meager salary: 275 rubles, with only about 60 left after all dues and rent had been paid. His wife could not find a job, and the housing situation was difficult.[65] "We were not doing well in Moscow," Regent later recalled.[66] The outbreak of war found all three family members in the Soviet Union. Regent's wife died in a sanatorium near Moscow in 1941. Regent himself lived until 1967, making him the last of our protagonists to pass away.

Regent's experience encapsulates the story of the postimperial generation's wanderings across Europe between the Adriatic and Siberia, suggesting the persistence of a certain continental integration in defiance of the new divisions. Regent's moves—Trieste, Ljubljana, Vienna, Paris, and eventually Moscow—were all possible in interwar Europe but would have been unimaginable after 1945, when borders became more strict and divides more rigid than ever.

Poland: Ignacy Daszyński, Herman Diamand, Stanisław Głąbiński

Between Moscow and Vienna lay another troubled successor state, Poland, which also succumbed to authoritarianism in the 1920s. Consisting of three parts that had long belonged to different empires, it was now independent after nearly 150 years of imperial rule. And like other successor states, it was ethnically diverse, with Ukrainians, Byelorussians, Germans, and Jews making up a significant percentage of the population. Torn between several political and cultural models, including the socialist left and the nationalist right, Poland gradually descended into chaos. By 1926 the new republic had seen fourteen different governments, each dissolved within a matter of months. Nor was this pattern like the cabinet reshuffling or rotation of ministers in Czechoslovakia; this was, rather, a case of the entire government being repeatedly forced to resign—a situation hardly conducive to stability.

This state of affairs culminated in a May 1926 takeover staged by General Józef Piłsudski, Poland's head of state (a position combining the duties of prime minister and president). As coups go, Piłsudski's had some share of noble motivation: he hoped to end the frequent governmental changeovers resulting from the ongoing confrontation between the two major camps, the socialists and the nationalists. In his new capacity as (among other titles) general inspector of the armed forces, Piłsudski monopolized control over the military and rotated civilian ministers and officials, favoring technocratic professionals over ideologues. The parliament was not dissolved, but subsequent elections were government-controlled. This was not a complete autocracy, and some institutional options remained open, but interwar Poland would never return to the level of (however flawed) democracy the country had briefly enjoyed.[67]

The crisis worsened in 1929 and 1930. Facing parliamentary opposition to his amendments of the constitution, Piłsudski first brought the military into the parliament and then in August 1930 ordered that body's closure.[68] The regime in Poland became even more rigid after Piłsudski's death in 1935, when the military took still greater control over the country.

Fragmented Opposition

Piłsudski's recourse to authoritarianism came as a shock even to some of his supporters—for instance, to Ignacy Daszyński. Daszyński had made a career in politics as one of Poland's leading socialists. The two men had been acquainted since before 1914. The political crisis thus entailed a personal crisis for Daszyński: the end of a friendship that had withstood the exigencies of empires, war, and postwar transition.

The post-1926 crisis between Daszyński and Piłsudski was, moreover, rooted in pre-1918 precedents, illustrating yet again the continuity of imperial-era practices across the ostensible 1918 watershed. Political violence had been a norm in the Russian Empire but an exception in its Habsburg counterpart. After 1918 Daszyński and Piłsudski continued to operate within the same ideological frameworks they always had: Piłsudski considered aggression an occasionally necessary if regrettable tactic; Daszyński found it entirely unacceptable. "We cannot adjust the constitution to the needs of each specific government," he wrote in the wake of Piłsudski's coup.[69] The new government, he emphasized, had failed to put an end to the chaos; Piłsudski himself had failed to restore democracy.[70]

Other socialists shared Daszyński's frustration. Herman Diamand had, like Daszyński, supported Piłsudski before, during, and after the war, but the events of 1926 came as a great disappointment. He had distinguished himself as a supporter of parliamentarianism, describing any attempt by the government to circumvent the parliament as dictatorship, equivalent to those in place in Soviet Russia and fascist Italy.[71] Diamand, however, did not rule out the possibility of cooperation with the government even after Piłsudski's takeover. When this did not materialize, he began to seek emotional—if not political—refuge outside of Poland. "The situation in Warsaw is not good," he wrote to his wife in December 1926.[72] Vienna, his second home under the empire, now seemed a haven: "Vienna makes a unique impression on me, different from other cities," he wrote his wife in November 1929. "I don't feel like a stranger here. I have invested so much work here, influenced the city's development. . . . People are amicable and brotherly to me here."[73] Many in his cohort shared similar sentiments, feeling split in their affections between several fatherlands.

Warsaw meanwhile became progressively more hostile. As an assimilated Jew, bilingual in Polish and German, Diamand experienced quite personally both the escalation in nationalism and the increasing hostility between the nationalist right and social democracy. Continuing his career specialization from the Habsburg period, in interwar Poland Diamand worked on the state's finances, in particular focusing on international relations. He spent much of the 1920s drafting Poland's trade agreements with Germany. His time in Berlin led Polish nationalists to denounce him as "a Jewish socialist who sympathizes with the Germans."[74] "They're calling me a Germanophile," he reported in a 1925 letter to his wife.[75] "Diamand's weakness," his fellow Jewish-descended Polish socialist Adam Pragier would comment in his memoirs, "was his limitless respect toward German Social Democracy, and his belief in the future of the Weimar Republic."[76] In 1928 Diamand still clung to the hope that democracy would return in Poland, declaring in the parliament that leftists like himself were willing to join the government.[77] He died in Lwów following a heart attack in 1931.

Nonsocialists who opposed Piłsudski, including the National Democrat Stanisław Głąbiński, were less apologetic in doing so; he was not, after all, their former comrade. Having made a political career in the Habsburg Empire as a deputy and minister, and thereafter in the Republic of Poland in its parliament and senate, Głąbiński now joined a cohort of political figures vociferously opposed to Piłsudski, whom he viewed as "a brave, daring, arrogant, vindictive, and sneaky man."[78] Yet in his approach to the Piłsudski phenomenon as to much else, Głąbiński was more akin to the Habsburg-bred socialist Daszyński than to the cothinkers he had among Polish nationalists from the former Russian Empire; the legacy of their respective imperial upbringings lived on among nationalists not just in the 1920s but through the 1930s.

Głąbiński, for example, was reluctant to endorse the use of force typically accepted by his compatriots from Russian Poland. The first major disagreement between Roman Dmowski, the leading Polish nationalist from the former Russian Empire, and Głąbiński had occurred upon the outbreak of the Great War, with the former endorsing Russia as a lesser evil compared to Germany and Austria, and Głąbiński remaining loyal to Vienna instead. When in 1926 Dmowski responded to Piłsudski's coup by organizing the Greater Poland bloc (Obóz Wielkiej Polski), meant to unite all nationalist organizations, Głąbiński refused to join. He did remain active within the National Democratic camp, serving as head of its caucus in the parliament from 1928 to 1935.[79] The unresolved conflict between Dmowski and Głąbiński was yet another example of the resilience of tradition and the troubled postimperial inheritance.

The history of Poland's crisis and its authoritarian regime bears many similarities with the story of authoritarianism in Austria. Both were products of tensions unresolved after 1918; in both cases, the historical legacy of confrontational relations between the two major parties backfired in the 1920s and 1930s, with consequences far more severe than anything seen under the Habsburgs. As in Austria and Italy, the opposition to authoritarianism in Poland was too fragmented to offer any substantive resistance. The failures to repair the damage would resonate still more direly during the Second World War.

Ukrainians between Authoritarianism and Communism

The crisis in Poland affected national minorities to a greater degree than it did ethnic Poles; intraethnic strife was of a correspondingly different scale as well. Before 1926, Poland's government, dominated by National Democrats, enforced assimilation in Galicia and Polish colonization in Volhynia—another region with a large percentage of Ukrainians and Byelorussians. These measures included the closure of Ukrainian schools or their replacement with bilingual Polish-Ukrainian institutions. Piłsudski opposed unilateral assimilation, favoring autonomy instead. After 1926 he reached out to politically moderate Ukrainians with an offer of compromise. Yet these efforts failed against the resistance of Ukrainian nationalists, who refused concessions and moderation and envisioned the destruction of the Polish state and Ukrainian independence as their ultimate and only acceptable goal. The escalation between the Polish government and Ukrainian nationalists came head to head during 1929–30, when, in response to Ukrainian political violence, Warsaw carried out a so-called pacification campaign against the Ukrainians on its eastern borderland, resulting in multiple deaths and the destruction of property.[80]

Poland's policies toward minorities and the Polish-Ukrainian crisis were consequential not only for the country itself but also for the inhabitants of territories across its border in the Soviet Union. In the 1920s and 1930s, the Soviets and Poles competed for the loyalty of Ukrainians at home and abroad. In the early 1920s, with its economic experimentation and tolerant national-minorities policy, the Soviet Union might have appeared a paradise of sorts to those aghast at the political and ethnic-based tensions escalating in Poland. If Poland was behaving as if it were a monoethnic state, the early Soviet Union, with its relatively tolerant policies and promises of national autonomy, was paradoxically something like a Habsburg reincarnation. As such, the Soviet state attracted some Ukrainians who, finding themselves in different European countries after 1918, were inclined to endorse Soviet Ukraine as the only extant form of Ukrainian statehood.

But as the 1920s drew to a close in the Soviet Union, the decade's progressive potential gave way to oppressive developments that were nightmarish. The year 1929 opened a ghastly period in Soviet history that would cost millions of citizens their lives: economic liberalization was halted, nationalities policies were reversed, and a wave of political persecutions commenced. In many cases, they particularly targeted members of national minorities who had thought they were trading their bourgeois comfort for the promise of ethno-cultural liberation under communism.

As described in chapter 7, those who fell under the spell of communist utopianism included Semen Vityk, a Ukrainian Social Democrat from Galicia. In 1925 he emigrated from Vienna to Kharkiv, the capital of Soviet Ukraine, endorsing the Soviet Union and all its policies. He was among many to experience the catastrophic consequences of this choice when in 1929 the "great turn" opened a period of repressions throughout the Soviet Union. Suspecting Ukrainians as potential bearers of cross-border influence from those who would destroy the Soviet Union, Stalin imprisoned or executed hundreds of thousands of them. Ukrainians originally hailing from Galicia fared worse than their peers from other parts of Ukraine, as their geographic origin made them particularly susceptible to the accusation of treason.

Vityk was arrested in March 1933 and sent to Siberia.[81] Even after being sentenced to labor camp, he continued to believe in the just workings of the system, sending numerous appeals to Soviet authorities in Moscow to complain of his treatment. Vityk described himself as a communist who had committed no crime. His pledges of having always supported the system made no difference. Vityk was eventually executed in 1937, one of many thousands who fell victim to the illusions of Soviet communism and Stalin's paranoia.

His story is both exemplary and unique among the cohort of protagonists discussed in this book. Facing the loss of the Habsburg Empire and then of Ukrainian independence, he became trapped in the post-1918 Europe with no clear sense of home and directions. Vienna provided a temporary respite, but it was the Bolsheviks—not the postimperial Austrians—who offered a new hope of salvation. Vityk was one of many descendants of Austro-Marxism who chose the radical left as an answer to the crisis of post-1918 Europe, and part of a larger cohort of Galician Ukrainians who endorsed the Soviet Union as a counterweight to Poland. Such was the result of the tragic choices of the many who felt trapped between the radical right and the radical left, between the East and the West, feeling homeless throughout.

Empire and Successor States, 1918–38

The post-1918 successor states all faced some of the same issues. They had emerged from an empire wherein ethnic heterogeneity had been accepted as the norm. All fashioned themselves as nation-states, specifically, as monoethnic states, each enforcing such policies with varying degrees of coercion.[82] These policies backfired: Germans in Czechoslovakia, Ukrainians in Poland, Croats and Slovenes in Yugoslavia, and Slavs and Germans in Italy never reconciled themselves with the unitary ambitions of their respective central authorities. Radical nationalism had hardly threatened the existence of the Habsburg monarchy prior to 1914, but in post-1918 Europe right-wing nationalism became a grave menace. And each of the successor states faced internal crises that in most cases resulted in authoritarianism or dictatorship. Italy fell to right-wing radicalism soon after the war. Poland became semiauthoritarian in 1926; Yugoslavia, a dictatorship in 1929; Austria, in 1933. All would eventually close their doors on the figures discussed in this study who sought refuge from political persecution in the new post-Habsburg space.

At the same time, several of these states retained elements of the bygone empire—even those that had not been part of it. Italy and the Soviet Union, for instance, make for unlikely "Habsburg successor states." But the Austrian imperial component was nearly as prominent in their interwar history as in that of such proper successor states as Poland and Czechoslovakia—sometimes even more so. For instance, the war did to Italy what the Habsburg collapse did to Czechoslovakia: make it a smaller replica of the empire. The Soviet Union too inherited part of the legacy of the late Habsburg Empire, for a time becoming its sole state upholder: Lenin took up the Austro-Marxist policy of ethnic tolerance, implementing it in the 1920s in the form of the Soviet nativization policy. A number of former Habsburg citizens took part in Austrian, Italian, and Soviet politics as ministers and state functionaries, influencing domestic politics and international affairs.

Unresolved ethnic tensions represented another legacy of the empire, and the conflicts that had germinated before 1918 took new form thereafter. Notably, the failure to address national integration facilitated outside aggression in the late 1930s. In 1939, a mere year after annexing Austria, Hitler moved into the Second Czechoslovak Republic on the pretext of defending the rights of ethnic German citizens supposedly insufficiently protected by Germany's recent annexation of the Sudetenland. Enthusiastic crowds had welcomed him in Vienna, and neither did Czechoslovakia offer any resistance. Germans in the Sudetenland in particular welcomed Hitler as their savior, while Ukrainians in eastern Poland hailed Soviet forces as they marched into the region in September 1939.[83] This enthusiasm dwindled with time, but the initial reception reflected the failures of interwar political settlements, which had exacerbated the crises leading to the Second World War. Such responses could only become possible because Poland had lost the propaganda war with the Soviet Union, and because Ukrainians in Warsaw's shadow remained almost oblivious to the atrocities Stalin had perpetrated on their conationals across the border in Soviet Ukraine.[84] Czechoslovakia also lost its battle with its ethnic minorities— or, to put it more charitably, lost its battle for their hearts and minds. Europeans would pay an impossible price for these failures.

The world of yesterday, to borrow Stefan Zweig's phrase, did not come to an abrupt end in 1918. Neither the First World War nor the civil wars and violence that followed after 1918 ultimately destroyed the practices and models from the Habsburg Empire. The gradual crisis that escalated from the 1920s onward with the concurrent radicalization of politics in several states shattered democratic institutions and undermined imperial practices without, however, totally destroying them. The overt military aggression of the late 1930s became the final blow, not only to democracy in interwar Europe but also to the Habsburg Empire, even if the latter's "official" death had come two decades earlier.

It was not 1918 but rather 1938–39 that brought an end to the Habsburg period in European history. The crisis in Europe, of course, did not start in 1938. Several states across Europe had experienced a political descent and crises of varying magnitude since 1918. The early 1930s became particularly problematic for many of those who came of age under the Habsburgs: Hitler's coming to power in Germany that year and the establishment of authoritarianism in Austria in 1934, after years of prolonged political dysfunction, created problems of enormous magnitude for those who had long regarded Austria and Vienna as a second home and safe haven. But it was only the outward German aggression in 1938 that ultimately destroyed democracy in large parts of Europe and reversed the institutional traditions that several of these countries and many of its citizens had carried from the pre-1918 period.

Epilogue

Empire, 1939–1945, and Beyond

"What is going to happen to Europe? I pray to God that he might bring people wisdom," wrote Alcide De Gasperi in April 1938, referring to Germany's annexation of Austria earlier that year.[1] Wisdom never arrived. Europeans looked away as Hitler moved on, and on March 15, 1939, German forces occupied the Sudetenland on the premise of defending its ethnic German inhabitants. The very ease of German expansion revealed the weakness of international institutions, and passivity led to further aggression. The year 1938 dispelled the illusion that democracy would be possible in Europe under current conditions.

The year 1938 likewise brought an end to an epoch that had started well before 1914 and lasted through the First World War and after it. Despite the severity of the political crisis and the onset of authoritarianism between 1918 and 1938, democracy had remained viable in much of Europe, including its eastern part. In fact the continent's East had been in some ways more stable than its West or South. The Habsburg legacy and its practices of institutional democracy persisted across geographical, national, and ideological divides. Institutional options had been dwindling, also across geographical divides, since the 1920s. But it was only outright military aggression that put an ultimate end to a specific political tradition that many countries, and all the protagonists of this book, inherited from the Habsburg Empire.

As Hitler tested European patience, his true ambitions lay in the East. In 1939 Germany and the Soviet Union signed the Molotov-Ribbentrop nonaggression treaty, a secret protocol stipulating the division of Poland. On September 1, Germany occupied western Poland, and two weeks later the Soviet Union took the east. The year 1941 marked another turning point in European history as, that June, Nazi Germany attacked the Soviet Union. Hitler had planned a quick advance, the Blitzkrieg strategy having been devised in light of the fact that Germany was not prepared to wage a prolonged war. But his designs went awry, and the fighting dragged on for years. In early 1943 German forces were defeated at Stalingrad, the beginning of a counteroffensive that ended with the Red Army's taking of Berlin in May 1945.

Hitler's aggression and the war that ensued reopened old wounds. During this conflict, the vanished empire revealed itself in a new light. It was a former imperial official—Emil Hácha—who, as president of Czechoslovakia, accepted Hitler's ultimatum that led to the Nazis' annexation of part of that country.[2] Another Austrian, also born in the empire, Otto Gustav von Wächter, served as the second governor of the Nazi-established District of Galicia from 1942 to 1944.[3] Even Hitler, born and raised in pre-1918 Austria, in a way paid homage to the empire he had detested: upon the organizing of the Waffen SS Division "Galicia" in 1944, he referred to its members as "Austrian Ruthenians"—the term by which Ukrainians were known in the empire until the late nineteenth century. In Trentino some ethnic Germans who had earlier protested their annexation to Italy now donned German military attire or offered their services to Nazi Germany in other capacities.[4]

Many of our protagonists lived to see the political escalation of the 1930s into the 1940s. Cesare Battisti was the only one discussed here to die before 1918. Three others—Heinrich Lammasch, Leon Biliński, and Mykola Wassilko—passed away in the early 1920s. Several others—Otto Bauer, Herman Diamand, Mykola Hankevych, Henrik Tuma, Karel Kramář, Valentino Pittoni, and Joseph Redlich—died in the 1930s, before the beginning of the Second World War. Semen Vityk perished in Siberia in 1937. The rest witnessed the outbreak of the Second World War, and several fell victim to it. The destruction inflicted by Nazism and Stalinism, separately and combined, was unprecedented, transforming Europe in a way that the fall of empires had not.

Austria and Czechoslovakia

Those who survived saw their lives turned upside down even before 1938. Otto Bauer experienced the crisis in Europe firsthand, spending the years from 1934 to 1938 in Brno after escaping civil war in Vienna. He hoped to return to Vienna from Brno, but in 1938 was forced to head westward to escape the Nazi expansion. That year he settled in Paris, where in July he suffered a heart attack that ended his life at age fifty-six.[5] Wilhelm Ellenbogen remained in Austria even after the 1934 crisis, but after 1938 had to run for his life: as an assimilated Jew, he would assuredly no longer be safe otherwise. He moved to New York, where he joined Austrian émigré circles and cofounded the Austrian Labor Committee. Having lived through the war and beyond it, still committed to Marxism and international socialism, Ellenbogen died in New York in 1951.

Austrian imperial politics had been tolerant, compromising, and in particular cosmopolitan, with a great number of Jews playing a prominent role. Their status became jeopardized in interwar Europe, but in the 1930s their personal safety was not yet under threat outside of Nazi Germany. Hitler's expansion into Eastern Europe changed everything. Ludwig Czech had experienced the effects of radical nationalism firsthand during the 1930s in Czechoslovakia, but nothing could have prepared him for what followed. The Brno section of the National Socialist Party obtained Hitler's permission to deport Czech to the Theresienstadt concentration camp, where he perished in 1942.[6]

Italy

The Nazi annexation of Austria affected the situation in Italy, just as had Vienna's entry into war back in 1914. Italy's entry into war on the Axis side proved still more consequential and devastating than Rome's joining of the Entente in 1915. Mussolini learned from the mistakes of his predecessors, aspiring to join the "winning" side early on. But the war also revitalized the opposition: some Italians who had suffered persecution under Mussolini now hoped that the military conflict could lead to the defeat of fascism.

Reflecting the divided Italian response to Mussolini were Alcide De Gasperi and Francesco Salata. De Gasperi reentered politics after 1941, attempting to mobilize opposition. In 1941 he renewed contacts with other former Popolari, and the next year he cofounded the Christian Democracy Party, which would be active through most of the twentieth century and whose successor organizations remain key players in Italian politics to the present day—thus standing as modern survivals of an entity (the PPI) founded just as the Habsburg Empire collapsed. In 1943 members of the Italian government ousted Mussolini, and Italy switched sides. On June 4, 1944, the Allies entered Rome, where a new government was formed. The Christian Democrats now became the country's dominant political force. De Gasperi became minister without portfolio and then foreign minister.

The nationalist Francesco Salata followed a different path. He supported Mussolini until the end, which caused tensions within his own family: his daughter Maria, the person closest to him after his wife passed away in 1922, opposed the fascists and during the war joined the resistance. Salata died in Rome on March 10, 1944.[7]

Between Trieste and Moscow

Some of those who had come to maturity under Habsburg rule found themselves trapped amid the conflicts between the Nazis, Italians, Soviets, and Serbian and Croatian nationalists. Consider the case, for instance, of Ivan Regent, a Slovene who had become a communist in post-1918 Italy, then escaped fascism to Yugoslavia, fled from Yugoslavia to Vienna and thence to Paris, finally settling in the late 1930s in Moscow. The war brought further challenges. Moscow was partly evacuated in 1941, and the Regents rode an overcrowded train for nine days—the time it took to cover the 1,200 kilometers from Moscow to Kuybyshev (now reverted to its original name of Samara), near Kazakhstan. Regent's wife, Malka, fell ill, and the family had to rely on the kindness of strangers to survive. Regent would later recall that journey to Kuybyshev as one of the most difficult moments in his life. But the family made it through and later returned to Moscow. In 1943–44 Regent oversaw a political reeducation program for Italian prisoners of war in the Soviet Union.[8]

For Regent, Moscow represented a safe harbor rather than an endpoint; over the years he never lost his sense of fatherland. The Second World War made it possible for him to go home. He traveled to Italy as part of a Soviet tank division and arrived in Trieste on May 3, 1945.[9] There he became involved in editing *Il Lavoratore,* now controlled by the communists. After 1945 he coordinated communist-led strikes, and was imprisoned as a result in 1947. Soon released, he emigrated yet again to communist-controlled Ljubljana and quickly rose through the party ranks, eventually becoming vice head of the Slovenian People's Assembly. Regent remained active in Yugoslavian politics through the 1950s, dying in that country in 1967—the last survivor of the cohort of men discussed in this book.

Poland

Austria, Yugoslavia, and Italy were gravely affected by the war, but Poland was all the more so, having become the primary zone of collision between the two totalitarianisms of Nazism and Stalinism, the country and its people suffering atrocities like nowhere else in Europe. Among the protagonists to directly experience the effects of Hitlerism and Stalinism was Stanisław Głąbiński. The fateful summer of 1939 found him vacationing with his family near Wilno (now Vilnius, Lithuania), from which they would return to Lwów in August. In early September, as the German invasion commenced, several National Democrats including Głąbiński discussed the possibility of forming a government abroad. To that aim, Głąbiński left Lwów, then still a free city, on the night of September 1, traveling to Paris for consultations on forming a Polish government in emigration. On September 16, the Red Army moved to occupy eastern Poland. As the Soviets took over Lwów, Wanda Wasilewska, a communist activist and writer based in Warsaw, reached out to Głąbiński, attempting to secure his endorsement of the Soviets' policy vis-à-vis Poland. He declined but also renounced the notion of armed resistance, appealing to his fellow citizens with calls for patience and calm.[10] On October 1 he returned to Soviet-occupied Lwów, having achieved nothing during his trip to Paris. On November 16 he attempted to go abroad again, hoping to make it to Bucharest on a freight train. This time he was arrested by Soviet police at the border crossing, then imprisoned in Lwów. He was later transferred to Kharkiv in Soviet Ukraine, where he died on August 14, 1941.[11]

Głąbiński was the second person discussed here, after Vityk, to perish at the hands of Soviet authorities. Just as the sense of despair among noncombatants in this period was of a greater magnitude than during the First World War, so too were the actual physical threats they lived under, with far more lives being claimed.

The Postwar Period: Alcide De Gasperi and the European Union

In 1945 Europe faced some of the same issues that had confronted it in 1918 and 1919: contested territories and zones of control (both military and civilian). But now there were different solutions, in part because of the lessons learned after 1918, and in part because democratic Europe was inclined to continue its passivity; the policy of nonintervention adopted before 1938 would endure. In 1945 democratic Europe indeed emerged victorious, but in ruins. Even before the war ended, at the Yalta Conference, the Western Allies ceded Eastern Europe to Soviet control in recognition of the Red Army's role in the victory over Nazism. Czechoslovakia, Poland, and Yugoslavia would now be guided from Moscow (although the latter of these countries managed to go its own way after 1948).[12]

Several of this book's protagonists made the most important decisions of their lives after the Second World War. Alcide De Gasperi is a notable example. In the 1930s he had argued that the Versailles system did not solve ethnic tensions, and that "internal divisions within European nations" would inevitably result in continental strife. Unity was Europe's only salvation.[13] In 1948 he became head of the European Movement, a precursor of the European Union. As he explained his vision of continental unity in a 1950 article for an Italian newspaper, "We should not consider a European union a new institution. . . . A European union is instead based on a reality that already exists. It is not a new creation. Now this existing phenomenon can be transformed into a superstructure."[14] Between 1950 and 1958, several political and economic treaties aimed at European unification were signed: notably, the Treaty of Rome in 1957 established the European Economic Community.

De Gasperi's worldview emblematizes the continuity of federative thinking between the Habsburg Empire and post-1918 Europe, persisting through the interwar era, the Second World War, and into the 1950s. Dying of heart failure in August 1954, De Gasperi did not live to see the European Union. But his ideas and ideals have survived to the present day—a piece of the Austrian imperial legacy, with its foregrounding of internationalism, living on in twenty-first-century Europe.

Europe's East

In the historiography of the post-1945 period, Europe is typically said to have undergone a remarkable recovery after the Second World War, but this would be true of only *part* of the continent.[15] The post-1945 divisions not only created rigid new barriers, they also refashioned Europe as a whole. For example, Czechoslovakia, which between the wars had stood as a symbol of relative stability and democracy, now became the opposite—part of the communist bloc, governed as more or less a puppet of Moscow. Other parts of the former

Habsburg Empire fared even worse after 1945. Eastern Galicia—part of Poland before 1939—was annexed to the Soviet Union.

The new realities in Eastern Europe reinvigorated historical memories; of the different regimes, Austrian imperial rule seemed by far the most beneficent. Habsburg nostalgia commenced even before 1939. In some quarters, it only grew as the twentieth century progressed, although the view of the Habsburg domain as everyone's favorite empire has often been stronger beyond Vienna than therein. The Habsburg Empire is truly unique among such polities of the continent, evoking mainly positive feelings among those, far and wide, whose ancestors once lived under its rule.

Fathers and Children

Such memories lived on especially in the children of the "last Austrians." That generation of fathers came to an end in 1939, though some did live beyond. Most of our protagonists had formed families prior to 1914, and some of their children remembered the breakup of the empire and the insecurity that followed. Some were close to their parents, but many others were not; their elders' professional lives and dedication to politics had often overshadowed family concerns, leaving their children with a sense of abandonment.

The most complicated case was that of the children of the "last Austrian Poles," seen for instance in the Głąbiński family. Stanisław Głąbiński had children late in life. Stanisław junior, born in 1924 when his father was sixty-two, would be raised in Lwów by nannies and relatives, his mother dying in 1926 when he was two and his father perennially preoccupied with work.[16] The son knew little about his mother other than tales of her exotic behavior recounted by his father. The elder Głąbiński withdrew from active politics in 1935 but continued to overschedule his life with academic and public speaking engagements.

Stanisław junior later remarked upon his feeling of abandonment: "When my father's memoirs came out in 1939, I was disappointed. It was all about politics; there was almost nothing there about me, as if personal life did not matter to him at all."[17] The younger Głąbiński, who would go on to become a successful diplomat, channeled his frustrations into a memoir tellingly titled *In the Shadow of My Father*.

In this milieu, it was particularly the Social Democrats who stood out for their tendency toward open relationships, extramarital affairs, and children born out of wedlock. One of these tradition flouters was Ignacy Daszyński, who had an affair and child with Felicia Nossig-Próchnik; the son, Adam Próchnik, was subsequently raised by Felicia's husband. Adam inherited his parents' passion for socialism but turned further to the left, becoming a communist; he would go on to become a writer, historian, and party member in communist Poland. Having been largely abandoned by Daszyński, he nevertheless remained a great admirer of his: "We all grew up under the spell of Daszyński," he commented later in life.[18] Daszyński was a presence in Adam's life, if not closely involved in it.

After Adam, Daszyński fathered five children, three sons and twin daughters, with his wife. This marriage also went awry, and the children would be raised primarily by their mother, Maria.[19] Daszyński married yet again late in life with Cecilia Kempner, twenty years his junior.[20] Despite various hardships, all these children received an education. Felix became an oil engineer and held jobs internationally, including in Ecuador. Stefan, the middle son, likewise studied engineering, in his case at the University of Pittsburgh, and worked in Colombia before returning to Poland. Jan, the youngest, remained in Lwów. One of the twin daughters, Hanna, became an actress. The other, Helena "Lula" (Rummel), studied economics in Cracow and later worked with the city council in Lwów.[21] These children, most of whom had been born under Habsburg rule, lived through the several systems that followed. Educated around the world, most eventually returned home to Poland.

Another of the flouters of traditional mores was Otto Bauer. Helena Landau, the daughter of a Polish-speaking family of assimilated Jews in Vienna, married him after divorcing her first husband. They had no children of their own, but Helena had two children from her first marriage. Bauer died in exile in Paris in 1938. Helena spent her last years in Zurich, where she moved to be with her daughter.

Still more complicated were the instances of children born out of wedlock to cross-ethnic couples. Mykola Hankevych's case, indeed, could merit a separate book, being the story of a problematic relationship exacerbated by ethnic divides. With Roza Vorzimmer, his Jewish socialist colleague, Hankevych had a son, Henryk. The couple later separated, and Henryk remained with his mother. He initially used his stepfather's family name, Vorzimmer, but changed it to Wereszycki in 1924. Henryk's choice of this surname was symbolic: having no connection to his family lineage, it referred, rather, to the Wereszycą River, the site of a battle in which he had fought against the Bolsheviks during the Polish–Soviet War.[22] His father Mykola Hankevych was a self-proclaimed

Ukrainian. His mother Roza was an assimilated Polish Jew. Henryk was raised as a Pole. The politicization of ethnicity in post-1918 Europe is starkly illustrated by the fact that, even though Hankevych later worked for Ukrainian independence, Henryk enlisted in the Polish army instead.[23] Henryk Wereszycki, Adam Próchnik, and Stanisław Głąbiński Jr. all grew up with a sense of alienation. The two former were raised by a different father, and the latter had a father who was largely absent both physically and emotionally. All were defined by their fathers' choices and life trajectories.

Other Social Democrats raised their children in defiance of ethnic conventions. Herman Diamand, an assimilated Jew raised in Galicia, communicated with his father in German throughout his life. But he opted to identify as culturally Polish, bringing up his children accordingly; the son and daughters received the traditional Polish names Zdisław, Milena, and Helena.[24] Or consider the extraordinary life and far-flung progeny of the Slovenian socialist Henrik Tuma. He grew up in a mixed Czech-Slovenian family, and his wife had been born and raised in Alexandria, Egypt. He lived in the Habsburg Empire, then Italy, then Yugoslavia, and raised eight children. All received good educations, studying in Italy, Yugoslavia, Germany, Austria, France, and Switzerland. Tuma died in 1935, but his children settled all over Europe from Sweden to Yugoslavia, defying Cold War divides.

Some "former Austrians" who found refuge in the Soviet Union were occasionally more fortunate. As mentioned, the Slovene Ivan Regent, a socialist turned communist, moved from Italy to Austria to Yugoslavia and eventually the Soviet Union. His daughter Mara followed suit. She inherited her father's passion for Marxism and also became a communist—a trajectory similar to that of Daszyński's son Adam Próchnik. Mara joined the party in Moscow and progressed through the ranks. During the war (possibly in 1944), she ran for and won a seat on the Moscow city council, forging a career as a communist far from her paternal home.[25]

Another socialist refugee from fascist Italy, the Italian Valentino Pittoni, spent the last years of his life in Vienna. His family facilitated the transition but stayed behind. While Pittoni resisted fascism passively, one of his daughters, Bianca, would take a more active stance during the war. Living in Paris, she joined the Italian socialist and communist circles in that city that formed part of the anti-Nazi resistance movement.[26]

Not all children, of course, followed in their fathers' political footsteps or endorsed their ideological choices. Such was the case with Francesco Salata, the only figure under discussion to have supported fascism and collaborated with Mussolini. During the Second World War, Francesco remained faithful to Mussolini, while his daughter Maria joined the antifascist resistance. But with her father physically frail, she continued to take care of him. In 1943 she brought him to Venice, where they spent the summer; in 1944, afraid to leave him on his own, she moved him to Rome, securing lodging for him at the Grand Hotel and taking care of him until his death in the spring of that year.

Another Maria (Romani)—De Gasperi's daughter—dedicated part of her life to promoting her father's legacy. She published a series of reminiscences of him and edited his correspondence and writings. It is due to her efforts that we know the nuances of De Gasperi's personal life. Marga Lammasch, Heinrich Lammasch's daughter, similarly worked to make her father's legacy accessible to a broad audience by arranging the publication of his works.

For some, the bonds formed in imperial days proved lifesaving in the new Europe. As Joseph Redlich witnessed the escalation of politics in Europe from a distance, spending most of his time in the United States, his son Hans Ferdinand was growing to be a prominent musicologist and composer in Germany. The father and the son were close: Joseph divorced his first wife back in 1908, when Hans was just five years old, and he became a sole guardian.[27] In the 1930s Hans became, along with so many other persons of Jewish descent, a target of Nazi persecution. Redlich had previously helped Jewish acquaintances to secure emigration papers as they fled this new extremist Europe, but he was unable to help his own son. Assistance came, fortunately, from the prominent British intellectual R. W. Seton-Watson, who intervened on Redlich's behalf and helped effect Hans's emigration to the United Kingdom. Redlich and Seton-Watson may or may not have been personally acquainted, but they did share a close friend in common: Tomáš Masaryk, the president of Czechoslovakia. During the First World War, Redlich had helped protect some of his Czech friends from the persecutions of the Austrian government. In the 1930s these contacts in turn helped save his son's life.

The children of the "last Austrians" were all too aware of the differences between the age of empires, which had shaped their fathers, and the world of their own, that of nation-states. Henryk Wereszycki experienced several different systems: the empire in which he was born, the transitional nation-state in which he came of age, the uncertainty of the interwar period, the Second World War, and the decades of his later life in communist Poland. Based on his career-long study of Galicia both in the empire and the Republic of Poland, and the problematic relationships between Poles and Ukrainians, he would ultimately blame Poland for squandering the democratic tradition it had inherited from the Habsburg Empire.

In 1987, writing from the standpoint of late communist Poland, Wereszycki made an interesting observation: the Polish socialist Bolesław Limanowski, who had lived through the 1930s and died at the age of ninety-nine, must have seen the institutional deterioration represented by Warsaw, the capital of independent Poland, as compared to the Austrian-ruled Lemberg/Lwów of 1910. Post-1918 Poland, Wereszycki wrote, had inherited the Austrian parliamentary tradition, which formed the basis of the new republic's democratic institutions, limited censorship, and independent judiciary. But opposed to this liberal political culture was another historical legacy: that of the Russian partition of Poland, with its inclination toward force rather than compromise.[28] Wereszycki grasped the essence of interwar Poland's intractable dilemma. The different political traditions, and the people representing them, were never fully reconciled. The independence to which Polish socialists had aspired before 1918 became problematic for all concerned; it became, indeed, the antithesis of democracy.

In 1989, as Poland was undergoing still another transformation from one-party communism to democracy, Wereszycki, shortly before his death (in Cracow in 1990), made public for the first time that Mykola Hankevych had been his biological father. Even before that, he had reflected with fondness on Hankevych's legacy in his publications—just as Adam Próchnik did in his work on Daszyński.[29]

These children were dispersed across the globe in a way their parents had not been: relocations, emigrations, and wars finally brought an end to a world that for so long had revolved around Vienna. But even amid tattered personal networks, standards of upbringing and education lived on. Given all the insecurity and trauma, it is all the more remarkable that most of our protagonists' children were so successful, several of them becoming prominent diplomats, entrepreneurs, cultural figures, and intellectuals. Hardly anyone may be said to have gotten "lost in history"—whether in the history of Eastern or Western Europe; the collective resilience of our protagonists' progeny is notable. Even though long gone, the Habsburg period remained alive in memory, especially for those in Europe's East, where, for many, everyone's favorite empire represented the best and most stable period in centuries of history.

Notes

Abbreviations

AAN   Archiwum Aktow Nowych, Warsaw, Poland

AcdS   Archivio Centrale dello Stato, Rome, Italy

PUL   Pełnomocznik Głównego Urędu Likwidacyjnego w Wiedniu (in AAN)

SNRÖ   *Stenographische Protokolle über die Sitzungen des Nationalrates der Republik Österreich*

SSPS   *Sprawozdanie stenograficzne z posiedzenia Sejmu,* Warsaw, Poland, 1919–1924

TsDAHO   Tsentralnyi derzhavnyi arkhiv hromadskych obiednan, Kyiv, Ukraine

TsDIAUL   Tsentral'nyi Derzhavnyi Arkhiv Ukrainy u L'vivs'kij oblasti, L'viv, Ukraine

Introduction

1. "Redlich to Hofmannsthal, Stanford University, 20.6.1928," in *Hugo von Hofmannsthal—Josef Redlich. Briefwechsel,* ed. Helga Ebner-Fußgänger (Frankfurt am Main: Fischer Verlag, 1971), 101.

2. On the Habsburg Empire as an embodiment of order and stability, see, most notably, Stefan Zweig, *The World of Yesterday,* trans. Anthea Bell (Lincoln: University of Nebraska Press, 2013).

3. Jana Osterkamp, *Vielfalt ordnen. Das föderale Europa der Habsburgermonarchie (Vormärz bis 1918)* (Munich: Vandenhoeck & Ruprecht, 2020); Helmut Rumpler, "The Habsburg Monarchy as a Portent for the New Europe of the Future," in *Die Habsburgermonarchie 1848–1918,* vol. 12, ed. Helmut Rumpler and Ulrike Harmat (Vienna: Austrian Academy of Sciences Press, 2018), 1–20.

4. On pan-Europeanism, see Dina Gusejnova, *European Elites and Ideas of Empire, 1917–1957* (Cambridge: Cambridge University Press, 2016), 69–71, 96.

5. See Quinn Slobodian, *The Globalists: The End of Empire and the Birth of Neoliberalism* (Cambridge, MA: Harvard University Press, 2018), 15–21, 104–117. On Mises's understanding of the Habsburg historical "mission," see Ludwig von Mises, *Erinnerungen von Ludwig Mises* (Stuttgart: Lucius & Lucius, 1978), 16.

6. On the "Habsburgian" philosophy of science in twentieth-century Europe, see Michael D. Gordin, "The Trials of Arnošt K.: The Dark Angel of Dialectical Materialism," *Historical Studies in the Natural Sciences* 47, no. 3 (2017): 320–348.

7. On legal, cultural, and architectural continuities, see Carlo Moos, *Habsburg post mortem. Betrachtungen zum Weiterleben der Habsburgermonarchie* (Vienna: Böhlau, 2016), specifically 12–15.

8. Trentino is the name of the region; Trento is its main city.

9. On "virtuous" nation-states and "vicious" empires, see Dominique Lieven, *Russia against Napoleon: The Battle for Europe, 1807–1814* (New York: Allen Lane, 2009), 13.

10. On the rejection of the Austrian imperial past and de-Austrianization, see Robert Gerwarth, *The Vanquished: Why the First World War Failed to End* (New York: Farrar, Straus and Giroux, 2016), 6; with particular regard to Czechoslovakia, see Andrea Orzoff, *Battle for the Castle: The Myth of Czechoslovakia in Europe, 1914–1918* (Oxford: Oxford University Press, 2009), 57.

11. On the demonization of empires, see Gerwarth, *The Vanquished*, 6.

12. Notable examples of research on the British and French imperial legacy in post-1945 Europe include Jordanna Bailkin, *The Afterlife of Empire* (Berkeley: University of California Press, 2012); Adom Getachew, *Worldmaking after Empire* (Princeton: Princeton University Press, 2019). On continuities after the collapse of the Ottoman Empire, see Michael E. Meeker, *A Nation of Empire: The Ottoman Legacy of Turkish Modernity* (Berkeley: University of California Press, 2002), esp. xii–xvii; Reşat Kasaba, *A Moveable Empire: Ottoman Nomads, Migrants, and Refugees* (Seattle: University of Washington Press, 2009), esp. 136; Theodora Dragostinova, *Between Two Motherlands: Nationality and Emigration among the Greeks of Bulgaria, 1900–1949* (Ithaca: Cornell University Press, 2001); and Ryan Gingeras, *Sorrowful Shores: Violence, Ethnicity, and the End of the Ottoman Empire, 1912–1923* (Oxford: Oxford University Press, 2011). On continuities between the Habsburg Empire and successor states, see Natasha Wheatley, *The Life and Death of States: Central Europe and the Transformation of Modern Sovereignty* (Princeton: Princeton University Press, 2023); Pieter M. Judson, *The Habsburg Empire: A New History* (Cambridge, MA: Belknap Press, 2016), esp. the epilogue; Paul Miller and Claire Morelon, eds., *Embers of Empire: Continuity and Rupture in the Habsburg Successor States after 1918* (New York: Berghahn Books, 2019); and Moos, *Habsburg post mortem*. On internationalism and international institutions, see Peter Becker and Natasha Wheatley, eds., *Remaking Central Europe: The League of Nations and the Former Habsburg Lands* (Oxford: Oxford University Press, 2020). On the continuum of politics, governance, and civil bureaucracy between the empire and post-1918 Austria, see Franz Adglasser and Fredrik Lindström, eds., *Habsburg Civil Service and Beyond: Bureaucracy and Civil Servants from the Vormärz to the Inter-War Years* (Vienna: Austrian

Academy of Sciences Press, 2019); John W. Boyer, *Culture and Political Crisis in Vienna: Christian Socialism in Power, 1897–1918* (Chicago: University of Chicago Press, 1995), 458–459; on this continuity in Czechoslovakia, see Tara Zahra, *Kidnapped Souls: National Indifference and the Battle for Children in the Bohemian Lands, 1900–1948* (Ithaca: Cornell University Press, 2008); Jeremy King, *Budweisers into Czechs and Germans: A Local History of Bohemian Politics, 1848–1948* (Princeton: Princeton University Press, 2002); on this continuity in Italy, see Marco Bresciani, "Conservative and Radical Dynamics of Italian Fascism: An (East) European Perspective (1918–1938)," in *Conservatives and Right Radicals in Interwar Europe,* ed. Marco Bresciani (New York: Routledge, 2021), 68–95; Marco Bresciani, "The Post-Imperial Space of the Upper Adriatic and the Post-War Ascent of Fascism," in *Vergangene Räume—Neue Ordnungen. Das Erbe der multinationalen Reiche und die Staatsbildung im östlichen Europa 1917–1923,* ed. Tim Buchen and Frank Grelka (Frankfurt an der Oder: Viadrina University Press, 2016), 47–64; Marco Bresciani, "Lost in Transition? The Habsburg Legacy, State- and Nation-Building, and the New Fascist Order in the Upper Adriatic," in *National Indifference and the History of Nationalism in Modern Europe,* ed. Maarten van Ginderachter and Jon Fox (London: Routledge, 2019), 56–80; Marco Bresciani, "The Battle for Post-Habsburg Trieste/Trst: State Transition, Social Unrest, and Political Radicalism (1918–23)," *Austrian History Yearbook* 52 (2021): 182–200; and Luciano Monzali, *Gli italiani di Dalmazia e le relazioni italo-jugoslave nel Novocento* (Venice: Marcilio, 2015).

13. On Austro-Marxism and Eurocommunism, see Michael Graber, "Der Austro-Eurokommunismus. Ein frühes Experiment," in Walter Baier et al., *Otto Bauer und der Austromarxismus. "Integraler Sozialismus" und die heutige Linke* (Berlin: Karl Dietz, 2008), 229–237. On definitions and origins of Eurocommunism, see Stephen Goode, *Eurocommunism* (New York: Franklin Watts, 1980), esp. 2; and Wolfgang Leonhard, *Eurocommunism: Challenge for the East and West* (New York: Holt, Rinehart and Winston, 1978), esp. 2–7.

1. Liberalism, Conservatism, Internationalism, and the End of Empire

1. Stefan Zweig to Romaine Rolland, October 14, 1918, cited in *Romain Rolland—Stefan Zweig. Briefwechsel 1910–1940,* ed. Waltraud Schwarze, trans. Eva und Gerhard Schewe and Christel Gersch (Berlin: Rütten & Loening, 1987), 380.

2. Zweig to Rolland, October 14, 1918, cited in *Romain Rolland—Stefan Zweig. Briefwechsel 1910–1940,* 380.

3. On transitions and continuities, in particular between the Habsburg Empire and the Republic of Austria, see Natasha Wheatley, *The Life and Death of States: Central Europe and the Transformation of Modern Sovereignty* (Princeton: Princeton University Press,

2023); Paul Miller and Claire Morelon, eds., *Embers of Empire: Continuity and Rupture in the Habsburg Successor States after 1918* (New York: Berghahn Books, 2019); Natasha Wheatley and Peter Becker, eds., *Remaking Central Europe: The League of Nations and the Former Habsburg Lands* (Oxford: Oxford University Press, 2020); and Carlo Moos, *Habsburg post mortem. Betrachtungen zum Weiterleben der Habsburgermonarchie* (Vienna: Böhlau, 2016). On the continuity of bureaucracy, in particular in Austria, see Franz Adlgasser and Fredrik Lindström, eds., *The Habsburg Civil Service and Beyond: Bureaucracy and Civil Servants from the Vormärz to the Inter-War Years* (Vienna: Austrian Academy of Sciences Press, 2018); and Pieter Judson, *The Habsburg Empire: A New History* (Cambridge, MA: Harvard University Press, 2016), 442–452.

4. On this argument, see Glenda Sluga, "Habsburg Histories of Internationalism," in Wheatley and Becker, *Remaking Central Europe,* 21.

5. For a biography of Lammasch, see Stephan Verosta, *Theorie und Realität von Bündnissen. Heinrich Lammasch, Karl Renner und der Zweibund (1897–1914)* (Vienna: Europa Verlag, 1971), 2. Marga Lammasch, "Mein Vater," in Marga Lammasch and Hans Sperl, eds., *Heinrich Lammasch. Seine Aufzeichnungen, sein Wirken und seine Politik* (Vienna: Franz Deuticke, 1922), 1–4. "Heinrich Lammasch," *Allgemeine Österreichische Gerichts-Zeitung,* May 22, 1915, 257.

6. Ulrike Harmat, "Untergang, Auflösung, Zerstörung der Habsburgermonarchie? Zeitgenössische Bedingungen der Erinnerung und Historiographie," in *Die Habsburgermonarchie 1848–1918,* vol. 12, ed. Helmut Rumpler and Ulrike Harmat (Vienna: Austrian Academy of Sciences Press, 2018), 50.

7. For recent analyses of Austrian liberalism and its collapse, see Judson, *Habsburg Empire,* 219–223; Pieter M. Judson, *Exclusive Revolutionaries: Liberal Politics, Social Experience, and National Identity in the Austrian Empire, 1848–1914* (Ann Arbor: University of Michigan Press, 1996); Jonathan Kwan, *Liberalism and the Habsburg Monarchy, 1861–1895* (London: Palgrave Macmillan, 2013); and John W. Boyer, *Culture and Political Crisis in Vienna: Christian Socialism in Power, 1897–1918* (Chicago: University of Chicago Press, 1995), 460–461.

8. On the importance of local administrations, see, for example, Judson, *Exclusive Revolutionaries,* 4.

9. On these continuities, see Helmut Rumpler, "The Habsburg Monarchy as a Portent for the New Europe of the Future," in *Die Habsburgermonarchie 1848–1918,* vol. 12, ed. Helmut Rumpler and Ulrike Harmat (Vienna: Austrian Academy of Sciences Press, 2018), 2.

10. On the pan-German movement and Schönerer, see Andrew G. Whiteside, *The Socialism of Fools: George Ritter von Schönerer and Austrian Pan-Germanism* (Berkeley: University

of California Press, 1975), 64–80. See also Carl Schorske, *Fin-de-Siècle Vienna: Politics and Culture* (New York: Vintage Books, 1981), 116–180.

11. Nancy M. Wingfield, *Flag Wars and Stone Saints: How the Bohemian Lands Became Czech* (Cambridge, MA: Harvard University Press, 2007), 57. On German nationalism in Austria, see also Lisa Kienzl, *Nation, Identität und Antisemitismus. Der deutschsprachige Raum der Donaumonarchie 1866 bis 1914* (Göttingen, Germany: V & R Unipress, 2014).

12. Judson, *Exclusive Revolutionaries,* 200.

13. Heinrich Lammasch, "Gegen den Völkerhaß" [published earlier in *Neuen Wiener Tagblatt,* no. 94, 1915], in Heinrich Lammasch, *Europas elfte Stunde* (Munich: Verlag für Kulturpolitik, 1919), 11.

14. Heinrich Lammasch, "Christentum und Völkrecht," in Lammasch, *Europas elfte Stunde,* 51.

15. For more detail on these movements as forming the postliberal trio, see Schorske, *Fin-de-Siècle Vienna,* 116–180.

16. Verosta, *Theorie und Realität von Bündnissen,* 4.

17. Joseph Redlich, "Heinrich Lammasch," *Journal of the Society of Comparative Legislation* 11, no. 2 (1911): 210. On Lammasch as a conservative, see "Lammasch gestorben," *Wiener Morgenzeitung,* January 8, 1920.

18. On Redlich and Masaryk's family ties, see Willy Lorenz, *Monolog über Böhmen* (Vienna: Herold Verlag, 1964), 116–117; and Zbyněk Zeman, *The Masaryks: The Making of Czechoslovakia* (London: Weidenfeld & Nicolson, 1976), 15–17.

19. Amy Ng, *Nationalism and Political Liberty: Redlich, Namier, and the Crisis of Empire* (Oxford: Clarendon Press, 2004), 27–38; R. W. Seton-Watson, "Joseph Redlich: Obituary," *Slavonic and East European Review* 16, no. 46 (1937): 200.

20. Ng, *Nationalism and Political Liberty,* 20.

21. On Redlich's nationalism and loyalty, see Ng, *Nationalism and Political Liberty,* 29.

22. Heinrich Lammasch, "Aus meinem Leben, 1899–1905," in Lammasch and Sperl, *Lammasch. Seine Aufzeichnungen, sein Wirken und seine Politik,* 10–19.

23. Lammasch, "Aus meinem Leben," 27.

24. A recent analysis of The Hague conference is Maartje Abbenhuis, *The Hague Conferences and International Politics, 1898–1915* (London: Bloomsbury Academics, 2019).

25. On the Institute of International Law, the Arbitration Court, and Lammasch's participation in both, see Gabriela A. Frei, "The Institut de droit international and the Making of Law for Peace (1899–1917)," in *Les défenseurs de la paix 1899–1917,* ed. Rémi Fabre et al. (Rennes, France: Presses Universitaires de Rennes, 2018), 127–133.

26. Jost Dülffer, *Regeln gegen dem Krieg? Die Haager Friedenskonferenz von 1899 und 1907 in der internationalen Politik* (Frankfurt am Main: Ullstein, 1981), 315.

27. On Lammasch's vision for the Court of Arbitration, see Heinrich Lammasch, *Die Ergebnisse der Haager Konferenzen das Kriegs-Verhütungsrecht. Zweite Abteilung. Die Lehre vor der Schiedsgerichtsbarkeit in ihrem ganzen Umfange* (Stuttgart: Verlag von W. Kohlhammer, 1914), 7.

28. On Lammasch's neutrality, see George Cavallar, "Eye-deep in Hell: Heinrich Lammasch, the Confederation of Neutral States, and Austrian Neutrality, 1899–1920," in *Neutrality in Twentieth-Century Europe: Intersections of Science, Culture, and Politics after the First World War,* ed. Rebecka Letteval et al. (New York: Routledge, 2012), 273–294.

29. Cavallar, "Eye-deep in Hell," 540.

30. Cavallar, "Eye-deep in Hell," 477.

31. Heinrich Lammasch, *Das Völkerrecht nach dem Kriege* (Kristiania, Norway: H. Aschehoug, 1917)

32. Lammasch, "Gegen den Völkerhaß," 11.

33. Joseph Redlich, *Emperor Francis Joseph of Austria: A Biography* (New York: Macmillan, 1929), 497.

34. Cited in Ng, *Nationalism and Political Liberty,* 79.

35. Alexander Watson, *Ring of Steel: Germany and Austria-Hungary in World War I: The People's War* (New York: Basic Books, 2014), 269; John R. Schnidler, *Fall of the Double Eagle: The Battle for Galicia and the Demise of Austria-Hungary* (Lincoln: University of Nebraska Press, 2015), 268.

36. A nuanced analysis of Austrian wartime policies and their contribution to the "unravelling" of the empire is John Deak and Jonathan E. Gumz, "How to Break a State: The Habsburg Monarchy's Internal War, 1914–1918," *American Historical Review* 122, no. 4 (October 2017): 1105–1136.

37. Ng, *Nationalism and Political Liberty,* 81; Kurt Ifkovits, *Hermann Bahr—Jaroslav Kvapil Briefe, Texte, Dokumente. Unter Mitarbeit von Hana Blahová* (Bern: Peter Lang, 2007), 235.

38. For a nuanced analysis of the Austrian occupation of Serbia and of Habsburg policy vis-à-vis the civilian population, see Jonathan Gumz, *The Resurrection and Collapse of Empire in Habsburg Serbia, 1914–1918* (Cambridge: Cambridge University Press, 2009).

39. Gumz, *Resurrection and Collapse,* 26–29.

40. On Meinl's political society, see Heinrich Benedikt, *Die Friedensaktion der Meinlgruppe 1917/18. Die Bemühungen um einen Verständigungsfrieden nach Dokumenten, Aktenstücken und Briefen* (Graz, Austria: Böhlau, 1962); and Friedrich Rennhofer, *Ignaz Seipel. Mensch und Staatsmann. Eine biographische Dokumentation* (Vienna: Böhlau, 1978), 84, 98. On the peace forum, see Rumpler, "The Habsburg Monarchy as a Portent," 2.

41. Heinrich Lammasch, "Abgestorbenes Völkerrecht," in Lammasch, *Europas elfte Stunde,* 128.

42. Heinrich Lammasch, "Erste Friedensrede im Herrenhause des österreichischen Reichsrates am 28. Juni 1917," in Lammasch, *Europas elfte Stunde,* 137.

43. Heinrich Lammasch, "Friedensversuche mit Präsident Wilson," in Lammasch and Sperl, *Lammasch. Seine Aufzeichnungen, sein Wirken und seine Politik,* 98.

44. Ng, *Nationalism and Political Liberty,* 83.

45. "Redlich to Bahr, 14.12.1914," in *Dichter und Gelehrter. Hermann Bahr und Josef Redlich in ihren Briefen 1896–1934,* ed. Fritz Fellner (Salzburg: Wolfgang Neugebauer Verlag, 1980), 103. Josef Redlich, *Austrian War Government* (New Haven: Yale University Press, 1929).

46. Ng, *Nationalism and Political Liberty,* 85.

47. "Redlich to Bahr, 13.07.1918," in *Dichter und Gelehrte,* 351. On the dangers of German nationalism, see also Redlich, *Austrian War Government,* 47.

48. "Redlich to Bahr, 3.01.1917," in *Dichter und Gelehrte,* 182.

49. Joseph Redlich, "German Austria and Nazi Germany," *Foreign Affairs* 15, no. 1 (October 1936): 184.

50. "Redlich to Bahr, 26.08 1917," in *Dichter und Gelehrte,* 253.

51. Redlich, *Austrian War Government,* 79. David F. Strong, *Austria (October 1918– March 1919): Transition from Empire to Republic* (New York: Columbia University Press, 1939), 71.

52. For these interpretations, see John Deak, *Forging a Multinational State: Statemaking in Imperial Austria from the Enlightenment to the First World War* (Stanford, CA: Stanford University Press, 2015), 265; Judson, *Habsburg Empire;* and Maureen Healy, *Vienna and the Fall of the Habsburg Empire: Total War and Everyday Life in World War I* (Cambridge: Cambridge University Press, 2004), 31.

53. Jana Osterkamp, *Vielfalt ordnen. Das föderale Europa der Habsburgermonarchie (Vormärz bis 1918)* (Munich: Vandenhoeck & Ruprecht, 2020).

54. Rumpler, "The Habsburg Monarchy as a Portent," 19.

55. On George Herron in English, see Mitchell Pirie Briggs, *George D. Herron and the European Settlement* (New York: AMS Press, 1971).

56. On the Wilsonian Fourteen Principles and self-determination especially as related to Eastern Europe, see Larry Wolff, *Woodrow Wilson and the Reimagining of Eastern Europe* (Stanford, CA: Stanford University Press, 2020).

57. Professor [George D.] Herron, "Heinrich Lammasch's Suggestion for Peace in Bern 1918," in Lammasch and Sperl, *Lammasch. Seine Aufzeichnungen, sein Wirken und seine Politik,* 189.

58. On Lammasch and his promotion of a Danubian confederation, see Rumpler, "The Habsburg Monarchy as a Portent," 2.

59. Wolff, *Woodrow Wilson,* 19.

60. For a detailed analysis, see Wolff, *Woodrow Wilson,* 19. A recent discussion of Wilson's Fourteen Points within the context of European politics is Jörn Leonhard, *Der überforderte Frieden. Versailles und die Welt 1918–1923* (Munich: Beck, 2018), 107–111.

61. On the new cabinet, see "Das Kabinett Lammasch," *Reichspost,* October 28, 1918, and "Die Kabinettsbildung Lammasch vollzogen," *Wiener Neuste Nachrichten,* October 28, 1918.

62. Verosta, *Theorie und Realität von Bündnissen,* 545.

63. On the confusion surrounding the actual date of the empire's end, see Judson, *Habsburg Empire,* 441.

64. "Lammasch gestorben," *Wiener Morgenzeitung,* January 8, 1920.

65. Heinrich Lammasch, *Woodrow Wilsons Friedensplan. Briefe, Schriften und Reden des Präsidenten* (Leipzig: E. P. Tal, 1919).

66. Heinrich Lammasch, *Völkermord oder Völkerbund* (The Hague: Martinus Nijhoff, 1920). On sovereignty, see 31–33. On potential opposition to an international league, 27. On war as an absolute evil, 33.

67. "Österreichs Schuldantheil, *Neue Züricher Zeitung,* 8. September 1919," in Verosta, *Theorie und Realität von Bündnissen,* 526.

68. A recent discussion of Austria, Versailles, Saint-Germain, and the post-1918 order is Arnold Suppan, *The Imperialist Peace Order in Central Europe: Saint-Germain and Trianon 1919–1920* (Vienna: Austrian Academy of Sciences Press, 2019).

69. Josef Redlich, "Heinrich Lammasch als Ministerpräsident," in Lammasch and Sperl, *Lammasch. Seine Aufzeichnungen, sein Wirken und seine Politik,* 154.

70. On post-1919 internationalism, see, for example, Glenda Sluga, "Remembering 1919: International Organizations and the Future of International Order," *International Affairs* 95, no. 1 (2019): 25–43; Wheatley and Becker, *Remaking Central Europe;* Volker Prott, *The Politics of Self-Determination: Remaking Territories and National Identities in Europe, 1917–1923* (Oxford: Oxford University Press, 2016), 3.

71. A good recent overview of the literature regarding the League of Nations is Susan Pedersen, "Back to the League of Nations," *American Historical Review* 112, no. 4 (October 2007): 1091–1117.

72. Fredrik Lindström, *Empire and Identity: Biographies of the Austrian State Problem in the Late Habsburg Empire* (West Lafayette, IN: Purdue University Press, 2008), 186.

73. Josef Redlich, *Das österreichische Staats- und Rechtsproblem. Geschichtliche Darstellung der inneren Politik der habsburgischen Monarchie von 1848 bis zum Untergang des Reiches,* vol. 1, *Der dynastische Reichsgedanke und die Enfaltung des Problems bis zur*

Verkündigung der Reichsverfassung von 1861 (Leipzig: Der Neue Geist Verlag, 1920). On dysfunctional administration and inefficient federalism as reasons for the monarchy's collapse, see vol. 2, 680. On incompetent bureaucracy as a cancer of the empire, see also Ng, *Nationalism and Political Liberty,* 40.

74. Lindström, *Empire and Identity,* 188.

75. Cited in Felix Frankfurter, "Josef Redlich," *Harvard Law Review* 50, no. 3 (1937): 1.

76. Josef Redlich, *Schicksaljähre Österreichs 1908–1919. Das politische Tagebuch Josef Redlich* (Graz, Austria: Böhlau, 1953), vol. 2, 326.

77. On cross-border family businesses and complications after 1918, see Eric W. Pasold, *Ladybird, Ladybird: A Story of Private Enterprise* (Manchester, UK: Manchester University Press, 1977), specifically p. 34. See also Patrick Crowhurst, *A History of Czechoslovakia between the Wars: From Versailles to Hitler's Invasion* (London: Bloomsbury Academic, 2015), 6–7.

78. Lothar Höbelt, *Die Erste Republik Österreich (1918–1938). Das Provisorium* (Vienna: Böhlau, 2018), 157.

79. Lindström, *Empire and Identity,* 154–155.

80. Hans Peter Hye, "Josef Redlich—ein österreichischer Historiker aus den böhmischen Ländern," in vol. 2 of *Die böhmischen Ländern in der deutschen Geschichtsschreibung seit dem Jahre 1848* (Prague: Ústí nad Labem, 1997), 69.

81. On Masaryk's offer, see Ng, *Nationalism and Political Liberty,* 118.

82. On the composition of the first parliament and government, and the Czech predominance in both, see Zdeněk Kárník, *České země v éře První republiky (1918–1938),* vol. 1, *Vznik, budování a zlatá léta republiky (1918–1929)* (Prague: Nakladatelství Libri, 2000), 72–73.

83. "Zweig to Rolland, 1 October 1920," in *Romain Rolland—Stefan Zweig. Briefwechsel 1910–1940,* 492. The episode is also discussed in Gerhard Oberkofler and Eduard Rabofsky, *Heinrich Lammasch (1835–1920). Notizen zur akademischen Laufbahn des großen österreichischen Völker- und Strafrechtsgelehrten* (Innsbruck, Austria: Universitätsverlag Wagner, 1993), 11.

84. On the Habsburg Law, see, for example, Gordon Brook-Shepherd, *The Last Habsburg* (London: Weidenfeld & Nicolson, 1968), 248, and Timothy Snyder, *The Red Prince: The Secret Lives of a Habsburg Archduke* (New York: Basic Books, 2008).

85. On this continuity, see Moos, *Habsburg post mortem,* 77. There is a large literature on federalism in the first Austrian republic. See, for example, Alfred Pfoser and Andreas Weigl, *Die erste Stunde Null. Gründungsjahre der österreichischen Republik 1918–1922* (Salzburg–Vienna: Residenz Verlag, 2017), 133; Höbelt, *Die Erste Republik Österreich,* 164; Walter Goldinger and Dieter A. Binder, *Geschichte der Republik Österreich 1918–1938* (Vienna: Verlag für Geschichte und Politik, 1992), 92.

2. Conservatives in the East

Part of chapter 2 has appeared as a separate article in Paul Miller and Claire Morelon, eds., *Embers of Empire: Continuity and Rupture in the Habsburg Successor States after 1918* (New York: Berghahn Books, 2019).

1. This compatibility of ethnic identification and imperial loyalty has received much attention in recent scholarship on the Habsburg Empire. Some notable examples include Pieter Judson, *The Habsburg Empire: A New History* (Cambridge, MA: Harvard University Press, 2015); Pieter Judson, "Wilson versus Lenin: The New Diplomacy and Global Echoes of Austria-Hungary's Dissolution," in *Die Habsburgermonarchie 1848–1918,* vol. 12, ed. Helmut Rumpler and Ulrike Harmat (Vienna: Austria Academy of Sciences Press, 2018), 385–396; and Daniel Unowsky, "Introduction: Imperial Loyalty and Popular Allegiances in the Late Habsburg Monarchy," in *The Limits of Loyalty: Imperial Symbolism, Popular Allegiances, and State Patriotism in the Late Habsburg Monarchy,* ed. Laurence Cole and Daniel Unowsky (New York: Berghahn Books, 2007), 1–10. On the overarching loyalty to the empire, especially in the military, see Laurence Cole, *Military Culture and Popular Patriotism in Late Imperial Austria* (Oxford: Oxford University Press, 2014). An older but still relevant book with a similar argument is István Deák, *Beyond Nationalism: A Social and Political History of the Habsburg Officer Corps, 1848–1918* (New York: Oxford University Press, 1990).

2. On continuities between the empire and Czechoslovakia, see, for example, Claire Morelon, "State Legitimacy and Continuity between the Habsburg Empire and Czechoslovakia: The 1918 Transition in Prague," in *Embers of Empire: Continuity and Rupture in the Habsburg Successor States after 1918,* ed. Paul Miller and Claire Morelon (New York: Berghahn Books, 2019), 41–54; Andrea Orzoff, *Battle for the Castle: The Myth of Czechoslovakia in Europe, 1914–1948* (Oxford: Oxford University Press, 2009); and Melissa Feinberg, *Elusive Equality: Gender, Citizenship, and the Limits of Democracy in Czechoslovakia, 1918–1950* (Pittsburgh: University of Pittsburgh Press, 2006).

3. A detailed discussion of the Polish partitions is provided in Jerzy Lukowski, *The Partitions of Poland: 1772, 1793, 1795* (London: Longman, 1999). On the history of the annexation and modernization of the province, see Iryna Vushko, *The Politics of Cultural Retreat: Imperial Bureaucracy in Austrian Galicia, 1772–1867* (New Haven: Yale University Press, 2015); Larry Wolff, *The Idea of Galicia: History and Fantasy in Habsburg Political Culture* (Stanford, CA: Stanford University Press, 2012), esp. 17–29; and Hans-Christian Maner, *Grenzregionen der Habsburgermonarchie im 18. und 19. Jahrhundert. Ihre Bedeutung und Funktion aus der Perspektive Wiens* (Münster, Germany: Lit Verlag,

2005), 27–77. On the population count by ethnicity, see Rudolf A. Mark, *Galizien unter österreichischer Herrschaft. Verwaltung—Kirche—Bevölkerung* (Marburg, Germany: Herder-Institut, 1994), 2.

4. David Rechter, *Becoming Habsburg: The Jews of Austrian Bukovina, 1774–1918* (Oxford: Littman Library of Jewish Civilization, 2013), 59.

5. For detailed statistics on Poles in Galicia and the monarchy in general, see Henryk Batowski, "Die Polen," in *Die Habsburgermonarchie 1848–1918,* vol. 3, part 1, ed. Adam Wandruszka and Peter Urbanitsch (Vienna: Austrian Academy of Sciences Press, 1980), 522–544; on Ruthenians, see Wolfdieter Bibl, "Die Ruthenen," in *Die Habsburgermonarchie 1848–1918,* vol. 3, part 1, 555–584.

6. The literature on Galician Jews is considerable. A good recent analysis of Jewish towns in Galicia is Börries Kuzmany, *Brody. Eine galizische Grenzstadt im langen 19. Jahrhundert* (Vienna: Böhlau, 2011).

7. For exact statistics for the year 1850, see Constantin Ungureanu, "Die Bevölkerung der Bukowina (von Besetzung im Jahr 1774 bis zur Revolution 1848)," *Romanian Journal of Population Studies* 5, no. 1 (2011): 117–143.

8. On territorial autonomy, see Maner, *Grenzregionen der Habsburgermonarchie,* 152.

9. For a detailed discussion of the distribution of positions, see Konstanty Grzybowski, *Galicja 1848–1914. Historia ustroju politycznego na tle historii ustroju Austrii* (Cracow: Ossolineum, 1959), 74–75.

10. A nuanced discussion of Galician autonomy within the broader context of the post-1867 Habsburg Empire is provided in Jana Osterkamp, *Vielfalt ordnen. Das föderale Europa der Habsburgermonarchie (Vormärz bis 1918)* (Munich: Vandenhoeck & Ruprecht, 2020), 248–250.

11. On Ukrainian demands for two provinces, see, for example, Maner, *Grenzregionen der Habsburgermonarchie,* 92.

12. Cited in Leon Biliński, *Znamiona polityki narodowej i krajowej* (Cracow: Nakładem autora, 1882), iii.

13. Biliński, *Znamiona polityki narodowej i krajowej,* ix.

14. On Polish conservatives and their political leverage, see Harald Binder, *Galizien in Wien. Parteien, Wahlen, Fraktionen und Abgeordnete im Übergang zur Massenpolitik* (Vienna: Verlag der Österreichischen Akademie der Wissenschaften, 2005), 39–41, and Philip Pajakowski, "The Polish Club, Badeni, and the Austrian Parliamentary Crisis of 1897," *Canadian Slavonic Papers / Revue Canadienne des Slavistes* 35, no. 1/2 (March–June 1993): 105–107.

15. On the "Polish government" in imperial Vienna, see Waldemar Łazuga, *"Rządy polskie" w Austrii. Gabinet Kazimierza hr. Badeniego 1895–1897* (Poznań, Poland: Wydawnictwo Naukowe UAM, 1991).

16. Ion Nistor, *Der Nationale Kampf in der Bukowina mit besondere Berücksichtigung der Rumänen und Ruthenen. Historisch Beleuchtet* (Bucharest: Institut de Arte Grafice, 1918), 18.

17. Nistor, *Der Nationale Kampf in der Bukowina,* 18.

18. For Wassilko's biography, see Oleksandr Dobrzhanskyi, "Nikolaj von Wassilko. Bukovinian Statement and Diplomat," *Codrul Cosminului* 25, no. 1 (2019): 187–188.

19. On national indifference, see Tara Zahra, "Imagined Non-Communities: National Indifference as a Category of Analysis," *Slavic Review* 69, no. 1 (Spring 2010): 93–119.

20. Mariana Hausleitner, "Konfliktfelder zwischen Rumänen und Ukrainern in der Bukowina zwischen 1910 und 1920," in *Mutter: Land-Vater: Stand. Loyalitätskonflikte, politische Neuorientierung und der Erste Weltkrieg im österreichisch-russlandischen Grenzraum,* ed. Florian Kührer-Wielach and Markus Winkler (Regensburg, Germany: Friedrich Pustet Verlag, 2017), 101.

21. "Politische Chronik," *Wiener Allgemeine Zeitung,* August 8, 1917; Czesław Partacz, *Od Badeniego do Potockiego. Stosunki polsko-ukraińskie w Galicji w latach 1888–1908* (Toruń, Poland: Wydawnictwo Adam Marszałek, 1997), 193. Hausleitner, "Konfliktfelder zwischen Rumänen und Ukrainern," 101.

22. On Wassilko's political leverage in Vienna, see, for example, an article from *Bukowiner Post,* no. 2198, March 8, 1908.

23. See Leon Biliński, *Wspomnienia i dokumenty 1846–1919,* vol. 2 (Warsaw: Nakładem Księgarni F. Hoesicka, 1925), 155.

24. On the "New Era," see Ihor Chornovol, *Pol's'ko-ukraiins'ka uhoda 1890–1894* (L'viv: L'vivs'ka akademiia mystetstv, 2000); on Vienna's role, see 11, 123. See also Dariusz Maciak, *Próba porozumienia polsko-ukraińskiego w Galicji w latach 1888–1895* (Warsaw: WUW, 2006); Partacz, *Od Badeniego do Potockiego,* 45–68.

25. On Biliński's role, see Leon Biliński, *Wspomnienia i dokumenty 1846–1919,* vol. 1 (Warsaw: Nakładem Księgarni F. Hoesicka, 1924), 159–160.

26. There is by now a relatively large literature on these compromises. On the various accords, see Gerald Stourzh, "Ethnic Attribution in Late Imperial Austria: Good Intentions, Evil Consequences," in *The Habsburg Legacy: National Identity in Historical Perspective,* ed. Ritchie Robertson and Edward Timms (Edinburgh: Edinburgh University Press, 1994), 67–83. On the 1905 Moravian compromise, see T. Mills Kelly, "Last Best Chance or Last Gasp? The Compromise of 1905 and Czech Politics in Moravia," *Austrian History Yearbook* 34 (2003): 279–301, and Jiří Malíř, ed., *Moravské vyrovnání z roku 1905. Možnosti a limity národnostního smíru ve střední Evropě—Der Mährische Ausgleich von 1905. Möglichkeiten und Grenzen für einen nationalen Ausgleich in Mitteleuropa* (Brno: Matica moravská, 2006), specifically chapters by Tara Zahra, Jeremy King,

and Peter Urbanitsch. The 1910 Bukovina compromise is discussed in Gerald Stourz, "Gelten Juden als Nationalität Altösterreich?," in *Prag–Czernowitz–Jerusalem. Der österreichische Staat und die Juden vom Zeitalter des Absolutismus bis zum Ende der Monarchie,* ed. Anna Maria Drabek et al. (Eisenstadt, Austria: Roetzer, 1984), 73–116. On the Galician compromise, see Börries Kuzmany, "Der Galizische Ausgleich als Beispiel moderner Nationalitätenpolitik," in *Galizien. Peripherie der Moderne—Moderne der Peripherie?* ed. Elisabeth Haid et al. (Marburg, Germany: Herder Institut Verlag, 2013), 123–144.

27. Osterkamp, *Vielfalt ordnen,* 253.

28. A nuanced discussion of these continuities is Stourzh, "Ethnic Attribution in Late Imperial Austria," 67–83.

29. On paramilitary violence in Eastern Europe during and after the First World War, see Mark Cornwall and John Paul Newman, eds., *Sacrifice and Rebirth: The Legacy of the Last Habsburg War* (New York: Berghahn Books, 2016), esp. chap. 2: Robert Gerwarth, "'War in Peace': Remobilization and 'National Rebirth' in Austria and Hungary," 35–52.

30. I am borrowing here from recent scholarship that has called for the extension of the chronology of the war in Eastern Europe. For example, see Peter Haslinger, "Austria-Hungary," in *Empires at War, 1911–1923,* ed. Robert Gerwarth and Erez Manela (Oxford: Oxford University Press, 2014), 74–95; Jochen Böhler, *Civil War in Central Europe, 1918–1921: The Reconstruction of Poland* (Oxford: Oxford University Press, 2018); and Jörn Leonhard, *Der überforderte Frieden. Versailles und die Welt 1918–1923* (Munich: Beck, 2018). For a similar chronological broadening of developments in the Russian Empire, see Peter Holquist, *Making War, Forging Revolution: Russia's Continuum of Crisis, 1914–1921* (Cambridge, MA: Harvard University Press, 2002).

31. For a nuanced account of Austria's policies in Bosnia, see Edin Hajdarpasic, *Whose Bosnia? Nationalism and Political Imagination in the Balkans, 1840–1914* (Ithaca: Cornell University Press, 2015). Also see Dževad Juzbašić, *Politika i priveda u Bosni i Hercegovini pod Austrougarskom upravom* (Sarajevo: Akademija Nauka i Umjetnosti Bosne i Hercegovine, 2002), 98, and Hamdija Kapidžić, *Bosna i Hercegovina za vrijeme austrougarske vladavine* (Sarajevo: Svjelost, 1968), 167. On Biliński in Bosnia, see Christopher Clark, *The Sleepwalkers: How Europe Went to War in 1914* (New York: HarperCollins, 2012), 394, and Srećko M. Džaja, *Bosnien-Herzegowina in der österreichisch-ungarischen Epoche (1878–1918). Die Intelligentsia zwischen Tradition und Ideologie* (Munich: R. Oldenbourg Verlag, 1994), 79.

32. Cited in Manfried Rauhensteiner, *The First World War and the End of the Habsburg Monarchy, 1914–1918,* trans. Alex J. Kay and Anna Güttel-Bellert (Vienna: Böhlau, 2014), 92.

33. For a detailed analysis, see Mark von Hagen, *War in a European Borderland: Occupations and Occupation Plans in Galicia and Ukraine, 1914–1918* (Seattle: University of Washington Press, 2007).

34. On Russian wartime policy in Galicia, see von Hagen, *War in a European Borderland,* esp. 23–28.

35. There is by now a relatively large literature on Brest-Litovsk. A recent detailed analysis of the treaties is Borislav Chernev, *Twilight of Empire: The Brest-Litovsk Conference and the Remaking of East-Central Europe, 1918–1918* (Toronto: University of Toronto Press, 2018). On the geopolitical shock of these developments, and the Bolsheviks' international legitimization, see Leonhard, *Der überforderte Frieden,* 107–129, and Frank Golczewski, *Deutsche und Ukrainer 1914–1939* (Paderborn, Germany: Ferdinand Schöningh, 2010), 65.

36. Ottokar Czernin, *Im Weltkriege* (Berlin: Ullstein, 1919), 336; Golczewski, *Deutsche und Ukrainer,* 190; Biliński, *Wspomnienia i dokumenty,* vol. 2, 170.

37. Biliński, *Wspomnienia i dokumenty,* vol. 2, 176.

38. On the conflict between colonial ambitions and self-determination, and the persistence of imperial practices across the 1918 epochal divide, see, for example, Erez Manela, *The Wilsonian Moment: Self-Determination and the International Origins of Anti-Colonial Nationalism* (Oxford: Oxford University Press, 2007). A good recent discussion of Wilsonian self-determination and its impact upon Eastern Europe is Larry Wolff, *Woodrow Wilson and the Reimagining of Eastern Europe* (Stanford, CA: Stanford University Press, 2020).

39. Steven Seegel, *Map Men: Transnational Lives and Deaths of Geographers in the Making of East Central Europe* (Chicago: University of Chicago Press, 2018), 77.

40. Volker Prott, *The Politics of Self-Determination: Remaking Territories and National Identities in Europe, 1917–1923* (Oxford: Oxford University Press, 2016).

41. Biliński, *Wspomnienia i dokumenty,* vol. 2, 165.

42. Stanisław Głąbiński, *Wspomnienia polityczne* (Pelplin, Poland: Nakładem i czcionkami Drukarni i Księgarni Sp. Z.O.O., 1939), 166.

43. Biliński, *Wspomnienia i dokumenty,* vol. 2, 156.

44. Cited in Caroline Fink, *Defending the Rights of Others: The Great Powers, the Jews, and International Minority Protection, 1878–1938* (Cambridge: Cambridge University Press, 2004), 111. For a full analysis of the pogrom, see 109–111.

45. On the anti-Jewish pogroms in Galicia in late 1918 and 1919, see "Ein furchtbarer Judenpogrom in Lemberg," *Neue Freie Presse,* no. 19490, November 27, 1918, 2–3; "Die Pogrome in Lemberg. Neukerungen von Dr. Leon Ritter v. Biliński, Finanzminister a. Oe.," *Neue Freie Presse,* no. 19491, November 28, 1918. In the literature, see Svjatoslav Pacholkiv, "Zwischen Einbeziehung und Ausgrenzung. Die Juden in Lemberg 1918–

1919," in *Vertaut und fremd zugleich. Jüdisch-christliche Nachbarschaften im Warschau-Lengnau-Lemberg,* ed. Alexandra Binnenkade et al. (Cologne: Böhlau, 2009), 155–216; Frank Golczewski, *Polnisch-jüdische Beziehungen 1881–1922. Eine Studie zur Geschichte des Antisemismus in Osteuropa* (Wiesbaden: Franz Steiner Verlag, 1981), 201; and Alexander Victor Prusin, *Nationalizing a Borderland: War, Ethnicity, and Anti-Jewish Violence in East Galicia, 1914–1920* (Tuscaloosa: University of Alabama Press, 2005), 75–91.

46. Biliński, *Wspomnienia i dokumenty,* vol. 2, 184.

47. On the importance of civil war in post-1918 Eastern Europe, see Robert Gerwarth, "Fighting the Red Beast: Counter-Revolutionary Violence in the Defeated States of Central Europe," in *War in Peace: Paramilitary Violence in Europe after the Great War,* ed. Robert Gerwarth and John Horne (Oxford: Oxford University Press, 2012), 52–71, and Jochen Böhler, *Civil War in Central Europe, 1918–1921* (Oxford: Oxford University Press, 2018).

48. On the "tripartite" divisions and difficulties of overcoming them, see R. J. W. Evans, "The Successor States," in Robert Gerwarth, ed., *Twisted Paths: Europe 1914–1945* (Oxford: Oxford University Press, 2007), 212. A nuanced recent analysis of the complicated integration is provided in Kathryn Ciancia, *On Civilization's Edge: A Polish Borderland in the Interwar World* (New York: Oxford University Press, 2021), chap. 3, "The Integration Myth."

49. Biliński, *Wspomnienia i dokumenty,* vol. 2, 201.

50. On the first Sejm, the number of deputies, and their party affiliations, see Michał Pietrzak, *Rządy Parlamentarne w Polsce w latach 1919–1926* (Warsaw: Książka i Wiedza, 1969), 87.

51. On the National Democratic [Endek] Party's campaign against Biliński, see "Powolanie Dr. Bilińskiego," *Czas,* 193 (August 1, 1919); "Biliński w Warszawie," *Kurier Polski,* no. 194 (July 29, 1919); J. D., "Dr. Biliński—ministrem skarbu," *Kurier Polski,* no. 197 (August 2, 1919).

52. Biliński, *Wspomnienia i dokumenty,* vol. 2, 147.

53. For a reference on the "Galician import" in Warsaw, see "Import galicyjski," *Czas,* March 5, 1919.

54. J. D., "Dr. Biliński."

55. Adam Pragier, *Czas przeszły dokonany* (London: B. Świderski, 1966), 227.

56. John Deak, *Forging a Multinational State: State Making in Imperial Austria from the Enlightenment to the First World War* (Stanford, CA: Stanford University Press, 2015), 225.

57. Large parts of Poland fell under German military occupation, and by 1918 the mark was the most common currency in all Polish territories.

58. See Diamand's speech to the Polish parliament on April 11, 1919, in Herman Diamand, *Przemówienia w Sejmie Rzeczypospolitej 1919–1930* (Warsaw: Nakładem Księgarni Robotniczej, 1932), 65.

59. Dominique Kirchner Reill, *The Fiume Crisis: Life in the Wake of the Habsburg Empire* (Cambridge, MA: Belknap Press, 2021).

60. Gábor Egry, "Negotiating Post-Imperial Transitions: Local Societies and Nationalizing States in East Central Europe," in Miller and Morelon, *Embers of Empire,* 15–42.

61. Seegel, *Map Men,* 79.

62. On the offices of propaganda, see Walentyna Najdus, *Ignacy Daszyński 1866–1936* (Warsaw: Czytelnik, 1988), 435–437; on the Allies' concerns over Polish actions during the war, see Klaus Schwabe, ed., *Quellen zum Friedensschluss von Versailles* (Darmstadt, Germany: Wissenschaftliche Buchgesellschaft, 1997), 342.

63. Biliński, *Wspomnienia i dokumenty,* vol. 2, 329.

64. For months, international efforts to stop new issuances led nowhere. See Alois Rasin, *Financial Policy of Czecho-Slovakia During the First Year of Its History* (Oxford: Clarendon Press, 1923), 19–22. On the negotiations between the Czechoslovak government and the bank, see *Vzpomínky z prvých dob ministerstva financí. Díl I. Část revuální.* V červnu 1928, https://www.mfcr.cz/assets/cs/media/Vzpominky-z-prvnich-dob-Ministerstva-financi-Dil-I.pdf, 28.

65. AAN, Pełnomocznik Głównego Urzędu Likwidacyjnego w Wiedniu (hereafter PUL): 24/III/1920, L: 932; AAN, PUL, no. 93: An Seine Exzellenz Herrn Vizegouverneur des österreichisch-ungarischen Bank von PAP in Wien 20 December 1919; AAN, PUL, no. 93, Likwidacja banku ausstro-wegerskiego: Sprawozdanie z posiedzeń Komitetu dyrektywnego i Rady Generalnej Banku austrowęgierskiego z 31 sierpnia 1920.

66. *Memoirs of Alexander Spitzmüller Freiherr von Harmersbach (1862–1953),* trans. Carvel de Bussy (Boulder, CO: East European Monographs, 1987), 247.

67. The Treaty of Saint-Germain was concluded in September 1919 between the victorious powers and Austria.

68. Jerzy Michalski, *Traktat pokojowy w Saint-Germain a obciążenie Polski* (Cracow: Nakładem Krakowskiej spółki wydawniczej, 1921), 13; "Die Nationalstaaten und der Goldschatz der Österreichisch-ungarischen Bank," *Neue Freie Presse,* no. 20291, February 23, 1921, 2.

69. SNRÖ, March 1, 1921, Karl Renner speech, 468.

70. Biliński, *Wspomnienia i dokumenty,* vol. 2, 342.

71. Biliński, *Wspomnienia i dokumenty,* vol. 2, 185.

72. See, for example, on Wassilko's efforts to expand Ukrainian schooling in Bukovina: "Der Zwift in der Bukowina," *Bukowiner Post,* March 27, 1913.

73. On Wassilko's wife, see his obituary in *Wiener Zeitung,* no. 178, August 4, 1924.

74. Wolfgang Pfeiffer-Belli, ed., *Harry Graf Kessler, Tagebücher 1918–1937* (Berlin: Insel Verlag, 1961), 351.

75. Caroline Milow, *Die ukrainische Frage 1917–1923 im Spannungsfeld der europäischen Diplomatie* (Wiesbaden: Harrassowitz Verlag, 2002), 198. See also Timothy Snyder, *The Red Prince: The Secret Lives of a Habsburg Archduke* (New York: Basic Books, 2008).

76. Cited in Felix Höglinger, *Ministerpräsident Heinrich Graf Clam-Martinic* (Graz, Austria: Böhlau, 1964), 203; cited in Milow, *Die ukrainische Frage,* 179.

77. On Ukrainians' distrust of Wassilko, see Isaak Mazepa, *Ukraina v ogni i buri revoliutsii* (Kyiv: Tempora, 2003), 248.

78. An excellent discussion of this in English is Snyder, *The Red Prince.*

79. Dmytro Doroshenko, *Moi spomyny pro nedavnie mynule* (Kyiv: Tempora, 2007), 236; Mazepa, *Ukraina v ogni i buri revoliutsii,* 287.

80. Ievhen Onatskyi, "Pid omoforom barona V. Vasylka," *Ukrainskyi istoryk* 65–68, no. 1–4 (1980): 122.

81. Biliński, *Wspomnienia i dokumenty,* vol. 2, 299.

82. On the Treaty of Warsaw, see, for example, Timothy Snyder, *Sketches from a Secret War: A Polish Artist's Mission to Liberate Soviet Ukraine* (New Haven: Yale University Press, 2007), 8.

83. A fine analysis of the Treaty of Riga is provided in Jerzy Borzecki, *The Soviet-Polish Peace of 1921 and the Creation of Interwar Europe* (New Haven: Yale University Press, 2008), 101–155. See also Snyder, *Sketches from a Secret War,* 139–141.

84. "Wassilko tritt zurück," *Wiener Morgenzeitung,* June 17, 1921.

3. Empire, Catholicism, and the Nation, 1880s–1920s

1. A detailed discussion of this meeting is provided in Friedrich Rennhnofer, *Ignaz Seipel. Mensch und Staatsmann. Eine biographische Documentation* (Vienna: Böhlau, 1978), 142.

2. The literature on Seipel is considerable, but most of it is dated, shaped by either unconcealed fascination with or outright antagonism toward him. One of the best biographies—dated but still relevant, and more balanced than most—is that of Klemens von Klemperer, *Ignaz Seipel: Christian Statesman in a Time of Crisis* (Princeton: Princeton University Press, 1972). The Deak quotation is cited here on p. 19. For a nuanced revision of Seipel's role in Austrian and European history, and of the Seipel myth in historiography, see John Deak, "Ignaz Seipel (1876–1932): The Founding Father of the Austrian Republic," in *Austrian Lives,* ed. Günter Bischof et al. (New Orleans: University of New Orleans Press, 2012), 32–55.

3. A discussion of this legacy and continuity between the nineteenth and the twentieth century is *Christdemokratie in Europa im 20. Jahrhundert,* ed. Michael Gehler et al.

(Vienna: Böhlau, 2001). For the Austrian case, see John W. Boyer, "Catholics, Christians and the Challenges of Democracy: The Heritage of the Nineteenth Century," in *Political Catholicism in Europe, 1918–1945*, vol. 1, ed. Wolfram Kaiser and Helmut Wohnout (London: Routledge, 2004).

4. On the "city revolution," see John W. Boyer, *Karl Lueger (1844–1910): Christlichsoziale Politik als Beruf. Eine Biografie* (Vienna: Böhlau, 2010), 226.

5. On Lueger as a "builder," see Richard S. Geehr, *Karl Lueger: Mayor of Fin de Siècle Vienna* (Detroit: Wayne State University Press, 1990), 143–144; on his welfare initiatives, see Boyer, *Karl Lueger,* 191–195. See also Johannes Hawlik, *Der Bürgerkaiser. Karl Lueger und seine Zeit* (Vienna: Herold Verlag, 1985), 153.

6. On the party's successes and legacy, see Timothy Kirk, *Nazism and the Working Class in Austria: Industrial Unrest and Political Dissent in the "National Community"* (Cambridge: Cambridge University Press, 1996), 24–25.

7. On this triangle of parties and their leaders, see Carl Schorske, *Fin-de-Siècle Vienna: Politics and Culture* (New York: Vintage Books, 1981), 116–180.

8. John W. Boyer, *Culture and Political Crisis in Vienna: Christian Socialism in Power, 1897–1918* (Chicago: University of Chicago Press, 1995), 460.

9. Paul Molisch, *Geschichte der deutschnationalen Bewegung in Oesterreich von ihren Anfängen bis zum Zerfall der Monarchie* (Jena: Gustav Fischer Verlag, 1926), 206–216.

10. Cited in Molisch, *Geschichte der deutschnationalen Bewegung in Oesterreich,* 155.

11. Boyer, *Karl Lueger,* 91.

12. Boyer, *Karl Lueger,* 165.

13. Boyer, *Culture and Political Crisis in Vienna,* 42.

14. Klemperer, *Ignaz Seipel,* 22.

15. On this alliance, see Klemperer, *Ignaz Seipel,* 43.

16. Ignaz Seipel, *Nation und Staat* (Vienna: Braumüller, 1910), 17, 64, 73, 90–91.

17. See Ignaz Seipel, *Der Kampf um die österreichische Verfassung* (Vienna: Braumüller, 1930), 9.

18. Seipel, *Der Kampf um die österreichische Verfassung,* 25.

19. Cited in Salvatore Sassi, *Alcide De Gasperi e il periodo absburgico* (Rome: Aracane, 2006), 26.

20. Statistics here are cited from Sassi, *Alcide De Gasperi e il periodo absburgico,* 26.

21. On the founding of this party, see Sassi, *Alcide De Gasperi e il periodo absburgico,* 74.

22. Stefano Trinchese, *L'altro De Gasperi. Un italiano nel'impero asburgico 1881–1918* (Rome: Laterza & Figli, 2006), xiv.

23. On the idea of a Christian republic, see Trinchese, *L'altro De Gasperi,* 81.

24. Sergio Zoppi, *Romolo Murri e la prima Democrazia Cristiana* (Florence: Valecchi Editore, 1986), 7; Benedetto Marcucci, *Romolo Murri. La scelta radicale* (Venice: Marsilio Editori, 1994), 43.

25. On De Gasperi and his federalist concepts, see Trinchese, *L'altro De Gasperi,* 87.

26. On De Gasperi's support of autonomy, see his speech in the Austrian parliament: Haus der Abgeordneten, 20. Sitzung der XXI. Session, October 25, 1911, 1177–1178.

27. On the university question and De Gasperi's stance on it, see Paolo Piccoli and Armando Vadagnini, *DeGasperi. Un trentino nella storia d'Europa* (Soveria Mannelli, Italy: Rubbettino, 2004), 27–45.

28. Alcide De Gasperi, "Lueger nel movimento cristiano-sociale. I funerali 'Il Trentino' (11 marzo 1910)," in *Scritti e discorsi politici,* vol. 1, *Alcide De Gasperi nel Trentino asburgico,* ed. Mariapia Bigaran et al. (Bologna: Il Mulino, 2006), 1065.

29. Alcide De Gasperi, "Lueger nel movimento cristiano-sociale—I Funerali Trento (11 marzo 1910)," in *Alcide De Gasperi nel Trentino Asburgigo,* 1065.

30. Luigi Sardi, *1914. De Gasperi e il Papa* (Trento: Curcu & Genovese, 2014), 43.

31. On the Vatican's diplomacy during the early stages of the war, see John F. Pollard, *The Unknown Pope: Benedict XV (1914–1922) and the Pursuit of Peace* (New York: Geoffrey Chapman, 1999), 59–96; Frank J. Coppa, "Mussolini and the Concordat of 1929," in *Controversial Concordats: The Vatican's Relations with Napoleon, Mussolini, and Hitler,* ed. Frank J. Coppa (Washington, DC: Catholic University of America Press, 1999), 83–84.

32. Piccoli and Vadagnini, *DeGasperi,* 103–104.

33. Giulio Andreotti, *De Gasperi e il suo tempo: Trento-Vienna-Roma* (Milan: Arnoldo Mondadori Editore, 1956), 68.

34. Piccoli and Vadagnini, *DeGasperi,* 99.

35. On this meeting and the discussions it involved, see *Alcide De Gasperi,* vol. 1, *Dal Trentino all'esilio in patria (1881–1943),* ed. Alfredo Canavero et al. (Rome: Rubbettino, 2009), 220.

36. Ignaz Seipel, "Die Erste Regierungserklärung" (from a speech at a session of the National Council in Vienna held on May 31, 1922), in *Seipels Reden in Österreich und anderwärts. Eine Auswahl zu seinem 50. Geburtstage,* ed. Josef Seßl (Vienna: Der Verlag "Heros," 1926), 18.

37. Seipel, "Die Erste Regierungserklärung," 18.

38. On Seipel's conservatism, see John W. Boyer, "Wiener Konservatismus vom Reich zur Republik—Ignaz Seipel und die österreichische Politik," in *Konservative Profile. Ideen und Praxis in der Politik zwischen FM Radetzky, Karl Kraus und Alois Mock,* ed. Ulrich E. Zellenberg (Graz, Austria: Leopold Stocker Verlag, 2003), 341–362.

39. Markus Benesch, *Die Wiener Christlichsoziale Partei 1910–1934. Eine Geschichte der Zerrissenheit in Zeiten des Umbruchs* (Vienna: Böhlau, 2014), 77.

40. For this argument, see John W. Boyer, "Boundaries and Transitions in Modern Austrian History," in *From Empire to Republic: Post–World War I Austria,* ed. Günter Bischof et al. (New Orleans: New Orleans University Press, 2010), 13–23.

41. Nathan Marcus, *Austrian Reconstruction and the Collapse of Global Finance, 1921–1931* (Cambridge, MA: Harvard University Press, 2018), 3.

42. On the postwar crisis in Austria, see Marcus, *Austrian Reconstruction;* Maureen Healy, *Vienna and the Fall of the Habsburg Empire: Total War and Everyday Life in World War I* (Cambridge: Cambridge University Press, 2004); Patricia Clavin, "The Austrian Hunger Crisis and the Genesis of International Organization after the First World War," *International Affairs* 90, no. 2 (March 2014): 256–278; and Patricia Clavin, *Securing the World Economy: The Reinvention of the League of Nations, 1920–1946* (Oxford: Oxford University Press, 2013), 18.

43. Klemperer, *Ignaz Seipel,* 114.

44. Marcus, *Austrian Reconstruction,* 106.

45. Marcus, *Austrian Reconstruction,* 104.

46. On Seipel's support of a Danubian federation, see Werner Thormann, *Ignaz Seipel. Der europäische Staatsmann* (Frankfurt: Carolus-Druckerei, 1932), 54.

47. Clavin, *Securing the World Economy,* 12.

48. I am borrowing here from Clavin, *Securing the World Economy,* 26.

49. On Seipel, Geneva, and the reduction of Austrian administration, see John Deak, "Dismantling Empire: Ignaz Seipel and Austria's Financial Crisis, 1922–1925," in Bischof, *From Empire to Republic,* 123–141.

50. See, for example, Gottlieb Ladner, *Seipel als Überwinder der Staatskrise vom Sommer 1922. Zur Geschichte der Enstehung der Genfer Protokolle vom 4 Oktober 1922* (Vienna: Stiasny Verlag, 1964).

51. Ignaz Seipel, "Auf der Brücke uber dem Abgrund" (from a speech on March 27, 1923), in *Seipels Reden,* 59.

52. Ignaz Seipel, "Das neue Österreich" (from a speech in Stockholm on March 22, 1926), in *Seipels Reden,* 309.

53. Cited in Thormann, *Ignaz Seipel,* 34. On Seipel's support of European unity, with Austria as a key component, see Klemperer, *Ignaz Seipel,* 247.

54. Ignaz Seipel, *Der Friede. Ein sittliches und gesellschaftliches Problem. Gleichwort von Rudolf Blüml* (Innsbruck, Austria: Tyrolia Verlag, 1937).

55. On the strained relationship between Vienna and the Länder, and how this affected the Christian Social Party, see Benesch, *Die Wiener Christlichsoziale Partei,* 138–140, 204.

56. On Seipel's resignation, see Klemperer, *Ignaz Seipel,* 244.

57. On the continuity in Christian Social politics between the empire and republican Austria, see Janek Wasserman, *Black Vienna: The Radical Right in the Red City, 1918–1938* (Ithaca: Cornell University Press, 2014), 9.

4. Empire and Nationalism, 1860s–1920s

1. Heinrich Lammasch, "Erste Friedensrede im Herrenhause des österreichischen Reichsrates am 28. Juni 1917," in *Heinrich Lammasch. Europas elfte Stunde,* ed. Fr. W. Ferster (Munich: Verlag für Kulturpolitik, 1919), 137.

2. Nancy M. Wingfield, *Flag Wars and Stone Saints: How the Bohemian Lands Became Czech* (Cambridge, MA: Harvard University Press, 2007), 315.

3. On national revolutions and the narratives of the empire's collapse, see Pieter Judson, "Afterwards," in *Embers of Empire: Continuity and Rupture in the Habsburg Successor States after 1918,* ed. Paul Miller and Claire Morelon (New York: Berghahn Books, 2019), 319. See also John Deak and Jonathan E. Gumz, "How to Break a State: The Habsburg Monarchy's Internal War, 1914–1918," *American Historical Review* 122, no. 4 (October 2017): 1106.

4. Ferdinand Peroutka, *Budování státu,* vol. 1, *1918–1919* (repr., Prague: Lidové noviny, 1991), 5.

5. Peroutka, *Budování státu,* vol. 1, *1918–1919,* 10–12. A recent nuanced discussion of the "peaceful" 1918 transition is John Deak, "The Great War and the Forgotten Realm: The Habsburg Monarchy and the First World War," *Journal of Modern History* 86, no. 2 (June 2014): 336–380.

6. Fulvio Suvich, who became Mussolini's foreign minister in the 1930s, is one of the most notable examples of this trend; see Fulvio Suvich, *Memorie 1932–1936,* ed. Gianfranco Bianchi (Milan: Rizzoli Editore, 1964).

7. A nuanced discussion of this nationalism that was compatible with imperial loyalty is provided in Gary B. Cohen, "Nationalist Politics and the Dynamics of State and Civil Society in the Habsburg Monarchy, 1867–1914," *Central European History* 40, no. 2 (June 2007): 241–278, esp. 242–245.

8. On the Głąbiński family, see Stanisław Głąbiński, *W cieniu ojca* (Warsaw: Książka i Wiedza, 2001), 15–16.

9. On Głąbiński's early career in the conservative camp, see Grzegorz Krzywiec, *Szowinizm po polsku. Przypadek Romana Dmowskiego (1866–1905)* (Warsaw: Wydawnictwo Neriton, 2009), 349.

10. Krzywiec, *Szowinizm po polsku,* 349.

11. Roman Wapiński, *Narodowa Demokracja 1893–1939. Ze studiów nad dziejami myśli nacjonalistycznej* (Wrocław, Poland: Zakład Narodowy im. Ossolińskich, 1980), 83.

12. Differences between representatives of the Russian and Habsburg Empires were universal; on their different political tactics in postimperial Poland, see, for example, Adam Pragier, *Czas przeszły dokonany* (London: B. Świderski, 1966), 226–227.

13. Brian Porter, *When Nationalism Began to Hate: Imagining Modern Politics in Nineteenth-Century Poland* (New York: Oxford University Press, 2000), 224.

14. Krzywiec, *Szowinism po polsku,* 105-109.

15. On National Democracy (with a focus on its development in Russian-ruled Poland), see Porter, *When Nationalism Began to Hate,* esp. chap. 8, 189-232. On National Democracy in Galicia, see Adam Wątor, *Narodowa Demokracja w Galicji do 1918 roku* (Szczecin, Poland: Wydawnictwo Naukowe Uniwersytetu Szczecińskiego, 2002), 53-55, 173-177; and Wapiński, *Narodowa Demokracja,* 122.

16. Głąbiński expressed his opposition to concessions to minorities in his speech to the Austrian parliament in October 1911: Haus der Abgeordneten, 45. Sitzung der XXI. Session, October 25, 1911, 1183. See also Stanisław Głąbiński, *Wspomnienia polityczne* (Pelplin, Poland: Nakładem i czcionkami Drukarni i Księgarni Sp. Z.O.O., 1939), 13.

17. Głąbiński, *W cieniu ojca,* 16.

18. Głąbiński, *W cieniu ojca,* 17-18.

19. A comprehensive discussion of Prague's Germans over the centuries is provided in Gary B. Cohen, *The Politics of Ethnic Survival: Germans in Prague, 1861-1914* (West Lafayette, IN: Purdue University Press, 2006).

20. Jeremy King, *Budweisers into Czechs and Germans: A Local History of Bohemian Politics, 1848-1948* (Princeton: Princeton University Press, 2002), 15.

21. Cohen, *Politics of Ethnic Survival,* 7, 20, 24; King, *Budweisers into Czechs and Germans,* 9.

22. Cited in Eagle Glassheim, *Noble Nationalists: The Transformation of the Bohemian Aristocracy* (Cambridge, MA: Harvard University Press, 2005), 30.

23. Tara Zahra, *Kidnapped Souls: National Indifference and the Battle for Children in the Bohemian Lands, 1900-1948* (Ithaca: Cornell University Press, 2008).

24. For exact numbers, see the 1910 census, listing 6.5 million Czechs in the Habsburg monarchy in general. These and other figures are included in Jiři Kořalka and R. J. Crampton, "Die Tschechen," in *Die Habsburgermonarchie 1848-1918,* vol. 3, part 1, ed. Adam Wandruszka and Peter Urbanitsch (Vienna: Austrian Academy of Sciences Press, 1980), 493-494.

25. On Prague's Germans and their decline, see Cohen, *Politics of Ethnic Survival,* 100-106, and Scott Spector, *Prague Territories: National Conflict and Cultural Innovation in Franz Kafka's Fin de Siècle* (Berkeley: University of California Press, 2000), esp. 13.

26. For a new and nuanced discussion of these considerations and of the failure of Bohemian autonomy, see Jana Osterkamp, *Vielfalt ordnen. Das föderale Europa der Habsburgermonarchie (Vormärz bis 1918)* (Munich: Vandenhoeck & Ruprecht, 2020), 263.

27. On the Young Czechs, see Bruce M. Garver, *The Young Czech Party, 1874–1901: The Emergence of a Multi-Party System* (New Haven: Yale University Press, 1978).

28. Useful recent discussions of the division of Prague University are provided in Jan Surman, *Universities in Imperial Austria, 1848–1918: A Social History of a Multilingual Space* (West Lafayette, IN: Purdue University Press, 2019), 180–187, and Michael Gordin, *Einstein in Bohemia* (Princeton: Princeton University Press, 2020), 21.

29. On Count Kasimir Felix Badeni's language regulations, see Glassheim, *Noble Nationalists*, 31; Berthold Sutter, *Die badenischen Sprachenverordnungen von 1897. Ihre Genesis und ihre Auswirkungen vornehmlich auf die innerosterreichischen Alpenländer,* 2 vols. (Graz, Austria: Böhlau, 1960); and John Deak, *Forging a Multinational State: State Making in Imperial Austria from the Enlightenment to the First World War* (Stanford, CA: Stanford University Press, 2015), 226. On the linguistic conflict and governmental crisis, see Philip Pajakowski, "The Polish Club, Badeni, and the Austrian Parliamentary Crisis of 1897," *Canadian Slavonic Papers / Revue Canadienne des Slavistes* 35, no. 1/2 (March–June 1993): 103–120.

30. John W. Boyer, *Culture and Political Crisis in Vienna: Christian Socialism in Power, 1897–1918* (Chicago: University of Chicago Press, 1995), 462. John W. Boyer, "Boundaries and Transitions in Modern Austrian History," in *From Empire to Republic: Post–World War I Austria,* ed. Günter Bischof et al. (New Orleans: University of New Orleans Press, 2010), 13–22.

31. On his childhood and early years, see Vladimír Sís, *Karel Kramář. Život a dílo. Skizza* (Prague: Knihovna Bozkopalova, 1930), 8–25; on the German middle school, see p. 9. On his family, see J. B. Shmeral, *Obrazovanie Chekhoslovatskoi respubliki v 1918 godu* (Moscow: Nauka, 1967), 203.

32. On Kramář's family and upbringing, see Robert W. Seton-Watson, "Karel Kramář: Obituary," *Slavonic and East European Review* 16, no. 46 (July 1937): 183.

33. Sís, *Karel Kramář,* 34.

34. *Paměti Dr. Karla Kramáře,* ed. Karel Hoch (Prague: Československý čtenář, 1938), 59.

35. *Paměti Dr. Karla Kramáře,* 59.

36. Karel Kramář, *Pět přednášek o zahraniční politice* (Prague: Tiskem a nákladem Pražské akciové tiskárny, 1922), 30.

37. For a detailed description of Czech realism, see Eva Schmidt-Hartmann, *Thomas G. Masaryk's Realism: Origins of a Czech Political Concept* (Munich: R. Oldenbourg Verlag, 1984).

38. Martin Kučera and Josef Tomeš, "Tomáš Garrigue Masaryk a Karel Kramář. K problematice jejich vztahu," in *T. G. Masaryk–Karel Kramář. Korespondence,* ed. Jan Bílek et al. (Prague: Masarykův ústav, 2005), 13.

39. On relations between Masaryk and Kramář, see Stanley B. Winters, "T. G. Masaryk and Karel Kramář: Long Years of Friendship and Rivalry," in *T. G. Masaryk (1850–1937)*, vol. 1, *Thinker and Politician*, ed. Stanlew B. Winter (London: Basingstoke, 1989), 153–190.

40. See Karel Kramář, *Das böhmische Staatsrecht* (Vienna: Die Zeit, 1896), esp. 8–18.

41. Kramář, *Das böhmische Staatsrecht*, 24–27.

42. Haus der Abgeordneten, 6. Sitzung der XX. Session, November 24, 1909, 370.

43. On Galician Russophilism, see Anna Veronika Wendland, *Die Russophilen in Galizien. Ukrainische Konservative zwischen Österreich und Russland 1848–1915* (Vienna: Verlag der Österreichischen Akademie der Wissenschaften, 2001).

44. Stanley B. Winters, "Austroslavism, Panslavism, and Russophilism in Czech Political Thought, 1870–1900," in *Intellectual and Social Developments in the Habsburg Empire from Maria Theresa to World War I*, ed. Stanley B. Winters and Joseph Held (Boulder, CO: East European Quarterly, 1975), 175–202.

45. Paul Vyšný, *Neo-Slavism and the Czechs, 1898–1914* (Cambridge: Cambridge University Press, 1977), 41.

46. E. P. Serapionova, *Karel Kramarz i Rosiia 1890–1937 gody. Ideinyie vozzrenia, politicheskaia aktivnost,' sviazi s rosiiskimi gosudarstvennymi i obschestvennymi deiateliami* (Moscow: Nauka, 2006), 18.

47. Zbyněk Zeman, *The Masaryks: The Making of Czechoslovakia* (New York: Barnes & Noble, 1976), 64.

48. Cited in Peter Haslinger, *Nation und Territorium im tschechischen politischen Diskurs 1880–1938* (Munich: Oldenbourg, 2010), 83.

49. Andrea Orzoff, *Battle for the Castle: The Myth of Czechoslovakia in Europe, 1914–1918* (Oxford: Oxford University Press, 2009), 37.

50. Orzoff, *Battle for the Castle*, 39–40; Mary Heimann, *Czechoslovakia: The State That Failed* (New Haven: Yale University Press, 2009), 26–28.

51. I am borrowing here from Pieter M. Judson, *Guardians of the Nation: Activists on the Language Frontiers of Imperial Austria* (Cambridge, MA: Harvard University Press, 2006), 233.

52. Ferdinand Peroutka, *Kdo nás osvobodil* (Prague: Nákladem Svazu národního osvobození, 1927), 10.

53. Peroutka, *Kdo nás osvobodil*, 40.

54. Heimann, *Czechoslovakia: The State That Failed*, 28.

55. A detailed account of Kramář's trial, with stenograms of the proceedings, is provided by *Proces dra Kramáře a jeho přatel*, 5 vols., ed. Zdenek Tobolka (Prague: Nákladem dra Zd. Tobolky, 1918–1920).

56. *Paměti Dra Aloise Rašína. Z otcovšína. Z otcových zápisku vydal Dr. Ladislav Rašín*, 2nd ed. (Prague: Tiskem Pražské akciové tiskárny, 1929), 132.

57. On the arrests and release of Kramář and Alois Rašin, see Jana Šetřilová, *Alois Rašín. Dramatický život českého politika* (Prague: Argo, 1997), 9, and "Úvod," in Alois Rašín, *Listy z vězení* (Prague: Nakladatelstvi Pražské akciové tiskárny, 1937), 9–14.

58. For more detail, see Zahra, *Kidnapped Souls,* 87.

59. Karel Kramář, *Die russische Krisis. Geschichte und Kritik des Bolschewismus,* trans. Alfred Schebek (Munich: Duncker & Humblot, 1925), viii.

60. SSPS, 28, February 10, 1921, Poseł Daszyński, p. ccviii/68.

61. Harald Binder, *Galizien in Wien. Parteien, Wahlen, Fraktionen und Abgeordnete im Übergang zur Massenpolitik* (Vienna: Verlag der Österreichischen Akademie der Wissenschaften, 2005), 87.

62. Głąbiński, *Wspomnienia polityczne,* 407.

63. Głąbiński, *Wspomnienia polityczne,* 232–234.

64. On Czechoslovakia's first parliament and government, see Josef Korbel, *Twentieth-Century Czechoslovakia: The Meaning of Its History* (New York: Columbia University Press, 1977), 42, and Hugh LeCaine Agnew, *The Czechs and the Lands of the Bohemian Crown* (Stanford, CA: Hoover Institution Press, 2004), 182. See also Lee Blackwood, "National Democracy at the Dawn of Independent Statehood, 1918–1919," *East European Politics and Societies* 4, no. 3 (Fall 1990): 469–487. On Czech National Democracy, see Stanley B. Winters, "Passionate Patriots: Czechoslovak National Democracy in the 1920s," *East Central Europe / L'Europe du Centre-Est* 18, no. 1 (1991): 55–68.

65. On cabinet arrangements, see Heimann, *Czechoslovakia: The State That Failed,* 40.

66. Poslanecká sněmovna—stenoprotokoly (Czechoslovakia parliamentary protocols), Čtvrtek 14. listopadu, 1918.

67. On the assassination, see "Masaryk to Nadezhda Kramářova," in Tomáš Masaryk, *Cesta Demokracie. Soubor projevů za republiku. Svazek prvni 1918–1920* (Prague: Čin, 1933), 64.

68. Haslinger, *Nation und Territorium im tschechischen politischen Diskurs,* 271.

69. Haslinger, *Nation und Territorium im tschechischen politischen Diskurs,* 47, 40.

70. Serapionova, *Karel Kramářz i Rosiia,* 407.

71. Haslinger, *Nation und Territorium im tschechischen politischen Diskurs,* 391.

72. Poslanecká sněmovna—stenoprotokoly (Czechoslovakia parliamentary protocols), 109. schůze (22. ledna 1920).

73. On Tusar's election, see LeCaine Agnew, *The Czechs and the Lands of the Bohemian Crown,* 182; Nancy Merriwether Wingfield, *Minority Politics in a Multinational State: The German Social Democrats in Czechoslovakia, 1918–1938* (Boulder, CO: East European Monographs, 1989), 17.

74. Shmeral, *Obrazovanie Chekhoslovatskoi respiubliki,* 204.

75. Hoch, *Paměti Dr. Karla Kramáře,* 84.

76. Hoch, *Paměti Dr. Karla Kramáře,* 121.

77. Peroutka, *Kdo nás osvobodil,* 6–7.

78. On Pětka, see Orzoff, *Battle for the Castle,* and Carol Skalnik Leff, *National Conflict in Czechoslovakia: The Making and Remaking of a State, 1918–1987* (Princeton: Princeton University Press, 1988), 57–62.

79. Poslanecká sněmovna—stenoprotokoly (Czechoslovakia parliamentary protocols), k rozpočtovému provisoriu pro první pololetí r. 1919, 12, Pátek 20. prosince 1918.

80. On the "myth" of Czechoslovak democracy and its debunking, see Orzoff, *Battle for the Castle,* and Heimann, *Czechoslovakia: The State That Failed.* On the failures of nationality policies, specifically toward Germans, see Patrick Crowhurst, *A History of Czechoslovakia between the Wars: From Versailles to Hitler's Invasion* (London: I. B. Tauris, 2015). On controversial minority policies, see Jan Kuklík and René Petráš, *Minorities and Law in Czechoslovakia, 1918–1922* (Prague: Karolinum Press, 2017).

81. On de-Austrianization, see Orzoff, *Battle for the Castle,* 57.

82. Karel Kramář, "Zůstaňte věrni našemu vlastenectvi (Projev k studentům 9 března 1936 ns valné hromadē. . . .)," in *Odkaz a Pravda Dr. Karla Kramáře,* ed. Vladimír Sís (Prague: Národní nakladatelství A. Pokorný, 1939), 17.

83. Karel Kramář, "Má víra a nadēje (Odpovēd Dr. Karla Kramáře na pojevy pocty jeho 75 naro . . . v sale Lucerny 29. Prosince 1935)," in *Odkaz a Pravda Dr. Karla Kramáře,* 14.

84. Poslanecká sněmovna—stenoprotokoly (Czechoslovakia parliamentary protocols), 109. schůze (22. ledna 1920).

85. Poslanecká sněmovna—stenoprotokoly (Czechoslovakia parliamentary protocols), 109. schůze (22. ledna 1920).

86. Cited in Małgorzata Wiśniewska and Lech Wyszczelski, *Bezpieczeństwo narodowe Polski w latach 1918–1938. Teoria i praktyka* (Toruń, Poland: Duet, 2009), 174.

87. Herman Diamand's speech to the parliament on March 18, 1919, in Herman Diamand, *Przemówienia w Sejmie Rzeczypospolitej 1919–1930* (Warsaw: Nakładem Księgarni Robotniczej, 1932), 46.

88. SSPS, 20 stycznia 1923, p. 18.

89. SSPS, 20 stycznia 1923, p. 18.

90. Andrzej Garlicki, *Piękne lata trzydzieste* (Warsaw: Prószynski i S-ka, 2008), 199.

5. Empire and Fascism, 1890s–1928

1. See Marco Bresciani, "Conservative and Radical Dynamics of Italian Fascism: An (East) European Perspective (1918–1938)," in *Conservatives and Right Radicals in Interwar Europe,* ed. Marco Bresciani (New York: Routledge, 2021), 68–95, and Marco Bresciani, "The Post-Imperial Space of the Upper Adriatic and the Post-War Ascent of Fascism," in *Vergangene Räume—Neue Ordnungen. Das Erbe der multinationalen Reiche*

und die Staatsbildung im östlichen Europa 1917–1923, ed. Tim Buchen and Frank Grelka (Frankfurt an der Oder: Viadrina University Press, 2016), 47–64.

2. I am borrowing here from James Gregor, *Marxism, Fascism, and Totalitarianism: Chapters in the Intellectual History of Radicalism* (Stanford, CA: Stanford University Press, 2009), 76.

3. Benito Mussolini, *Il Trentino visto da un socialista* (Trento: La Finestra, 2003), 39–40.

4. Accounts of Italian fascism and its origins are numerous. One of the best analytical presentations of fascism and its historiography is Robert O. Paxton, *The Anatomy of Fascism* (New York: Knopf, 2004).

5. On fascism in Italy's eastern borderlands, see Marco Bresciani, "Lost in Transition? The Habsburg Legacy, State- and Nation-Building, and the New Fascist Order in the Upper Adriatic," in *National Indifference and the History of Nationalism in Modern Europe,* ed. Maarten Van Ginderachter and Jon Fox (London: Routledge, 2019), 56–80, and Annamaria Vinci, *Sentinelle della patria. Il fascismo al confine orientale 1918–1941* (Bari, Italy: Laterza, 2011).

6. Elio Apih, *Italia. Fascismo e antifascismo nella Venezia Giulia (1918–1943). Ricerche storiche* (Bari, Italy: Laterza, 1966), 27; Angelo Visintin, *L'Italia a Trieste. L'operato del governo militare italiano nella Venezia Giulia 1918–1919* (Gorizia, Italy: LEG Edizioni, 2000), 79. On Trieste, see Roberta Pergher, *Mussolini's Nation-Empire: Sovereignty and Settlement in Italy's Borderlands, 1922–1943* (Cambridge: Cambridge University Press, 2017), 1–31. A nuanced recent discussion of fascism in Trieste is Marco Bresciani, "The Battle for Post-Habsburg Trieste/Trst: State Transition, Social Unrest, and Political Radicalism (1918–23)," *Austrian History Yearbook* 52 (2021): 194.

7. On the importance of the Adriatic region in Italian nationalist discourse, see, for example, Marina Cattaruzza, *L'Italia e il confine orientale 1866–2006* (Bologna: Il Mulino, 2007), 16, and Bresciani, "Post-Imperial Space," 11.

8. See Dominique Kirchner Reill, *Nationalists Who Feared the Nation: Adriatic Multi-Nationalism in Habsburg Dalmatia, Trieste, and Venice* (Stanford, CA: Stanford University Press, 2012), esp. chap. 4.

9. On this argument, see Fabio Capano, "From a Cosmopolitan to a Fascist Land: Adriatic Irredentism in Motion," in *Nationalities Papers* 46, no. 6 (2018): 976–991.

10. For the exact numbers, see Marina Cattaruzza, "Slowenen und Italiener in Trieste (1850–1914)," in *Die Moderne und ihre Krisen. Studien von Marina Cattaruzza zur europäischen Geschichte des 19. und 20. Jahrhunderts,* ed. Sacha Zala (Göttingen: V & R Unipress, 2012), 219.

11. On this argument, see Angelo Ara, "The 'Cultural Soul' and the 'Merchant Soul': Trieste between Italian and Austrian Identity," in *The Habsburg Legacy: National Identity*

in Historical Perspective, ed. Ritchie Robertson and Edward Timms (Edinburgh: Edinburgh University Press, 1994), 58–66.

12. Vanni d'Alessio, *Il cuore conteso. Il nazionalismo in una comunità multietnica. l'Istria asburgica* (Napoli: Filema, 2003), 17.

13. Alessio, *Il cuore conteso,* 93.

14. For a useful recent discussion of the historiography of Italy and the First World War, see Roberta Pergher, "An Italian War? War and Nation in the Italian Historiography of the First World War," *Journal of Modern History* 9, no. 4 (December 2018): 863–899.

15. On the proposed annexations, see Margaret Macmillan, *Paris 1919: Six Months That Changed the World* (New York: Random House, 2001). On the territorial conflict with Yugoslavia, see specifically p. 110.

16. On parallels between Italian territories and Galicia, see Francesco Frizzera, *Cittadini dimezzati. I profughi trentini in Austria-Ungheria e in Italia (1914–1919)* (Bologna: Il Mulino, 2018), 61.

17. Luca Riccardi, *Francesco Salata tra storia, politica e diplomazia* (Udine, Italy: Del Bianco Editore, 2001), 127–131.

18. For a nuanced discussion of the intersection of geography and politics in the early twentieth century, see Steven Seegel, *Map Men: Transnational Lives and Deaths of Geographers in the Making of East Central Europe* (Chicago: University of Chicago Press, 2018).

19. See Francesco Salata, *Il diritto d'Italia su Trieste e l'Istria. Documenti* (Turin: Bocca, 1915), and Riccardi, *Francesco Salata,* 127. His views on Istria are available in Francesco Salata, *Patria e storia. Discorso al Congresso biennale della Società istriana di archeologia e storia patria. Pirano, 18 settembre 1927* (Parenzo, Italy: Stab. Tip. Gaetano Coana & Figli, 1927).

20. On Idla, see Riccardi, *Francesco Salata,* 193.

21. On this role, see Maura Hametz, *Making Trieste Italian, 1918–1954* (Trowbridge, UK: Wiltshire, 2005), 16.

22. A detailed description of territories is included in Dennison I. Rusinow, *Italy's Austrian Heritage, 1919–1946* (Oxford: Clarendon Press, 1969), 9–13.

23. On the ethnic composition of Fiume, see Luigi Emilio Longo, *L'esercito italiano e la questione fiumana (1918–1921),* vol. 1 (Rome: Stato Maggiore Esercito, Ufficio Storico, 1996), 13.

24. Mario Dassovich, *I molti problemi dell'Italia al confine orientale,* vol. 1, *Dall'armistizio di Cormons alla decadenza del patto Mussolini-Pašić (1866–1929)* (Udine, Italy: Del Bianco Editore, 1989), 195–196.

25. Howard M. Sachar, *The Assassination of Europe, 1918–1942: A Political History* (Toronto: Toronto University Press, 2015), 36.

26. The literature on Fiume is enormous. A new account is Dominique Kirchner Reill, *The Fiume Crisis: Life in the Wake of the Habsburg Empire* (Cambridge, MA: Belknap Press,

2020). On the contests over Fiume, see Antonella Ercolani, *Da Fiume a Rijeka. Profilo storico-politico dal 1918 al 1947* (Milan: Rubbettino, 2009).

27. See Francesco Piazza, *L'altra sponda adriatica. Trieste, Istria, Fiume, Dalmazia 1918–1998. Storia di una tragedia rimossa* (Verona: Cierre, 2001), 16.

28. An excellent recent analysis of Trieste's transition from the Habsburg to Italian rule is Marco Bresciani, "The Battle for Post-Habsburg Trieste," 182–200.

29. On the Danubian basin and Trieste, see Pasquale Cuomo, *Il miraggio danubiano. Austria e Italia, politica ed economia 1918–1936* (Milan: FrancoAngeli, 2012), 59.

30. Cattaruzza, *L'Italia e il confine orientale,* 61.

31. On Trieste's economic decline after 1918, see Giulio Sapelli, *Trieste italiana. Mito e destino economico* (Milan: FrancoAngeli, 1990), 91–100, and Cattaruzza, *L'Italia e il confine orientale,* 61.

32. Reill, *The Fiume Crisis.*

33. On the continuity of bureaucracy in Trentino and South Tyrol, see Andrea di Michele, *Die unvollkommene Italianisierung. Politik und Verwaltung in Südtirol 1918–1943,* trans. Julia Becker and Patrick Bernard (Innsbruck, Austria: Universitätsverlag Wagner, 2008), 28–32. On similar continuities along the Adriatic, see Marco Bresciani, "Lost in Transition?," 56–80.

34. Hametz, *Making Trieste Italian,* 17; Rusinow, *Italy's Austrian Heritage,* 62, 109. See also Apih, *Italia. Fascismo e antifascismo nella Venezia Giulia,* 78.

35. "Galli to Sonnino, Rome, 17.10.1918," in Carlo Galli, *Diarii e lettere. Tripoli 1911–Trieste 1918* (Florence: Sansoni, 1951), 311.

36. I am borrowing here from Hametz, *Making Trieste Italian,* 123.

37. Cited in Angelo Visintin, *L'Italia a Trieste. L'operato del governo militare italiano nella Venezia Giulia 1918–1919* (Venice: Istituto regionale per la storia del movimento di liberazione nel Friuli-Venezia Giulia, 2000), 79.

38. Antonio Mosconi, *I primi anni di governo italiano nella Venezia Giulia* (Bologna: L. Capelli, 1924), 21.

39. Rusinow, *Italy's Austrian Heritage,* 103, 109. On Nitti and his policies, see Andrea di Michele, *Die unvollkommene Italianisierung,* 69, and Apih, *Italia. Fascismo e antifascismo nella Venezia Giulia,* 78.

40. A nuanced analysis of Rome's post-1918 policies in Trentino is provided in Roberta Pergher, "Staging the Nation in Fascist Italy's 'New Provinces,'" *Austrian History Yearbook* 43 (2012): 98–115; on the term *allogeni,* see 103. See also A. Angeli, "Gli autonomisti giuliani e l'avvento del fascismo," in *Il fascismo e le autonomie locali,* ed. Sandro Fontana (Bologna: Il Mulino, 1973), 198.

41. Di Michele, *Die unvollkommene Italianisierung,* 112.

42. On the office's founding, see Almerigo Apollonio, *Dagli Asburgo a Mussolini. Venezia Giulia 1918–1922* (Gorizia, Italy: LEG Edizioni, 2001), 187.

43. Ester Capuzzo, "Francesco Salata e il problema dell'autonomia nelle nuove province," in *Autonomia e federalismo nella tradizione storica italiana e austriaca,* ed. Maria Garbari and Davide Zaffi (Trento: Società di studi trentini di scienze storiche, 1996), 148.

44. Riccardi, *Francesco Salata,* 302. See also Angeli, "Gli autonomisti giuliani e l'avvento del fascismo," 183.

45. Alfredo Canavero, "L'esperienza del Partito Popolare (1918–1926)," in *Alcide De Gasperi,* vol. 1, *Dal Trentino all'esilio in patria (1881–1943),* ed. Alfredo Canavero et al. (Soveria Mannelli, Italy: Rubbettino, 2009), 200.

46. On the chaotic annexation, see Angelo Ara, "Una fonte austriaca per la storia triestina fra le due guerre mondiali," in Angelo Ara, *Fra Austria e Italia. Dalle Cinque Giornate alla questione alto-atestina* (Udine, Italy: Del Bianco Editore, 1987), 217–226.

47. "La depredazione delle Terre Liberate," *Il Giornale del Popolo,* June 16, 1920.

48. "La depredazione delle Terre Liberate," *Il Giornale del Popolo,* June 16, 1920.

49. On De Gasperi's parliamentary inquiry, see Francesco Salata, "Decentramente e autonomie. Communicazioni alla commissione consultative centrale. Seduta pomeriediana del 7 giugno 1922," in Francesco Salata, *Per le nuove provincie e per l'Italia. Discorsi e scritti con note e documenti* (Rome: Stabilimento poligrafico per l' amministrazione della guerra, 1922), 83.

50. Francesco Salata, "Le nuove provincie e il Tesoro. Discorso alla commissione consultativa centrale. Seduta antimeridiana dell' 8 giugno 1922," in Salata, *Per le nuove provincie e per l'Italia,* 103.

51. AcdS, Ministero del'Interno, Atti Amministrativi. Direzione Generale AA.GG.PP. Divisione del personale. Affari diversi, 1861–1952. Busta 9: "Spunti Polemici," *Il Nuovo Trentino,* 26.03.1923: Il Trentino in arretrato di cinquant'anni.

52. Cited in *Alcide De Gasperi,* vol. 1, *Dal Trentino all'esilio in patria (1881–1943),* ed. Alfredo Canavero et al. (Rome: Rubbettino, 2009), 387.

53. On pro-Austrian sentiment, see Ara, "Una fonte austriaca per la storia triestina," 217.

54. Adrian Lyttelton, *The Seizure of Power: Fascism in Italy, 1919–1929* (Princeton: Princeton University Press, 1988), 112.

55. Lyttelton, *Seizure of Power,* 114.

56. On liberals' attitudes toward the fascists, see Lyttelton, *Seizure of Power,* 112–114.

57. Lyttelton, *Seizure of Power,* 96.

58. Riccardi, *Francesco Salata,* 292.

59. For more on the office, see Vinci, *Sentinelle della patria,* 31.

60. On the PPI, see Michael Burleigh, *Sacred Causes: The Clash of Religion and Politics, From the Great War to the War on Terror* (New York: HarperCollins, 2007), 33–34.

61. Canavero, "L'esperienza del Partito Popolare," 303.

62. Alcide De Gasperi, "Preface," in *Le battaglie del Partito Popolare. Raccolta di scritti e discorsi politici dal 1919 al 1926,* ed. Paolo Piccoli and Armando Vadagnini (Rome: Edizioni di Storia e Letteratura, 1992), x.

63. "L'attività del Partito popolare italiano (Relazione di Alcide De Gasperi al V Congresso nazionale del Partito popolare italiano, 28–30 giugno 1925)," in *Alcide De Gasperi nel Partito popolare italiano e nella Democrazia cristiana. Un'antologia di discorsi politici 1923–1954,* ed. Giovani Allara and Angelo Gati (Rome: Edizioni Cinque Lune, 1990), 65.

64. *Alcide De Gasperi,* vol. 1, *Dal Trentino all'esilio in patria,* 303.

65. "La situazione politica e parlamentare dalla crisi Facta all'avvento di Mussolini (Relazione di Alcide De Gasperi al IV Congresso nazionale del Partito popolare italiano. Torino 12–14 Aprile 1923)," in *Alcide De Gasperi nel Partito popolare italiano e nella Democrazia cristiana,* 46.

66. "L'attività del Partito popolare italiano," 65.

67. On those disagreements, see John N. Molony, *The Emergence of Political Catholicism in Italy: Partito Popolare, 1919–1926* (London: Croom Helm, 1977), 77. The PPI's agrarian program is discussed in Francesco Piva and Francesco Malgeri, *Vita di Luigi Sturzo* (Rome: Edizione Cinque Lune, 1972), 222.

68. Anthony Rhodes, *The Vatican in the Age of Dictators (1922–1945)* (New York: Holt, Rinehart and Winston, 1973), 27.

69. Rhodes, *The Vatican in the Age of Dictators,* 32.

70. Rhodes, *The Vatican in the Age of Dictators,* 45.

71. Philip Morgan, *Italian Fascism* (New York: St. Martin's Press, 1995), 19.

72. Milica Kacin-Wohinz, *Narodnoobrambno gibanje primorskih Slovencev v letih 1921–1928,* vol. 2 (Koper–Trieste: Založba Lipa Koper and Založništvo Tržaškega Tiska, 1977), 174.

73. Alcide De Gasperi, "La nostra autonomia. Il testo del discorso tenuto il 24 giugno," orig. published in *Il Trentino,* July 4, 1921, repr. in De Gasperi, *Le battaglie del Partito Popolare,* 228.

74. On Matteotti's murder, see Lyttelton, *Seizure of Power,* 197.

75. On charges of Austrophilism in post-1918 Trieste, see Bresciani, "The Battle for Post-Habsburg Trieste," 189.

76. Giorgio Vecchio, "'Esule in patria'. Gli anni del fascismo (1926–1943)," in *Alcide De Gasperi,* vol. 1, *Dal Trentino all'esilio in patria,* 408.

77. "Alcide De Gasperi to Carlo [his wife's brother], 16 marzo 1927," in Alcide De Gasperi, *Lettere dalla prigione 1927–1928* (Milan: Arnoldo Mondadori Editore, 1955), 13.

78. The episode is described in Paolo Piccoli and Armando Vadagnini, *DeGasperi. Un trentino nella storia d'Europa* (Soveria Mannelli, Italy: Rubbettino, 2004), 171.

79. Piccoli and Vadagnini, *DeGasperi. Un trentino nella storia d'Europa,* 169.

6. Democratic Socialism and Left-Wing Radicalism

1. The official beginning of this school is usually traced to 1903 and 1904 articles in the Austrian Marxist journal *Marx-Studien* that elaborated the premises of Austro-Marxism. See Ernst Glaser, *Im Umfeld des Austromarxismus. Ein Beitrag zur Geistes-geschichte des österreichischen Sozialismus* (Vienna: Europa Verlag, 1981), 17–22, and Hermann Böhm, *Die Tragödie des Austromarxismus am Beispiel von Otto Bauer. Ein Beitrag zur Geschichte des österreichischen Sozialismus* (Frankfurt am Main: Peter Lang, 2000), 15–23.

2. On Austro-Marxism and democracy, see Böhm, *Die Tragödie des Austromarxismus,* 22. On the "third way," see Peter Goller, *Otto Bauer–Max Adler. Beiträge zur Geschichte des Austromarxismus (1904–1938)* (Vienna: Alfred Klahr Gesselschaft, 2008), 9, and Helmut Gruber, *Red Vienna: Experiment in Working-Class Culture, 1919–1934* (Oxford: Oxford University Press, 1991), 38. On "socialism with a human face," see Böhm, *Die Tragödie des Austromarxismus,* 25.

3. See Norbert Leser, *Zwischen Reformismus und Bolschewismus. Der Austromarxismus als Theorie und Praxis* (Vienna: Europa Verlag, 1968).

4. On this historiographical neglect, see Anson Rabinbach, *The Crisis of Austrian Social-ism: From Red Vienna to Civil War, 1927–1934* (Chicago: University of Chicago Press, 1983), 2.

5. Some notable examples are Peter Kulemann, *Am Beispiel des Austromarxismus. So-zialdemokratische Arbeiterbewegung in Österreich von Hainfeld zur Dolfuß-Diktatur* (Hamburg: Junius, 1979), 13, and Detlev Albers et al., eds., *Otto Bauer und der "Dritte" Weg. Der Wiederentdeckung des Austromarxismus durch Linksozialisten und Eurokommu-nisten* (Frankfurt am Main: Campus Verlag, 1979).

6. Cited in Rabinbach, *Crisis of Austrian Socialism,* 2. One recent example of this ap-proach is Ernst Hanisch, *Der große Illusionist. Otto Bauer (1881–1938)* (Vienna: Böhlau, 2011).

7. On Austro-Marxism as intertwined with the empire, see Rabinbach, *Crisis of Austrian Socialism,* 13.

8. I am borrowing the concept of "milieu" from Glaser, *Im Umfeld des Austromarxismus,* 61.

9. Hanisch, *Der große Illusionist,* 74.

10. George G. Rundel, "Wilhelm Ellenbogen und Italien," in *Wilhelm Ellenbogen. Aus-gewälte Schriften,* ed. Norbert Leser and George G. Rundel (Vienna: Österreichischer Bundesverlag, 1983), 22.

11. Johann Wolfgang Brügel, *Ludwig Czech. Arbeiterführer und Staatsmann* (Vienna: Verlag der Wiener Volksbuchhandlung, 1960), 26.

12. On Šmeral's father, see Jan Galandauer, *Bohumír Šmeral 1810–1914* (Prague: Svoboda, 1981), 12.

13. Jakub S. Beneš, *Workers and Nationalism: Czech and German Social Democracy in Habsburg Austria, 1890–1918* (Oxford: Oxford University Press), 184.

14. Gruber, *Red Vienna,* 30.

15. On Bauer's "overshadowing" of Renner, see Gruber, *Red Vienna,* 33.

16. Ellenbogen, for example, referred to Bauer as "an old friend." See Sitzung des Nationalrates der Republik Österreich, December 2, 1922, 4947.

17. On the control of trade unions, see Beneš, *Workers and Nationalism,* 185.

18. On Social Democrats' anticlericalism, see John W. Boyer, *Culture and Political Crisis in Vienna: Christian Socialism in Power, 1897–1918* (Chicago: University of Chicago Press, 1995), 204–206.

19. On Neudorf and illegality, see Herbert Steiner, *Die Arbeiterbewegung Österreichs 1867–1889. Beiträge zu ihrer Geschichte von der Gründung der Wiener Arbeiterbildungsvereines bis zum Einigungsparteitag in Hainfeld* (Vienna: Europa Verlag, 1964), 95.

20. For a discussion of this transition, see Wolfgang Maderthaner, "Die Entstehung einer demokratischen Massenpartei. Sozialdemokratische Organisation von 1889 bis 1918," in *Die Organisation der österreichischen Sozialdemokratie 1889–1995,* ed. Wolfgang Maderthaner and Wolfgang C. Müller (Vienna: Löcker Verlag, 1996), 21–92, esp. 33.

21. On the importance of this "limited toleration," see Beneš, *Workers and Nationalism,* 25.

22. On the participants, see Fritz Kaufmann, *Sozialdemokratie in Österreich. Idee und Geschichte einer Partei von 1889 bis zur Gegenwart* (Vienna: Amalthea, 1978), 110.

23. Hans Mommsen, *Die Sozialdemokratie und die Nationalitätenfrage im habsburgischen Vielvölkerstaat* (Vienna: Europa Verlag, 1963), 80, 94.

24. A detailed analysis of this in English is Ladislav Cabada, *Intellectuals and the Communist Idea: The Search for a New Way in Czech Lands from 1890 to 1938* (Lanham, MD: Lexington Books, 2010), chap. 2.

25. Ludwig Brügel, *Geschichte der österreichischen Sozialdemokratie,* vol. 5, *Parlamentsfeindlichkeit und Obstruktion/Weltkrieg/Zerfall der Monarchie* (Vienna: Verlag der Wiener Volksbuchhandlung, 1925), 77.

26. For a detailed discussion of the debates within the Czech party, see Ludwig Brügel, *Geschichte der österreichischen Sozialdemokratie,* vol. 5, 77–105. See also Mommsen, *Die Sozialdemokratie und die Nationalitätenfrage im habsburgischen Vielvölkerstaat,* 86, 96.

27. Beneš, *Workers and Nationalism,* 4.

28. Beneš, *Workers and Nationalism,* 185.

29. On the Brno program, see "Nationalities Program of the Austrian Social Democratic Workers' Party" (adopted at the Brün Party Congress, 1899), in Mark E. Blum and

William Smaldone, eds., *Austro-Marxism: The Ideology of Unity,* vol. 2 (Leiden, Netherlands: Brill, 2016), 24–25.

30. Karl Renner, "Nation and State," in *Discourses of Collective Identity in Central and Southeastern Europe (1770–1945): Texts and Commentaries,* ed. Ahmet Ersoy et al. (Budapest: CEU Press, 2010), 13.

31. Otto Bauer, *The Question of Nationalities and Social Democracy,* trans. Joseph O'Donnell (Minneapolis: University of Minnesota Press, 2000), 144.

32. Bauer, *Question of Nationalities and Social Democracy,* 259–309.

33. Bohumír Šmeral, "The National Question and the Social Democrats," in Ersoy, *Discourses of Collective Identity in Central and Southeastern Europe (1770–1945),* 418.

34. Paul Reimann, *Geschichte der kommunistischen Partei der Tschechoslowakei* (Hamburg: Verlag Carl Hoym Nachfolger, 1931), 26–27.

35. On Bauer's vision of Austro-Marxism, see Otto Bauer, "Austromarxismus," in *Austromarxismus. Texte zu "Ideologie und Klassenkampf,"* ed. Hans-Jörg Sandkühler and Rafael de la Vega (Frankfurt: Europäische Verlagsanstalt, 1970), 50.

36. Otto Bauer, *Zwischen zwei Weltkriegen? Die Krise der Weltwirtschaft der Demokratie und des Sozialismus* (Bratislava: Eugen Prager, 1936), 194.

37. For Bauer's arguments, see Otto Bauer, "Gefahren des Reformismus," in *Der Aufstieg zur Massenpartei. Ein Lesebuch zur österreichischen Sozialdemokratie 1889–1908,* ed. Brigitte Keppinger (Vienna: Löcker, 1990), 123–124.

38. Wilhelm Ellenbogen, "Karl Kautsky," in Wilhelm Ellenbogen, *Ausgewälte Schriften,* ed. Norbert Leser and George G. Rundel (Vienna: Österreichischer Bundesverlag, 1983), 74.

39. Mommsen, *Die Sozialdemokratie und die Nationalitätenfrage im habsburgischen Vielvölkerstaat,* 128. Kautsky's role in drafting the Hainfeld program is discussed in Christoph Butterwegge, *Austromarxismus und Staat: Politiktheorie und Praxis der österreichischen Sozialdemokratie zwischen den beiden Weltkriegen* (Marburg, Germany: Verlag Arbeit und Gesellschaft, 1991), 61.

40. On the Socialist International and Germans' predominance in it, see Julius Braunthal, *History of the International,* 2 vols., trans. John Clark (New York: Frederick A. Pragier, 1967), vol. 1, 200.

41. On the Austro-Marxists' rejection of Bolshevism, see Walter Baier, "Integraler Sozialismus und radikale Demokratie," in *Otto Bauer und der Austromarxismus. "Integraler Sozialismus" und die heutige Linke,* ed. Walter Baier et al. (Berlin: Karl Dietz, 2008), 20–21.

42. On Stalin's and Trotsky's stays in Vienna in 1913, see Frederic Morton, *Thunder at Twilight: Vienna 1913–1914* (Cambridge, MA: Da Capo Press, 2001), specifically 5–23.

43. The pre-1917 Bolsheviks included only four members from Georgia. See Liliana Riga, *The Bolsheviks and the Russian Empire* (Cambridge: Cambridge University Press, 2012), 186.

44. On Georgian revolutionaries and the Bolsheviks, as well as Stalin and his Georgianness, see chap. 2 in Erik R. Scott, *Familiar Strangers: The Georgian Diaspora and the Evolution of Soviet Empire* (New York: Oxford University Press, 2016).

45. For Stalin's essay on nationality, see Joseph Stalin, "Marxism and the National Question," in J. V. Stalin, *Works,* vol. 2, *1907–1913* (Moscow: Foreign Language Publishing House, 1953), 300–381.

46. Leon Trotsky, *My Life: An Attempt at an Autobiography* (New York: Pathfinder Press, 1970), 217.

47. Trotsky, *My Life,* 217.

48. Hanisch, *Der große Illusionist,* 126.

49. Otto Bauer speech, "Parteitag 1909," in Otto Bauer, *Werkausgabe,* vol. 5 (Vienna: Europa Verlag, 1978), 15.

50. Otto Bauer speech, "Parteitag 1913," in Otto Bauer, *Werkausgabe,* vol. 5, 99–103.

51. Wilhelm Ellenbogen, "Nieder mit der Privilegienparlament," in Wilhelm Ellenbogen, *Ausgewälte Schriften,* 194.

52. Boyer, *Culture and Political Crisis in Vienna,* 452–455.

53. On the crisis within the Second International in 1914, see Georges Haupt, *Socialism and the Great War: The Collapse of the Second International* (Oxford: Clarendon Press, 1972), specifically 204. A useful if dated analysis of 1914 and the collapse of the Socialist International is provided in Braunthal, *History of the International,* vol. 2.

54. Haupt, *Socialism and the Great War,* 204.

55. Friedrich Weissensteiner, "Dr. Wilhelm Ellenbogen—Persönlichkeit und Werk," in Wilhelm Ellenbogen, *Menschen und Prinzipen. Erinnerungen. Urteile und Reflexionen eines kritischen Sozialdemokraten,* ed. Friedrich Weissensteiner (Vienna: Böhlau, 1981), 23.

56. Gustav Habrman, *Mé vzpomínky z války. Črty a obrázky o událostech a zápasech za svobodu a samostatnost* (Prague: Ústřední dělnické, 1928), 65.

57. On the Adler family and the father-son split, see Julius Braunthal, *Victor und Friedrich Adler. Zwei Generationen Arbeitsbewegung* (Vienna: Verlag der Wiener Volksbuchhandlung, 1965).

58. Braunthal, *Victor und Friedrich Adler,* 85.

59. On Bauer's imprisonment and his transport to Siberia, see Hanisch, *Der große Illusionist,* and Verena Moritz, *1917. Österreichische Stimmen zur Russischen Revolution, mit einem Beitrag von Wolfgang Maderthaner* (Vienna: Residenz Verlag, 2017), 233.

60. Otto Bauer, *Das Weltbild des Kapitalismus* (1924; repr., Frankfurt am Main: Makol Verlag, 1971). On his sympathy for the February 1917 revolution, see Butterwegge, *Austromarxismus und Staat,* 187.

61. On the Stockholm conference and its failures, see Braunthal, *History of the International,* vol. 2, 149.

62. Butterwegge, *Austromarxismus und Staat,* 187–188.

63. Butterwegge, *Austromarxismus und Staat,* 90.

64. Richard Saage, *Der erste Präsident. Karl Renner—eine politische Biographie* (Vienna: Paul Zsolnay Verlag, 2016), 134; Raimund Löw, *Otto Bauer und die russische Revolution* (Vienna: Europa Verlag, 1980), 33.

65. Otto Bauer, "Bolshewismus oder Sozialdemokratie?," in Bauer, *Werksaufgabe,* vol. 5. See esp. the preface and 345–347; Bauer, *Zwischen zwei Weltkriegen?,* 298.

66. For more detail, see Gruber, *Red Vienna,* esp. 21, and Rabinbach, *Crisis of Austrian Socialism,* 18.

67. Hans Hautmann, *Die Anfänge der linksradikalen Bewegung und der Kommunistischen Partei Deutschösterreich 1916–1919* (Vienna: Europa Verlag, 1970), 44.

68. Sitzung der provisorischen Nationalversammlung für Deutschösterreich am 30 October 1918, p. 24.

69. Sitzung der provisorischen Nationalversammlung für Deutschösterreich am 30 October 1918, 38.

70. Sitzung der provisorischen Nationalversammlung für Deutschösterreich am 30 October 1918, 67.

71. Zdeněk Kárník, *Habsburk, Masarykči Šmeral. Socialisté na rozcestí* (Prague: Universita Karlova, 1996), 92.

72. Ferdinand Peroutka, *Budování státu,* vol. 1, *1918–1919* (Prague: Lidové noviny, 1991), 30.

73. On citizenship in the empire, see, for example, Annemarie Steidl, *On Many Routes: Internal, European, and Transatlantic Migration in the Late Habsburg Empire* (West Lafayette, IN: Purdue University Press, 2020), 36–38.

74. Hanisch, *Der große Illusionist,* 165.

75. Otto Bauer, *The Austrian Revolution,* trans. H. J. Stenning (London: Leonard Parsons, 1925), 71.

76. Bauer, *Austrian Revolution,* 71.

77. Bauer, *Austrian Revolution,* 110.

78. I am borrowing here from Rabinbach, *Crisis of Austrian Socialism,* 2.

79. Rabinbach, *Crisis of Austrian Socialists,* 20.

80. Bauer, "Parteitag 1919," in Otto Bauer, *Werkausgabe,* vol. 5, 165.

81. The concept is defined in Wilhelm Ellenbogen, "Sozialisierung in Österreich," in Ellenbogen, *Ausgewahlte Schriften,* 232.

82. For more detail on the nationalizations, see Erwin Weissel, *Die Ohnmacht des Sieges. Arbeiterschaft und Sozialisierung nach dem Ersten Weltkrieg in Österreich* (Vienna: Europa Verlag, 1976), 285.

83. On Bauer's time in government and his resignation, see Carlo Moos, *Habsburg post mortem. Betrachtungen zum Weiterleben der Habsburgermonarchie* (Vienna: Böhlau, 2016), 44–55.

84. Hanisch, *Der große Illusionist,* 201.

85. Otto Bauer, *Austrian Democracy under Fire* (Bratislava: Labor Publications Department, 1934), 222.

86. There is a relatively large literature on "Red Vienna." For some examples, see Gruber, *Red Vienna,* and Rabinbach, *Crisis of Austrian Socialism.* Citation here is from Rabinbach, p. 29.

87. On continuities of Austrian socialists' practices between the empire and the first republic, see Rabinbach, *Crisis of Austrian Socialism,* 29.

88. For the numbers, see Hugh LeCaine Agnew, *The Czechs and the Lands of the Bohemian Crown* (Stanford, CA: Hoover Institution Press, 2004), 182.

89. Bernard Wheaton, *Radical Socialism in Czechoslovakia: Bohumír Šmeral, the Czech Road to Socialism and the Origins of the Czechoslovak Communist Party (1917–1921)* (Boulder, CO: East European Monographs, 1986), 15.

90. Poslanecká sněmovna—stenoprotokoly (Czechoslovakia parliamentary protocols), 66. schůze (obsah, pořad, přílohy), Čtvrtek 13. ledna 1921.

91. Poslanecká sněmovna—stenoprotokoly (Czechoslovakia parliamentary protocols), 66. schůze (obsah, pořad, přílohy), Čtvrtek 13. ledna 1921.

92. Paul Reimann, *Geschichte der kommunistischen Partei der Tschechoslowakei* (Hamburg: Verlag Carl Hoym Nachfolger, 1931), 91.

93. Ferdinand Peroutka, *Budování státu,* vol. 1 (Prague: Lidové Noviny, 1991), 326, 333.

94. Peroutka, *Budování státu,* vol. 1, 333.

95. Peroutka, *Budování státu,* vol. 2, 536.

96. Bohumír Šmeral, *První cesty do země Leninovy* (Prague: Práce, 1973), 20.

97. Jacques Rupnik, *Histoire du parti communiste tchécoslovaque. Des origines à la prise du pouvoir* (Paris: Presses de la Fondation Nationale des Sciences Politiques, 1981), 69.

98. Zdenek Suda, *Zealots and Rebels: A History of the Ruling Communist Party of Czechoslovakia* (Stanford, CA: Hoover Institution Press, 1980), 5–35. On Muna's role in Czechoslovak communism, see Ladislav Cabada, *Komunismus, levicová kultura a česká politika 1890–1938* (Plzeň, Czech Republic: Vydavatelstvi Aleš Čeněk, 2005), 35.

99. On the Kyiv and Petrograd groups, see, Suda, *Zealots and Rebels,* 15–17, and H. Gordon Skilling, "The Formation of a Communist Party in Czechoslovakia," *American Slavic and East European Review* 14, no. 3 (October 1955): 347.

100. On Šmeral and his "homegrown" communism, see Suda, *Zealots and Rebels,* 36.

101. Wheaton, *Radical Socialism in Czechoslovakia,* 24.

102. On the formation and ethnic composition of the CPC, see Suda, *Zealots and Rebels,* 46, and Cabada, *Komunismus, levicová kultura a česká politika,* 60–64.

103. On Germans' joining in, see S. V. Kretinin, *Sudeto-nemetskaia sotsial-demokratiia. Stranitsy politicheskoi istorii* (Voronezh, USSR: Voronezhskii Universitet, 1968), 65.

104. Kretinin, *Sudeto-nemetskaia sotsial-demokratiia,* 66.

105. Cited in Paul Reimann, *Geschichte der kommunistischen Partei der Tschechoslowakei* (Hamburg: Verlag Carl Hoym Nachfolger, 1931), 187.

106. Leszek Kolakowski, *Main Currents of Marxism,* vol. 2, *The Golden Age,* trans. P. S. Falla (Oxford: Clarendon Press, 1978), 18.

107. Josef Stalin, "The Communist Party of Czechoslovakia: Speech Delivered in the Czechoslovak Commission of the Communist International, January 17, 1925," in Josef Stalin, *Works,* vol. 7, 1925; available online at the Marxist Internet Archive, https://www.marxists.org/reference/archive/stalin/works/1925/03/29.htm#1, 106.

108. See Šmeral's speech against the arrests: Poslanecká sněmovna—stenoprotokoly (Czechoslovakia parliamentary protocols), 66. schůze (obsah, pořad, přílohy) 368, 1. X. 1925; 871. XI.

109. H. Gordon Skilling, "The Comintern and Czechoslovak Communism: 1921–1929," *American Slavic and East European Review* 19, no. 2 (April 1960): 236.

110. On Gottwald and his relationship with the Comintern, see Skilling, "The Comintern and Czechoslovak Communism," 234.

111. In the first years of its existence, the party claimed some 350,000 members, many of them non-Czech leftists who after 1918 were marginalized by mainstream parties. See Kretinin, *Sudeto-nemetskaia sotsial-demokratiia,* 78.

112. Suda, *Zealots and Rebels,* 36.

113. On Germans' opposition to Czechoslovakia, see Harry Klepetař, *Seit 1918 . . . Eine Geschichte der Tschechoslowakischen Republik* (Mährisch Ostrau, Czechoslovakia: Verlag Julius Kittls Nachfolger, 1937), 13.

114. Poslanecká sněmovna—stenoprotokoly (Czechoslovakia parliamentary protocols), 66. schůze (obsah, pořad, přílohy) 87, 19. X. 1921; 50. IV. (něm. 102).

115. Poslanecká sněmovna—stenoprotokoly (Czechoslovakia parliamentary protocols), 66. schůze (obsah, pořad, přílohy) 87, 19. X. 1921; 50. IV. (něm. 102), 96.

7. From Promise to Terror

1. One example of a study that claims to trace the Austro-Marxist legacy in post-1918 in Poland is Ewa Czerwinska, *"Nurt mediacji," Austromarksizm i jego recepcja w Polsce. Studium myśli filozoficznej i społeczno-politycznej* (Poznań, Poland: Instytut Filozofii UAM, 1985).

2. See, for example, two works on Galician socialism: Kerstin Jobst, *Zwischen Nationalismus und Internationalismus. Die polnische und ukrainische Sozialdemokratie in Galizien von 1890 bis 1914. Ein Beitrag zur Nationalitätsfrage im Habsburgerreich* (Hamburg: Dölling und Galitz Verlag, 1996), and John-Paul Himka, *Socialism in Galicia: The Emergence of Polish Social Democracy and Ukrainian Radicalism (1860–1890)* (Cambridge, MA: Harvard Ukrainian Research Institute, 1983).

3. Himka, *Socialism in Galicia,* 71.

4. On Limanowski and his move to Galicia, see Walentyna Najdus, *Polska Partia socjalno-demokratyczna Galicji i Śląska 1890–1919* (Warsaw: Państwowe wydawnictwo naukowe, 1983), 61, and Marian Żychowski, *Bolesław Limanowski 1835–1935* (Warsaw: Książka i Wiedza, 1971), 144.

5. On socialist expats from the Russian Empire, see Himka, *Socialism in Galicia,* 37. Jobst, *Zwischen Nationalismus und Internationalismus,* especially p. 32.

6. Walentyna Najdus, *Ignacy Daszyński 1866–1936* (Warsaw: Czytelnik, 1988), 21. See also Himka, *Socialism in Galicia,* 72.

7. Herman Diamand, *Pamiętnik Hermana Diamanda. Zebrany z wyjątków listów do żony* (Cracow: Nakładem Towarzystwo Uniwersytetu Robotniczego, 1932), 6–9.

8. For Hankevych's biography, see Oleh Zhernokleev and Ihor Raikivs'kyi, *Lidery zakhidnoukrains'koii social-demokratii. Politychni biografii* (Kyiv: Osnovni tsinnosti, 2004), 146–171. On Hankevych's family, see Andrzej A-Zięba, "Altenbergowie, Vorzierowie, Hankiewicz," in Elżbieta Oran and Antoni Cetnarowicz, eds., *Henryk Wereszycki. Historia w życiu historyka* (Cracow: Historia Jagellonica, 2001), 73–119.

9. For Vityk's biography, see Zhernokleev and Raikivs'kyi, *Lidery zakhidnoukrains'koii social-demokratii,* 97–118.

10. Jobst, *Zwischen Nationalismus und Internationalismus,* 35–38.

11. On dual membership, see, for example, Jobst, *Zwischen Nationalismus und Internationalismus,* 80.

12. Jobst, *Zwischen Nationalismus und Internationalismus,* 89.

13. Raimund Löw, *Der Zerfall der "kleinen Internationale." Nationalkonflikte in der Arbeitsbewegung des alten Österreich (1889–1914)* (Vienna: Europa Verlag, 1984), 41; Najdus, *Polska Partia socjalno-demokratyczna Galicji i Śląska,* 139–144.

14. Zhernokleev and Raikivs'kyi, *Lidery zakhidnoukrains'koii social-demokratii,* 151.

15. Zdeněk Kárník, *Habsburk, Masaryk či Šmeral. Socialisté na rozcestí* (Prague: Svoboda, 1996), 19.

16. Haus der Abgeordneten, 41. Sitzung der XXI. Session, December 12, 1911, 2129.

17. Haus der Abgeordneten, 41. Sitzung der XXI. Session, December 12, 1911, 207.

18. Jobst, *Zwischen Nationalismus und Internationalismus,* 139.

19. On this celebration, see Kazimiera Janina Cottam, *Bolesław Limanowski (1835–1935): A Study in Socialism and Nationalism* (Boulder, CO: East European Quarterly, 1978), 186, and Żychowski, *Bolesław Limanowski,* 305.

20. Henryk Wereszycki, "Życzymy ci towarzyszu Limanowski wolnej Warszawy. Wspomnienie mówione," in Henryk Wereszycki, *Niewygasła przeszłość* (Cracow: Społeczny Instytut Wydawniczy Znak, 1987), 234.

21. Volodymyr Levyns'kyi, *Narys rozvytku ukrainskogo robitnychogo rukhu v Gałychyni* (Kharkiv, Soviet Ukraine: Derzhavne vydavnytstvo Ukrainy, 1930), 74.

22. On the Hankevych brothers, see Antin Czernets'kyi, *Spomyny z mogo zytia* (Kyiv: Osnovni Tsinnosti, 2001), 39.

23. Harald Binder, *Galizien in Wien. Parteien, Wahlen, Fraktionen und Abgeordnete im Übergang zur Massenpolitik* (Vienna: Verlag der Österreichischen Akademie der Wissenschaften, 2005), 483.

24. He was accused of using party funds to support the election campaign of a nonsocialist Ukrainian candidate, Ievhen Petrushevych. See Binder, *Galizien in Wien,* 160.

25. Jobst, *Zwischen Nationalismus und Internationalismus,* 243.

26. On the Bund, see Joshua D. Zimmerman, *Poles, Jews, and the Politics of Nationality: The Bund and the Polish Socialist Party in Late Tsarist Russia, 1892–1914* (Madison: University of Wisconsin Press, 2004).

27. Jobst, *Zwischen Nationalismus und Internationalismus,* 59.

28. Joshua Shanes, *Diaspora Nationalism and Jewish Identity in Habsburg Galicia* (New York: Cambridge University Press, 2012).

29. Henryk Piasecki, *Sekcja Żydowska PPSD i Żydowska Partia Socjalno-Demokratyczna* (Wrocław, Poland: Ossolineum, 1982); on Diamand's opposition, see 78–81. Also see Henryk Piasecki, "Herman Diamand w latach 1890–1918," *Biuletyn Żydowskiego Instytutut Historycznego w Polsce* 2, no. 106 (1978): 38.

30. Otto Bauer, "Die Nationalfrage und die Sozialdemokratie," in Otto Bauer, *Werkausgabe,* vol. 1 (Vienna: Europa Verlag, 1975), 414–424, and Ernst Hanisch, *Der große Illusionist. Otto Bauer (1881–1938)* (Vienna: Böhlau, 2011), 54.

31. Hanisch, *Der große Illusionist,* 54.

32. Diamand, *Pamiętnik Hermana Diamanda,* 131.

33. Diamand, *Pamiętnik Hermana Diamanda,* 141.

34. Ignacy Daszyński, *Cztery lata wojny. Szkice z dziejów polityki Polskiej Partyi Socjalno-Demokratycznej* (Cracow: Nakładem Posła Zygmunta Klemensiewicza, 1918), 10.

35. Diamand, *Pamiętnik Hermana Diamanda,* 144.

36. "Wniosek na posiedzeniu Komisiji Politycznej Koła Polskiego w sprawie odbudowy państwa polskiego. 1. V. 1916," in Ignacy Daszyński, *Teksty,* ed. Jerzy Myśliński and Jacek Szczerbiński (Warsaw: Czytelnik, 1986), 185.

37. Haus der Abgeordneten, 53 Sitzung der XXII. Session, January 22, 1917, 2817.

38. Haus der Abgeordneten, 53 Sitzung der XXII. Session, January 22, 1917, 2817.

39. On support of the monarchy during the war, see Jerzy Holzer, *Polska Partia Socjal-istyczna w latach 1917–1919* (Warsaw: Państwowe Wydawnictow Naukowe, 1962), 88.

40. A-Zięba, "Altenbergowie, Vorzimerowie, Hankiewicz," 98.

41. Haus der Abgeordneten, 91. Sitzung der XXII. Session, October 19, 1918, 4594.

42. Sprawozdanie z 55 posiedzenia Sejmu, 25.06.1919, LV/65.

43. Najdus, *Ignacy Daszyński,* 425.

44. On Daszyński's support of autonomy, see Najdus, *Ignacy Daszyński,* 444.

45. Diamand, *Pamiętnik Hermana Diamanda,* 208.

46. Diamand, *Pamiętnik Hermana Diamanda,* 213.

47. Bernard Singer, *Od Witosa do Sławka* (Paris: Instytut Literacki, 1962), 48–49.

48. Singer, *Od Witosa do Sławka,* 24.

49. Stanisław Głąbiński, *Wspomnienie polityczne* (Pelplin, Poland: Nakładem i czcionkami Drukarni i Księgarni Sp. Z.O.O., 1939), 313.

50. Diamand, *Pamiętnik Hermana Diamanda,* 226.

51. A-Zięba, "Altenbergowie, Vorzimerowie, Hankiewicz," 114.

52. Najdus, *Ignacy Daszyński,* 376.

53. Christoph Mick, *Kriegserfahrung in einer multiethnischen Stadt. Lemberg 1914–1947* (Wiesbaden: Harrassowitz Verlag, 2010), 238. The pogrom against Jews in Lwów in November 1918 has been analyzed in great detail by historians. A good critical analysis in Polish is Jerzy Tomaszewski, "Lwów, 22 listopada 1918," *Przegląd Historyczny* 75 (1984): 279–285.

54. A-Zięba, "Altenbergowie, Vorzimerowie, Hankiewicz," 102.

55. "Mykola Hankevych, Ukraina i Polscha," *Sotsialistychna dumka,* September 3, 1921.

56. "Mykola Hankevych, Ukraina i Polscha," *Sotsialistychna dumka,* September 3, 1921.

57. "Holosy z kruhiv partjinykh tovaryshiv v spravi vykliuchennia Mykoly Hankevycha," *Vpered,* no. 12 (745), January 18, 1922.

58. "Holosy z kruhiv partjinykh tovaryshiv v spravi vykliuchennia Mykoly Hankevycha," 145; the reference here is to deputies specifically of the former Austrian imperial parliament.

59. "Holosy z kruhiv partjinykh tovaryshiv v spravi vykliuchennia Mykoly Hankevycha," 151.

60. "Holosy z kruhiv partjinykh tovaryshiv v spravi vykliuchennia Mykoly Hankevycha," 145.

61. Cited in Liongyn Tsegel'skyi, *Vid legendy do pravdy* (L'viv: Svichado, 2003), 138.

62. Nadiia Surovtsova, *Spohady* (Kyiv: Vydavnyctvo Oleny Telihy, 1996), 151.

63. Surovtsova, *Spohady,* 151.

64. On the Soviet funding of *Nova hromada,* see Surovtsova, *Spohady,* 139.

65. TsDAHO, Fund 269, Op. 1, Spr. 250, Semen Vityk to Volodymyr Starosolskyi, Vienna, May 16, 1923, 81.

66. Vityk to Starosolskyi, 81.

67. On Ukrainians in the Bolshevik party, see Liliana Riga, *The Bolsheviks and the Russian Empire* (Cambridge: Cambridge University Press, 2012), 152–153.

68. A good recent discussion of the nominally independent Soviet Ukraine and the centralized communist party is Olena Palko, "Social and/or National Revolution? Ukrainian Communisms in the Revolution and Civil War," *Socialist History* 53 (2018): 69–90.

69. Francine Hirsch, *Empire of Nations: Ethnographic Knowledge and the Making of the Soviet Union* (Ithaca: Cornell University Press, 2005), 25.

70. Joseph Stalin, "Marxism and the National Question," in J. V. Stalin, *Works,* vol. 2, *1907–1913* (Moscow: Foreign Language Publishing House, 1953), 300–381; on the dangers of national autonomy, see 323. On the Bolsheviks' views of the nationality issue, see Hirsch, *Empire of Nations,* 26–27, and Terry Martin, *The Affirmative Action Empire: Nations and Nationalism in the Soviet Union, 1923–1939* (Ithaca: Cornell University Press, 2001), 4–5.

71. On Lenin's vision of self-determination, see Vladimir Ilyich Lenin, "The Right of Nations to Self-Determination," in Lenin, *Collected Works,* vol. 20 (Moscow: Progress Publishers, 1972), 393–454; on the right of independent statehood, see 395. Available online at the Marxists Internet Archive, https://www.marxists.org/archive/lenin/works/1914/self-det/.

72. On Stalin's support of federalism, see Jeremy Smith, *The Bolsheviks and the National Question, 1917–1923* (New York: St. Martin's Press, 1999), 28. On "accidental federalists," see Stephen Kotkin, *Stalin: Paradoxes of Power, 1878–1928* (New York: Penguin, 2015), 346. On the Bolsheviks' nationalities program, see Smith, *The Bolsheviks and the National Question,* 18–31.

73. I borrow the phrase "Wilsonian moment" from Erez Manela, *The Wilsonian Moment: Self-Determination and the International Origins of Anticolonial Nationalism* (Oxford: Oxford University Press, 2007). On the scholarly neglect of Lenin's conception of national self-determination, see Eric D. Weitz, "Self-Determination: How a German Enlightenment Idea Became the Slogan of National Liberation and a Human Right," *American Historical Review* 120, no. 2 (April 2015): 484–485. See also the old but still relevant Arno Mayer, *Wilson vs. Lenin: Political Origins of the New Diplomacy* (New York: Meridian Books, 1969).

74. Martin, *The Affirmative Action Empire.*

75. "Semen Vityk. Svoiim chy chuzhym," *Nova hromada,* nos. 2–4 (1924): 15.

76. The trip is described in Nadiia Surovtsova, *Lysty,* vol. 1, ed. Olena Serhiienko (Kyiv: Vydavnyctvo Oleny Telihy, 2001), 626.

77. Surovtsova, *Lysty,* 626.

78. Oksana Pylat, "Hromads'ko-politychna diialnist' Semena Vityka" (dysertatsiya na zdobuttia naukovogo stupenia kandydata istorychnykh nauk, Universytet Ivana Franka, L'viv, 2007), 152.

79. Pylat, "Hromads'ko-politychna diialnist' Semena Vityka," 152.

80. Surovtsova, *Spohady,* 151.

81. On security missions, see Pylat, "Hromads'ko-politychna diialnist' Semena Vityka," 152.

82. Pylat, "Hromads'ko-politychna diialnist' Semena Vityka," 152, 22.

83. TsDIAUL, F. 309, Op. 1, Spr. 2258, Vityk to Hankevych, Kharkiv, January 14, 1926, 21.

84. Antin Chernetskyi, *Spomyny z mogo zhyttia* (Kyiv: Osnovni tsinnosti, 2001), 72.

85. "Partijna narada," *Vpered,* no. 13 (746), January 19, 1922.

86. Cited in Janusz Dadziejowski, *Komunistyczna partia zachodniej Ukrainy 1919–1929. Węzłłowe problemy ideologiczne* (Cracow: Wydawnictwo Literackie, 1976), 25. On the infiltration of the USDP by the communists, see also Matvii Stakhiv, *Khto vynen? Z istorii komunistychnogo rukhu ta ioho pomichnykiv* (L'viv: Nakładem Hromads'koho holosu, 1936), 37.

87. On dangers of the KPZU, see Timothy Snyder, *Sketches from the Secret War: A Polish Artist's Mission to Liberate Soviet Ukraine* (New Haven: Yale University Press, 2007), 30.

8. Nationalism, Marxism, and Communism

1. See, for example, Hans Mommsen, *Die Sozialdemokratie und die Nationalitätenfrage im habsburgischen Vielvölkerstaat* (Vienna: Europa Verlag, 1963). For an attempt to reverse this trend, see Marina Cattaruzza, *Socialismo adriatico. La socialdemocrazia di lingua italiana nei territori costieri della Monarchia asburgica 1888–1915,* 2nd ed. (Rome: Gennaio, 2001).

2. On the impact of Austro-Marxism on post-1918 Italy, see, for example, Elio Apih, *Italia. Fascismo e antifascismo nella Venezia Giulia (1918–1943). Ricerche storiche* (Bari, Italy: Editori Laterza, 1966), 33.

3. On national historiographies of socialism in Trieste, see Sabine Rutar, *Kultur-Nation-Milieu. Sozialdemokratie in Triest vor dem Ersten Weltkrieg* (Essen: Klartext, 2004), 20–23.

4. Cattaruzza, *Socialismo adriatico,* 8.

5. On Trieste as a major Slovenian city, see Sabine Rutar, "Die slowenische Sozialdemokratie in Triest (1896–1918)," *Südostforschungen* 57 (1998): 169–171.

6. Eduard Winkler, *Wahlrechtsreform und Wahlen in Triest 1905–1909* (Munich: R. Oldenbourg Verlag, 2000), 83.

7. Rutar, "Die slowenische Sozialdemokratie in Triest," 175.

8. For more on this, see Cattaruzza, *Socialismo adriatico,* 42–43.

9. Rutar, "Die slowenische Sozialdemokratie in Triest," 176. On the founding of the South Slavic Social Democratic branch in Trieste, see Rutar, "Die slowenische Sozialdemokratie in Triest," 177–78, and Boris Gombač, "Ustanovitec Yugoslovanske socialdemokratske stranke v Trstu," *Jadranski koledar* (1976): 198–210.

10. Winkler, *Wahlrechtsreformen und Wahlen in Triest,* 84. The original title of the party read as "Partito operaio socialista in Austria, sezione adriatica."

11. On their marginal status within imperial social democracy, see Mommsen, *Die Sozialdemokratie und die Nationalitätenfrage im habsburgischen Vielvölkerstaat,* 238. On their continual marginalization, see also Cattaruzza, *Socialismo adriatico,* 7. On the founding of these parties, see William Klinger, "Crepuscolo adriatico. Nazionalismo e socialismo italiano in Venezia Giulia (1896–1945)," *Quaderni* 23, no. 1 (2012): 81–82.

12. On Pittoni's role in Italian socialism, see, for example, Klinger, "Crepuscolo adriatico," 85.

13. Elio Apih, "Valentino Pittoni fra Austria e Italia," in Elio Apih, *Il socialismo italiano in Austria. Saggi* (Udine, Italy: Del Bianco Editore, 1991), 40–42.

14. Apih, "Valentino Pittoni fra Austria e Italia," 41. On Adler's influences over Pittoni, see also Almerigo Apollono, *La "Belle Époque" e il tramonto dell'Impero asburgico sulle rive dell'Adriatico (1902–1918)* (Trieste: Deputazione di Storia per la Venezia Giulia, 2014), 88.

15. Apih, "Valentino Pittoni fra Austria e Italia," 47.

16. Ivan Regent, "Nekaj o socialistočnem gibanju na primorskem in v Istri," in Ivan Regent, *Poglavja iz boja za socializmem,* vol. 3 (Ljubljana: Cankarjeva Založba, 1961), 27.

17. Ennio Maserati, *Il sindicalismo autonomista triestino degli anni 1909–1914* (Udine, Italy: Del Bianco, 1965), 28.

18. Maserati, *Il sindicalismo autonomista triestino,* 27–60.

19. Cited in Apih, "Valentino Pittoni fra Austria e Italia," 41.

20. Apih, "Valentino Pittoni fra Austria e Italia," 49.

21. Benito Mussolini, *Il Trentino visto da un socialista* (Trento: La Finestra, 2003), 39–40.

22. Claus Gatterer, *Cesare Battisti. Ritratto di un "Alto traditore"* (Florence: La Nuova Italia, 1976), 196; Cesare Battisti, "Discorso pronunciato al Parlamenti di Vienna il 28 ottobre 1911," in *Scritti politici di Cesare Battisti,* ed. Ernesta Bittanti ved. Battisti (Florence: Felice le Monnier, 1923), 131–132.

23. Haus der Abgeordneten, 19. Sitzung XXI. Session, October 24, 1911, 1126.

24. On Slovenian socialists' support of federalization, see Mommsen, *Die Sozialdemokratie und die Nationalitätenfrage im habsburgischen Vielvölkerstaat,* 263.

25. Rutar, *Kultur-Nation-Milieu.*

26. A brief political biography of Tuma is provided in Jože Pirjevec, "Henrik Tuma e il socialismo," *Prispevki za novejšo zgodovino* 17, nos. 1–2 (1977): 75–87.

27. "Tuma to Fran Erjavec, Trst, 30 marca 1917," in Henrik Tuma, *Pisma. Osebnosti in dogodki (1893–1935),* ed. Branko Marušič (Ljubljana: Inštitut Milka Kosa/Založba Devin, 1994), 86.

28. Henrik Tuma, *Iz mojega življenja. Spomini, misli in izpovedi* (Ljubljana: Naša Založba, 1937), 257–267.

29. Tuma, *Iz mojega življenja,* 292.

30. "Dovol J. 'Delavski list' 17.1.1908," in Ivan Regent, *Poglavja iz boja za socializmem,* vol. 1 (Ljubljana: Cankarjeva Založba, 1958), 13.

31. Vlado Strugar, *Jugoslavenske socijaldemokratske stranke 1914–1918* (Zagreb: Jugoslavenska akademija znatnosti i umjetnosti, 1963), 263; Tuma, *Iz mojega življenja,* 319; Rudolf Golouh, *Pol stoletja spominov. Panorama političnih bojev slovenskega naroda* (Ljubljana: Inštitut za zgodovino delavskega gibanja, 1966), 19–25.

32. On Austrian political persecutions on the southern borderland, see John Paul Newman, *Yugoslavia in the Shadow of War: Veterans and the Limits of State Building, 1903–1945* (Cambridge: Cambridge University Press, 2018), 119.

33. Apih, "Valentino Pittoni fra Austria e Italia," 62.

34. Apih, "Valentino Pittoni fra Austria e Italia," 61–62; Gatterer, *Cesare Battisti,* 196.

35. Giovanni Lorenzoni, *Cesare Battisti and the Trentino* (New York: Italian Bureau of Public Information, 1919), 23.

36. "Lettera aperta a B Mussolini, pubblicata da 'L'Avanti,' 14.09.1914," in Bittanti, *Scritti politici di Cesare Battisti,* 189.

37. Paolo Maranini, *Cesare Battisti* (Milan: Casa Editrice Bietti, 1935), 18.

38. Gatterer, *Cesare Battisti,* 230–232.

39. On the Battisti myth, see Massimo Tiezzi, *L'eroe conteso. La costruzione del mito di Cesare Battisti negli anni 1916–1935* (Trento: Fondazione Museo Storico Trentino, 2007); for the citation, see p. 7.

40. Apih, "Valentino Pittoni fra Austria e Italia," 64.

41. Apollono, *La "Belle Époque" e il tramonto,* 670–672.

42. Apollono, *La "Belle Époque" e il tramonto,* 1118.

43. Apollono, *La "Belle Époque" e il tramonto,* 66.

44. Giuseppe Piemontese, *Il movimento operaio a Trieste. Dalle origini alla fine della prima guerra mondiale* (Udine, Italy: Del Bianco Editore, 1961), 159.

45. Dušan Kermavner, *"Regent Ivan." Slovenski biografski leksikon. Slovenska biografija* (Ljubljana: ZRC SAZU, 2013).

46. Tuma, *Iz mojega življenja,* 340–341.

47. Tuma, *Iz mojega življenja,* 387.

48. Tuma, *Iz mojega življenja,* 351; Rutar, "Die slowenische Sozialdemokratie in Triest," 193.

49. "Tuma to Bauer, Karl Renner, Dr. Gottlieb Šmeral, Modráček Franz, Trieste, 11 Dezember 1917," in Tuma, *Iz mojega življenja,* 13.

50. Glenda Sluga, *The Problem of Trieste and the Italo-Yugoslav Border: Difference, Identity, and Sovereignty in Twentieth-Century Europe* (Albany: State University of New York, 2001), 41.

51. Golouh, *Pol stoletja spominov,* 44.

52. Vlado Strugar, *Jugoslavenske socijaldemokratske stranke,* 276.

53. On this merger, see "Il convegno dei socialisti sloveni della Venezia Giulia 21.09.1919, Trieste," in *Viri za zgodovino komunistične stranke na Slovenskem v letih 1919–1921,* ed. J. Fischer and J. Prunk (Ljubljana: Inštitut za zgodovino delavskega gibanja, 1980), 316–317. See also Marina Rossi, "Ivan Regent a Mosca nei documenti riservati dell'archivio del P.C.U.S. ed in alcune fonti autobiografiche ed epistolari (1931–1945)," *Acta Historiae* 17, no. 4 (2009): 685, and Marco Bresciani, "The Battle for Post-Habsburg Trieste/Trst: State Transition, Social Unrest, and Political Radicalism (1918–23)," *Austrian History Yearbook* 52 (2021): 190.

54. The right-left divides are discussed in Helmut König, *Lenin und der italienische Sozialismus 1915–1921. Ein Beitrag zur Gründungsgeschichte der kommunistischen Internationale* (Tübingen, Germany: Böhlau, 1967), 23, 29. See also Geatano Arfé, *Storia del socialism italiano 1892–1926* (Turin: Piccola Biblioteca Einaudi, 1977), 239–251.

55. Albertina Vittoria, *Storia del PCI 1921–1991* (Rome: Carocci Editore, 2006), 11.

56. Tommaso Detti, *Serrati e la formazione del partito comunista italiano* (Rome: Editori Riuniti, 1972), 46.

57. On debates between Lenin and Giacinto Menotti Serrati, a leading Italian communist, on issues of autonomy and centralization, see Detti, *Serrati e la formazione del partito comunista italiano,* 45.

58. On Italian communists' reliance on Moscow as a counterweight to Italian fascism, see Aldo Agosti, "The Comintern and the Italian Communist Party in Light of New Documents, 1921–1940," in *International Communism and the Communist International, 1919–1943,* ed. Tim Rees and Andrew Thorpe (Manchester, UK: Manchester University Press, 1999), 104.

59. On Pittoni's friendship with Oberdorfer, see "Pittoni to Signor Prof. Angelo Treves, 13.12.1919," in Apih, *Il socialismo italiano in Austria,* 94.

60. Aldo Oberdorfer, "Le condizioni e i problemi della Venezia Giulia, Firenze, lunedi di Pasqua 1919," in Aldo Oberdorfer, *Il socialismo del dopoguerra a Trieste* (Florence: Vallecchi, 1922), 15–16.

61. Oberdorfer, "L'evoluzione dei socialisti Giuliani," in Oberdorfer, *Il socialismo del dopoguerra a Trieste,* 29.

62. On the communist takeover, see Bresciani, "The Battle for Post-Habsburg Trieste," 192.

63. "Pittoni to Marina, Milan, 26.11.1922," in Apih, "Valentino Pittoni fra Austria e Italia," 95–96.

64. Apih, "Valentino Pittoni fra Austria e Italia," 80.

65. Oberdorfer, "Le condizioni e i problemi della Venezia Giulia," 17.

66. Oberdorfer, "Non-socialisti sloveni, Maggio 1919," in Oberdorfer, *Il socialismo del dopoguerra a Trieste,* 37.

67. On the tensions between Italian and Slovenian socialists during the September 1919 congress of the PSI, see "Antonio Mosconi, Il Comissario Generale Civile to Ministero dell'Interno Trieste, 25.11.1918," in Fischer and Prunk, *Viri za zgodovino komunistične stranke na Slovenskem,* 333–334.

68. Angelo Visintin, *L'Italia a Trieste. L'operato del governo militare italiano nella Venezia Giulia 1918–1919* (Gorizia, Italy: LEG Edizioni, 2000), 106–107.

69. Ivan Regent and Ivan Kreft, *Progresivna preusmeritev političnega življenja med vojnama v Sloveniji in Trstu* (Murska Sobota, Slovenia: Pomurska Založba ČZP Pomurski tisk, 1962), 25.

70. Oberdorfer, "Non-socialisti sloveni, Maggio 1919," 36.

71. Ivan Regent, *Spomini* (Ljubljana: Cankarjeva Založba, 1967), 114.

72. Regent, *Spomini.*

73. Cited in Strugar, *Jugoslavenske socijaldemokratske stranke,* 296.

74. Tuma, *Pisma. Osebnosti in dogodki,* 87.

75. Tuma, *Pisma. Osebnosti in dogodki,* 87.

76. "Henrik Tuma to Ivan Regent, 1.10.1924," in Tuma, *Pisma. Osebnosti in dogodki,* 424.

77. Regent and Kreft, *Progresivna preusmeritev političnego življenja,* 29.

78. Regent and Kreft, *Progresivna preusmeritev političnego življenja,* 154.

79. Regent and Kreft, *Progresivna preusmeritev političnego življenja,* 29.

80. Regent, *Spomini,* 157.

9. Radical Politics, Conservative Responses

1. Julius Deutsch, "Erinnerungen an Ludwig Czech," in Johann Wolfgang Brügel, *Ludwig Czech. Arbeiterführer und Staatsmann* (Vienna: Verlag der Wiener Volksbuchhandlung, 1960), 18.

2. A nuanced discussion of federative ideas in Europe, specifically during the interwar period, is provided in Holly Case, "The Strange Politics of Federative Ideas in East-Central Europe," *Journal of Modern History* 85, no. 4 (December 2013): 833–866. See also the older but still relevant Vojtech Mastny, "The Historical Experience of Federalism in East Central Europe," *East European Politics and Societies* 4, no. 1 (Winter 2000): 64–96.

3. A considerable literature exists on the League of Nations. For a useful recent analysis of the League's limitations and its decline through the 1930s, see Marco Duranti, *The Conservative Human Rights Revolution: European Identity, Transnational Politics, and the Origins of the European Convention* (New York: Oxford University Press, 2017), 60. A nuanced overviews of the League, its successes, and its limitations is Susan Pedersen, "Back to the League of Nations," *American Historical Review* 112, no. 4 (October 2007): 1091–1111.

4. On the Schutzbund, see Barbara Jelavich, *Modern Austria: Empire and Republic, 1815–1986* (Cambridge: Cambridge University Press, 1987), 183.

5. Anson Rabinbach, *The Crisis of Austrian Socialism: From Red Vienna to Civil War, 1927–1934* (Chicago: University of Chicago Press, 1983), 2.

6. Excerpts from the Linz program have been published in Gerd Storm and Franz Walter, *Weimarer Linkssozialismus und Austromarxismus. Historische Vorbilder für einen "Dritten Weg" zum Sozialismus?* (Berlin: Europäische Perspektiven, 1984), 9. For an interpretation of the program, see Rabinbach, *Crisis of Austrian Socialism,* 46–47.

7. On Bauer's role in the drafting of the Linz program, see Otto Leichter, *Glanz und Ende der Ersten Republik. Wie es zum österreichischen Bürgerkrieg kam* (Vienna: Europa Verlag, 1964), 38.

8. Otto Bauer, "Austromarxismus," in *Austromarxismus. Texte zu "Ideologie und Klassenkampf,"* ed. Hans-Jörg Sandkühler and Rafael de la Vega (Frankfurt: Europäische Verlagsanstalt, 1970), 50.

9. Rabinbach, *Crisis of Austrian Socialism,* 29.

10. Anton Pelinka, *Die gescheiterte Republik. Kultur und Politik in Österreich 1918–1938* (Weimar: Böhlau, 2017), 61.

11. On Seipel's antirepublicanism and flexibility, see Pelinka, *Die gescheiterte Republik,* 53, 61.

12. Pelinka, *Die gescheiterte Republik.*

13. On Seipel's resignation, see, for example, "Demission Dr. Seipels. Die bürgerliche Einheitsfront bleibt aufrecht," *Wiener Journal,* April 4, 1929; "Der Rücktritt der Bundesregierung," *Wiener Zeitung,* April 5, 1929.

14. John Deak, "Ignaz Seipel (1876–1932): Founding Father of the Austrian Republic," in *Austrian Lives,* ed. Günter Bischof et al. (New Orleans: University of New Orleans Press, 2012), 32–55; the citation is from p. 55.

15. For more on this subject, see Lothar Höbelt, *Die Erste Republik Österreich (1918–1938).* *Das Provisorium* (Vienna: Böhlau, 2018), 195, and Barbara Jelavich, *Modern Austria: Empire and Republic, 1815–1986* (Cambridge: Cambridge University Press, 1987), 186.

16. See John T. Lauridsen, *Nazism and the Radical Right in Austria, 1918–1934* (Copenhagen: Museum Tuscolanum Press, 2007), 184–198.

17. On the founding of the party and its major principles, see Bernd Vogel, *Die "Blauen" der Zwischenkriegszeit. Die Großdeutsche Volkspartei in Vorarlberg* (Regensburg, Germany: Roderer Verlag, 2004), 17.

18. Sitzung des Nationalrates der Republik Österreich, December 2, 1922, 4947. Christiane Rothländer, *Die Anfänger der Wiener SS* (Vienna: Böhlau, 2012), 22.

19. On the Greater German People's Party, see Gerhard Botz, *Nationalsozialismus in Wien. Machtübernahme, Herrschaftssicherung, Radikalisierung 1938/39* (Vienna: Mandelbaum, 2008), 15–16, and Radomír Luža, *Austro-German Relations in the Anschluss Era* (Princeton: Princeton University Press, 1975), 20.

20. On the history of the coalition and the problematic relations between the Heimwehr and the government, see Lauridsen, *Nazism and the Radical Right in Austria,* 245–254.

21. On the Austrian corporate state, see Bertrand Michael Buchmann, *Insel der Unseligen. Das autoritäre Österreich 1933–1938* (Vienna: Molden, 2019), 12, and Julie Thorpe, *Pan-Germanism and the Austrofascist State, 1933–38* (Manchester, UK: Manchester University Press, 2011), esp. 4–7.

22. Lucian O. Meysels, *Der Austrofaschismus. Das Ende der ersten Republik und ihr letzter Kanzler* (Vienna: Amalthea, 1982), 61.

23. Julius Braunthal, *Auf der Suche nach dem Millennium* (Vienna: Europa Verlag, 1964), 263.

24. A recent analysis of the July coup attempt is provided in Höbelt, *Die Erste Republik Österreich,* 318–319.

25. Höbelt, *Die Erste Republik Österreich,* 328.

26. Höbelt, *Die Erste Republik Österreich,* 333.

27. Ernst Hanisch, *Der große Illusionist. Otto Bauer (1881–1938)* (Vienna: Böhlau, 2011), 298–303.

28. Joseph Buttinger, *In the Twilight of Socialism: A History of the Revolutionary Socialists of Austria,* trans. E. B. Ashton (New York: F. A. Praeger, 1953), 42.

29. Otto Bauer, *Austrian Democracy under Fire* (Bratislava: Labor Publications Department, 1934), 41.

30. Bauer, *Austrian Democracy under Fire,* 42.

31. Bauer, *Austrian Democracy under Fire,* 52.

32. Bauer, *Austrian Democracy under Fire,* 49.

33. On Bauer's illusions in exile, see Peter Eppel, "Österreicher im Exil 1938–1945," in *NS-Herrschaft in Österreich 1938–1945,* ed. Emmmerich Tálos et al. (Vienna: Verlag fur Gesselschaftskritik, 1988), 558.

34. Friedrich Weissensteiner, "Dr. Wilhelm Ellenbogen—Persönlichkeit und Werk," in Wilhelm Ellenbogen, *Menschen und Prinzipen. Erinnerungen, Urteile und Reflexionen eines kritischen Sozialdemokraten,* ed. Friedrich Weissensteiner (Vienna: Böhlau, 1981), 31.

35. Charles A. Gulick, *Austria from Habsburg to Hitler,* vol. 2, *Fascism's Subversion of Democracy* (Berkeley: University of California Press, 1948), 1035.

36. Gulick, *Austria from Habsburg to Hitler,* 1316.

37. Doris A. Corradini, "Between Scholarship and Politics: Josef Redlich and the United States of America," in *Narratives of Encounters in the North Atlantic Triangle,* ed. Waldemar Zacharasiewicz and David Staines (Vienna: Austrian Academy of Sciences Press, 2015), 145–158.

38. "Redlich to Hofmanstahl, Stanford University, 20.6.1928," in *Hugo von Hofmannstahl—Josef Redlich. Briefwechsel,* ed. Helga Ebner-Fußgänger (Frankfurt am Main: Fischer Verlag, 1971), 101.

39. On the Creditanstalt crisis, see Aurel Schubert, *The Credit-Anstalt Crisis of 1931* (Cambridge: Cambridge University Press, 1991), and Nathan Marcus, *Austrian Reconstruction and the Collapse of Global Finance, 1921–1931* (Cambridge, MA: Harvard University Press, 2018), 299–301.

40. Corradini, "Between Scholarship and Politics," 156; "Austrian Finance Minister's Resignation Said to Be Due to His Jewish Origin," *Jewish Telegraphic Agency,* October 7, 1931.

41. Robert W. Seton-Watson, "Joseph Redlich: Obituary," *Slavonic and East European Review* 16, no. 46 (July 1937): 202.

42. Joseph Redlich, "German Austria and Nazi Germany," *Foreign Affairs* 15, no. 1 (October 1936): 179–187.

43. Hamilton Fish Armstrong, *Peace and Counterpeace: From Wilson to Hitler: Memoirs of Hamilton Fish Armstrong* (New York: Harper & Row, 1971), 496.

44. Seton-Watson, "Joseph Redlich: Obituary," 200.

45. "Skandal um Habsburg-Rede: 'Fußballmatch auf dem Heldenplatz,'" *Der Standard,* March 14, 2008, https://www.derstandard.at/story/3258746/skandal-um-habsburg-rede -fussballmatch-auf-dem-heldenplatz.

46. H. James Burgwyn, *Italian Foreign Policy in the Interwar Period, 1918–1940* (Westport, CT: Praeger, 1997), 141.

47. Luca Riccardi, *Francesco Salata tra storia, politica e diplomazia* (Udine, Italy: Del Bianco Editore, 2002), 399.

48. Alcide De Gasperi, "Le ragioni di una rubrica, 1–15 1933," in *De Gasperi e l'Europa degli anni trenta,* ed. Angelo Paoluzi (Rome: Edizione Cinque Lune, 1974), 65.

49. Alcide De Gasperi, "Gli Asburgo tornano in Austria, 1–15 agosto 1935," in Paoluzi, *De Gasperi e l'Europa,* 137.

50. For this argument, see Timothy Snyder, *Bloodlands: Europe between Hitler and Stalin* (New York: Basic Books, 2012).

51. *První ministerský předseda ČSR. Dr. Karel Kramář* (Prague: Společnost Dr. Karla Kramáře, 1938).

52. H. Gordon Skilling, "The Comintern and Czechoslovak Communism: 1921–1929," *American Slavic and East European Review* 19, no. 2 (April 1960): 236–237.

53. Johann Wolfgang Brügel, *Ludwig Czech. Arbeiterführer und Staatsmann* (Vienna: Verlag der Wiener Volksbuchhandlung, 1960), 47.

54. Brügel, *Ludwig Czech,* 72.

55. S. V. Kretinin, *Sudeto-nemetskaia sotsial-demokratiia. Stranitsy politicheskoi istorii 1918–1938* (Voronezh, USSR: Voronezhskii Universitet, 1968), 83.

56. Jörg Kracik, *Die Politik des deutschen Aktivismus in der Tschechoslowakei 1920–1938* (Frankfurt am Main: Peter Lang, 1999), 307.

57. On Alexander's dictatorship, see Dejan Djokić, *Elusive Compromise: A History of Interwar Yugoslavia* (New York: Columbia University Press, 2007), 68–69.

58. "Henrik Tuma to Ivan Regent, 26.03.1925," in Henrik Tuma, *Pisma. Osebnosti in dogodki (1893–1935),* ed. Branko Marušič (Ljubljana: Inštitut Milka Kosa/Založba Devin, 1994), 426.

59. "Henrik Tuma to Ivan Regent, 26.03.1925," 426–427.

60. "Henrik Tuma to Ivan Hribar, Ljubljana 2.07 1934," in Tuma, *Pisma. Osebnosti in dogodki,* 159.

61. Tuma, *Pisma. Osebnosti in dogodki,* 536.

62. Ivan Regent, *Spomini* (Ljubljana: Cankarjeva Založba, 1967), 191.

63. On Regent in Moscow, see Marina Rossi, "Ivan Regent a Mosca nei documenti riservati dell'Archivio del P.C.U.S. ed in alcune fonti autobiografiche ed epistolari (1931–1945)," *Acta Historiae* 17, no. 4 (2009): 681–719.

64. Patricia Albers, *Shadows, Fire, Snow: The Life of Tina Modotti* (Berkeley: University of California Press, 2002), 249.

65. Rossi, "Ivan Regent a Mosca," 221.

66. Regent, *Spomini,* 257.

67. There is a large literature on Piłsudski's coup. For a detailed analysis in English, see, for example, Joseph Rothschild, *Piłsudski's Coup d'Etat* (New York: Columbia University Press, 1966), and Antony Polonsky, *Politics in Independent Poland, 1921–1939: The Crisis of Constitutional Government* (Oxford: Clarendon Press, 1972).

68. On the arrests and the so-called Brest trials (most were detained at the prison in Brest), see Andrzej Garlicki, *Od Brześcia do maja* (Warsaw: Czytelnik, 1986), specifically 13–50. On the 1930s, see Andrzej Garlicki, *Piękne lata trzydzieste* (Warsaw: Prószyński i S-ka, 2008).

69. Ignacy Daszyński, "Przemówienie sejmowe w obronie parlamentu wygłoszone po przewrocie majowym J. Piłsudskiego," in Ignacy Daszyński, *Teksty,* ed. Jerzy Myśliński and Jacek Szczerbiński (Warsaw: Czytelnik, 1986), 296.

70. Ignacy Daszyński, "Końcowe uwagi ze stadium politycznego w pierwszę rocznicę przeworotu majowego," in Daszyński, *Teksty,* 314.

71. See, for example, Diamand's speeches to the parliament on February 13, 1920, and October 23, 1923, in Herman Diamand, *Przemówienia w Sejmie Rzeczypospolitej 1919–1930* (Warsaw: Nakładem Księgarni Robotniczej, 1932), 98, 427.

72. Herman Diamand, *Pamiętnik Hermana Diamanda. Zebrany z wyjątków listów do żony* (Cracow: Nakładem Towarzystwo Uniwersytetu Robotniczego, 1932), 273.

73. Diamand, *Pamiętnik Hermana Diamanda,* 302.

74. Diamand, *Pamiętnik Hermana Diamanda,* 189.

75. Diamand, *Pamiętnik Hermana Diamanda,* 254.

76. Adam Pragier, *Czas przeszły dokonany* (London: B. Świderski, 1966), 455.

77. See Diamand's speech to the parliament on June 8, 1928, in Herman Diamand, *Przemówienia w Sejmie Rzeczypospolitej 1919–1930* (Warsaw: Nakładem Księgarni Robotniczej, 1932), 509.

78. Stanisław Głąbiński, *Rządy sanacje w Polsce (1926–1939),* available online at http://wsercupolska.org/przeczytaj/Stanislaw_Glabinski-Rzady_sanacji_w_Polsce.pdf, 2.

79. Stanisław Głąbiński, *W cieniu ojca* (Warsaw: Książka i Wiedza, 2001), 38.

80. An excellent analysis of Polish–Ukrainian relations and the pacification campaigns is provided in Timothy Snyder, *Sketches from a Secret War: A Polish Artist's Mission to Liberate Soviet Ukraine* (New Haven: Yale University Press, 2005), and Timothy Snyder, *The Reconstruction of Nations: Poland, Ukraine, Lithuania, Belarus, 1569–1999* (New Haven: Yale University Press, 2003), 150.

81. Nadiia Surovtsova, *Lysty,* vol. 1, ed. Olena Serhiienko (Kyiv: Vydavnyctvo Oleny Telihy, 2001), 626.

82. For a similar argument, see Robert Gerwarth, *The Vanquished: Why the First World War Failed to End* (New York: Farrar, Straus and Giroux, 2016), 9.

83. Jan T. Gross, *Revolution from Abroad: The Soviet Conquest of Poland's Western Ukraine and Western Belorussia* (Princeton: Princeton University Press, 2002).

84. The Polish–Soviet propaganda war is discussed in Snyder, *Sketches from a Secret War.*

Epilogue

1. Alcide De Gasperi, "Timori per l'Europa (1–15 aprile 1938)," in Angelo Paoluzi, *De Gasperi e l'Europa degli anni trenta* (Rome: Edizione Cinque Lune, 1974), 67–68.

2. On Hácha, see Chad Bryant, *Prague in Black: Nazi Rule and Czech Nationalism* (Cambridge, MA: Harvard University Press, 2007), 38–43.

3. Olesya Khromeychuk, *"Undetermined" Ukrainians: Post-War Narratives of the Waffen SS "Galicia" Division* (Oxford: Peter Lang, 2013), 19.

4. Denisson I. Rusinow, *Italy's Austrian Heritage, 1919–1946* (Oxford: Clarendon Press, 1969), 4.

5. Ernst Hanisch, *Der große Illusionist. Otto Bauer (1881–1938)* (Vienna: Böhlau, 2011), 365.

6. J. W. Brügel, *Ludwig Czech. Arbeiterführer und Staatsmann* (Vienna: Verlag der Wiener Volksbuchhandlung, 1960), 157.

7. Luca Riccardi, *Francesco Salata tra storia, politica e diplomazia* (Udine, Italy: Del Bianco Editore, 2001), 410–411.

8. Ivan Regent, *Spomini* (Ljubljana: Cankarjeva Založba, 1967), 230.

9. Regent, *Spomini,* 243–246.

10. Stanisław Głąbiński, *W cieniu ojca* (Warsaw: Książka i Wiedza, 2001), 70.

11. Krzysztof Kaczmarski, *Studia i szkice z dziejów obozu narodowego* (Rzeszów, Poland: Instytut pamięci narodowej, 2010), 210.

12. On Yalta, see Serhii Plokhy, *Yalta: The Price of Peace* (London: Penguin Books, 2011).

13. Cited in Piero Craveri, *De Gasperi* (Bologna: Il Mulino, 2006), 489–491.

14. Alcide De Gasperi, "L'Unione Europea, Dichiarazione fatta al giornale 'Il Popolo' 20 febraio 1950," in *De Gasperi e l'Europa. Scritti e discorsi,* ed. Maria Romana De Gasperi (Brescia, Italy: Morcelliana, 1979), 81.

15. Tony Judt, *Postwar: A History of Europe Since 1945* (London: Penguin Press, 2005).

16. Głąbiński, *W cieniu ojca,* 16–17, 33.

17. Głąbiński, *W cieniu ojca,* 18.

18. Stanisław Sławomir Nicieja, *Adam Próchnik. Historyk, polityk, publicysta* (Warsaw: Państwowe Wydawnictwo Naukowe, 1986), 27.

19. Walentyna Najdus, *Ignacy Daszyński 1866–1936* (Warsaw: Czytelnik, 1988), 456.

20. Najdus, *Ignacy Daszyński,* 506.

21. Najdus, *Ignacy Daszyński,* 362, 460, 505.

22. "Wielcy Lwowianie: Henryk Wereszycki," http://kresy24.pl/13-grudnia-1898/.

23. Andrzej A-Zięba, "Altenbergowie, Vorzimerowie, Hankiewicz," in *Henryk Wereszycki. Historia w życiu historyka,* ed. Elżbieta Oran and Antoni Cetnarowicz (Cracow: Historia Jagellonica, 2001), 101. On Vorzimmer's family and their fate during World War II, see also *Najmniej jestem tam gdzie jestem . . . Listy Zofii i z Vorzimmerów Breustedt z Warszawy i getta warszawskiego do córki Marysi w Szwajcarii (1939–1942),* ed. Elżbieta Orman (Cracow: Księgarnia Akademicka, 2016).

24. "Hermeine [Diamand] to [Herman] Diamand, Letter, 18.7.1927," in Naukova Bibioteka im. Vasylia Stefanyka, L'viv, Ukraine. Manuscript Division, Diamand no. 52, p. 42.

25. Regent, *Spomini,* 257.

26. On Bianca Pittoni in Paris during the Second World War, see Renato Monteleone, *Filippo Turati* (Turin: Unione Tipografico–Editrice Torinese, 1987).

27. Amy Ng, *Nationalism and Political Liberty: Redlich, Namier, and the Crisis of Empire* (Oxford: Clarendon Press, 2004), 12.

28. Cited in Henryk Wereszycki, "Życzymy ci towarzyszu Limanowski wolnej Warszawy. Wspomnienie mówione," in Henryk Wereszycki, *Niewygasła przeszłość* (Cracow: Społeczny Instytut Wydawniczy Znak, 1987), 237.

29. Henryk Wereszycki, *Historia polityczna Polski 1864–1918,* 2nd ed. (Wrocław, Poland: Ossolineum, 1990), 143.

Acknowledgments

This book is the product of many years of work and adventures across continents. I first conceived the idea for this study in 2010, while on a fellowship at Harvard University. I immersed myself in the project while on another fellowship in 2011–12 at Imre Kertész Kolleg in Jena, Germany. I am particularly grateful to this institute's directors—Joachim von Puttkamer and the late Włodzimierz Borodziej—for supporting the project and inviting me to join in the first cohort of Imre Kertész fellows. The concept grew in conversations with many scholars in residence in Jena that year, in particular with Anna Veronika Wendland, Stanislav Holubec, Jochen Böhler, and Holly Case. From 2010 to 2022 I researched and worked on the book in the United States, Germany, Austria, Poland, Italy, the Czech Republic, and Ukraine. The Institute for Human Sciences in Vienna provided an intellectual home for me over the years, for which I am most grateful.

My colleagues at Hunter College—CUNY in New York City provided a remarkably amicable environment in which I could grow as both a scholar and a teacher, and they made me feel truly at home. I am particularly grateful to Mary Roldán for her unconditional support and to Dániel Margócsy, Ben Hett, Elidor Mëhilli, and Jill Rosenthal for helping me navigate the city and the CUNY system, as well as for reading and commenting on portions of this manuscript and being good friends.

My colleagues at Princeton believed in the project from the beginning, supported me through the pandemic and the war in Ukraine, and above all offered the most rigorous and nuanced feedback at different stages of the writing. Many of them have read and commented on parts or all of the manuscript. I am particularly grateful to Stephen Kotkin, Katya Pravilova, Michael Gordin, Jeremy Adelman, and Harold James, who read several drafts of the entire manuscript, as well to Angela Creager and Yaacob Dweck, with whom I have discussed the study at length. David Bell offered very helpful suggestions on how to reframe the introduction. Pieter Judson, Robert Gerwarth, and Charles King read and commented on an earlier draft during a book writing workshop at Princeton at the height of the Covid pandemic in May 2020. Keith Wailoo discussed the project with me and helped arrange the writing workshop, as well as an invaluable year of sabbatical leave that enabled me to revise and almost entirely rewrite the manuscript. Also very supportive over the years, both personally and professionally, has been Susan Ferber.

Several scholars have read and commented on particular chapters devoted to countries within their expertise, helping me to avoid errors and misinterpretations. I am particularly grateful to Stanislav Holubec for his feedback on the Czechoslovak component of the book; Ke-Chin Hsia for his expertise on Austria; Federico Marcon, Marco Bresciani, and Bianca Centrone for their readings of Italian sections; and Jadwiga Biskupska for assistance with the book's Polish topics. Emily Greble read parts of an earlier draft of the manuscript.

Many other colleagues and friends have helped with research and writing over the years. My doctoral advisor, Timothy Snyder, supported the project from the outset, and Marci Shore contributed numerous suggestions, both personal and professional. Jadwiga Biskupska guided me through job talks, book proposals, and numerous chapter drafts. This book also grew in conversation with Princeton graduate students: at the latest stages of writing, Camilla Pletuhina-Tonev read and commented on several chapters, and Bianca Centrone reviewed most of the manuscript, offering essential feedback and correcting many typos. Two anonymous peer reviewers also provided invaluable feedback, which is reflected in the final version of the book. My editor, Avram Brown, did wonders for my writing, making adjustments throughout the text and correcting multiple errors; this book is more readable because of him. Jaya Chatterjee of Yale University Press has efficiently shepherded this book through the review process, for which I am very grateful. Mary Pasti at Yale University Press has been truly amazing through the last stages of copyediting, proofs, and production.

Over the years, I have presented this book project at different workshops and conferences—too many to mention here—across the continents. Part of chapter 2 has appeared as a separate article in Paul Miller and Claire Morelon, eds., *Embers of Empire: Continuity and Rupture in the Habsburg Successor States after 1918* (New York: Berghahn Books, 2019), and a brief article giving a general outline of the argument was published in *Passato e Presente* 106 (2019).

My family members around the world have also lived with this book for many years. My son, Henryk, born in 2018 (not to be confused with any of my protagonists and not named after any of them), has been a bright light amid a great deal of recent darkness. My mother, Stefania Vushko, supported me over the years in ways I cannot even begin to enumerate. She succumbed to Covid in 2021. I dedicate this book to her, with the hope that I can give my son the love and care that she has given me over the decades.

Index

Page numbers in italics indicate a figure.